KNOW THE TRUTH

KNOW
THE TRUTH

A MEMOIR

George Carey

HarperCollins*Publishers*

HarperCollins*Publishers*
77–85 Fulham Palace Road,
Hammersmith, London w6 8jb

www.harpercollins.co.uk

Published by HarperCollins*Publishers* 2004

1

A catalogue record for this book
is available from the British Library

ISBN 0 00 712030 3

Set in PostScript Linotype Minion with
Castellar and Photina display by
Rowland Phototypesetting Ltd,
Bury St Edmunds, Suffolk

Printed and bound in Great Britain by
Clays Ltd, St Ives plc

CONTENTS

ILLUSTRATIONS

Unless otherwise stated, all photographs are from the author's collection.

On holiday with my parents as a teenager.

My father at the age of about sixty-five, on holiday in the Lake District.

Dreaming of travelling the ocean waves, I broke the rules by applying to be a Sea Cadet at the age of twelve, when the entry level was thirteen.

National Service as a signals operator in the RAF. I was stationed in Egypt, and then at Shaibah, near Basra in Iraq.

A moment of leisure during my posting at Shaibah.

Marriage to Eileen, 25 June 1960.

Wild West Week at St Mary's, Islington, in the summer of 1964.

Eileen and me with Rachel, Mark and Andrew in 1966.

My first visit to the Vatican, in 1977, when I met Pope Paul VI.

A rare picture of me actually teaching as Principal of Trinity Theological College in Bristol.

My consecration as Bishop of Bath and Wells by Robert Runcie on 3 December 1987.

As Bishop of Bath and Wells with our beloved King Charles spaniel, Buccleuch.

Ordeal by photocall in Wells on the day of the announcement of my nomination as Archbishop of Canterbury in 1990.

With John Major in January 1991.

My first overseas trip as Archbishop, to Papua New Guinea in 1991.

With John Habgood, the Archbishop of York.

Meeting Nelson Mandela for the first time in January 1993, when he came to address the leaders of the Anglican Communion in Cape Town.

With Yasser Arafat at Lambeth Palace in December 1993.

vii

Dr Mohammed Sayed Tantawi, Grand Imam of Al-Azhar, who hosted the gathering of faith leaders which led to the Alexandria Declaration.

It was often my privilege to escort the Queen Mother at state banquets.

With Dinka children in Sudan, 1993.

Uganda, 1994. Crowds lining the road to greet the Archbishop of Canterbury.

With Patriarch Illya II of Georgia on a river boat on the Thames in June 1995.

Perhaps our most harrowing overseas visit of all, to Rwanda in 1995, only months after the genocide in the country.

With United Nations Secretary General Kofi Annan in Uganda in 1995.

Desmond Tutu's retirement service as Archbishop of Cape Town in 1996.

With Tony Blair at the TUC in 1997.

Eileen and I greet Princess Margaret to an Ash Wednesday community Eucharist at Lambeth Palace in 1999.

In the summer of 1999 human chains were formed as part of the Jubilee 2000 campaign to call for the cancellation of debt on behalf of the world's poorest economies.

With Pope John Paul II in the Vatican in 2000.

Eileen and me with President George W. Bush at the White House on 24 April 2001.

On a rainy day in June 2002 the Queen came to a Lambeth Palace garden party to celebrate her Jubilee with children from local schools. *(Camera Press)*

With His Royal Highness Prince El Hassan bin Talal of Jordan and the Chief Rabbi Jonathan Sachs.

FOREWORD

At first sight *Know the Truth* may seem a dogmatic, preachy title, chosen by a writer who is determined to get his point across. I will have to leave my readers to judge if that is actually the case. All I can say by way of disclaimer is that the phrase is not mine, but comes from the famous words of Jesus in John's gospel: 'You shall know the truth and the truth shall set you free.' The words were chosen because the verse is the motto of the Anglican Communion, and expresses the aspiration of this great tradition in Christianity to be a faithful witness to the love of God in Jesus Christ. For me, as a former President of the Communion, they have special relevance and meaning.

I do not deny that this memoir is incomplete – as the story of any individual's life must be. No one can tell 'the whole truth' about themselves, because other people's experiences and memories are part of the fuller and richer picture. All I can say is that as far as I am aware, based as it is on a daily diary I have kept over the years, supplemented by the records of my former staff at Lambeth Palace, what is recorded here is an accurate account of a complex public life. I have not shirked from revealing worries and frustrations, as well as something of the fun and joy along the way – indeed, there has been a lot of that. Sadly, it has proved impossible to record everything. In my eleven and a half years as Archbishop I visited over eighty countries, and paid visits to many dioceses up and down the country. Only a tiny fraction of those visits is recorded in this book.

When, halfway through my archiepiscopate, I decided to write my memoirs it came as a surprise to discover that I would be the first of the 103 Archbishops to have done so. Admittedly Archbishop

Thomas Secker in the eighteenth century set out on the task, but his sudden death left his memoirs unfinished. This book is a reflection on a ministry of which Archbishop Cosmo Lang said in the year of my birth: 'The post [of Archbishop of Canterbury] is impossible for any one man to do, but only one man can do it.' Any holder of this historic office – one of the oldest in the United Kingdom – knows from first-hand experience that its demands, expectations and opportunities take one to the edge of human endurance, and require of its holders a recognition of our frailty and our need of God's everlasting grace.

There have been times in recent years when I have wondered ruefully why I ever committed myself to writing an autobiography. I have had to ask myself whether I was doing so in order to justify my actions, to get my own back on my adversaries, to give my own version of events. As far as I know my own heart, I have endeavoured to reflect on my life, experiences and work from the viewpoint of someone who simply wishes to offer this memoir as a gift to the Church. I have no wish to justify my actions, to defend my record or to hurt others. I trust that *Know the Truth* will be seen for what it is intended to be: an honest account of a pilgrimage that I hope will assist others treading a similar lonely path in leading and serving others. I offer it to all people of goodwill in the hope that it might enrich their journey into the love of God.

Few spiritual journeys are ever walked alone. So many people have travelled with me, and I shall remain everlastingly grateful for their patience, kindness, friendship and support. Pride of place goes to my wife Eileen, whose rock-like place in my life and work is evident throughout this journey. What a great friend she has been over these tumultuous years, and what times have we shared together. Then there are our parents, who though now out of our sight through death, are never out of our minds and grateful hearts. We think of our brothers and sisters, whose lives are inextricably linked with our story, and of our beloved children and their husbands and wives, who have shared our joy and pain over some difficult years. Thank you, Rachel and Andy, for your love and care for us at the Old Palace; and Mark and Penny, Andrew and Helen and Lizzie and Marcus – not forgetting thirteen wonderful grandchildren. Thank you, each one of you, for constantly reminding us that life is a gift to be enjoyed.

In the making of this book there are a number of people who should be thanked and appreciated. I am grateful to Julia Lloyd, who spent a whole year at Lambeth going through the records and recording speeches, travel journals and staff records in such a way that my task was made much easier. Thank you, Julia, for introducing me to zip drives! My son Andrew has also been a tower of strength, going over the draft chapters with a careful eye, reminding me of incidents I had forgotten – and in some cases those I wanted to forget! I am grateful to him for his thoroughness, wisdom, insight and incisiveness. Thanks must go to Sir Philip Mawer, Richard Hopgood and Richard Lay for their help with the chapter on the Church Commissioners; to Dr Mary Tanner for her careful insights on the ecumenical chapter; to Canon Andrew Deuchar, Canon Roger Symon and Dr Alistair Macdonald-Radcliffe for their suggestions with respect to the chapters dealing with the Anglican Communion; to Canon Andrew White and Canon David Marshall for positive comments on the inter-faith chapter; and to the Very Reverend Michael Mayne and Sir Ewan Harper for helpful criticisms of the chapter on the Royal Family. I alone am responsible for the use I have made of all the assistance offered; any shortcomings are entirely my fault.

I also wish to record my debt of gratitude to those who may not feature a great deal in this narrative but whose contribution is deeper than I can possibly state. To Dr Ruth Etchells, whose friendship goes back many years, and whose wisdom has always been there and often sought. To Dr James and the Reverend Elisabeth Ewing, two dear American Christians, whose grace has touched the lives of our family so many times over the last decade. To Sir Siggy and Lady Hazel Sternberg and Lord Greville Janner, wonderful Jewish friends whose kindness has reminded us of the '*hesed*' love of God in the Hebrew scriptures. To Professor Richard McBrien, Professor of Theology at Notre Dame University; Beverley Brazauskas; and Professor Gerry O'Collins of the Gregorian University, Rome, for their rich Catholic contribution to our lives.

Finally, a word of gratitude to my publishers, HarperCollins, and the genial and caring oversight of my editors Michael Fishwick and Robert Lacey.

GEORGE CAREY
March 2004

I

1

No Backing Out

'It is perhaps significant that though state education has existed in England since 1870, no Archbishop has so far passed through it. The first Prime Minister to do so was Lloyd George. Nor has anyone sat on St Augustine's Chair, since the Reformation, who was not a student at Oxford or Cambridge. Understandably nominations to Lambeth have been conditioned by the contemporary social climate, but such a limitation of the field intake is doubtless on the way out. It is inconceivable that either talent or suitability can be so narrowly confined.'

Edward Carpenter, Cantuar: The Archbishops in Their Office *(1988)*

AS THE DOOR OF THE OLD PALACE BANGED behind Eileen and the family as they departed for the cathedral, I was left alone in the main lounge to await the summons that would most certainly change the direction of my life. At lunchtime with my family around the kitchen table there had been nervous laughter as Andrew, who had had his hair cut that morning, recounted hearing another customer talk about the 'enthornment' of the new Archbishop. We all agreed that that was a great description of it, although another of the family volunteered, 'At least he didn't say "entombment".'

Somewhere in the building Graham James, my Chaplain, was sorting out the robes I would shortly wear. From the lounge window I could see and hear the crowds of people teeming around the west front of the cathedral. They were there to capture a glimpse of the Princess of Wales and other dignitaries including the Prime Minister,

John Major. I could not help thinking wryly that within twenty yards of where I was standing another Archbishop of Canterbury, Thomas Becket, had met his death in the same cathedral on 30 December 1170. My journey from this room was not going to lead me to his fate, but it was bound to bring me too in touch with opposition and conflict, as well as with much joy and fulfilment. The massive, enduring walls of the cathedral overshadowing the Old Palace however were a reassuring sign that the faith and folly, the strengths and weaknesses, the boldnesses and blunders of individual Archbishops are enveloped by the tender love of God and His infinite grace.

The television was on in the room, and I could hear Jonathan Dimbleby and Professor Owen Chadwick solemnly discussing the significance of the enthronement of the 103rd Archbishop of Canterbury. Professor Chadwick, a well-known Church historian, was reminding the viewers of the significance in affairs of state of the role of the Archbishop, an office older than the monarchy and integral with the identity of the nation.

Graham swept in with the first set of clothing I had to wear. 'We'd better get you dressed, Archbishop,' he said. 'There's no backing out now!'

I put on my cassock as I heard Owen Chadwick say that today, 19 April, was the Feast Day of St Alphege, a former Archbishop of Canterbury who, in 1012 AD in Greenwich, was battered to death by Vikings with ox bones because he refused to allow the Church to pay a ransom for his release. It seemed a hazardous mantle I was about to don.

Suddenly a great deal of noise erupted outside, and we walked over to the window to see the Prime Minister arrive with several other Ministers of State. He waved to the crowds and was ushered into the cathedral.

The whole world, it seemed, was present at the service in one way or another. Not only all the important religious leaders in the country – Cardinal Hume and Archbishop Gregorius, Moderators of the Church of Scotland, the Methodist Church and the Free Churches

– but also the Patriarchs of the four ancient Sees of Constantinople, Alexandria, Jerusalem and Antioch. Billy Graham was present as my personal guest and as someone whose contribution to world Christianity was unique and outstanding. Cardinal Cassidy represented Pope John Paul II and the Pontifical Council for Christian Unity. Every Archbishop in the Anglican Communion was present, as was every Bishop in the Churches of England, Wales, Scotland and Ireland.

Behind me Dimbleby and Chadwick were now speculating about the new Archbishop. I caught several of the comments: 'A surprising appointment . . . he has only been a Bishop less than three years . . . Yes, an evangelical, but open to others . . . was born in the East End of London . . . working class . . . No, certainly not Oxbridge, but has taught in three theological colleges and Principal of another . . . comes with experience of parish life as well as being Chairman of the Faith and Order Advisory Group . . . I think he will be an unpompous Archbishop.'

Mention of my background brought home to me how much I owed to my godly and good parents, who sadly were not here to share in today's momentous events. How proud, and yet how humble, they would have felt. I smiled to myself as I recalled my mother's loud comment when in 1985 I was made Canon in Bristol Cathedral: 'Now I know what the Virgin Mary must have felt like!' Eileen, rather shocked, wheeled on her: 'Mum, that's blasphemy!' Mother, unrepentant, just smiled.

Yes, how thrilled Mum and Dad would have been; but as realistic Christians they would not be glorying in the pomp and majesty of the day, so much as in the service it represented. They would also be sharing in the tumult of my feelings, and my apprehension as I faced a new future.

Actually, I was not the slightest bit ashamed of my working-class background, which I shared with at least 60 per cent of the population. The popular press had of course milked the story thoroughly, and it was the usual tale of 'poor boy makes good' by overcoming huge obstacles to 'get to the top'. How I hated that kind of language of 'top' and 'success'. It encouraged the stereotype that I was a 'man of the people', and therefore in tune with the vast majority of the populace. There was no logic in that, as a moment's thought should have reminded such journalists that David Sheppard's background – to take one example of many – did not prevent him from being closely in touch with the underprivileged. Nevertheless, I hoped with all my heart that it was true, and it was very much at the centre of my ministry to represent the cares and interests of ordinary people, with whom I could identify in terms of background.

Some writers, astonishingly, had drawn the conclusion that because I came from an evangelical background my politics were essentially conservative. That was clearly not the case, but neither did it mean that I automatically identified with any particular political party. I saw my role as Archbishop as a defender of the principles of parliamentary democracy. I wanted to support those called to exercise authority, and I would later remind Prime Ministers of both major parties that I saw it as my duty to confront them if they embarked upon policies which I felt undermined the nation in any way.

But what kind of Archbishop was I going to be? As the 103rd Archbishop I was spoiled for choice if modelling myself on any of my predecessors was the way to proceed. Becket feuded so regularly with his King that he spent most of his time in exile. No, that was not for me. The quiet, scholarly Cranmer, perhaps, with whose theology I could identify; but, then again, he was too vacillating and cautious. Nearer my time perhaps one of the greatest of them all, William Temple – scholar, activist, social reformer and inspirer. Yes, a giant among Archbishops, but he was Archbishop of Canterbury for a mere two years during wartime. As a model for this post there were many great men to consider. It struck me that whatever inspiration I received from my illustrious predecessors, I had to be my own man. One thing I could depend upon was that the same divine grace and strength that the previous Archbishops had received was available to me too.

'It's time to go, Archbishop,' said a smiling Graham, handing me my mitre, and then with a prayer we walked towards the door, leaving the television commentary still describing the scene within the cathedral as we advanced to be part of it.

2

East End Boy

'Perhaps more typical of the period after 1940, when the war settled down into the long slog that it became for most non-combatants is the comment of an old lady from Coventry. Asked by her priest what she did when she heard the sirens, she replied: "Oh, I just read my bible a bit and then says 'bugger 'em' and I goes to bed."'

W. Rankin

THE WORLD INTO WHICH I WAS BORN on 13 November 1935 was a very troubled and insecure one. The nations were just emerging from the effects of the devastating Wall Street crash that had led to thousands of bankruptcies and to the ruin of many millions of ordinary people around the world. Europe had been badly affected by the Depression, and the rise of fascism was beginning to trouble many. The United Kingdom was not immune from the turmoil and confusion of the period, with unemployment blighting the lives of millions. An absorbing and important sideline was the worrying problem of the monarchy, that would very shortly lead to the abdication of Edward VIII and the accession to the throne of George VI.

To what extent my working-class parents shared in these questions and concerns I have no knowledge, although poverty was an abiding reality in our home. Number 68 Fern Street, Bow, London E3, was a typical working-class terrace house, with two bedrooms and a toilet upstairs, and two rooms and a scullery downstairs. I never heard my parents complain about their council home. They kept it clean and were proud of it.

It was a very happy and loving home into which I was born. I was the eldest of five children. Dennis, the twins Robert and Ruby, and Valerie followed at roughly two-year intervals. It was our privilege to have two wonderful parents.

To outward appearances, there was nothing remarkable about them. Their marriage certificate declared that our father, George Thomas Carey, was a labourer at the time of my birth. His schooling had stopped at fourteen years of age, and from birth until well into his teenage years he was the beneficiary of cast-off clothes and shoes. His background was impressive only for the extent of its poverty and deprivation. He was eight months old when his father died in St Bart's Hospital as a result of an appendicitis operation at the age of twenty-five. His earliest memory was of his mother's second marriage to an Irish Roman Catholic, a street trader, who was habitually drunk and who often beat his wife when under the influence of alcohol.

In addition to his older brother John, Dad's mother gave birth to a further eight children. She only married her Catholic husband on the clear understanding that the two sons of her first marriage were brought up in the Church of England faith. She often took them to Bow Church, which to this day occupies a position of prominence on Mile End Road.

My father told me that two moments of his childhood stand out. His maternal grandparents were both born blind, and when his grandmother passed away his grandfather joined this already very large family. The cramped house necessitated grandson and blind grandfather sharing a single bed. A close relationship grew between them, and the old man devoted many hours to teaching the boy to read. My father was encouraged to recite huge passages of the Bible that later in life he could still recall and repeat. At the age of ten, Dad was due to go on a school trip to Regent's Park Zoo. The day before the trip, Granddad gave his daughter some money, with the mysterious instruction that should anything happen to him, nothing should stop George going to the zoo. Dad was suddenly woken up during the night and transferred into another bed without knowing why. On his return home from the zoo the following day his mother told him gently that his dear grandfather had died in the night with his arms around him. A very special bond was broken – but Dad remained devoted to the memory of his blind grandfather throughout his life.

Dad's second memory was of a night in his early teens when he was woken by loud screaming and the sound of breaking furniture. Fearfully he crept out of bed, and struggled downstairs. The screaming was his mother's. Candles were the only form of lighting, so it was with some difficulty that he found his way to her bedroom. Suddenly, confronting him was his stepfather, breathing heavily and clearly the worse for drink.

'What's the matter, Georgie?' came the harsh voice.

'I heard Mum scream, and it frightened me,' the boy said.

His stepfather replied, 'Go to bed, George. Your mother is all right.'

The following day he found out that his older brother had also heard the screaming and had pulled their drunken stepfather off their mother, who had been savagely beaten. He in turn was practically strangled before Nell, one of the stepsisters, was able to rescue him. Mother, son and stepdaughter were thrust from the house and spent the remainder of the night at an uncle's home. The battered face of his mother the following day told the sorry story of the power of drink in his stepfather's life. Apparently he could be the most charming of men when sober, but rarely did my father talk of him. There was, however, no mistaking the depth of the love between my father and his mother. Although I have no recollection of her whatsoever, the fragrance of her presence was almost tangible in my father's life. Few of us realise how lasting is the impact that such caring and close relationships have on our children.

My mother, Ruby Catherine Gurney, came from a more secure and more prosperous working-class home – although the same struggle for existence blighted her life too. Looking at the earliest photos I possess of my mother, she was clearly a good-looking and gentle woman, intelligent, full of life with a great sense of humour. She too was from a large family, and like my father did not have the chance of a decent education.

It was not until many years later that I discovered the extraordinary fact that my mother's side of the family had close links with Canterbury. My mother's great-great-grandparents, Thomas and Mary Gurney, were born in Canterbury and baptised in St Alphege's Church, just fifty yards away from the Old Palace. Their son James was married to Louisa Dawson in the same church on 26 March 1849, and their place of residence was recorded as Archbishop's Palace, Canterbury. The Gurney family later moved to the East End of London, where my mother was born and grew up. One firm recollection of my parents, sharply etched in my memory, is the fact that they remained in love and cherished one another throughout their lives. I have no memory of them ever having an argument, and with their children they would rely on kindness and good humour to resolve any tense situation.

At some point shortly before the war my parents moved to Dagenham in Essex, which was just as well, as 68 Fern Street was badly damaged during the Blitz. We moved to a larger council house with three bedrooms. The houses around swarmed with young families, and the small number of cars on the roads meant that children could play safely on most of the sidestreets. Impromptu football matches started after school on most days. At the age of five I was enrolled at Monteagle Primary and Junior School, just a few minutes' walk from home. Later in life I was surprised to discover that my academic year at Monteagle School was not only to yield a future Archbishop of Canterbury, but also a senior officer in the Royal Air Force and the captain of a Cunard liner.

My recollections of those early years are exceedingly vague, and consist of a kaleidoscope of war memories: the excitement of being bundled into underground shelters, the shattering of the calm order of life through three evacuations to Wiltshire, the drone of planes overhead, the sound of the dreaded 'doodlebugs' and the destruction they wrought. A tremendous camaraderie developed among the families in our road, and people went to great lengths to support one another, even to the degree of sharing rations if the children did not have enough to eat. Dad became very accomplished at making toffee, and Mum's cooking became highly inventive, as she had to make do with whatever ingredients she had to hand to produce food for us all. Dad was not called up, but was involved in 'essential services', working at Ford's motor company churning out tanks and armoured vehicles for the army. Often after work he had to take his turn of duty as one of the Home Guard. As youngsters we were tickled pink to see our father donning his uniform, cleaning his Lee-Enfield rifle and parading with other members of his brigade to different parts of the city. In later years I could never watch BBC TV's *Dad's Army* without thinking of my father.

At times in the early days war did seem exciting and rather intoxicating. A sense of urgency gripped the nation, and that feeling of living on the edge of survival penetrated even the world of children of my age. It was impossible to escape the business of war. We knew we were living in desperate days. During the day barrage balloons filled the sky, and the unmistakable traces of fighter-plane tracks high in the heavens were witnesses to the dogfights going on far above us. I became all too familiar with the sound of the 'doodlebug', the German V1 rocket, which did so much damage to the East End. I learned that if you could hear it you were safe. It was when the engine cut out that you knew its journey was over, and you had better run for cover. Sadly, my best friend at school, Henry, was badly injured in a doodlebug attack. War invaded our daily lives – everyone, it seemed, had at least one relative in the forces, and at school assemblies prayer was earnest. All children learned how to put gas-masks on, and took in their stride regular visits to the air-raid shelters in the back garden – even though the dirty conditions and the presence of spiders made such times less than appealing.

War also intruded on our diet, in the form of rationing, which affected every person in Britain. Everyone had a ration book, and food was rigidly controlled, with priority given to expectant mothers and children. With five children, my parents had a hard time ensuring that we all received adequate nourishment. But while everyone was hungry in wartime Britain, no one starved. The irony is that, despite people having to go without, on the whole rationing meant that the nation was better fed than it had been in the 1930s. People preferred equality to a free-for-all in which the well-off might stockpile food and the poor starve. Poorer families such as ours were entitled to free school meals. Some of my most exciting memories are of my father saving enough sugar to make fudge for all the family.

There were periods when the level of bombing in London meant that children had to be evacuated to safe country areas. That happened to us three times, but thankfully, at least when we had to leave the security of home – in spite of the dangers of bombs – we had the reassuring presence of our mother with us. Many a London child of my generation has reason to be grateful for the wonderful care of country people who could not have been kinder and more welcoming to the city kids with their unruly behaviour and their ignorance of the ways of rural communities.

There was, however, one terrible experience which was imprinted on the memory of us all, when Mother fell out with a family with whom we were staying in Warminster. A deserter came to the door one day asking for bread, and Mum gave him some. The woman who owned the house was furious with her, and a violent argument ensued. The woman then told Mother that she was totally fed up with us all – we must go. We left in a hurry, and returned to London. But Mum only had enough money to reach Paddington, and Dad had no idea we were on our way home. It was very late in the evening when the train arrived, and we were all wretchedly tired. I remember that the younger ones were crying, and Mum was forlorn and exhausted. Suddenly, to our relief and joy, a neighbour recognised Mum and greeted her: 'Ruby! What on earth are you doing here so late?

Why, you all look in need of a good meal.' Mum, in tears, explained her predicament, and the good Samaritan bought us all fish and chips and gave us the money to complete our journey home. It was one of those moments forever treasured in our family history. For my parents it was a real sign that 'Someone' was watching over us all.

But we could not stay in Dagenham, it was far too dangerous, and once more we were evacuated – this time to Bradford-on-Avon and to a remarkable family, the Musslewhites, whose kindness we always remembered. Mr Musslewhite was the billeting officer and also churchwarden of Christ Church, Bradford-on-Avon. It was his job to match children and families with hospitable homes. I was told by one of his children that when he came face-to-face with Mrs Ruby Carey and her five offspring he was so touched by this very close family that, acting on impulse, he decided: 'We will take in this family ourselves.'

We stayed with them for several weeks before a house was found on White Hill, which became our home until it was safe to return to Dagenham. Mr Musslewhite and his family also helped us in more than practical ways. He helped to reconnect us with our church, because it was entirely natural to go to his church every Sunday and to enter into the rhythm of worship and praise, community life and the care of one another. For us children it also meant education at the local church school, which we greatly appreciated. Ever since those days Bradford-on-Avon has had a special place in our affections.

I have little recollection of the many schools I must have entered during those years, except the shock of sitting the eleven-plus examin-ation in 1946, and failing it. Of course, most working-class people then – and possibly even today – gave very little thought to such exams. Life had dealt them such a poor hand that they became accustomed to failure and constant disillusionment. I don't recall my parents being terribly bothered by my failure, but I myself was keenly aware of its momentous significance. Looking back, I am sure that the shock of failing the eleven-plus had a very important part in my later determination to succeed academically. Even at that age I was aware that this exam could determine, to a large degree, the trajectory of one's life. I was shaken, angry and very disappointed with myself.

So to Bifron's Secondary Modern School I went. It wasn't such a bad place for a boy keen to learn, and I quickly made friends. 'Speedy Gonzales' was my father's nickname for me, because I always had my head in a book, and 'speedy' was, to be honest, the last thing I was. School reports from the period inform me that I was regularly in the top three places in most subjects. My favourite teacher, Mr Kennedy, a delightful Scot who had entered the teaching profession directly from the navy, taught English. He opened to me the riches of literature, and I borrowed book after book from him. To this day I owe him so much – for teaching me, with his softly-spoken Scottish accent, the power of literature and the need for precision in language. I recall one time when I had to read out an essay I had composed to the class. I felt very proud to be chosen, and weaved into it a few newly discovered words. Suddenly I came to 'nonchalantly'.

'What do you mean by that word, Carey?'

'Well, sir, I think it means "carelessly".'

'Then why didn't you use the word "carelessly", because all of us know that word better than "nonchalantly"!'

Afterwards, Mr Kennedy said, 'A good essay, George, but don't use language to show off!'

And then there was the Headmaster, Mr Bass, who always wrote in green ink. His impact on my life was his belief in me. I remember the time when Alec Harris, my best friend, and I played truant. Alec had been asked by his mother to do some shopping. No shopping was in fact done. With the money burning a hole in his hand, Alec and I went to Barking cinema – known as the 'fleapit' – instead, where a horror film banned to children was the main attraction. We attached ourselves to an obliging man and spent Mrs Harris's money on the tickets, ice cream and sweets. We got our just deserts, because the film was particularly horrible, with realistic scenes of a hand that strangled people. Leaving the cinema, both of us realised the even more horrifying consequences of what we had done. Not only had we played truant, but we had spent someone else's money on a film we were not entitled to see. Mrs Harris was, not surprisingly, angry, and reported us both to the school. I was caned, but long after the pain had subsided the rebuke in Mr Bass's voice hurt me more: 'I am disappointed by you, Carey. You have let yourself down. You are worthy of better things than this.'

What made this incident particularly distressing was that the late forties were very tough for ordinary people. Employment was not a great problem and most men found work quickly, but wages were low, and poverty dogged the steps of most working-class families. Mrs Harris had every right to be profoundly distressed. Luckily I was able to keep the story from my parents, who would have been appalled by my behaviour. As for our family, Dad continued to work at Ford, and brought home just enough for us to pay the rent and get by. Life was hard, but we were a happy family, and entertainment came from fun in the home, close friendships at school, and of course from the radio, or 'wireless' as everyone called it.

One day the wireless packed up. We were dismayed beyond measure, but Dad reassured us that we would get a new one, although as we could not afford to buy it outright, it would have to be on hire purchase. I shall never forget the day the salesman came to agree terms with our parents. Soon we would be the proud owners of a new radio, and for the five children it was a moment to savour and look forward to. After the man had left, one look at Dad's face told the story – he did not earn enough to pay the monthly instalments for a new radio; we had to settle for a second-hand one that Mother bought with some saved housekeeping money the following day. I would not go so far as to say that that incident alone made me conscious of the unfairness of life, and the way that a privileged class controlled the rest of us. It is true to say, however, that the form of Christian faith I espoused later in life had a clear social and political foundation. If it did not make a difference to life, it could never be for me a real faith.

Party politics did not intrude greatly into our home. Mum and

Dad were working-class Conservatives, as far as political affiliation was concerned. My father was an intelligent man and enjoyed a good argument. His daily paper was the *Express*, and every Sunday the *People* was read from cover to cover. They were Tory papers. He had no time for socialism, believing it to be allied to Communism, and therefore in his view opposed to everything that made Britain great and free. Our parents were also unashamedly royalist, principally, I believe, because the monarchy gave a visible form to British traditions and values.

Nevertheless, even as a young teenager I could not help wondering, as I watched our two happy parents, what the Conservative Party had ever done for them. 'Look at how poor you are. Look at the way you struggle to make ends meet,' I thought. I could not understand their acceptance of the way things were. Deep down I felt that there ought to be, indeed must be, a better way.

Shortly after the war we moved again, this time to a three-bedroom council house in Old Dagenham. Our parents had a modest bedroom overlooking the rear garden, which was bigger than our previous one, the girls were in a pokey 'box room', and the three boys shared a larger room overlooking the road. It was a house full of noise and fun. Most evenings we listened to the radio which engaged with our imaginations with serials like *Dick Barton, Special Agent* and many other favourites. We were encouraged to read, and the local library was a great resource. Whenever he had time Dad would disappear into the shed where his tools were stored and make toys for us all. Alas, I never did acquire his practical ability, although my brother Dennis did in abundance.

With romantic notions of the ocean, I decided to join the Sea Cadets at the age of twelve, and I stayed with this great youth organisation until I was sixteen. Admittedly I had to lie to get in, as the minimum age of entry was thirteen, but I was a tall, strong lad and managed to convince the CO that I was old enough. The Sea Cadets helped me to mix with other teenagers and gave me confidence in holding my own with them.

At thirteen I was able to sit another examination to see if I was up to the level to attend high school, and this time I passed. I can still remember the feeling of happiness. I was not a failure after all. But then came another let-down – my parents visited Mr Bass, and the conclusion of the meeting was that there was more to be gained by my staying at Bifron's than moving on at that stage. I was not unhappy with the decision, because I was comfortable at the school, was cruising through the classes and had made many friends. The blow was to come when, at the age of fifteen and a half, I had to leave Bifron's with no qualifications whatsoever. Secondary-modern pupils did not sit the matriculation examination.

This did not bother me at first, because I did not realise the significance of matriculation. My reading had made me thirsty for adventure, and I dreamed of joining the Merchant Navy and becoming a Radio Officer – no doubt the legacy of Mr Kennedy's tales of his life in the Royal Navy before he became a teacher. The outside world, however, brutally woke me up to reality. For the vast majority of working-class children, school ended at fifteen and work beckoned. So I was suddenly pitched into the world of employment, and became an office boy at the London Electricity Board in East India Dock Road, Bow.

The adult world I now found myself a member of was certainly not dull or lacking interest. On the contrary, it was a bustling, urgent world of caring for customers and serving others. As office boy I was at the bottom of the heap, and the servant of all. At the top of the pile was Mr Vincent, a tall, emaciated figure who swept through the outer offices to sycophantic calls of 'Good morning, sir! Good morning, Mr Vincent.' Without acknowledging any of the greetings he would disappear into his office, closing the door sharply behind him.

I fell foul of Mr Vincent in my second week. I was summoned into his office and given instructions to go to a shop in Whitechapel and collect some goods he had ordered. He gave me £5 to cover the cost. I was thrilled at this opportunity to show him that I was up to scratch. I jumped on the bus happily and then, for some reason known only to the brain of an absent-minded fifteen-year-old, I started to clear out my pockets of their debris, discarding some items and shredding others. I arrived at the shop, and after I had been handed the parcel I reached for the note I had put into my top pocket. With mounting horror, I realised what I had done. From my pocket I withdrew – half of a fiver. The shopkeeper refused the tattered remains of the note point-blank, and with panic I returned to face the music, knowing that my job was on the line.

A stern-looking Mr Vincent heard me out in total silence. 'Now go to the bank,' he ordered, 'and in return for the half of the banknote, you may be able to get a new £5 note – otherwise you will have to pay for this yourself.' As that represented at least two weeks' salary for an office boy, I was relieved when the bank gave me a whole £5 note for the fragment I sheepishly presented. It was not a happy start to my working life.

There was, however, another side to this unpopular boss whose grumpy personality made him seem a tyrant to his staff. One lunch-time Mr Vincent found me in the corner of the open office reading a book I had withdrawn from the local library. As I was by far the youngest in the office I had no one of my own age to chat with, and reading was the only way to pass the time – not that I, of all people, complained. No doubt Mr Vincent had observed me reading on other occasions, but this time he approached me with a book.

'Carey. Have you read much of Charles Dickens?' he asked.

I replied that I had not.

'A pity,' he said. 'He is in my opinion one of the greatest writers in the English language. Here, borrow this book, and tell me what you think.' He disappeared into his office, slamming the door behind him.

Within a few days I had read *Nicholas Nickleby* and returned it. The following day I was called into Mr Vincent's large office and, standing on the other side of his desk, I was required to give him a critique of *Nicholas Nickleby*. His muttered grunts indicated approval, and another Dickens novel was passed across the desk. I must have read my way through most of Dickens's *oeuvre* before I left to do my National Service at the age of eighteen. How I thank God for Mr Vincent for giving me such a wonderful apprenticeship in learning. It dawned on me later that it wasn't only the reading of Dickens he encouraged in me, but the articulation of ideas. He made me use words more effectively, and made me listen to the rolling cadences of prose. 'Read that again,' I was often ordered. 'Do you see the way he was combining nouns, adverbs and verbs to bring the reader into the story?' He made me pay attention to the uses of language, as well as to its beauty.

But another discovery – an even more important discovery – happened during this period. I discovered there was a God.

My family was not religious – at least, not in the sense of feeling a need to go to church and worship. To this day I am not religious in that way. Worship is of course important, and people who claim to be Christian should belong to a congregation and attend as regularly as they can. But if worship is the outward badge of being a Christian, putting one's belief into practice will always be its heart.

It was Bob, one of the twins, four years my junior, who first started going to Old Dagenham Parish Church. From the back of our three-bedroom council house at 198 Reede Road we could see the tower of the church in the old village of Dagenham. Bob loved the people he met there, and told me about them. So after work one day I decided to go along to the Youth Club that met on a Monday evening.

I made friends instantly. Every Monday the open Youth Club met, and on Tuesdays there was a meeting of 'Christian Endeavour'. It was these that really interested me. They took the form of a service lasting one hour, led, in the main, by young people. Most of them were from lower-middle-class backgrounds, and they were zealous and bright. A few of them stood out, and would become special friends: Ronald Rushmer, Edna Millings, and the twins David and John Harris.

They were all a year or two older than myself, and I was impressed by the depth of their faith, the rigour of their thinking and the breadth of their lives. There was nothing 'holy' or 'religious' about them. They seemed to me to be whole people, and their interests were certainly mine. The fact is that, whether religious or not, I was deeply interested in philosophy, and particularly the meaning of life. I can't even begin to date this interest, although I know that as soon as I was old enough to get a library ticket I started to read books by great thinkers. I vividly remember reading a book by Bertrand Russell for over an hour at Becontree library, and being asked to leave by an impatient member of staff who wanted to lock up.

The war had deeply unsettled my generation, and led many of us to ask fundamental questions about the meaning of freedom, democracy and peace. Working-class men returning from six years of conflict were determined to put behind them forever the nightmare of the thirties. Winston Churchill's stock in the country was still high, but it was felt that even he represented a period that demeaned the vast majority of people in the land – as was demonstrated by his defeat in the general election of July 1945.

War affected me too: not in the sense of unsettling me psychologically, so much as making me aware that there were exciting questions concerning the meaning of life. Later I would find that Immanuel Kant's classic formulation expressed my search succinctly: 'What can I know? What must I do? What can I hope for?' The three questions, focusing on epistemology, morals and the future of humankind, seemed to me to identify the truly crucial issues. For me as a teenager, however, the questions took a less sophisticated form: 'Is there a God? If so, what is He like? Is He knowable?'

Old Dagenham Parish Church, with its open and evangelical style, suited me perfectly. A new vicar had arrived, the Reverend Edward Porter Conway Patterson – or 'Pit-Pat', as the young people instantly baptised him. Pit-Pat had recently returned from service in Kenya as a missionary. His preaching was direct, and always contained an appeal for people to turn to Christ. Many did, and the congregation grew. There could be no denying Pit-Pat's great abilities and focus. His theology was Christ-centred and Bible-based. He was against anything that watered down the heart of what he believed to be Anglican theology, and particularly disapproved of Catholicism in any shape or form. If there was anything worse than Roman Catholicism, it was Anglo-Catholicism. He urged his congregation to abstain from drink and to avoid cinemas and theatres: 'Come out from among them and be separate' was one of his favourite Pauline texts.

Pit-Pat's great strengths were his directness and simplicity; his weaknesses were the same. It did not take me very long to discover this, and in time I became concerned that he was projecting a joyless and stern gospel that fell short of the faith I was discovering for myself. Sadly, the negative influence of his teaching resulted in my feeling guilty for the next ten years whenever I saw a film or drank even a glass of beer or wine.

Worship puzzled me as well as impressed me. It was always based on the Book of Common Prayer, and a great deal of it seemed boring. It was the sermon we looked forward to, and following the service those young people who wanted to would go to the curate's house for coffee and a discussion of the sermon. As time went on, however, I began to appreciate the framework of worship. Because of my growing love for the beauty of language, I came to find the Prayer Book evocative and wonderfully inspiring, and it took root in me. There are times even now when I wonder if the Church took a wrong turn in developing modern liturgies from the 1960s onward. We have certainly lost 'common prayer'. In my youth, every parish church was bound together by the 1662 Prayer Book, even though it was expressed in many different ways. Sadly, today 'uncommon prayer' is closer to the truth, and many evangelical churches have departed from authorised forms altogether.

My intellectual development continued when the Harris twins began to interest me in music. Until then my musical education had been limited to what I heard on radio, which was largely the popular music of the time. I was, and continue to be, a fan of big bands and jazz. Ted Heath and his orchestra, Dizzy Gillespie, Stan Kenton and his band were among my favourites. One day John Harris said to me, 'George, do you fancy coming round to our house on Saturday afternoon to listen to music?' I readily accepted, expecting that we would be listening to jazz. Not a bit of it. I found myself listening entranced to classical music for three hours. This became a regular feature of my weekends, listening to great music, which like literature and philosophy took root in me – Elgar, Beethoven, Chopin, Bach, Mozart and other great composers. Ironically for a developing evangelical, Elgar's *Dream of Gerontius* had a major impact on my emotional and theological development. It remains to this day one of the finest pieces of music I have ever heard. Through the influence of John and David Harris, music became an essential element of my growing faith. In time I was able to say with Siegfried Sassoon:

> From you, Beethoven, Bach, Mozart,
> The substance of my dreams took fire.
> You built cathedrals in my heart,
> And lit my pinnacled desire.
> You were the ardour and the bright
> Procession of my thoughts toward prayer.
> You were the wrath of storm, the light
> On distant citadels aflame.

As my thinking progressed, so did my journey into the Christian faith. I bought my first Bible, and read it avidly. At the same time I was reading Christian writers such as Leslie Weatherhead, the great Methodist teacher. Pit-Pat, recognising my thirst for reading, lent me books on prayer and spirituality, on faith and doubt, on doctrine and dogma. The focus of my interest was the person of Jesus Christ. His claims, and the claims that the Church made about Him, were so remarkable that I was forced to ask: Is it true that He is the hinge of history, that decisive omega point, by which all faith is assessed? The point came when I passed from a vague belief in God to a firm and joyful conviction that Jesus is the Son of God, Saviour of the

World and, what seemed more important at the time – my saviour and Lord. There was no blinding Damascus experience, rather a quiet certainty that many of my questions had been answered, and my Christian life had begun.

I told Pit-Pat, and he was thrilled, although his response unnerved me: 'I want you to read John 1.1, and memorise it to the end. Come back next week and recite it to me. Now, next Sunday, after the evening service we are going to have an open-air service in the banjo directly opposite your house. I want you to give your testimony.'

The first request was easy, but the thought of giving a testimony, a familiar practice in evangelical circles, terrified me. Because the 'banjo' (a familiar pattern on council estates, with houses arranged in the shape of a banjo around a small green) was opposite my house, all our neighbours would be able to see me standing on a soapbox, and would hear me speak. The implications were horrifying. My parents would be ashamed. But Pit-Pat would not hear of me backing down. 'You have committed yourself to Christ. Now nail your colours to the mast!'

The following Sunday evening after the service, about thirty of us were there on the green, and a simple service began with a few hymns, a speaker and my 'testimony'. I doubt if it lasted more than two minutes, but it was enough to satisfy Pit-Pat. In his opinion George Carey, at the age of nearly seventeen, had declared himself a believer.

Looking back fifty years, I have no doubt in describing it as a real conversion experience which changed the pathway of my life. It was forged from reading, from worship, fellowship and prayer. But it was only a beginning. Other great moments of discovery were to follow, and one can only call such youthful moments of conversion authentic in the light of what develops from them.

Great joy was to follow as other members of our family followed Bob and myself on this journey of faith. Our sisters Ruby and Val attended a church camp, and returned with a story of a commitment to Christ. And then our parents quite unexpectedly followed. I will never forget the moment Mum and Dad committed themselves to Christ. They had watched their children's spiritual development with curiosity mixed with joy and, no doubt, alarm. That they did not know what was going on was evident, but they were pleased with the difference faith made to our lives.

Youth for Christ rallies were held regularly in Dagenham at that time, and we had invited Mum and Dad along to one particular meeting. The preacher invited all those who wanted to follow Jesus Christ to come to the front. To my amazement our parents walked hand-in-hand up the aisle. For both of them it was a 'coming home'. They had been brought up as Christians, and had gone to church as youngsters. My father's life, especially, had been irradiated with the spiritual through the influence of his blind grandfather. Now both of our wonderful parents were convinced Christians.

Dennis, eighteen months younger than me, was in the meantime going out with Jean, his future wife, and missed the spiritual revolution going on in the family. Although sad that this was not to be his story too, he was never made to feel excluded in any way. Indeed, I always felt very close to him, and knew that the Christian faith was also real to him, although expressed in a different way.

The impact of my father's dramatic conversion revealed itself a few weeks later. Dad said early one Sunday morning, 'I'm not going to church today, because I've got to put something right.' He explained that when he was fourteen he had worked for a Christian man named Mr Zeal in Forest Gate, and had stolen some money. 'But he must be dead by now!' said Mother, amazed by Dad's insistence that he had to at least try to make amends.

Later that day, Dad returned from his journey with a glad and triumphant smile on his face. He had gone to the nonconformist church where Mr Zeal worshipped and had been informed that Mr Zeal was still alive, but was not very well. Dad went round to his former employer's house, reintroduced himself and confessed that he had taken a small amount of money. Mr Zeal looked at him with complete amazement and joy. 'You know, Carey,' he finally said, 'I knew you had taken the money, and I have been praying for you ever since.' What a shot in the arm for my father's faith that was, and what a lot it taught us all about the power of prayer.

Even as a youngster I could tell what that commitment to Christ did for my mother and father. It changed them both, and gave them a great thirst to know more not only about the Christian faith, but about how to apply that knowledge to life around them. The limited education my father had received made it impossible for him to do anything other than lowly jobs, and soon after his conversion he became a porter at Rush Green Hospital in Romford, where he made a deep impact on the lives of many patients through his Christian goodness and kind words.

As for me, my learning too continued. My work at the London Electricity Board did not tax me, and I was eager to move on. The opportunity came when, not long before my eighteenth birthday, I received a letter informing me that I was due for my National Service call-up. I was delighted. It was time for me to move from my secure home, and I was ready to go.

3

Signals

'Why couldn't Quirrell touch me?'

'Your mother died to save you. If there is one thing Voldemort cannot understand it is love . . . love as powerful as your mother's leaves its own mark. Not a visible sign . . . but to have been loved so deeply, even though the person who loved us is gone, will give us some protection forever.'

J.K. Rowling, Harry Potter and the Philosopher's Stone

WITH A YOUTHFUL IMAGINATION fired by Mr Kennedy's stories of the Royal Navy, and fed by my experience in the Sea Cadets, my preference was to do my National Service in the navy. Unfortunately, the Royal Navy did not accept conscripts at that time, so it had to be the Royal Air Force. As it turned out I was not to be disappointed in the slightest. For a young man eager to explore life and widen his horizons, the Air Force suited me down to the ground.

First came a week of 'kitting out' at RAF Cardington, where hundreds of dazed and subdued eighteen-year-olds gathered to be allocated to billets, receive severe haircuts and don the blue uniform of the youngest service. Pit-Pat's final advice to me the previous day seemed particularly daunting: 'George, you must disclose that you are a Christian right from the start. Don't be ashamed of your faith. When lights go out, kneel by your bed and say your prayers.' This had seemed easy enough to agree to when in church, but I confess that as I surveyed the crowded billet on my first evening, with the good-natured banter of high-spirited young men all around me, my resolve wavered. Nevertheless, taking a deep breath, I knelt and spent several minutes in prayer.

The reaction was interesting. First there was a quietening-down of voices as everyone realised I was praying and, unusually courteously, gave me space for prayer. The second reaction – clearly predicted by Pit-Pat – was that it marked me out as someone who took his faith seriously. The following day at least six young men in the billet took me aside and declared that they were practising Christians. By the end of the second day we were told of a SASRA (Soldiers and Sailors Scripture Readers' Association) Bible-study meeting that evening. SASRA was particularly favoured by nonconformist and evangelical Christians, and throughout my National Service I found it a wonderful source of fellowship and support.

I never found that my practice of public praying, which I kept going for a great deal of my time in the Air Force, limited or negatively affected my relationships with other servicemen. To be sure, there were often jokes when I knelt down to pray. There were several times when things were thrown at me, and once my left boot was stolen while I was on my knees – just minutes before an inspection. Somehow I managed to keep to attention with one boot on and one off as the officer advanced through the billet.

Years later, in fact just a few weeks before I retired, I was touched to receive a letter from a Mr Michael Moran, who wrote to my secretary at Lambeth Palace:

> Dear Sir,
> Are you able to tell me whether George Carey spent the early years of his National Service at the basic training camp at RAF Cardington? When I was there at that time I was deeply impressed (and this has remained with me ever since) by the devotion and courage of an eighteen-year-old named George who knelt to pray at the side of his barrack-room bed. At no time in the following two years did I see anyone else show such evidence of his faith.

I was rather uncomfortable to receive such praise, because I did not kneel down to impress people by my courage, or to be the odd man out. In fact, I shrank from doing so. I did it simply because I felt Pit-Pat was absolutely right: if prayer is important, and if one is in a communal setting with no private place to pray, one ought not to be ashamed or embarrassed to be known as someone who loves God and worships Him. Later in life I would put the issue as a question to others: 'Muslims aren't ashamed to pray publicly, so why should Christians feel embarrassed? If it is a good way of praying when one is alone, why should we be ashamed of acknowledging a relationship with God when we are with others?'

The relative calm of the kitting-out week was followed by eight weeks' hard square-bashing at West Kirby, near Liverpool. To this day, while I am left with many questions about the psychology behind the tyrannising and brutal attitude of the Platoon Leaders and Sergeants, there can be little dispute that it is a highly efficient way of moulding young men into effective members of a military unit. For eight weeks we were terrorised by screaming NCOs who told us in unambiguous terms that we were the lowest forms of life ever to appear on earth: 'You are a turd of unspeakable putrefaction', 'a cretin with an IQ lower than a tadpole', 'You are the scum of the earth! What are you? Repeat it after me: the scum of the earth', 'You are hopeless, hopeless, hopeless.'

The verbal ingenuity of some descriptions was rehearsed in the billet long into the evening, as we sympathised with victims or rejoiced at the misfortune of a rival platoon. There were times when I too became the object of the Squad Corporal's wrath. 'Carey, you little bleeder!' he screamed into my face, his saliva making my eyes water, 'I am about to tear your ****ing left arm off and intend to beat your ****ing 'ead in with the bloody end, until your brains – if you have any – are scattered far and wide.' Imagine my disappointment when I discovered later that this threat was far from original, and was in fact a tried and trusty favourite of that particular NCO.

I was able to gauge attitudes to the Church from the viewpoint of the ordinary conscript. The vast majority of my 'mates' had no contact with institutional religion. Although most of them, deep down, had faith, few of them had the ability to convert it into anything of relevance. They were not, on the whole, helped by the Chaplains, who held officer rank and talked down to the conscripted men. We all had to go to compulsory religious classes, and I can only say that from a Christian point of view these were something to be endured rather than enjoyed. The talks were usually moralistic, and the most embarrassing were about sex, a subject on which the Chaplains were definitely out of touch with the earthy culture of working-class people. I remember asking myself: 'Why are they so shy about talking about the subject where they are expert? About the existence of God, about spirituality and prayer, about Jesus Christ and His way?'

Even more frustrating to me was the fact that I never saw a Chaplain visiting the men, either in the mess or in the billets. Far more effective was the ordinary 'bloke' from SASRA, who at least had the courage to meet the men where they were. Church parades were no different. The hymns were sung indifferently, and the sermons went over the heads of all. I was often embarrassed by the effete way services were conducted, and felt that overall they did more harm than good to the Church.

Although I was glad when the square-bashing was over, I have to admit that it taught me a lot about myself and how to cope when pushed to one's limit. At the end of the eight weeks I was posted to RAF Compton Bassett in Wiltshire to train as a Wireless Operator. If I was not able to be a Wireless Officer in the Royal Navy, well, being a Wireless Operator in the Royal Air Force seemed an interesting challenge. And so it turned out to be. The training took twenty weeks, and included elementary electronics as well as having Morse code so drummed into us that by the end of it most of us were able to send and receive Morse at over twenty words a minute. As VHF was still in its infancy even in the RAF at that time Morse code was a reliable and efficient form of communication, though of course very slow.

At Compton Bassett we were able to participate in many activities, ranging from sport to hobbies of all kinds. Discipline continued to be very strict, but we were now finding that the ordered life enabled work and leisure to function smoothly. I played a lot of football, and enjoyed running as well. At weekends evening worship at Calne Parish Church was certainly far more authentic than the formal and compulsory church parades.

At the end of the training, everyone waited with impatience for their postings. I was astonished to be selected for the post of Wireless Operator on an air–sea rescue MTB (motor torpedo boat) operating out of Newquay in Devon. It seemed that at last my dreams would be fulfilled. If not the Royal Navy, at least I would be at sea with the RAF. But it was not to be. Two days before taking up my posting I was told to report to the CO's office, where I was given completely different instructions – to go home on leave immediately, and to report to Stansted airport the following Sunday evening for an unknown destination.

I was among twenty or so extremely puzzled airmen on a York aircraft which left Stansted that September Sunday evening in 1955. To the question I put to the Sergeant on duty I received the friendly rejoinder, 'You'll know soon enough where you are when you land, laddie.'

Sure enough, I did. The following morning I found myself in Egypt, and the same day I started work as a Wireless Operator (WOP) at RAF Fayid – a huge RAF camp alongside part of the Suez Canal known as the 'Bitter Lakes'. With a large group of other WOPs work began in earnest, handling signals from Britain and the many RAF bases in the Middle East. In my leisure time I enjoyed exploring beyond the base and discovered many things about Egypt, its culture and life. I settled down to church life on the base, and made many friends.

After three months at RAF Fayid I was sent to RAF Shaibah – a posting which was greeted by howls of sympathy by my colleagues. Shaibah was a tiny base about fifteen miles from Basra, at the top of the Persian Gulf. It is very hot most of the year, and the temperature rarely falls below 120 degrees in the shade in summer. With just 120 airmen to service the squadron of Sabre jets and cover the region I was told that it was a deadly appointment, and that I was to be pitied.

On the way to Shaibah a bizarre incident took place that was to make me chuckle often in later life. The journey began with a flight to Habbaniyah, a large RAF camp close to Baghdad, from where I was to make my way by train to Basra. I boarded the plane and was shown to my seat by the WOP, who told me, 'Carey, your lunch is on your seat. Make yourself at home,' before disappearing into the cockpit alongside the pilot. There were no other passengers, but I noticed that there was another lunchbag on the seat alongside mine. Surely this was for me too, I concluded. It was, I admit, naïve of me to suppose that the RAF would offer me two lunches and without hesitation I scoffed both of them. To my surprise the plane landed in the Transjordan, and as we taxied towards the concourse the terrible truth dawned on me – we were about to pick up another passenger, and I had eaten his lunch.

The passenger in question was an elderly clergyman, who was greeted with deference by the crew and shown to his seat alongside mine. We had a brief chat, and the plane took off. The moment came when he reached for his lunchbox, and I had to stammer out an apology for having eaten his lunch. He made light of it, and we relaxed into a pleasant conversation in which he showed great interest in my welfare and future. On landing at Habbaniyah I was impressed to see a red carpet laid out to welcome somebody – I knew it was not for me. The top brass were all there alongside the CO. The elderly clergyman paused to say goodbye to me, then turned to the steps to be greeted by the CO and whisked away.

'Who was that?' I asked the WOP.

'Oh, that's Archbishop McInnes, Archbishop of Jerusalem and the Middle East,' came the reply.

Sadly, I never had an opportunity to apologise again to Archbishop George McInnes for having eaten his lunch that day; but at least I was later able to tell his son, Canon David McInnes, of the incident. David had followed his father into the Church, and completed a very distinguished ministry as Rector of St Aldate's, Oxford. He was sure that his father would have been delighted and thoroughly amused that the culprit was a future Archbishop of Canterbury.

Despite the warnings of my colleagues at Fayid, Shaibah was to prove a wonderful posting for me. I was one of eight WOPs who had a special role as High Frequency Direction Finding Radio Operators (known as HF/DF Operators). So primitive and sensitive was this means of communication that it required the erection of special radio huts three miles from the camp, out in the desert. On each side of the hut stood four large aerials which received signals from transport planes, and which provided an accurate beam by which a plane could determine its position and find its way to us.

Operators were on duty in these isolated huts for eight hours at a time, and for many months we worked around the clock. The duty was often boring, very hot and lonely. There were however times when the importance of our work was driven home. On one occasion several Secret Service personnel called on me to help trace the position of a Russian radio network which was proving to be a nuisance to the RAF. Another time, a two-engine transport plane from Aden to Bahrain was in serious trouble, with one engine on fire and the other causing problems. To this day I recall the SOS ringing through my headphones, and the signal telling me that the plane needed help urgently as it was about to crash. All the training I had received was focused at that very moment on giving the crew directions on how to find their way to Shaibah, then alerting the main camp and the emergency services that a crippled plane was in need of help. As a member of the air–ground rescue team I would be required to switch instantly to new responsibilities if the plane crashed in the desert. Fortunately I was able to help nurse the plane to the base, where it made an emergency landing and all was well.

It was a lonely job most of the time, but I loved it. It gave me time to read and reflect. When things were quiet and no planes were within a two-hundred-mile radius it was safe to walk a short way from the hut and explore the desert. The idea that the desert was void of life, I discovered, is quite erroneous. There were always fragile, tiny yet beautiful flowers that one could find, and the place teemed with insects, snakes and scorpions. As for human contact, I often met passing Bedouin tribespeople: sometimes shy, giggling young girls hidden behind their flowing black robes, herding their black goats; sometimes their more confident brothers and fathers. They were always friendly, even though we could only communicate through signs and through my limited Arabic, which caused great merriment. In exchange for water, which I had in abundance, I would often receive figs, dates and other fruits. Their simple, uncomplicated lives seemed attractive and natural. It was always a joy to meet them, and for a few moments share a common humanity in a hostile terrain.

I do recall though one terrifying time when I wandered a little too far, and could not find my little signals hut in the expanse of desert. The realisation that I was totally lost, without water, and that my replacement would not arrive at the hut for six hours panicked me greatly. I tried to take my bearings from the puffs of smoke coming from the distant oilwells in Kuwait, but to no avail. I walked carefully north, hoping to find some clue that might orient me. Then, with relief, I heard the sound of singing, and into view came some of my Bedouin friends. They were shocked to see me so exhausted, and after a drink of water I was taken back to the hut. Perhaps only forty minutes had passed, but it made me aware of how fragile life is, and how the desert can never be taken lightly.

In our leisure time there was opportunity to explore the sur-rounding region, including the teeming city of Basra, a forty-minute car ride away. Every Sunday evening dozens of us would go to worship at St Peter's Church, where there was a hospitable expatriate congre-gation. I confess that I can scarcely recall the services at all, and the only thing I remember is the vicar's fascination for the card game Racing Demon, that was played every Sunday evening following choral evensong. But the worship was excellent, and almost without realising it I was nurtured and sustained by it.

Several of us went on a number of trips to the ancient Assyrian site of Ur of the Chaldees, home to Nebuchadnezzar. Time had reduced this great archaeological site to pathetic heaps of stone, but its grandeur and imposing scale was undiminished.

It was the living, vibrant Iraq that intrigued me, however, and I went out of my way to find out more about the life of its people. I made some enquiries at the Education Centre on the base, and enrolled in a class to learn Arabic. In this way I encountered Islam as a living faith. I was the only pupil in the class, and I took advantage of such personal tuition. My teacher was an intelligent middle-aged Iraqi named Iz'ik, who took great delight in teaching me the rudiments of a graceful language. In addition to the language, he introduced me to his faith. Through his eyes I gained a sympathy towards and an interest in Islam that has endured until the present time.

I was impressed by my teacher's deep spirituality and devotion to God. It was not uncommon to see Muslim believers serving on the camp lay out their prayer mats wherever they were and turn to Mecca at the set times of the day. Many of my fellow airmen mocked them, but I could not. I sensed a brotherhood with them in their devotion and their openness about their spirituality. Although sharp differences exist between the two world religions, the way that Islam affects every aspect of life continues to impress me.

I was led also to appreciate the overlap between the Christian faith and Islam. I discovered its deep commitment to Jesus – a fact hardly known to most Christians – who is seen as a great prophet who will come as Messiah at the end of time. I began to appreciate the remarkable role of Mohammed in Islam, and the way in which he is a role model for male Muslims. Perhaps one of the most striking things that Iz'ik revealed to me was the fact that in Iraq Christians had been living alongside Muslims for centuries in complete harmony. In time I met a number of Assyrian Christians whose faith was deep and real.

Iz'ik and I often discussed the areas of faith and life where our religions diverged. Among these was the Trinity, and I hope that my youthful explanation led my teacher to understand that Christianity is monotheistic, and not polytheistic as many Muslims believe. I argued as strongly as I could for the relevance of Jesus Christ and the determining significance of Him for faith. As I saw it then – and still do – one can have a high regard for Jesus (as Muslims un-doubtedly do), yet fail to see that unless He is central to the faith, that faith is inadequate without Him. Some thinkers have termed this the 'scandal' of Christianity, and the reason it can be seen as uncompromising and exclusive.

Perhaps above all I was led to appreciate the spirituality of Islam, and its devotion to prayer and the disciplined life. Although, as a young evangelical, I was perhaps over-eager to convince Iz'ik of the truth of Christianity, he would give as good as he got, and we both enjoyed our weekly discussions. Later in life those times would help me to treat Islam not as a faith hostile to Christianity, but as a religion with many virtues and many similarities to our own. Sadly, when I left Shaibah I left the study of Arabic behind me as well. In 1956 I did not consider it remotely possible that I would ever find the language useful in the days to come. How wrong I was.

The months passed quickly because there was so much to do. As the Wireless Operator of an air–ground rescue crew, I enjoyed several weekends on practices in the wonderful Iraqi marshes, which in recent years Saddam Hussein has so destructively drained. In the 1950s it was a fertile area for wildlife and fishing, and if the truth be known, the air–ground rescue practices were in fact an opportunity for the CO to indulge his love of shooting game. Besides being the wireless link with the base, my other job was to pluck and skin the beautiful pheasants he shot. Ironically, on one of these weekends an aircraft actually did crash in Kuwait, and an *ad hoc* rescue team had to be formed to do what we were supposedly training to do.

Because the desert ground was so hard, and the heat so debilitat-ing, free time was passed in less strenuous activities, and the open-air swimming pool was our daily centre when off-duty. I was keen on other sports too, and accompanied a friend who was a dedicated runner in punishing laps of the perimeter of the airfield. The daily routine of work and sport allowed time for Christian fellowship as well. Of the 120 men on the base, there was a small but healthy number of practising Christians of all denominations and traditions. There was no Chaplain, so we had to create our own worship, which usually took the form of Bible study with hymns and prayers.

Towards the end of my time at Shaibah I found an old building left open for spring cleaning. Shaibah had been a huge base during the Second World War, and most of the former camp was now closed up. To my surprise I found myself in a well-kept Anglican chapel. I immediately conferred with some of my friends, and we agreed that it would be good to keep it open – that is, if the CO agreed. He did, but for a limited time only. So for several weeks we held services according to the Book of Common Prayer rite and I celebrated holy communion – quite illegally, of course. I don't suppose for one moment that the Almighty was bothered that in the absence of a priest a group of young men took it in turns to use the words of the 1662 Prayer Book and to celebrate communion.

Once a week a flight from RAF Habbaniyah would bring us one of the latest films being shown in the UK, and we would gather in the open air to watch them. I well remember one which suggested to me the residual hostility some people felt towards the Church of England. The title I cannot remember, but one of the characters, a vicar, was a detestable man out to con an old woman of her wealth. When he was shown putting on his dog collar, jeers and whistles of disgust drowned out the soundtrack. The moment seemed to show that young people felt alienated from the life of the Church. That of course had not been so in my case, but I had to remember that not everyone had had good experiences of clergymen.

There was a darker side to service life which brought home to me the value of a faith, with its framework of moral values. Several times a week men would visit the brothels of Basra, and sometimes they returned with the unexpected fruits of pleasure – in the form of gonorrhoea, syphilis and other sexually transmitted diseases. This meant that we had to endure horrific educational films on the dangers of these diseases, which certainly disturbed many of us, but did not seem to dampen the ardour of others. I did not see it as my job to reprove them, although I would certainly put my view forward. Neither was I immune from the temptation that led them to succumb, but I suppose I felt that my faith expected me to honour women, and not to treat them as mere objects of sexual gratification.

As time drew close to my demob, the next stage on my journey increasingly occupied my mind and prayers. One evening when I was on a late shift, the silence of the desert called me to reflect deeply on the future. When the shift ended I signed the usual summary of work, then waited outside for the car that would bring out my replacement and take me back to the camp. I could not but marvel at the beauty and brilliance of the night sky from the darkness of the desert in which I stood. Thousands of stars illuminated the heavens, and seemed within an arm's length of me. As I drank in the awesome scene, I was overcome by the finiteness and smallness of man when measured against the age of the universe. And yet, that did not intimidate me. Later Gerard Manley Hopkins's great poem 'The World is Charged with the Grandeur of God' would become one of my favourites, and would capture for me the feeling of awe I felt then.

It has sometimes puzzled me that the size of the universe has led thinking people into agnosticism. Some have said to me, 'How can you possibly believe in a personal deity when our planet is a third-rate planet in a tenth-rate galaxy in one of countless solar systems?' I would usually reply that this was making too good a case for the earth, but that size has little to do with it. If the Almighty is so awesome that He has created as many galaxies as there are grains of sand in a million deserts, that same awesome God may still love us and be our heavenly Father. Pascal's cry, 'The silence of eternal space terrifies me,' did not stop him trusting in the maker of all things.

It was those evenings in the southern Iraqi desert, under the velvety blanket lit by the brilliance of thousands of stars, that led me to take an interest in cosmology and the mystery of creation. I have not read anything since that has caused me to falter in my conviction that a personal faith in a loving God is not irrational or incredible. But it is not faith that drives people to serve God and others, so much as love. I was convinced of the love of God for all, and that was the element that energised my response perhaps more than any other.

But that moment beneath the stars also crystallised a question that had been on my mind for months: what was I going to make of my life on my return to England in a few weeks? Teaching was an admirable profession. Social work too attracted me. But the tug at my heart was definitely the ordained ministry, and in prayer I tried to put into words my deep desire to serve God and humankind with all my heart.

I had no qualifications to speak of, just an overwhelming longing to make something of my life with all the energy and ability I had been given. Yet even with the optimism and self-confidence one has at that age, I was conscious of the huge challenge ahead of me. But under that wonderful night sky the thought began to enter my head that ordination might not be beyond me. I might lack academic qualifications, but I did not lack ability or a great desire to do something useful with my life. I was still young enough to learn. I could only do my very best, and rely on God's grace.

4

Shaken Up

'Don't trouble because you think you are not fit. Of course
you are not fit. The greatest saint is not fit for the service of
God: but there is a wise saying that God does not choose what
is fit but he fits what he chooses ... the sense of unfitness is
one of the signs of vocation.'

The Spiritual Letters of Father Hughson (1953)

AT THE END OF JANUARY 1956 I was demobbed, and exchanged
the heat of Shaibah for the cold of Dagenham. I received a wonderful
reception from my parents and family, and it was so good to be
home. Later in life T.S. Eliot's wonderful poem 'East Coker' would
become one of my favourites. It includes the simple line 'Home is
where we start from'. Eliot was making the point that home is the
cultural, spiritual and social start for us all – and for me it was
certainly all of those things. Returning home made me realise what
I missed those many months but had never pined for, because the
security of a good home gives one the strength not to rely on it as
a crutch, but to know it as a resource. Nevertheless, it was a great
homecoming, and the future beckoned.

A few days after my return the church had its annual New Year
party, and of course I wanted to be there. It was a foggy evening
when I set out, and on the ten-minute walk I had to cross a footbridge
over a railway line. I could hear footsteps approaching, and out of
the fog appeared a young lady of about seventeen. We recognised

one another from the church youth group, and walked together to the party, chatting happily and catching up on one another's news. Her name was Eileen Hood. She was working as a nanny and studying for her NNEB (National Nursery Examination Board), and was intending to become a nurse when she qualified. She was an intelligent girl, and she was also very good-looking. Later, as I became increasingly drawn towards her, I found I had some rivals to see off, but at that time romance was not high on my or her agenda. A friendship developed, however, and we began to see a lot of one another.

Of greater concern to me at that moment was my future, and the tug I felt in my heart to be ordained. I resumed my job with the London Electricity Board, but made no secret of the fact that I did not see my long-term future there. I was moved by the understanding and encouragement of Mr Vincent and other senior staff. They may not have shared my goals or my religious commitment – though some certainly did – but they knew that another kind of career beckoned.

The problem was my lack of academic qualifications, which I felt keenly. It came home to me with a particular shock when a few months after demob I served on a youth camp. Also helping out were a few students from Ridley Hall, Cambridge, one of the Church of England's theological colleges. One of them, a few years older than me, asked what I was going to do in life. I replied rather hesitantly, 'I feel the call of ordination.'

I shall never forget the look of incredulity on his face. 'Forget it!' he said instantly. 'You'll never make it!'

I never did ask him to explain himself. Such a crushing retort momentarily knocked the stuffing out of me. If that was how a fellow young Christian could react to another's aspirations, what future did I have in the ministry?

A clue to the answer came in a much more encouraging form from the curate at Dagenham Parish Church, Eric Vevers. Mr Vevers was in his thirties, and had been a carpenter before training for the ministry at Oak Hill Theological College. When I told him I wanted to be ordained, he gripped me by the shoulders and said fiercely, 'Don't do it, George. Don't be ordained.' Seeing my startled response, he continued, 'You must not even consider the idea of ordination unless you feel in your heart that this alone is what you want to do, and that God is calling you and is confirming it through His Church – otherwise it will be the most terrible of all professions.'

His words struck home, and I had to reflect deeply on what constituted the character of vocation to the ordained ministry. It seemed to consist of three elements. The priesthood had to attract. I could say without any equivocation that it did. There was the intellectual challenge it offered, the centrality of people and community, the joy of speaking of one's faith – all this and more appealed to me greatly. Then one's own personal abilities and qualifications came into it. Long before intellectual attainment one must have qualities that are 'ministerial' in character. My family and friends were telling me that I got on well with all sorts of people, that I had the ability to communicate, that I possessed the basic knowledge of scripture, that I was eager to learn. Above all I had a passion for Christ and His Kingdom. Lastly, I recognised that no good thing came without some sacrifice. I had to be prepared to accept the cost. The priesthood then – and now, but especially then – was very poorly paid, and vocation entailed accepting this as a precondition of service. I was ready for that too.

Pit-Pat, our vicar, was of great help. In spite of the differences in our understanding, which had deepened since my return, he was a constant encouragement and support. Indeed, in his time as vicar at least six young men sought and eventually received ordination – remarkable for anywhere, let alone a place like Dagenham. He knew of my great desire, but was also well aware that unless I had an opportunity to matriculate to university I had no chance whatsoever. He brought to my attention the work of the Reverend 'Pa' Salmon, who lived in Rock House, Woldingham, Surrey. Pa was a rich evangelical clergyman who used his wealth to help disadvantaged young people. To my delight I learned that he would not only provide board for me in his home, but would give me uninterrupted time to study for matriculation, and would provide a tutor. I leapt at the offer, said goodbye to the London Electricity Board and moved to Rock House.

Pa Salmon's remarkable offer felt like an answer to prayer, and I shall never forget the warmth of his family and the privilege it was to study in his house with six other young men. It was, I suppose, a kind of monastic community as we gathered each day for study, for fellowship, for prayer and for work. We were led by the Reverend John Bickersteth, who kept an eye on us all, guided us in our various studies and, week by week, gave the most insightful Bible studies, drawing imaginatively on the Greek text of the New Testament. John was the ideal person for this kind of ministry. He was just twelve or so years older than most of us, and well able to connect with our aspirations. He gave great personal encouragement to me, and I flowered under his leadership.

I had set myself the goal of studying for three 'A' levels and six 'O' levels, and my target date was a mere eighteen months ahead. There was a lot to do, and very little time. But I was hungry to learn, and highly motivated. I discovered the joy of studying systematically, reflecting and arguing with texts. The days, weeks and months raced away as my studies deepened. And of course I grew as a person. It is difficult for people who are used to speaking with fluency and ease to understand that others may find social communication simply terrifying. So it was with me – I felt awkward and very aware of my working-class background and speech. However, my confidence developed as I discovered that I could hold my own in argument; that I was as bright as, if not brighter than, some of those I envied for their social ease.

I saw a lot of Eileen, who was also working for exams. We were falling in love although I could not understand what she saw in me. She knew the way my life might turn out, and we discussed whether she really wanted to be the wife of a clergyman. Her immediate future, as she saw it, lay in nursing, which she also regarded in terms of vocation and as a Christian ministry. It was her intention that once we were married she would continue in her profession, as well as giving herself unstintingly to a common life with me serving our Lord. I could not have asked for more.

At last the exams came, and when the results arrived I had passed in all subjects – three 'A' levels and six 'O' levels in eighteen months. I made sure to thank all those who made it possible – Pit-Pat, Eric Vevers, the church family, and above all Pa and John Bickersteth. At last, I felt, I was really on my way.

Almost at the same time as I sat the exams I was required to attend an Ordination Selection conference, or as people of my generation called it, a CACTM (the Church's Advisory Council for the Training of Ministry) conference. It was a nerve-racking experience to be one of thirty or so young men grilled by half a dozen experts over a twenty-four-hour period. Two things I especially remember. The first was a group session, designed to allow the Selectors to assess the would-be ordinands' social and group skills. I enjoyed this a lot, but I was disconcerted by some of the assumptions that prevailed. One that particularly shocked me was a discussion as to whether or not Baptists were actually Christians. If the fact that we were discussing such a question surprised me, still more troubling was the discovery that a significant number of the group actually thought the Baptist tradition was sub-Christian. This made me aware that I was one of just a handful of evangelicals on that Selection conference. At that time evangelicals were few in the leadership of the Church, and as far as I can remember there was not one evangelical among the Selectors. Later the subject of ecclesiology was to become an important element in my theological thinking (see Chapter 5), but at that moment I was only aware of deep differences in the family of the Church, and that the tradition I had come from was in a minority.

My second memory was of an enjoyable conversation with the educational Selector. He asked me about my reading, and I spoke with great gusto of books that had influenced me, and others that I was currently reading. 'Such as?' he threw at me. I replied that I had just finished Bertrand Russell's *Why I Am Not a Christian*, then gave a résumé of the book and why I found it unconvincing.

The Selector said with a quizzical smile, 'Well now, imagine that one day you bumped into Bertrand Russell in Blackwell's bookshop and you were given the opportunity to show why you are a Christian. What would you say?'

With some rapidity I gave my answer. The Selector looked at me, still smiling broadly, and said after a long pause, 'Well, Carey, I hope you don't meet him for a very long time!' It was a response I deserved. I had a long way to go in understanding the difficulties of those who honestly cannot believe, as well as in appreciating the deeper issues of philosophy, science and epistemology that separate unbelief from faith.

A few weeks later I was informed that the Selection Board had recommended me for training, and I was given the green light to go to college that autumn, at the age of twenty-two. But which college? Pit-Pat was desperate for me to go to either Wycliffe Hall, Oxford, or Ridley Hall, Cambridge. If neither of these appealed to me, he felt I should choose a clear-cut evangelical college such as Oak Hill or, preferably, Tyndale Hall, Bristol, where he had trained for the ministry.

I was open to all suggestions, and visited six or so colleges in rapid succession. Each was excellent, but one stood out for me – one that Pit-Pat did not know well and did not care for particularly, the London College of Divinity, at Northwood. LCD, as it was known, was the former St John's, Highbury, which was destroyed by enemy action in the war. The Principal responsible for the college's move to Northwood was Dr Donald Coggan, who in 1956 became Bishop of Bradford, and was later to become Archbishop of Canterbury. Now, under the principalship of an Irishman, Dr Hugh Jordan, LCD was enjoying great popularity and attracting many students.

There were two reasons why LCD appealed to me. It was an evangelical college, but it was not narrow or partisan. I must have felt instinctively that I needed a broader theological education, and that LCD would suit my temperament. The second reason was equally important. I was attracted by the intellectual rigour of the London Bachelor of Divinity course, with its emphasis on languages, philosophy and historical theology. The course taught at both LCD and King's London offered all I was most anxious to study. It did not worry me that I was bypassing colleges at Oxford and Cambridge. I was fully aware of the excellence of theological education in those venerable universities, as well as the snob value of an Oxbridge degree, but I was quite satisfied that the London BD offered a more satisfying course that would stretch me fully.

For non-degree students the basic course for those under thirty was the three-year ALCD (Associate of the London College of Divinity) course. Those who had matriculated to do the degree course, such as myself, were required to do the four-year course, which included the ALCD.

It was with some nervousness that in September 1958 I entered the gates of the London College of Divinity and set out on a four-year programme that was to change me forever. Deep friendships were developed, and the rigorous academic regime was punctuated with much fun and fellowship. One particularly memorable moment was when Eileen paid her first visit to the college. It was an inflexible rule that girlfriends could only visit at the weekends, and then only with the Principal's approval. On the last Saturday of the Michaelmas term I went to the station to meet Eileen. During my absence the other students covered the walls of my room with pictures of their girlfriends. Eileen's astonishment and my dismay at seeing photographs of dozens of girls caused great amusement, but I had trouble persuading her that they had nothing to do with me. The embarrassment was completed when later that evening, having returned from taking Eileen to the station for her journey back to London, I found that the lock had been changed on my room and my bed was now outside the Principal's office. I was grateful that Dr Jordan was able to see the joke.

Compared to today, the theological training of my day was monastic and Spartan. The few married students in college were required to live apart from their wives, with only two free weekends per term. Permission to marry during one's training had to be obtained from the Principal and one's Bishop. The day started with worship at 7.15 a.m., and failure to be there meant an explanation to the Principal. The mornings were given over to lectures, and the afternoons devoted either to sport or manual work around the grounds. Further study followed from 4.30 p.m., and after evening prayer and supper, study continued until 9.30 p.m. Compulsory silence was demanded from 11 p.m. until 6 a.m.

For those of us newly returned from National Service, and especially for someone like myself, for whom education had come at such a price, this discipline hardly seemed draconian. Indeed, I soon found that I wanted more time to study, because I enjoyed it so much. Although I pitched myself into the social life of the college and had a regular place in the football team, I felt that I had to discipline my use of time so as to squeeze as much as I possibly could from the hours given to me. I found that by getting up slightly earlier than the others, going to bed slightly later, spending a little less time drinking coffee after supper and so on, I had more time for the reading and study I so relished.

There was no protection from the world of hard ideas and difficult questions. The staff was dedicated and talented. I particularly remember Victor McCallin, the Vice Principal, another Irishman from Trinity, Dublin, who gave us splendid, though whimsical, lectures in philosophy. 'Never avoid critical questions during your time here,' he would warn successive generations of students, 'because if you do, when you are alone later in ministry they will come and grab you by the throat.'

I was not alone in finding many of my ideas and beliefs being challenged. Degree students such as myself were required to prepare for a university entrance exam at the end of our first year, so the work was thorough and searching. It seemed at times as if the faculty intended to drive every certainty from us: our Old Testament study focused on the historicity of the texts, and took us into the arid wastes of dry Germanic scholarship; New Testament study seemed designed to show that we could know very little of the Jesus of history; philosophy led us to questioning certainty of any kind; and history and comparative religion forced us to consider the competing claims of other religions and other denominations. That we did not cave in under this avalanche of critical theology owes much to the rhythm of worship which underpinned our studies, as well as to the caring teaching we received. We were in no doubt that each member of the staff was a practising and believing Christian, and that they were always on hand to explain and assist if any student floundered intellectually or spiritually.

All this was grist to my mill. To swim as a tiny minnow in this ocean of ideas and follow in the wake of great giants like Augustine, Thomas Aquinas, Martin Luther, Karl Rahner and William Temple was a wonderful privilege. Although an evangelical and thoroughly committed to a belief in the authority of the Bible, I was unable to accept narrow theories of inerrancy, in which the Bible was held to be historically accurate as well as literally 'true' in every detail. I did not, for example, see a scientific world-view as incompatible with the world view of the scriptures. Many evangelicals may have believed the world was created in seven days, but that was not my interpretation of the Book of Genesis. As time went on I realised that there was nothing preventing me from accepting with conviction the trustworthiness of the Old Testament in its fundamental purpose of disclosing God's will for His chosen people Israel, and the unfolding drama of redemption leading to the coming of Jesus. In short, I did not require a book devoid of human error, corrupted texts or mistakes.

When later in my first year I asked a prominent evangelical preacher to explain to me why 2 Chronicles was so different from 2 Kings when both books were largely describing the same historical events, his reply astonished me. 'The difference,' he opined, 'is that similar to a photograph and a portrait. The books of Kings describe what actually happened, but the books of Chronicles are looking at it from an artistic point of view.' Even though I had just commenced Old Testament studies, I was staggered by the ignorance of this answer, although no doubt the speaker truly believed what he said. I remember thinking at the time that if that was an accurate expression of evangelical orthodoxy, it was too facile for me. No serious student of the texts could dismiss the profound differences between the two books in such a simplistic way. However, the answer that I found so unsatisfactory led me to dig deeper, and it took me months to acknowledge that I had to face up to the fact that the two books of Kings as well as Chronicles were primarily theological works, in which the writers were reflecting on history as well as seeking to write it. To this day I remain dismayed that many evangelical clergy seek to shield their congregations from critical scholarship. It need not disturb trusting belief – on the contrary, it will often lead to the strengthening and maturing of faith.

My faith was greatly shaken by the rigorous studies at LCD. But such shaking is an important element within the strengthening of faith. My knowledge was broadening out to include new ways of understanding God's truth. Of course, holding together the content of faith – namely God as understood through Jesus Christ – as trustworthy and reliable is only possible through the lived experience of knowing Him and walking with Him. This, for me and for my colleagues, took the form not only of regular worship in chapel, but also the discipline of private prayer and reflection on scripture. This practice has continued through my life and ministry, and is the foundation of what I am and what I do. My experience echoes the wonderful answer given by Carl Jung, the famous psychologist, when he was asked towards the end of his life, 'Do you believe in God?' To which he gave the breathtaking answer: 'I don't believe – I know, I know.' My studies of philosophy showed that epistemology (the science of knowing) takes many forms, in which analytical knowledge – two and two makes four – is but a small part of what we can grasp as truth. Indeed, analytical knowledge is not without its difficulties, as its truth derives from the self-contained world of arithmetical knowledge. Knowledge as we normally understand it emerges from reflection on experience, and is as foundational for every area of life as it is for theology.

At the end of my first year at LCD the Reverend E.M.B. Green, a dynamic young evangelical scholar, joined the staff and sharpened the missionary focus of the college. Michael arrived with an impressive reputation as a scholar and teacher. He was the possessor of first-class degrees in classics and theology, and the author of several studies of New Testament subjects. To have him as one of our faculty was a great coup for the college, and he did not disappoint. We were riveted by his challenging teaching and the depth of his lectures. He was also a gifted evangelist, and many of us went on unforgettable parish missions with him. His love of God and willingness to share his conviction made a lasting impression on my life and ministry. The combination of classics and theology that Michael brought was a great gift to us all, and my understanding of the Greek text of the New Testament deepened, just as my knowledge and grasp of Hebrew flourished under the wise teaching of Mr Jordan, our Principal.

As my theological knowledge and my experience of faith developed, so did my relationship with Eileen. We had already committed ourselves to one another in a long engagement that had started on her eighteenth birthday, but now, two years later, we were anxious to get married well before I was ordained. The problem was that the rule of the Church then was very firm: marriage and ordination training did not mix, so marriage had to be delayed. I was not convinced by this logic. Nervously I approached both Bishop and Principal, and presented the strongest arguments I could muster. To our great delight both gave their full agreement, and we made plans to marry on 25 June 1960, after a three-year engagement and halfway through my studies.

This was perilously close to the prelims of the degree course, and to my dismay I discovered that the first paper in Hebrew, which was mandatory for honours degree students, was scheduled for the Monday following our wedding. The shock was compounded by the fact that we had planned to take our honeymoon in Dunoon, on the Clyde, where Eileen's mother had been brought up. How on earth could I possibly square this circle – to marry on Saturday, 25 June in Dagenham, fly up to Glasgow, and take a Hebrew exam two days later at the University of London? It was agreed that I could sit the exam at the University of Glasgow – but what would Eileen say about this? Fortunately, instead of throwing up her hands in horror at this intrusion into our honeymoon she saw the funny side, and agreed that somehow the exam had to be included in our plans.

Our wedding was a wonderful celebration and commitment. Dagenham Parish Church was packed with family and friends. Pit-Pat took the service, and preached on the text from Joshua 24: 'As for me and my house, we will serve the Lord' – a verse that would continue to inspire and guide us through the years. Although Eileen gave the traditional promise to 'obey' her husband, both of us knew that our marriage would not and could not be based on inequality. True marriage, we knew, was a mutual obeying, trusting and learning. I realised that I had much to learn from Eileen, and I hoped that I could offer something to her as well.

We had a wonderful honeymoon, despite the interruption. While I sat in an examination hall in Glasgow University, Eileen waited on a park bench outside in glorious sunshine. I remember going into the examination in a carefree mood – I was rather surprised to find out much later that I had passed comfortably.

After an engagement lasting three years it was a relief to live together as man and wife. Today, the distinctions between married and single life have largely gone, and many cohabit without any sense that it might be wrong. I regret the loss of innocence that this implies, and the fact that it suggests that marriage is no longer special. This may be dismissed as the thoughts of someone out of touch with modern culture. So be it. I remain unconvinced that society has improved on God's will for His people by such laxity in sexual matters. We have lost the grandeur of holiness and the personal discipline involved in keeping oneself solely for another precious person.

Back from honeymoon we settled in Northwood, sharing a house with another newly married couple, Bill and Maggie Barrand, who became lifelong friends, especially Maggie, who had earlier distinguished herself as a member of the England badminton team. Eileen began work as a staff nurse at Mount Vernon Hospital, where she worked with terminally ill carcinoma patients.

Towards the end of my final year at LCD the security of our faith and the calmness of our lives were shaken by the loss of our first child. We had both been thrilled when Eileen became pregnant. She had a very good pregnancy, and was physically well throughout it. She reached full term, and we awaited the birth with enormous excitement. The days dragged by, until fourteen days later she was admitted to Hillingdon Hospital to be induced. After examining her carefully, the doctor shook his head and told us with great sympathy that the baby was dead. To this day I admire so much that young woman who, at the age of twenty-three, had to endure twelve hours of agony, knowing that at the end of it a dead baby would be the issue.

After her ordeal we clung together tightly, wordlessly, helplessly, and found comfort in one another. So much joy and happiness had been invested in that baby – a boy, to whom we had already given the names Stephen Andrew. In the delivery room I held him in my arms, and could not believe he was dead, he seemed so beautifully formed. Eileen was not so fortunate. She only saw him briefly, because the Sister firmly believed it was not in the mother's interest to hold him. In her kindly Irish Catholic way she told me firmly, 'Don't worry, dear. We Catholics believe he lives in a special place called Limbo.' It was meant to be helpful. We did not find it especially so.

We emerged from the hospital reeling, empty-handed and wounded. Where is God when bad things happen to good people? Neither of us was so naïve as to believe that our happiness and welfare was the test of God's existence and His providence. We knew we lived in a world shot through with tragedy and the effects of man's sinfulness. As Christians we were also aware that membership of God's family did not give us a cast-iron guarantee that we would float through life trouble-free. But this was our first personal experience of suffering, and our thoughts constantly turned towards that vulnerable and helpless baby who never had an opportunity to live.

Two things, I believe, kept us going – personal experience and fellowship. We knew we lived in God's love, and were aware of His presence beside us. Our tragedy also made us aware of how precious it was to belong to a tightly-knit Christian community. At its best the Church is a wonderful source of friendship and kindness – and that is what we found at college, where we were supported and embraced by affection and prayer. Almost immediately we found that our suffering became part of our lives and ministry. To our astonishment we realised that other young couples had also suffered the death of a child, and we were able to share our experience and share in their suffering. But, of course, one can never forget. On every 2 April we think of Stephen Andrew and remember him in silent prayer, wistfully wondering what kind of person he would have become.

Both of us returned to work, and I had to focus on my finals. I was determined to give of my very best, and studied night and day until the examinations which fell at the end of June – then waited anxiously for the results. I was overjoyed to see my name among those awarded a 2.1 honours degree. As I stood there looking at the board outside the Senate House in Gower Street, I thanked God for His grace which had led me to this day. Now I had to take the learning, the knowledge and the training gathered over the years, and put it to work.

I visited a few parishes to see if I was acceptable to the incumbent. One experience hurt me a little. The Principal wished me to see Canon Tom Livermore, a prominent evangelical and the Rector of Morden in Surrey. I made the journey by train, then walked to the

Rectory. Canon Livermore was expecting me, and to my surprise he had his overcoat on. Without inviting me inside he said, 'Let's take a walk around the parish.'

As we walked he interviewed me, but I had a sneaking feeling that he had already made up his mind about me. We walked past the old parish church, then into a council estate and past the mission church. 'That is where I would put you, Carey,' he said, 'if I had a job to offer, but only a few days ago I offered the curacy to somebody else.' By this time we were almost at the station: 'Now, how much was your fare? Well, here it is. Goodbye.'

I could not believe that anybody could be so cruel. I felt I had been dismissed as a working-class lad who could only work in one culture. Later I got to know Canon Livermore, and found him to be a friendly man and an effective leader. Everybody, I suppose, can have an off day.

Happily, we were soon offered a post at St Mary's, Islington, in north London, where Prebendary Peter Johnston was the vicar. After years of sensing a vocation, facing the doubts, the rejections, the obstacles and the sheer hard work of intense theological study, my ministry was about to begin.

5

—◦—

A Changing Church

'He never attempted brilliance, but thoroughness; he thought
more of conscience than genius; more of great futures than
little results. He was deaf to the praise or blame of the world.'

Tribute to Archbishop Frederick Temple

OUR FIRST VISIT TO ST MARY'S to meet Peter Johnston and his
wife Phyllis, and to see the church and parish, was an unforgettable
moment in our lives. After a distinguished ministry at St John's,
Parkstone, Dorset, Peter had only been instituted a few months before
our arrival, and was beginning to find his feet in this very different
parish. He was a bluff, determined and clear-sighted man with firm
objectives and a steady evangelical spirituality. Phyllis was a sparkling
woman a few years older than her husband. As they had married
late in life, the energy and love they might have poured into family
life they gave instead in generous commitment to others. Their open
home and commitment to building Christian community became a
lifelong model for us. We were immediately attracted to them, and
an instant friendship developed. Phyllis took Eileen under her wing,
and through the training and leadership I received at his hands Peter
was to become one of the greatest influences on my development as
a minister.

We joined a large and vigorous team. St Mary's was – and continues to be – a leading London church. Under Peter's predecessor

Maurice Wood, later to become Bishop of Norwich, it had become very popular with students and nurses. Peter did not want to diminish this ministry, but he did want to make St Mary's a church for those who actually lived in the parish, and this became the central plank of his policy. Islington in the sixties was not the 'yuppie' place it is today. It was a predominantly working-class district with a great deal of poverty, and there were many destitute families and desperate, housebound elderly people. Situated at the southern end of the A1, the church received more than its share of 'gentlemen of the road' – so much so that one of Peter's initiatives included turning the crypt into a night shelter for the homeless.

St Mary's was also distinguished for its firm commitment to the evangelical tradition. In the nineteenth century Prebendary Wilson had founded the Islington Clerical Conference, which had become a major annual gathering of evangelical clergy for fellowship and teaching, in reaction to the increasing 'Catholicising' of the Church of England through the Oxford Movement. Peter continued the Conference, and indeed developed it, broadening its emphasis to take into account relevant themes confronting the Church. However, he used to joke that St Mary's was more famous for its curates than its vicars, and would trot out such names as the great hymn-writer and Methodist leader Charles Wesley, Donald Coggan, who was later to become Archbishop of Canterbury, and a future Bishop of Liverpool, David Sheppard.

My predecessor, David Fletcher, had been a very popular teacher and evangelist. I felt unworthy to be stepping into his shoes, and was secretly afraid that I might let Peter down. The senior curate was Michael MacGowan, and we were soon joined by five other staff members: David Green, Chrisanther de Mel, David Boyes, Tom Jones and John Barton. Peter was assembling a new team to serve the community.

Together with my fellow curate David Green and at least forty other young men, I was ordained Deacon of St Mary's in St Paul's Cathedral on Michaelmas Day 1962 by the Bishop of London, Robert

Stopford. I cannot recall much of the service, except my very strong feeling of unworthiness and helplessness. I was only too well aware of my shortcomings, and the burden of my background seemed a weight too great to bear. However, I was equally aware that the grace of God was more than a promise – it was a fact in the lives of those who took the plunge. And so it proved to be.

Eileen and I lived in a tiny cottage in the grounds of the church, and there in the course of the next four years we were to bring into the world our three eldest children, Rachel, Mark and Andrew. We were poor but very happy. My stipend was very low, and Eileen recalls that her housekeeping amounted to £3.15s. a week. We could not afford a car, but through the generosity of a friend were never without one to get away on our day off. We did not have a washing machine or any of the gadgets that most young married people now take for granted.

The cottage, the oldest building in Islington, was very damp, but we managed to bring up three very healthy children in it. In spite of living on our beam ends, it was a wonderful four years of training in a great parish and at a significant cultural period. London was the pulsating centre of the 'swinging sixties'. Rock and roll was in the ascendant, and the Beatles were making their way into the hearts of the young everywhere. A heady and optimistic excitement about the future prevailed, accompanied by a cynicism towards spiritual values and tradition. The witty but irreverent *That Was the Week That Was* expressed the mood of the decade. The Church was not immune from the spirit of enquiry and the culture of the age. Across the River Thames, the diocese of Southwark appeared to be the vanguard of new ideas, new experiments in ministry and new approaches to gender and sexuality. In America as well as in Britain, certain theologians affirmed 'the death of God', by which they meant the demise of traditional ways of conceiving of Him. Harvey Cox, one of the most radical and interesting of the new wave of theologians, predicted the death of orthodox theology by the end of the century. In Britain John Robinson, Bishop of Woolwich, produced a sensational book, *Honest to God*, which seemed to call into question the nature of the Christian faith. In the view of the press and the chattering classes it signalled that the Church had realised at last that traditional ways of talking about God were no longer relevant. The Church was at a crossroads: either it entered this heady new world where everything was being questioned and nothing was sacred, or it lived on as an out-of-touch irrelevance in a buzzing, exciting new age.

In reality there was nothing new in Robinson's book – it was little more than a scaled-down popularising of the thinking of such theologians as Paul Tillich, who had posited the image of God as 'ground of being' (rather than an external deity), Rudolf Bultmann and Dietrich Bonhoeffer, a Lutheran pastor who resisted the Nazis and claimed that man had come of age. It caused an instant sensation, however, and made Robinson famous and the book a bestseller. Within weeks Archbishop Michael Ramsey, greatly alarmed by the furore aroused by *Honest to God*, responded with a devastating riposte arguing that, while Robinson's concerns were very real, orthodox teaching properly understood and interpreted had the depth and strength to give confidence in the Christian faith. The irony is that today, despite the sales of *Honest to God* it now appears dated, whereas Michael Ramsey's reply to it has a timeless quality.

The intellectual storm created by *Honest to God* was far from altogether negative. At St Mary's, with an intelligent and discerning congregation, the opportunity was taken by the staff to preach on the themes of Robinson's book, and we were not afraid to encourage the congregation to read it. One of my responsibilities was for the thirty-to-forty age group, which met following the Sunday-evening service. We usually numbered in excess of fifty, and sometimes up to a hundred if I managed to tempt a popular speaker to address us. In addition, I started a fortnightly study group for those who wished to explore the Christian faith more deeply, and a regular membership of twenty to thirty was soon established.

Peter was a disciplined leader whose expectations were high.

Visiting the parish systematically was a priority, and each of the staff had to make twenty-five calls a week, which had to be written up with a verbal report to be presented at the Monday staff meeting. To start with I found this a great irritant, but as time went on I grew to appreciate its thoroughness and the concern for people that it demonstrated.

Without realising it at the time, I caused a small sensation in my first week by going to the local town hall and asking if I could speak to the person in charge of Social Services. I managed to see the Chief Social Officer, and after explaining who I was, asked him whether, as I would be visiting a great many people in the months and years to come, he did not agree that there would be some virtue in my knowing who was concerned with the elderly, handicapped and others from the standpoint of the Social Services. Could not some collaboration be considered?

I recall to this day the look of astonishment that passed over his face. 'In all my years of working,' he slowly remarked, 'a representative of the church has never bothered to contact us or made a suggestion of this kind. I think it is a splendid idea, and we must make sure we are in touch.' Peter Johnston was contacted later that week, and was delighted that official links would be established between Social Services and the church. For myself, I was startled that everyone found the approach so remarkable. I thought it was obvious. It was illustrative of the wide gap between the church and the community which still exists to this day. It also highlighted an unwillingness on the part of many clergy to work with other professionals.

As a curate I was required to attend Post-Ordination Training with other Deacons and young clergy in the diocese of London. 'Potty' training, as it was known to us all, consisted of lectures on themes related to the ordained ministry, together with essays that we had to submit at regular intervals. I had heard from others that the training was unsatisfactory, and decided to approach the Bishop of London with another idea – could I be allowed to enrol at King's College, London to pursue a master of theology degree? Permission was given, and soon after ordination to the priesthood I began research on the Apostolic Fathers. At college I had become aware of the importance of a collection of writings – some obscure, others less so – that appeared at the end of the New Testament era and at the beginning of the second century A.D. This little-known period is of critical importance for the study of the Church and its ministry, known as ecclesiology because it was then that the Church first wrestled with vital principles relating to its development and growth throughout the Mediterranean region. I was fully aware that it would be very difficult to balance the demands of parish and family life with the obligations of a research degree, but I was determined to try. Eileen was also keen for me to do postgraduate work, and I duly registered and obtained the services of Professor H.D. McDonald, Vice Principal of London Bible College, as my supervisor. 'Derry-Mac', as he was popularly known, was an Irish nonconformist scholar of great erudition and ability. We clicked immediately, and the work began.

Central to my desire to study this period of the Church's life was a fascination with the Catholic tradition of the Church, especially Roman Catholicism. All I knew of Roman Catholicism had been derived from books, largely anti-Rome, and from the partisan sermons of Pit-Pat. I was unable to accept that the Roman Catholic Church was as heretical and unreformed as I had been led to believe, and believed that research into the Apostolic Fathers would help to answer many of my questions.

I was fortunate that my study coincided with the Second Vatican Council, called by Pope John XXIII in 1959 and concluded in 1965. Although John XXIII was an old man, dismissed by many as a 'caretaker' Pope, his decision to call a General Council revolutionised the Catholic Church through its policy of '*aggorniamento*' (renewal). It was a breathtaking decision. From that moment on the Roman Catholic Church entered upon an engagement with the world, other Churches and other religions that allowed it to speak again with authority.

The Second Vatican Council was having an effect at the local level too. I was asked by the Bishop of London to join a small Roman Catholic/Church of England study group to study the impressive documents of the Council. If I had any prejudices or suspicions about Catholicism, this encounter with Roman Catholic priests, religious and lay people, laid them to rest entirely. I particularly recall a Bible study when a nun of my age exclaimed, 'We must go back to the scriptures and find our unity there!' The statement surprised and angered me at first, but the more I thought about it, the more it appealed to me. My anger evaporated as I found myself thinking, 'What do you mean, "get back to the scriptures"? You Catholics are the ones who have left them behind through teaching things which are not found in them.' But I knew instinctively that such a possessive attitude to scripture was wrong, however disagreeable I might consider some aspects of RC teaching to be. She was correct – the only way forward was to go back to our common roots. Only by doing that could we find unity, by seeing one another as brothers and sisters bound by a common commitment to Jesus Christ, and not as two warring groups, each claiming to possess the whole truth and denying the other's version.

I completed my fifty-thousand-word dissertation for the M.Th., sat a three-hour paper on the Apostolic Fathers, and then shortly before Christmas 1965 had to appear before the leading theologian Professor Eric Mascall and another examiner for the 'viva'. It seemed to go well, but towards the end of the session I was longing for someone to put me out of my misery – had I passed or not? I didn't feel I could ask, and believed that the examiners would certainly not tell me. But as Professor Mascall walked me to the door, he reached out his hand and, looking me intently in the eye, said, 'You WILL have a very happy Christmas!'

All I could reply was, 'Thank you, sir. I am so glad to hear it. Happy Christmas to you.' I think I floated home to tell my patient wife what Eric had said. He was an outstanding scholar, and it was a privilege to have been taught by him and to have known him. I still feel a tinge of sadness that, although I regard the ordination of women as a wholly positive and necessary thing, and am delighted that under my leadership the Church of England had the courage to legislate for it, the decision caused Eric so much distress in his old age, as he felt our Church lacked the authority to take such a momentous decision alone.

Despite my other activities, ministry in the parish was certainly not neglected. I poured myself into the responsibilities entrusted to me – the work with adults, and also the Sunday school. With the help of Liz Salmon the Sunday school became a thriving and important part of the church's mission. Liz became a friend of the family for life, and remained a committed member of St Mary's as a church-warden and a great supporter of missionary work abroad.

I felt strongly that the Sunday school could not rely simply on children coming to a dreary church hall on a Sunday afternoon – we had to supplement it with exciting initiatives to reach into the homes of the parish. I started a Boys' Club, and established a football team. This certainly helped attract boys in football-mad Islington, the home of Arsenal FC. Every year during the Easter holidays several of us held a Children's Holiday Club that attracted many youngsters. The theme varied: one year it was a 'Wild West Week', another the 'Jungle Holiday Club', another 'Treasure Island'. Church members were roped in to assist, and we had considerable success in reaching out to the local schools and community.

The work was serious, but there were many funny moments too. One that stands out was my attempt to procure a horse and wagon for the Wild West Week. While I found a man with a horse and wagon – which in Islington was not easy – he would only hire them out if his pet monkey was also employed. There was much bemusement and laughter as I paraded through the streets of Islington dressed as a cowboy, with a monkey perched on my shoulder. It pulled in the children, however.

One of our most mischievous boys was a ten-year-old called Billy Budd. The reason I still remember his name forty years on was he was left behind in Southend when three coachloads of children went to the seaside for our annual summer outing. The trip was planned thoroughly, and considered foolproof; we did not take into account, however, the mischievousness of London children. Each child was given a card with details of the trip, the church and telephone numbers in case they got lost or needed help. Those were the days when one could take children to the seaside and let them roam at will. We drummed into the boys and girls the importance of being back at the coach station at 6 p.m.

The day was sunny and warm, and the trip was a great success. Most of the children stayed with their appointed leaders. When 6 o'clock came we did a thorough round-up – or thought we did. I counted all the heads in my coach and called out names; but somehow Billy fell through the net. Later we found that one of his friends had put up his hand when Billy's name was called.

The next day was Sunday, and Mrs Budd came along to the hall that afternoon with a tired-looking Billy holding her hand. Looking accusingly at me, she said: 'You left Billy behind yesterday, you know.'

I was startled, and laughed, 'Certainly not, Mrs Budd. We counted everybody.'

She replied, 'You did, you know. When he got to the coach park at 7 p.m. the coaches had left. He went to the police station and they put him in a comfortable cell, and I returned with him this morning on the milk train at 5 a.m.'

I stammered out an apology, and her tone softened immediately. She said, smiling, 'I thought you would like to know.' I dread to think what would be a parent's reaction today.

In my third year at St Mary's Peter asked me if I would be prepared to do a little teaching at Oak Hill Theological College in Southgate, as the member of staff teaching the doctrine paper for the London BD was sick. I was delighted, and accepted immediately, reasoning that as well as assisting the college, it would provide me with an opportunity to consolidate my knowledge. I was just about to register for a doctorate. I had decided so because just a few weeks previously I had received an envelope enclosing £50 with a one-sentence note: 'For your Ph.D.' Eileen was convinced – correctly, as it later turned out – that this kind and generous gesture had come from Peter Johnston's wife Phyllis.

Spurred on by such belief in me, I registered for a doctorate in ecclesiology whilst still juggling the demands of the parish, family life and teaching at Oak Hill. It was a busy existence, but I loved it. If in later life I achieved anything at all it was due to the thorough training I received from Peter Johnston: his love of people and that rare gift of giving the other person instant and total attention; his thorough sermon preparation; his confidence in the gospel and evangelical witness; his humanity and tolerance of human weakness; his strategies for church growth – all these, and much more, were his legacies to his curates. He was never a soft touch, however. Never once in my four years working with him did I dream of calling him 'Peter' – he was always 'the Vicar' or 'Mr Johnston'. He expected the highest standards from us, and showed his disapproval clearly when it was necessary. I remember being angry with him once in my first year when I turned up for the Sunday services in a pair of brown shoes – my black pair were unfit to wear. Mr Johnston took one look at them and said, 'You can't possibly process in brown shoes – go and sit in your stall at once.' I did so in silence, feeling indignant that he did not allow me to explain that at the moment we did not have enough money to buy a new pair of shoes.

On another occasion I had agreed to speak at a meeting on my day off and I went to see the vicar to get my day off changed. He heard me out, then said: 'George, I want you to learn that a day off is very important, and it should be only for emergencies that it is ever changed. No, you can't have a different day. Fulfil that engagement, and learn the lesson.' I did so, very quickly.

Peter Johnston was in every sense of the words a thorough professional in all he did. He was convinced that those who served Christ in the ordained ministry must give of their very best, and be a disciple and learner until their time was over. He was not a particularly exciting preacher, but his talks were learned, well prepared and biblical. He built up St Mary's to be at the heart of the community and relevant to its needs because he understood that the Christian faith spoke directly to the hearts of all. Yet he had his Achilles' heel. He often compared himself unfavourably with Maurice Wood, his predecessor, because he did not possess a degree. He had gone to Oak Hill College straight from the navy, and felt inadequate as a result. Of course he should never have thought that. His intelligence and wide reading made him an outstanding evangelical leader, and I am not alone among his many curates in testifying to the way he prepared us for our ministries ahead.

Our time at St Mary's was drawing to an end. Eileen too had found it a place of growth. I marvelled at her ability not only to create such a warm family life but to open our home to all comers, as well as taking a full part in parish life alongside Phyllis. It was typical of Peter to mark our departure with a hint of humour. I preached for the last time on the evening before we left, and following my address I was astonished to hear Peter stand and say: 'Our final hymn is "Begone, Unbelief, our Saviour is near!"'

'Could any ministerial work be better and happier than St Mary's, Islington?' I asked myself as we followed the van containing our belongings in a friend's car. Prebendary Maurice Wood had asked me months before if I would join his staff at Oak Hill, and I had agreed after much consultation. I regretted leaving parish life behind, as I had only ever thought of my ministry in terms of working with ordinary people and leading them to our Lord. I had never thought of myself as a teacher, and this invitation had taken Eileen and me by surprise. But instinctively we felt that it was right to accept.

We joined a strong and happy faculty with members of the calibre of Maurice himself, a gifted pastor and evangelist; John Taylor the Vice Principal, a superb Old Testament teacher later to be Bishop of St Albans; Alan Stibbs, the *éminence grise* of the college, whose biblical expositions were outstanding; John Simpson, who taught history, and would become Dean of Canterbury Cathedral during my time as Archbishop; and a number of other impressive teachers.

It was my task to take on the bulk of teaching doctrine for the London BD and Dip.Th. courses, which was an extremely heavy load. Considering that I was just thirty – younger than many of the students – I had every reason to worry if I would be up to it. I need not have done so: I managed to keep slightly ahead of the students in the first term, and then quarried away until I was on top of the material.

We had a very happy four years at Oak Hill, during which I completed most of my dissertation for the Ph.D as well as having time to reflect more on the challenges facing the Church, and the desperate need for unity. In particular I began to wonder if I was truly at home in the evangelical tradition. I felt guilty about even entertaining the question. After all, everything I had received and everything I was, I owed to this noble tradition.

As I wrestled with the issue, I realised that it was not the substance of evangelicalism I was doubting, so much as the superficial assumptions many evangelicals made. It was depth that they seemed to lack. When I considered the books on my study shelves it was clear to see the influence of a godly liberal tradition ever since I had started to become a thinking Christian. Furthermore, I was uncomfortably conscious that, even at Oak Hill, there was too much superficial teaching and intolerance concerning other traditions in the Church, especially any form of Catholicism. More to the point, I was finding myself increasingly drawn towards that tradition. Just a few miles away in Cockfosters was a small Roman Catholic monastic community, and on the occasions when I was there for an act of worship I found it inspiring and moving. I could not accept that Christ was absent from that small band who, though no doubt different from me in many respects, were just as devoted as I was to the Christian faith.

I realised that I could be of best service to Oak Hill if I used these feelings, doubts and questions to inform my teaching and to challenge those listening to me. My focus became the intention to help evangelicals to become as inclusive as I believed the Christian faith to be – in other words, to be aware of the strength of other traditions as well as the strength of their own.

I was helped by a sad incident. That laid-back philosopher Victor McCallin, Vice Principal of the London College of Divinity, had just left the college to become vicar of Jesus Church, Enfield, a few miles from Oak Hill. It seemed an unusual post for a Low Church Irishman, because Jesus Church was notoriously 'High'. Nevertheless, I was delighted to have my old teacher and friend so close. No sooner had Victor started his new work than he asked me if I would cover his services while he and his wife Joan took two weeks' holiday. I was glad to agree, but within a few days I was told that on the eve of his holiday Victor had collapsed, and had been rushed to hospital. Eileen and I visited him, little suspecting that anything was seriously wrong – but we were told that Victor had leukaemia, and was not expected to live. Within days he was dead.

We could scarcely take in the suddenness of his death. It hardly seemed possible that the smiling, relaxed Irishman with his kindly and gentle humour was no longer with us. Instead of covering his services for two weeks, I became the resident minister and priest for nine months. The congregation of Jesus Church were shattered by Victor's death, and I did my best to provide cover and care during this period. It meant learning the ropes of doing things the 'Anglo-Catholic' way, and I began to respect the thorough and painstaking character of Catholic worship. Donning chasubles and copes eventually became second nature. Students from Oak Hill came across to preach and share in the life of the church, and they too began to appreciate the strength of a tradition so different from their own.

In 1970 I joined the staff of St John's College, Nottingham. This sideways move was not made because I had been unhappy at Oak Hill. For some time Michael Green, who had replaced Hugh Jordan as Principal at the London College of Divinity, had kept me in touch with the exciting plans to move LCD to Bramcote, Nottingham, where it became St John's, Nottingham. The invitation to return to my old college as a staff member was an exciting one, and I was attracted by the teaching I was offered and the more historical approach it would enable me to take. An additional attraction was that St John's would be a constituent college of the University of Nottingham, which would bring me into contact with a wider range of fellow teachers.

The difference between St John's and Oak Hill lay not in evangelical character so much in ethos and style. The students at St John's were on the whole much younger, with a greater number of graduates. There was a heady buzz about the place, with a strong missionary focus and great intellectual content. The students were lively, and were not content with half-baked views or shoddy thinking. Spirited discussion shaped the life of the place, and a deep and healthy spirituality fused academic and worshipping life. Some of the friendships we made with students continued for the rest of our ministry – particularly with Paul and Mary Zahl. Paul, a very bright American, was reading for a master's degree, and later went on to complete his doctoral studies at Tübingen under Professor Jurgen Moltmann. He would later become Dean of Birmingham, Alabama, where his scholarship and effective preaching increased the cathedral congregation significantly, and where he developed an international ministry. Paul was not the only high flier at St John's by any means; there were others there whose academic prowess may have been less distinguished, but who were not lacking in other skills and abilities. The chemistry of intellectual vigour, spiritual commitment and deep interest in engaging with the contemporary world made the college an exciting place to be in the 1970s.

The staff was the most able and happiest team I have been privileged to be part of. Michael Green led us with typical enthusiasm and enormous commitment to the gospel, and there was little doubt that his presence drew many students to the new college. Julian Charley, the Vice Principal, had just joined the newly formed Anglican/Roman Catholic International Commission as its only evangelical scholar. The awakening of evangelical interest in and sympathy towards Catholicism owes a great deal to Julian's dedicated interest in the Roman Catholic Church, which took a personal form in his deep friendship with Father Jean Tillard, one of the Catholic representatives on the Commission. Sadly, Julian's outstanding ability was never fully recognised by the Church, and he was never offered a senior office commensurate with his gifts.

Colin Buchanan was another outstanding teacher whose energy, entrepreneurial ability and scholarship made a breathless and dynamic contribution to the college. Possessor of one of the sharpest brains in the Church, Colin was also a man of integrity and deep faith. His combative personality and direct, uncompromising style earned him a few enemies over the years, but his pastoral concern and commitment to people won him more friends than he lost.

Charles Napier taught doctrine alongside me, and brought something very special and distinctive to the college. Brought up as a Roman Catholic and ordained a Roman Catholic priest following advanced studies at Louvain University, Charles had left his Church and had become an Anglican. He contributed a deep stillness and a lovely debunking attitude that gently put any bumptious student – or staff member, for that matter – in his or her place.

Within a short while St John's became the largest and most popular college in the Church of England. Whilst clearly within the evangelical tradition, its stance on most things was refreshingly radical, in the biblical sense of being rooted in a commitment to New Testament orthodoxy, yet open to all that God wanted to give us together. The Charismatic Movement was now beginning to make inroads in all Churches and it was hardly surprising that it soon found a home at St John's. At first the form this took was in new songs, and especially a beautiful Polkingham sung mass that we used at every college communion service. Later it manifested itself in several students claiming that if one desired to be empowered, 'baptism in the Holy Spirit' was necessary. I found myself in strong conflict with this theology, although not in opposition to the spiritual awakening it brought. In my view, the idea that there could be a special group of Christians, superior to others by reason of a second baptism, flew in the face of Christian thought. There could only be one baptism for the forgiveness of sins.

Before very long I found myself somewhat embarrassed by an event that was to change me dramatically, and that made me more sympathetic to Charismatic theology. Things were going well at St John's. I had finished my Ph.D, and I was thoroughly enjoying the intellectual challenge of the work and the close friendships with students. But I was beginning to be aware that my spiritual life was lagging behind my intellectual development. I was at a loss to know what to do about this. I realised that part of the problem stemmed from the nature of priesthood. When one is a priest, and particularly when one is associated with such a clear-cut tradition as evangelicalism, the pressure to conform and to give the impression that one's faith is impervious to doubt and unbelief is enormous. Unlike the Catholic tradition with its time-honoured policy of spiritual direction, the individualism of the evangelical tradition had no comparable support structure. There was no one to whom I could turn and talk things through frankly. Even to admit to questioning the essence of Christianity in a theological college where I, as one of the teachers, was a purveyor of certainty, seemed shameful. Although I knew I could have trusted any of my colleagues, I was reluctant to do so. I felt trapped.

As I analysed my problem, I detected a layer of fear in myself that I had never encountered before, including fears of death and dying. These surprised me, and I had no idea where they had come from. At first I wondered if they originated in the study I was doing at the time on existentialist thinkers such as Kierkegaard, Jean-Paul Sartre, Albert Camus and others. This focused on the principles that seemed to underpin modern life and culture, and I was enjoying this particular dimension of thought. The fears, however, were real, and faith seemed so insubstantial. The challenge of the 'absence of God' coincided with a spiritual barrenness that I was palpably aware of. Worship seemed boring and unreal; God Himself seemed remote and without substance, and the arguments for His existence weak and foolish. Even Jesus Christ, for so long the heartbeat of my faith, now appeared to be little more than a vague historical figure, incapable ever again of inspiring enthusiasm and commitment in me.

In the priesthood, the job and life are one. I was in my mid-thirties, still very young in ministerial terms, and merely to go through the motions was hypocritical and out of the question. I knew that if I could not sort this out, I was finished as a priest. I was faced with a dreadful reality – all that I had worked for and stood for seemed perilously close to disappearing.

I tried to confide my feelings to Eileen, but she was bearing the burden of a growing family, and as a protective father and husband I felt inhibited from sharing them fully with her. Much later I realised that I was wrong to carry this all alone – Eileen was more than capable of understanding, and would have been an enormous help. Nevertheless, only those who know something of the 'dark night of the soul' can comprehend the darkness I was feeling then. Of course, as anyone in the priesthood knows – and for that matter anyone in any profession where strong convictions prevail – one can fool people a great deal of the time, and I am sure that few of those around me knew anything of my inner turmoil. But one cannot fool oneself. These struggles went on for many months, and were resolved in an unexpected manner.

The summer of 1972 was spent in London, Ontario, with Eileen's widowed mother, and her sister Evelyn and brother-in-law Roy and their family, who had moved to Canada some years earlier. We were now a family of six, as Elizabeth had joined our brood eight months earlier. It was a delightful holiday with much bonding, laughter and fun. I took time out to study the Canadian Church, and read a great deal besides.

I refused all offers to preach or lecture – except one, to preach at Little Trinity, Toronto. Little Trinity, a large evangelical church, was led then by Harry Robinson, a dynamic minister and a very effective leader in the Canadian Church. The engagement necessitated a trip on my own, and I was put up in a community house on the evening prior to my sermon. I shall never forget what happened after

I was shown to my room. I walked across to the bookshelves and saw a charismatic book that was very popular at the time, *Aglow with the Spirit* by Robert Frost. As I skimmed through its pages, I seethed with indignation at the author's interpretation of the work of the Holy Spirit. Uncharacteristically I tossed the book away from me in disgust, and to my shame it hit a picture, which fell to the floor with a crash. As I walked over to replace the picture and retrieve the book, I found myself thinking that it is easy enough to throw away a book, but that what I could not discard was the faith, the confidence and the sheer joy of the Christian life.

I sat down and began thinking more about my faith, my spiritual state and my hopes for the future. I thought back to the start of my spiritual journey and the deep convictions I had had then, and which I no longer felt. I traced that journey of faith from my origins in the East End of London to Dagenham, and to the trust that others had placed in me. I knew that I still longed to serve God, but my personal integrity was crucial to my survival as a believer. In that quiet Toronto room I began to wonder if it was possible to recover my former assurance when it seemed that the iron of deep unbelief had entered my soul.

I decided to bury my pride, and fell to my knees. I remained wordless for a very long time. Then a prayer started to form which was, I suppose, in essence a confession of failure and an admission that intellectual pride and human arrogance had stopped me hearing God's voice. How I longed to come home, I said to myself and to that 'Other' who was listening. Then something happened. There was no answering voice, no blinding light or angelic appearance – only a deepening conviction that God was meeting me now. I felt the love of God and His tenderness towards me. As I prayed out loud – a practice I strongly recommend – I felt a sense of joy and elation, of reassurance and hope as I resumed my walk with God.

I returned to my feet after what had been a very long period of quiet prayer, reflection and encounter. Even now, many years later, it is impossible to say why that moment was so important to my life and experience. Was I so longing to believe that I made myself believe? That might be possible, but so strong in me is the spirit of enquiry that such an interpretation could not sustain me in the long run. I am not the kind of person who is afraid of doubt – indeed, I regard it as an essential component of faith. The steadiness of my faith since that encounter in 1972 is for me an assurance of the reality of faith, not an illusion. It represented a 'coming home' to the roots that alone hold one fast. The nearest approximation I have read to what I felt then is by the scientist F.C. Happold, who in his book *Religious Faith and the Twentieth Century* recounts his own experience:

> It happened in my room at Peterhouse in the evening of Feb
> 1st 1913 when I was an undergraduate at Cambridge . . . When
> I tried to record the experience at the time I used the imagery
> of the Holy Grail; it seemed just like that. There was, however,
> no sensible vision. There was just the room, with its shabby
> furniture and the red shaded lamp on the table. But the room
> was filled with a presence which in a strange way was about
> me and within me, like light or warmth. I was overwhelmingly
> possessed by Someone who was not myself, and yet I felt I
> was more myself than I had ever been before.

That seemed to capture the essentials of my experience.

Two things flowed immediately from this unspectacular but important event. First, the grave doubts and spiritual darkness were a thing of the past. I was now able to move on with contentment and trust – and with no little joy. Of course, such experiences of God's love do not mean the end of doubt or distrust. Any thinking Christian will encounter the unknown, the darkness within and without. Doubt, as I have observed, is an important element for faith and may at times even be the engine that drives trust. But what I had dealt with – or rather, what God had sorted out in me – was that terrifying shadow that had clouded my faith and work.

The second result of that meeting with God was that it denoted for me an awareness of the Holy Spirit and, as a consequence, an experiential discovery of the Trinity. I guess that many evangelicals encounter God through Jesus, and this can result in an overfamiliar view of God that scorns mystery, distance and wonder. In the same way, there are Catholics whose Christian experience seems wholly theistic, avoiding any personal intimacy with Jesus Christ. I recall once overhearing a Bishop say: 'I'm a God-the-Father kind of Christian' – a code that intimated that he found 'Jesus' talk too embarrassing to handle.

My Toronto experience unexpectedly opened up the Trinity for me in a most exciting way. It dawned on me that I had never thought much about the Holy Spirit, who up to that point had been for me either a doctrine in the Creed or a mysterious force at work in the Bible. Now I saw Him as a living reality in the Church today, and at the heart of what we mean when we say 'God'. This led me to a greater sympathy with Charismatic theology and practice, whilst still rejecting the two-stage baptismal theology that some believed in. Where I found myself overlapping with Charismatic thought was in the realisation that there was so much to discover, experience and understand about God's love. In the wonderful words of John Taylor, Bishop of Winchester: 'Every Christian is meant to possess his possessions and many never do.'

This new experience of God's love in Christ, made known again to me through the Holy Spirit, was like a second wind to me in my work. I returned to St John's bursting with energy and eager to get on with the job. The remaining three years of my time at the college were very creative ones, in which I completed my first book, *I Believe in Man*, which explored human nature and sexuality. But the Toronto experience led me to reconsider my future. After nine years in two theological colleges it was time to move on, and put into practice all I had gained in theology and experience. In 1975, at the age of thirty-nine, I became vicar of St Nicholas's, Durham.

6

Challenges of Growth

'I have no difficulty in saying how I conceive the work of a
parish priest. My object is first of all to gather a congregation;
large, converted, instructed and missionary-hearted and then
set it to work. Forge, temper and sharpen your sword – then
wield it.

Peter Green of Salford

THE DECISION TO LEAVE ST JOHN'S and return to parish ministry was not taken lightly. There were those who felt that I should
stay on at St John's and consolidate my work, but the 'Toronto
experience' had given me a thirst to work out what I felt God was
teaching me. I considered a number of parishes which the Bishop of
Southall asked me to visit, but an invitation to St Nicholas's, Durham,
caused my heart to beat in excitement. St Nic's, as generations of
Durham undergraduates still call it affectionately, is a leading evangelical church in the marketplace of Durham, with a distinguished
teaching ministry. Interestingly, the previous incumbent was also a
'George' and his wife an 'Eileen'. George Marchant had served for
twenty-five years as vicar of St Nic's before becoming Archdeacon
of Auckland. A fine scholar and pastor, he had served the church
devotedly and would be a hard act to follow.

Our first visit to St Nic's confirmed my suspicions that there was
much to do there, but that suited me down to the ground. I needed
a real challenge, and a cosy bolt-hole was not for me. We met the

churchwardens, Gerald Brooke and Dick Bongard, and hit it off with them at once. They were frank about the church's problems, which were many. The local congregation was very small; there was hardly any youth or Sunday-school work to speak of; the buildings were in bad shape; the student congregation had shrunk ever since George Marchant had left, wooed away by the Charismatic, Catholic style of another city-centre parish, St Margaret's; giving was appalling; and there was too much reliance on a small but dedicated lay team who had struggled manfully during the interregnum.

I was to learn some very important lessons during the exciting seven years I spent at St Nic's. First, one has to have a clear theological vision. I made no secret of mine when the churchwardens and the Church Council asked me what I stood for. I replied that I was first of all a Christian who accepted other Christians of all mainstream traditions as full members of the Body of Christ. Although the Church is hopelessly divided, all baptised Christians are members of God's one family. I remember quoting the statement attributed to Archbishop William Temple: 'I believe in one holy, catholic and apostolic church – but regret that it doesn't exist.' I went on to say that I was a cradle Anglican, able to work and live with people from other traditions in one Church. Although an evangelical – and absolutely convinced of the role of the Bible as the ultimate authority in matters of faith and morals – I did not regard the evangelical tradition as the repository of the total truth about God. Furthermore, I continued, I believed that the emerging Charismatic Movement in the Church of England had much to teach us. It would be my intention, subject to Church Council agreement, to bring in some of these new elements in worship and their spiritual gifts to make the faith more appealing and exciting. I am glad to say that the Council were prepared to take a risk by giving their wholehearted backing to this vision of change.

Secondly, I found that one has to have clear objectives. For me the overall objective was to make St Nic's an open, accessible church where everyone was welcome. I believed in growth, and aimed to increase the congregation and improve the giving. The church was positioned perfectly at the heart of the small city but was closed six days a week, when shoppers, workers, students and tourists crowded the streets, and only open on Sunday, when there was hardly anybody around. I wanted St Nic's to be available to all, truly a serving and caring church.

In order to achieve this objective of growth, the character of worship had to change. Worship at St Nic's was solidly morning and evening prayer according to the Book of Common Prayer, but there was no choir to lead or enliven it. With a heavy heart I came to realise that the services were, frankly, very boring. Furthermore, the coldness of the church building meant that there was little that might attract casual worshippers to come regularly. Although there was a regular 8 a.m. communion service every Sunday, celebrations of the Holy Communion at other times amounted to the final part of the 1662 Service, used after a morning or evening service for the handful of worshippers who remained. This was plainly unsatisfactory. The missionary situation the Church was now in demanded a fresh approach to worship – it had to be accessible, friendly, joyful, yet also reverential. I was confident that we could make it so, with the talents of the many able people in the congregation. Indeed, as I drew upon these talents in creating a music group, and in encouraging children to bring their instruments along when a church orchestra was formed, the congregation increased and with it a deepening sense of fellowship.

Not everyone liked the changes to the worship, of course. A small core of devoted members of the congregation felt that I was changing the character and identity of St Nic's to such an extent that it was no longer their church. One evening in my second year a former churchwarden asked me to meet twenty-two mainly elderly members of the congregation. I was shocked and saddened to learn of their deep distress. The last thing I wanted was to cut them off from their spiritual home. As we talked I realised that the conversation was wholly one-sided. They were only concerned about their worship, what the church meant to them and how important the Book of

Common Prayer was to them. There seemed to be no awareness of the missionary context of the Church, and the necessity of adapting to meet the needs of a new hour. The Church of England had been experiencing years of decline, which accelerated during the 1960s and 1970s as I began my own ministry. The situation was so serious that no regular churchgoer could afford to be sanguine. The need for change, I felt, should have been obvious to all.

I realised that there was no real meeting of minds; yet it was important to keep everyone within the family of the church. We therefore replaced the 8 a.m. communion service with a new traditional service at 9 a.m. All the services with their new styles of worship attracted greater numbers, including this one, although its growth was more modest.

This was a very important lesson to me, showing that it was possible – indeed, essential – to include the more traditional element in church life. That is not to say that the other services were extreme, by any means. I saw no reason to depart from the Church's expectations that clergy should use the official prayers and should robe properly. It was and remains my conviction that liturgies, appropriately and imaginatively used, and the traditional dress of clergy are not barriers to understanding.

Another lesson I learned at St Nic's was that if there is to be growth in church life, it cannot be accomplished by the clergy alone. It is imperative to utilise the gifts and abilities of lay people. The problem was that at the beginning I had to do everything. This was a shock to the system, having served my curacy at St Mary's, Islington, where I was used to working in a team, and having attended two theological colleges where manpower was readily available. I realised that I had to bring about a change of culture in which the leadership of the church was corporate rather than singular. Of course there were lay leaders there from the beginning, but there were many others whose talents were not being tapped. Over the next few years I gradually broadened the leadership team.

This was not without its problems. One of the main challenges when lay people bring their gifts and skills to the task of leadership is the tension between the corporate and the specific responsibility for the 'cure of souls' entrusted to the clergy. The church, through the Bishop, had given me responsibility for building up the congregation, and the Bishop's words at my induction rang through my mind again and again: 'Receive this charge which is both yours and mine.' I could not democratise this role too much without completely abdicating from it. On the other hand, neither could I run away from a desire to share my leadership, and to accept the challenge when somebody else came up with a brilliant idea or when I found myself in a minority.

In my third year this became a very real issue. I began to feel uncomfortable and even threatened by the fact that more and more people were sharing the exercise of leadership. At about this time I shared the platform at a meeting with a leading clinical psychologist, Dr Frank Lake. I told him privately that although the work was going well at St Nic's, I had a problem: 'As I widen the team I'm finding that I'm delegating areas of ministry where I'm strong, and being left with areas of ministry where I'm weak –'

Before I could finish, Frank beamed at me and said, 'That's wonderful, George! How few clergy have the grace and ability to surrender what they're strong at and bear the burden of weakness!' Without another word, he left for another seminar he was leading.

Frustrated, I initially did not consider this to be an adequate reply to my comment, but as I drove home I began to see that he had in fact given me a profound response. He was saying: 'Leadership includes the ability to trust others and give them freedom to flourish. A true leader keeps watch on the whole, but is prepared to exercise humble ministries as well.' That was an important lesson, and my sense of feeling threatened when leadership was shared diminished – indeed, my confidence in the exercise of my own leadership deepened.

Another thing I realised was that we had a very serious problem, in that there was hardly any children's work going on. Even though St Nic's was fortunate to have its own youth centre, it was rarely used. A young priest, Graeme Rutherford, who was doing a master's degree at the university, was attempting to create an open youth club, but it was an uphill struggle and the results were meagre as far as church attendance was concerned.

It was the condition of the church accounts that gave the impetus to a change of attitude. As I pored over the accounts prior to my first Annual General Meeting of the Church Council, it dawned on me that they were a very good indicator of what we considered important. Our spending showed very bleakly that mission did not matter to us, and that areas like Sunday school and youth work were deemed unimportant. Indeed, the finances showed that the church was interested in maintaining itself only by spending money on buildings, repairs and heating.

I set the church a challenge. From now on, I said, our missionary giving must start at 10 per cent of gross income, and not what we can spare when all expenses are paid. Furthermore, I continued, we must have a realistic budget for children and youth work, for the reason that a church that does not invest in the young is doomed. Again the Parochial Church Council backed this overwhelmingly, but sadly the Treasurer himself was the first casualty of the strategy. He resigned because 'the church would not be able to afford it'. The interesting thing is that when a congregation is set a healthy challenge, it will respond to it. This proved to be the case at St Nic's. Giving soared as we created a missionary budget aimed not at simply maintaining ourselves, but at attracting new members.

Perhaps one of the most exciting developments was the creation of 'Watersports'. The idea started when a new member of the congregation, David White, came to me one day and said hesitantly, 'I know you're appealing for people to help with youth work. At the age of sixty-two I'm hardly the sort that youth workers are made of, but I have a boat, and I'm prepared to take children sailing.' From this small beginning developed a number of children's and youth activities which continued for many years. Many dozens of families from inside and outside the church community, as well as a number of youngsters from areas of social deprivation, learned sailing and canoeing with the church in the Lake District. As a consequence many new children were fed into the Sunday schools, and often their parents began to attend the church.

I wanted the church to serve the wider community. For me, Christianity was too important to be left to churches and Christians. My theology was, and is, that God is at work in the world, and uses people of all faiths and none to further His purposes. Furthermore, caring practically for the body and the mind is as much a priority of the gospel as caring spiritually for the soul – indeed, the two cannot be separated. So I had no hesitation in raising the question: How may we serve our community better? As I saw it, healthy churches are relevant to the needs of those they serve.

It was difficult at first to see how St Nic's was serving the wider community. I decided to do my own private survey, by going to people outside the church to see what they thought of it and what suggestions they might have. I approached the Mayor, the Chief Executive of the city council, market traders, shopkeepers, shoppers and others. The results were sobering as well as challenging. For the majority of them St Nic's was 'just there', part of the landscape of Durham, and they had no expectations of it. But when I pressed the question: 'What would you like to see the church providing?' the answers were positive. Some wanted the church to be open, so they could go in and pray. Others suggested that they would like to see church people more involved in the life of the city, and St Nic's more visible in providing help to the elderly, the young and the destitute.

This deepened my own resolve to get involved in the life of the city. I became a part-time Prison Chaplain at Low Newton Prison, which held over three hundred young men and about forty women. I spent up to twelve hours a week in the prison, and found it a healthy balance to the middle-class life of St Nic's. I also became Chaplain to the Royal Air Force Club, where as an ex-RAF man I was made very welcome. This brought me into close contact with another side of Durham life, that of ordinary citizens very similar to the people I grew up with in Dagenham. Another area occupied a great deal of my time – I chaired the local committee of the Cyrenaian organisation, which dedicates itself to serving homeless people. From my days in Islington I felt I had a calling to help the members of this underclass, who usually drop out of mainstream community life. Today they constitute an even more serious problem than they did then. I and two other men of my age, one an agnostic, the other an atheist, made an unlikely trio as we set about helping such people get back on their feet by overseeing the management of a hostel where they could stay. Homeless men were frequent visitors to the vicarage as well, especially around dinnertime, when Eileen would make up a sandwich and a cup of tea for them.

Largely as a result of my desire to make St Nic's more central to the life of the community, we set about a radical reordering of the building. From my first visit to the church I realised it had huge problems, but equal potential. It was ideally and excitingly positioned in a busy market square, yet it was in a very rundown state. The interior was gloomy and unattractive. The pews, many in very bad condition, made it difficult to adapt the space for anything other than worship. Heating was supplied by a temperamental coal boiler which, I was told, was the last solid-fuel boiler in the diocese, and which required stoking from Friday onwards before the Sunday services could be comfortably held. There were also serious leaks in the roof – six or so buckets were placed by the church cleaner, Mrs Simpson, at the offending places. If one adds to the list of problems the fact that the church interior was defiantly puritan in its ugliness and tastelessness, something radical had to be done.

The creation of an attractive interior that provided facilities which could be used seven days a week became the mirror image of the spiritual pilgrimage of the congregation at the same time. I learned the lesson that no reordering of any building should happen without the spiritual reordering of people. That we were able to raise £350,000 within two years at a time when inflation was raging at around 20 per cent was only slightly short of miraculous. I remain convinced to this day that many congregations do not properly see that buildings may either be part of their successful outreach into the community or, in the majority of cases, significant reasons for the decline of church life.

It is said in the Old Testament that Jacob's love for Rachel was so special that his seven years of service 'seemed but a day'. My time at St Nic's was sometimes tough and always exhausting, but it stands out as perhaps the most significant period of our joint ministry. Eileen was blissfully happy bringing up our four children and sharing energetically in our work together. All of the children started school in Durham, and our eldest, Rachel, went away to college in London, while our sons Mark and Andrew completed 'A' levels and 'O' levels respectively. Our youngest, Lizzie, was in primary school by the time we left. We lived in a beautiful seven-bedroomed vicarage overlooking the cathedral and castle, with grand, high-ceilinged rooms for entertaining, and a garden filled with adventure for the children and bushes packed with summer fruits. The whole family were to remember Durham with great fondness; it was an idyllic place to grow up.

Eileen's ministry developed to such an extent in the church family that she provided much of the hospitality offered by St Nic's, and opened the vicarage for bed-and-breakfast in order to raise money for the building project. Eileen's mother, Margaret Daisy Hood, now in her eighties, came to live with us, having spent the last ten years of her widowhood with Eileen's sister in Canada. It was clear that Mrs Hood was suffering from dementia, and this became very distressing for us all. Sometimes she would wander from the house, to be found in a confused state in some part of the city and be brought back by a kindly and sympathetic neighbour. This certainly added to the stress on Eileen. Alas, both her mother and my father died within a short while of each other towards the end of our time at St Nic's. Both were wonderful Christian people whose influence on us was great. I particularly felt the death of Dad as his passing was so sudden – he had a severe heart attack and died instantly. His funeral in Dagenham Parish Church took the form of deep thanksgiving for the rich life of a truly humble man whose legacy was considerable.

In my second year at St Nic's an unexpected phone call from Christopher Hill, on the staff at Lambeth Palace, affected my life greatly. Christopher's responsibility was for ecumenical relationships. I remember that November morning very well.

'Would you like to spend three weeks in Rome?' was the strange question.

Looking out of my office window on a very bleak and cold Durham, I replied, 'Yes please. But tell me more.'

I was told that the following February the Anglican Centre in Rome would be hosting a three-week course for representatives of all Provinces of the Anglican Communion, organised by the Pontifical Council for Christian Unity. John Moorman, the former Bishop of Ripon and now retired to Durham, was to lead the course. I had been chosen to represent the Church of England.

It was a life-changing experience. Ever since my Oak Hill days I had been becoming closer and closer to Christians of other denominations, especially in the Roman Catholic Church. In Durham warm relationships with Father John Tweedy, the local Roman Catholic priest, were quickly established and we worked closely together. I was also a regular visitor to Ushaw Seminary, a few miles outside the city. The visit to Rome made me aware that this great Christian city was part of my heritage of faith, and Roman Catholicism entered my understanding of theology. The place overwhelmed me, and in my spare time from the lectures and sessions of the course I would walk for miles – retracing the journey of many a martyr from the Colosseum to the catacombs. In the crypt of St Peter's I would linger and pray at the very place where the bones of St Peter were laid.

Bishop John Moorman, a renowned authority on St Francis, was a splendid leader. Other teachers shaped our thinking – including a youthful Terry Waite, who was then working for the Roman Catholic Mission Department, and Professor Gerry O'Collins, New Testament theologian at the Gregoriana who later became a dear friend. Among fellow Anglicans was Miseri Kauma, Bishop of Namirembe in Uganda, an inspiring and dynamic missionary Bishop. The three weeks in Rome gave us all an opportunity to study Catholicism, not only through the lectures and reading but also through rare opportunities to meet representatives of the many 'dicasteries', or departments, that comprise the Vatican.

But this three-week study course was not an unembroidered charm offensive by the Roman Catholic Church. It was a deliberate attempt to open the Church to others. I was especially struck by our private audience with Pope Paul VI. A deeply holy man, he was frank about the problems of his Church following the Second Vatican Council. As he saw it, the Council, which concluded its work in 1965, and with which he clearly identified, had left the Church divided. Implementation of its vision had fallen to him but was proving difficult to achieve, although much had been done. Now, in the twilight of his life and ministry, he was showing signs of great weariness, yet a serene spirit in Christ came through strongly to us.

On the course we were invited to put our toughest questions to our Catholic friends. As the only evangelical present, my theological questions concerned the infallibility of the Pope, the Marian dogmas, the authority of the Church, and prayers to the saints. While I was by no means fully satisfied by the responses given, I was better informed when I returned home. Two years later I made a private visit to consolidate my knowledge and to study in greater depth the significance of the Virgin Mary.

In my sixth year at St Nic's I began to receive letters, phone calls and personal messages asking me to consider putting my hat in the ring for the Principalship of Trinity College, Bristol. I rejected all these overtures for a number of reasons. The first, and most important, was that my work at St Nic's was not over. I could not leave when there was still a large amount of money to raise and the building work had not yet begun. A second reason which appeared to make it unlikely that I would be offered the post was that Trinity College's theological tradition seemed far removed from mine. It stood for a reformed evangelical doctrinal commitment which seemed to me narrow, negative, anti-Rome, and puritanical. Perhaps this perception of Trinity was ill-founded, but it was shared by many other people in the Church at that time. Strong appeals to consider the post, however, made Eileen and me waver. What should we do?

I decided to get my Bishop's advice. I did not know the Bishop of Durham, John Habgood, very well, though I had met him many times. He was an excellent speaker, preacher and scholar, but seemed rather remote to ordinary mortals. He had no capacity for small-talk, and most clergy in the diocese dismissed him as a pastor. This latter estimate, I knew first-hand, was mistaken. Two years before I had had a car crash and had ended up in hospital, following which I had required several weeks' convalescence. On hearing this, John Habgood made available a sum of money to allow me to have a proper rest. I knew that, in spite of the impression he could give at times, he was a caring man, and would answer every question with great insight. I outlined my predicament to him, and without hesitation he gave his opinion that Trinity needed to be brought into the Church of England, and that I was ideally positioned to do it. He urged me to be positive about meeting the College Council, but said that I must make it clear to them that I had to finish the building project at St Nic's before I could possibly take up the position.

In the light of that advice I accepted the invitation to visit the college and meet the Council. To my surprise, I found that it was set up as a formal interview. As I was not convinced I should even be considering the post, I had not prepared myself to argue my corner. Before the interview I met Archdeacon Trevor Lloyd, the other person being interviewed that day, who shared with me his opinion that Trinity was at a crossroads – unpopular with Church of England ordinands, it was having to rely on American students from nonconformist traditions who were beginning to change the culture of the college. Trevor's verdict was that Trinity was in a make-or-break situation, and that the appointment of the next Principal would be decisive for its survival. That was a sobering thought to take into the interview. However, the meeting with the Council went very well. I made it abundantly plain that I was not seeking a new post at the moment, and would have to have very good reasons to move from St Nic's, where I was very happy. To my utter astonishment, at the end of the day I was summoned to meet the Council again, and was offered the post of Principal of Trinity College, Bristol.

I returned home on the train stunned. Eileen had not bothered to come with me, because neither of us had believed that this move could possibly be right for us. But as I told her about the day's events we began to see that this could be the next step for us. It was a real and demanding challenge. The more we thought about it, the more we could see that my experience of theological education and parish life fitted me well for the post. We had to admit that once the building project at St Nic's was complete my presence was not necessary for the next stage, which was to use the buildings for the wider community.

The lay leaders of the church were wonderful in their acceptance of our decision and their willingness to release us once the building work had been completed. The next nine months sped by quickly – we raised the remaining £50,000; indeed we exceeded that amount – and a week of celebrations were held, with the Bishop of Durham leading a service of blessing for the development. The farewells were sad and generous, and we travelled to Bristol with heaviness of heart but much gratitude to God for all we had learned at St Nic's. We had been blessed beyond belief.

All my fears concerning Trinity College were confirmed when I began my new work as Principal in September 1982. Life at St Nic's had been tough enough, especially in the first four years, but I seemed to have fallen from the frying pan into the fire. There were structural problems with the constituent colleges in the union. Tyndale College, associated with the famous names of Stafford Wright and Jim Packer, was renowned for its emphasis on uncompromising and clear evangelical teaching rooted in the inerrancy of scripture. Clifton Theological College, associated with Alex Motyer, had been established in protest to Tyndale and took a milder line on doctrinal matters, although it was still clearly evangelical. The Women's College, which was itself an amalgam of St Michael's House, Oxford, and Dalton House, had buildings across the Downs. Years earlier Oliver Tompkins, Bishop of Bristol, had issued an ultimatum to the three evangelical colleges to amalgamate, and they had done so with a lot of grumbling and not a little feuding.

When I arrived, the amalgamation was not complete. An independent body called the Clifton College Trust still held the deeds of the main building, and was reluctant to surrender them because of suspicions that the ethos of Tyndale would dominate. I found myself regarded with no small suspicion. Older Council members representing the Tyndale tradition were worried that my more open style would undermine a clear-cut evangelical tradition, whilst some of the Clifton College fraternity were fearful that I would be taken over by the dominant Tyndale group. It was clear that if this division were to be overcome – by love and persuasion – it would take some time to achieve.

In the short term the college was in a mess, partly due to its undeserved reputation in the Church of England, which I myself had shared. I realised from my first day that the college was served by an able and highly dedicated faculty who could hold their own with any theological department in the country. Nevertheless, the immediate future was troubling. The break-even financial figure was 105 students, but four weeks before the beginning of term only just over eighty had enrolled to join us. We were heading towards a huge deficit. Of those likely to join us, only forty-eight were ordinands, even though the Church's allocation of ordinands to Trinity was eighty. The bursar told me that nothing could be done to tackle that year's deficit.

I was dismayed, but I was also quite sure that a great deal could be done. To begin with, it was important to restore confidence in the college, starting with the staff. Once again the theological vision had to be shared and owned. I was delighted to find no objection to my desire to do something about the worship, which I felt must combine that Anglican balance of word and sacrament. I knew that with talented students the musical standard, and therefore the quality of worship, would steadily improve. When the students arrived our policy was to help them to realise that they had come to the best theological college in England. There was, I felt, a natural and healthy pride in speaking confidently of this. Another part of my job as Principal was to promote the college and make it visible in the structures of the Church. This was done in a variety of ways.

First, I accepted many speaking engagements, as a means to promote the college and to inform as many people as possible that Trinity gave a first-class theological education. Second, I revived a practice which Maurice Wood had developed at Oak Hill, of staff and students spending long weekends in parishes talking about the call of ordination. Third, I kept in close touch with some of the large parishes which were key providers of ordinands, especially at Oxford and Cambridge. My former Principal Michael Green was now at St Aldate's, Oxford, and his church became a particular quarry for excellent and gifted ordinands.

The students themselves were a good bunch on the whole, but I was worried about the quality of some of the non-ordinands. It is understandable, if not excusable, for Principals to admit people simply to make up numbers. A few of the students at Trinity were plainly unable to cope with the college's demanding intellectual disciplines, and were there hoping that the course would provide a back door into ordination.

If this troubled me, I had a greater shock when I received worrying reports about one particular student. The first complaints came from two of the women students, who reported that he was sexually harassing them. I called him in at once. He was from a breakaway Christian group, and was hoping to obtain a degree so that he might be ordained in his own Church. He listened to the complaints in an untroubled way, and it was clear that he had pestered the women but was completely free of shame. I gave him a lecture on the kind of behaviour I expected from students at Trinity. However, his view of sexuality appeared to amount to nothing more than an expectation of gratification. He assumed it was obvious that, as a single man, he had sexual needs that should be fulfilled. I asked him to square this with his theology and the discipline of the college. Sending him away again with a warning, I felt with sinking heart that I was encountering a wholly new phenomenon in my experience – a Christian who felt that there were no rights or wrongs in the area of sexual morality. My fears were realised as I and his tutor watched the man's progress. Besides his inappropriate behaviour with female members of the college he was a practising homosexual. And then he mentioned without a trace of shame that he paid weekly visits to his 'hooker' in a nearby village. My mouth must have dropped. Perhaps I had misheard. 'My hooker,' he repeated. He did not last long in Trinity after that.

The episode prepared me for aspects of culture that I was to meet later in my ministry as Archbishop – namely the erosion of holiness by a cultural view that sexual intercourse is of little more significance than shaking hands. When this is combined with a view of the Bible as itself being culturally conditioned, with no authority in matters of sexuality, the drift into hedonistic narcissism becomes inevitable. The Church which blesses such immorality, or calls it holy, ends up as nothing more than a benign religious club.

Returning to theological education after seven years away in parish ministry brought to the surface some of my deepest questions and worries about the purpose and success of our colleges and courses in turning out effective ministers and priests with the leadership skills to work with others and to build up congregations. Was it our aim to produce theologians? Or to produce pastors and teachers? The curriculum of most colleges and courses did not make the purpose transparent. From my experience of three theological colleges it was clear that the majority of their staffs had little experience of parish life, and even less of leading congregations into growth. But it was also true that the brightest and most visible of students did not necessarily make the most dedicated and effective clergy.

These two facts worried me a great deal. If the task of the Church of England's colleges and courses is to turn out godly men and women with fire in their bellies to teach, evangelise, pastor and build up congregations, then the logical conclusion is that that task is closer to vocational training than it is to making men and women academics. But compelling though this argument was, it was not without problems. My own experience told me that we could not ignore the intellect. While I wanted my students to leave college with a clear focus, dedication and enthusiasm for building up churches, I was also concerned to equip them to handle ideas, and that meant taking theology seriously. How could one square that circle?

I had also become aware of a very significant difference between Catholic and Anglican models of theological education. The Roman Catholic model focused on ministerial formation, whereas the Anglican model was more intent on information. It seemed as if we attempted to prepare people by loading them with knowledge, while Roman Catholic priests were formed in their spirituality and the application of theological knowledge to the life of the Church.

I found myself arguing more and more for two significant changes in theological teaching. First, that the present basic education of three years for those under thirty, and two years for those over, was woefully inadequate. Our starting point should be four years for those under thirty and three years for those older. Furthermore, my experience suggested to me that the best way to prepare would be by sandwich training, with substantial time spent learning from effective ministers and priests. Lastly, the whole purpose of theological education and training must be earthed in prayer and spiritual transformation. I was convinced that effective ministers – of all traditions – shared one striking characteristic: they had a burning love of God and a yearning to share Him with others. However, the responsibility for delivering such radical changes in ministerial formation was not mine – it belonged to the Church centrally.

My thoughts about the necessity of changes for the future of the Church's ministry did not stem from any misgivings about my students. We were able to attract men and women of great ability, and student numbers grew to such an extent that by the time I left Trinity in 1987 it was the largest theological college in the Church of England. Furthermore, the divisions between the Clifton College Trust and Trinity had been resolved to everyone's satisfaction.

At the end of my fifth and final year at Trinity one of our most gifted students, Phil Potter, mentioned to me in passing that there was a lot of talk about my becoming Bishop of Bath and Wells. I was flabbergasted to learn this, but what I was even less prepared for was the way that the thought both disturbed me and prompted unhealthily ambitious thoughts. Up to that point, senior office in the Church had not entered my head. I was prepared to stay at Trinity until my work was over, and then return to parish ministry. But ambition now began to enter my psyche, and I both liked it and loathed it. Looking back on that time, I am still not sure how to interpret the ambition I felt. Of course, ambition is not always unhealthy. When one has gifts to offer any organisation, the desire to give leadership for the good of the whole is not bad. A part of me was suggesting that I had proved myself for a wider leadership role, and that there was nothing wrong in this unexpected desire to become a Bishop. However, to this day I feel that I was encountering something within me that was not good. I was desiring the role of Bishop more than the task of leadership it demanded. It was important to resolve this, which I attempted by an honest analysis of my desires and by taking them to God in prayer.

In my journal from this period I wrote: 'It's an awful cancer. I know at the level of my mind that this is all about baubles; that serving Christ is the most important thing. That being faithful, obedient and ready is all He requires. But deep within there is a demon which loves power and authority, and he will be disappointed if nothing comes.' A realisation dawned that I needed to rededicate myself to the work of Trinity College. And in prayer I dedicated myself to God's work rather than my own concerns. I found this liberating, as though a weight had been lifted from me.

Two days later, on 23 June 1987, an envelope dropped through our letterbox from Number 10 Downing Street. The letter, signed by the Prime Minister Mrs Thatcher, simply said that the Crown Appointments Commission had put my name forward, and that she hoped I would accept this offer. After careful thought and prayer I did, and was consecrated Bishop of Bath and Wells on 3 December 1987.

7

Letters from Number 10

'What the average Englishman wanted was a Church which would respond to his needs, teaches a message which he could understand, and lift him to a higher level of life – but, this, somehow, was just what he never got.'

Ronald Jasper, A.C. Headlam *(1960)*

THE MOVE TO WELLS WAS NOT without its sadness. We had enjoyed our time in Bristol greatly, living for the first time in our married life not in a college community or a house tied to a church, but in a normal street. And so much had been achieved at the college. With the co-operation of the faculty and council the college was now united, phase one of an exciting building programme was complete, and Trinity was full and attracting ordinands from throughout the Church of England.

True, an intriguing future beckoned, although aspects of it terrified me. Not the actual work, because I was comfortable with a leadership role and the speaking and teaching that went with it. But I was ignorant of the secondary aspects of being a Bishop – what one had to wear, what the expectations were, and what were the different responsibilities in a diocesan team.

Of course there were people I could rely on for advice and information. The suffragan Bishop of Taunton, Nigel McCulloch, a young and very popular Bishop, offered his assistance readily, as did David

Hope, the Bishop of Wakefield, later to become Bishop of London and then Archbishop of York. Both were from the Catholic wing of the Church, and were on hand to show this evangelical what to wear and when to wear it. Not that copes, mitres and chasubles bothered me much. Although I preferred to dress simply, my attitude was that if this was what the Church wanted me to wear, then I was quite prepared to don the unfamiliar for the dignity of the office.

First I had to be ordained for this ministry, and a date was fixed for 3 December 1987 at Southwark Cathedral. Up to that point I had not met Robert Runcie, the 102nd Archbishop of Canterbury. From a distance Robert seemed a reserved and lofty figure. He had the reputation in evangelical circles of being wobbly and indecisive on doctrinal and ethical issues, and the only contact I had had with Lambeth Palace as a Principal was distinctly unpromising. An able ordinand had resigned over the statements of David Jenkins, the then Bishop of Durham. As a result I had written to the Archbishop expressing my concern that a Bishop of the Church should express his doubts so freely about the resurrection of Christ. I received what was obviously a standard letter, signed by a staff member, to the effect that David Jenkins's views did not state the mind of the Church. I was not impressed.

I met Robert for the first time on the evening before my consecration. The convention is for the family of the new Bishop to stay overnight with the Archbishop. Our large family was delighted and excited to accept this kind invitation, and it turned out to be a wonderful occasion. Before dinner Robert and I had a thirty-minute conversation, and my opinion of him changed as we spoke together. I could not fail to notice his evident spirituality, his wry sense of humour and his distinct love of people. But he seemed terribly tired and preoccupied.

The reason for this became apparent during dinner. I was sitting next to Lindy Runcie, whose direct and candid observations on every subject made her an entertaining companion. Looking across at Robert, she suddenly exploded and said, 'Poor Robert is under such pressure. That wretched man!' As the adjective was clearly not aimed at her husband, I asked her what she meant. Out poured a great deal of vitriol directed at Dr Gary Bennett, then Chaplain of New College, Oxford, and a leading Anglo-Catholic theologian, who she believed was the author of the Preface to the new edition of *Crockford's Clerical Directory*, which by tradition was written anonymously by a prominent cleric. The Preface was critical of Robert's liberalism, and accused him of packing the House of Bishops full of his cronies. As I was hardly one of these I could barely contain my mirth, but Robert and Lindy were obviously most distressed. This was my first encounter with the demands of the Archbishop's office and the way criticism could work its way under one's skin, causing real emotional pain.

The service in Southwark Cathedral the following day lived up to my expectations. Robert led it very well, and Canon Roy Henderson, Chairman of Trinity Council, gave an inspiring address. I had asked the cathedral if the college music group could lead some devotional songs during the offering of communion, and they did so very beautifully indeed.

The press were out in force after the consecration to cover what seemed to be a developing civil war in the Church. Robert was besieged by photographers and cameramen, and journalists clamoured for him to give his view of the damaging Preface, and to offer an opinion about the identity of the author. Of course he declined because it was not the time or place to comment upon such a matter.

If the Preface did originate from Gary Bennett, it was unworthy of a writer of such distinction. As it happened I knew him well, and liked him, although we had clashed ideologically as fellow members of a Commission which had been brought together to examine the theology of the Episcopate, and the Preface's style was certainly similar to his. It was a commonly held view that Gary was ambitious to be a Bishop, and very bitter towards the two Archbishops, who he felt were blocking his chance of higher office. The story was to end tragically a week later, when Gary committed suicide after having been exposed as the author of the Preface on the front page of the *Sun* newspaper.

Looking back on that episode, which brought such shame on the Church of England, I doubt very much if there ever was a liberal conspiracy. The Crown Appointments system does not operate like that. Archbishops have considerable but not final influence in deciding which names are put forward for appointment. The truth was possibly more mundane – that the Anglo-Catholic tradition had declined from greatness to a less pivotal position in the Church. Was it any longer able to provide men with the ability and vision needed to lead churches into mission and life? In my judgement it now appeared to be obsessed with issues which were of secondary importance to most members of the Church, such as the ordination of women. It was a tradition in crisis.

What kind of Bishop did I want to be? This question was very much in my mind from the moment the offer had come from the Crown. I spent many hours considering it and praying over it, and two conclusions emerged.

First, all I could offer was myself in all my humanity. I was overcome by the thought of being a Bishop and there was every reason for trepidation. Few people from my kind of background ever came this close to senior office in the Church. With genuine humility I could only offer my unworthiness and weakness, and ask that this sacrifice of love might be pleasing in God's sight. The day before my consecration as Bishop I had read 2 Chronicles 1, and had written in my private diary the following words: 'Reading from 2 Chron. 1 this morning the words leapt out: God said "Ask what I shall give you?" Solomon replied: "Wisdom and knowledge to go out and to come in before thy people." How relevant! I feel I need this too but combined with an unflinching faith in the power of the Gospel and an undying love of God. Only if I truly love Him will I love others.'

Second, I believed I was called to be a Bishop-in-mission. As I considered what was expected of me, I felt dissatisfied with the traditional role of being a Bishop, just as the traditional role of being a clergyman had not satisfied me in Durham. It was assumed that I would pastor clergy, confirm and institute them into new work and generally oversee the work of the diocese. There would certainly be enough to do even if I restricted myself to such a traditional role. Bath and Wells was one of the larger dioceses, with about 590 churches and over three hundred clergy, four hundred Readers and many thousands of active Anglicans. But the traditional role would not satisfy me – for several reasons.

For a start, it was clear that though the Church was still very influential in Somerset community life, it was not attracting enough people to regular worship. A different approach was required if we were to reverse years of decline in a changing society. An equally serious reason was that the clergy seemed embattled and ill-equipped to handle a different kind of community from the one they been trained for – one in which they now had to go out and sell their wares. Trained, by and large, for traditional ministry, in which pastoring and leading worship were the major elements, they were now required to build Christian congregations and lead others to faith. Though they were highly dedicated and very able, their sense of self-worth was being undermined by lack of affirmation in the community and poor responses to their overtures. It was obvious that I needed to build up the confidence of the clergy and people, and lead by example.

I also knew that I had much to learn myself, and there were many wise and experienced priests who could help me to be a trustworthy and faithful Bishop. I did not have to wait long for a few useful lessons to arrive. My very first confirmation service was at High Ham, a small village about nine miles from Wells. It was a Deanery confirmation service, which meant that fifteen or so clergy would be there to see this new Bishop take his first service. I was keen to do my best, and prepared well. Everything ran smoothly until the very end. The choir preceded me to the door of the church, and I turned to face them to say the words: 'Go in peace to love and serve the Lord,' to which the response was: 'In the name of Christ. Amen.' As I started the sentence, I realised that my pastoral staff was well and truly jammed in a grating at my feet. Laughter rang around the church as I, mortified, tugged in vain to free it. It stood upright and defiant in the grating until someone strong enough was able to release it.

Disrobing in the vestry, I had a chat with Peter Coney, who was Diocesan Communication Officer. 'Peter,' I said, 'I am keen to learn. How did it go?'

Tenderly, Peter held my arm and said, 'Bishop George, you were appointed because the Church wanted you – not somebody else.'

That was the most comforting thing anybody could have said. His message was very clear: 'Be yourself and use your gifts. Don't try to be something other than yourself.'

If Peter was a valued friend who helped me to relax into the ministry of Bishop, Douglas White helped me to see the ministry through the eyes of clergy. Douglas was eighty-four years of age when in my first year I took a service in his church near Yeovil. He had been incumbent since 1948 or so, and therefore was not bound by the official retirement age of seventy, which came into force in 1978. He had married Yolanda, a bride of thirty-seven, at the age of sixty-four, and they had two teenage girls. Even though he was going blind he was determined to resist all attempts to move him from office. We robed in his kitchen and prepared to go across the beautifully-kept churchyard to the lovely small church just thirty yards away.

'Bishop,' said Douglas, turning to me, 'may I say just one thing? I really am not used to Bishops being around. Do forgive me if anything goes wrong in the service.'

I was touched by this, and suddenly became aware that Bishops could overawe even the most experienced of godly priests. Very moved by his transparent honesty, I held his arm and said, 'Douglas, if you only knew the fear of this very inexperienced Bishop every time I take a service. Come on. Let's go out there and face them together.'

And we did. The church was packed, and it was obvious that Douglas was a devoted clergyman, loved by the village and very popular with children. The service was not without its comical moments. Douglas was more blind than he let on, and he relied on his memory to get him through the Book of Common Prayer. Now and again his memory would fail him, and members of the congregation would assist. He began: 'Dearly beloved brethren, the scripture moveth us in . . . er . . . in, er . . .' From the back came a loud whispered voice prompting 'sundry places'. Others picked this up, and 'sundry' rang out from several pews. Douglas then continued: 'Oh yes, sundry places.'

There was a lovely symbiosis between Douglas and his congregation, of the kind expressed perfectly by the seventeenth-century poet and priest George Herbert in *The Country Parson*: 'So the country parson who is a diligent observer and tracker of God's ways, sets up as many encouragements to goodness as he can, both in honour, and profit, and fame that he may, if not the best way, yet any way, make his parish good.' That was Douglas's way. He died in harness at the age of ninety-two, full of years and full of faith.

Douglas's fear made me realise that one is put on a pedestal as a Bishop, and that it was important to hold on to two crucial facts: one should never demean or undermine the office by one's behaviour; but at the same time one should never hide behind the office or use it to promote one's own importance. Douglas's statement led me to recall what someone had said to me following my consecration: 'George, from now on two things will happen to you. You will never lack for a good meal, but from now on, no one will ever tell you the truth.' I was determined to have my ear close to the ground, so that I could learn – and face the truth, whatever it was.

Being a missionary Bishop means being a missionary with others. It was therefore crucial to assemble a team of lay people around me, and to offer my help to parishes and deaneries. I invited Brian Pearson, a non-stipendiary priest who was then Vice Principal of a college in Brighton, to join me as a Chaplain and to head up the team. We then secured the services of a group of musicians, dramatists and other lay leaders to assist. Thus commenced a programme of what became 'Teaching Missions', of which there were fifteen during the nearly three years I was Bishop of Bath and Wells.

The format was nearly always the same. They would last about five days, and each evening there was a main teaching slot which I would give in the context of a lively and varied programme. Each day there would be a variety of activities which included visits to schools, youth events and meetings with local men's and women's groups. I made it clear that a Teaching Mission was not an evangelistic event. Nevertheless, I was convinced that the faith could be taught in such a way that people would understand it and form a judgement. It was my hope that by teaching the faith, and not ducking the challenging questions that thinking people would ask, they might hear the fresh and hopeful tones of the gospel.

So it proved. The very first one at the parish church in Wellington was memorable for both the congregation and my fledgling team. The Anglo-Catholic church was rather fearful of the word 'mission', and Father Terry Stokes, the parish priest, had urged me to bear this in mind. I had no difficulty in assuring him that my approach would be cerebral, not emotional, and that it was my desire to fit in with the tradition of the parish which hosted the mission. We hit upon the theme 'A Faith to Have and to Hold', based on words from the marriage service, which formed a wonderful centre around which the events in schools, clubs and pubs could cohere. I was told that it proved to be a turning point in the life of this church, encouraging faith and deepening confidence in its mission.

Teaching Missions became a vital lifeline between me and local communities, reminding me constantly that the role of a Bishop has to be measured by his relationship with society at large, not merely his diocese and church. I found them so valuable for my own ministry, and for bringing new life and confidence to local churches, that as Archbishop I continued to lead missions in the diocese of Canterbury.

A Bishop is of course more than merely a local Bishop. He is a national figure, at once a performer on the wider stage. I was keen to develop the national ministry, even though it would be some years before my turn came to be introduced into the House of Lords. Through my reading I had come across the scathing comment of Archbishop Benson, written a hundred years earlier, on Bishops who never ventured forth from their dioceses: 'Bishops of their dioceses were not so much Bishops of England.'

I had already accepted the Archbishops' invitation to chair the Faith and Order Advisory Group, the Church's central committee for handling theological issues related to unity. This gave me an immediate entrée into the wider ecumenical scene both at home and abroad. I knew there would be other invitations for national ministry, but for the moment I was happy to wait.

However, membership of the House of Bishops was a major commitment. I disapproved of clergy isolating themselves from the wider Church by not attending Synods and diocesan events, and had expressed myself forcefully on that point at times. I therefore believed it was my duty to make the House of Bishops a priority in my diary. It was later to be a sadness during my time as Archbishop that this commitment was by no means universally shared. There were always a few who took their attendance at meetings of the House of Bishops lightly, and this seemed to me symptomatic of the state of the clergy generally – a half-hearted commitment to the institutional Church, suggesting a weak understanding of a theology of obedience.

Notwithstanding this, I quickly came to the conclusion that if one's commitment to the House of Bishops was formed with reference to the actual quality of its meetings, truancy was entirely understandable. They seemed to be arranged so as to forbid participation. Organised as it was then by Douglas Pattison, Secretary General of Synod, conduct of business seemed limited to the two Archbishops, a few senior Bishops, and those who were bold enough to speak up and who sat close enough to the front to understand what was going on. The rest sat in the semi-circular chamber facing a large table behind which the two Archbishops, Douglas Pattison and a few lay staff sat. There were no microphones to aid communication.

Robert made no secret of the fact that the House of Bishops bored him, and allowed the Archbishop of York, John Habgood, to take the lead on the majority of occasions. John had a very quiet voice, which added to the already overwhelming atmosphere of an impenetrable club in which new members could barely hear what was said, let alone contribute. Consequently few did, in many cases because they were too terrified to speak up unless invited to do so.

I remember being greatly struck in my early days in the House of Bishops by three of my senior colleagues whose rhetorical skills were outstanding, but were not always employed constructively. David Jenkins, Bishop of Durham, could always be relied upon to speak entertainingly and often brilliantly, but I felt that he had spent so many years in academic teaching that his concerns were not always grounded in real life and the experience of people in his diocese. Bill Westwood, Bishop of Peterborough, was popular with the media and was also effective in raising emotions in the House, but he worried me by his tendency to pour doubt on all diocesan efforts to raise funds or enthusiasm. 'We have tried it in Peterborough and it doesn't work,' seemed to be his constant and discouraging refrain. I recall arriving at a House of Bishops late one day because of a train delay, and asking Bill, 'How's it going?' To which he replied, 'All right, but it's becoming increasingly difficult to be a Christian here.' I thought that was a little rich. David Lunn, Bishop of Sheffield, a fierce defender of the Prayer Book and of Catholic life, was another whose eloquence was often unintentionally destructive through its gloomy diagnoses and assumptions. I have often wondered if the three men realised how negative they appeared to be.

Although these three Bishops did not represent mainstream thought in the House of Bishops, they undoubtedly affected its mood, as pessimism and despondency always will. Mark Santer, Bishop of Birmingham, was one of the most articulate and probing of the Bishops and a joy to hear, especially on ecumenical matters. David

Sheppard, Bishop of Liverpool, and Jim Thompson, at that time Bishop of Stepney, spoke up passionately for the Church's involvement in society, and were very much behind the report *Faith in the City* which had caused such a furore a few years before, and which was about to take a practical form through the implementation of one of its recommendations, the Church Urban Fund.

The Church Urban Fund was a test of our mettle as Bishops, and although a majority of us voted to go ahead with it, I was troubled by a clear lack of enthusiasm among some of our number. We were not agreed on the principle of raising substantial funds for the urban Church, and some were convinced that the proposed figure of £20 million could not be raised in the economic climate of the late 1980s. It was a moderate triumph that we eventually agreed to raise this sum, which in my view was a very modest goal. The Fund was launched in Westminster Abbey in 1989, and attracted great publicity because there was so little government money going into urban development at the time. That the Church of England was prepared to pour so much money into our cities was a vigorous sign of our mission to the nation.

As far as Bath and Wells was concerned, our mainly rural diocese was expected to raise £350,000, which to my delight we managed relatively easily. Indeed, we gave £500,000 to CUF, and could have raised much more. Most dioceses reached their targets with ease, and in some cases – Oxford and Lichfield – raised substantially greater sums which were used to fuel diocesan projects. It has always seemed to me a pity that we had not started with the aim of raising twice as much money, although that would have met many objections.

As it happened, the way the Fund operated meant that far more than £20 million was given to our cities. Because a great number of the grants were offered on a matching basis, or initiated other giving, it is possible that the CUF in reality made £40 million available. Later, as Archbishop, I was able to see at first hand what a difference the Fund made to our mission. I recall visiting Barking and Dagenham, and seeing six CUF projects. I was amazed to find so many people in those churches supporting the vulnerable. When I asked the Archdeacon of West Ham, Tim Stevens, what difference the Fund had made to my old haunts, he replied simply, 'It has made us credible.' On the present level of funding grants, the CUF will come to an end in 2007. Will the Church have the courage and faith to relaunch it? We shall see.

If I had worries that Church of England Bishops were disunited, my experience of the Lambeth Conference of 1988 raised major questions in my mind about the state of worldwide Anglicanism. As the Conference fell just seven months after I had taken up office as Bishop, I was one of the newest there, and found myself rubbing shoulders with such giants as the Nobel Prize-winning Desmond Tutu and many others. On the face of it the Conference was a splendid show of Anglican strength and the growth of the Communion, especially in the developing world. I was, and am, proud to belong to a tradition which emphasises incarnational ministry among the very poor and the distressed. Desmond's outstanding ministry in South Africa was greatly applauded, as was the fine work of Archbishop David Gitari in Kenya, whose bold condemnation of corruption had put him at great risk. Archbishop Robin Eames's attempts to reconcile divided communities in Northern Ireland were also honoured, as was Bishop Samir Kaffity's impassioned representation of the Palestinians.

But there was another side to Lambeth 1988, in spite of Robert Runcie's gentle, wise and humorous leadership. I saw for the first time how easy it is for contentious matters to be 'spun' by the press. There were a number of Bishops who were able to use the media very cleverly. Bishop Jack Spong, Bishop of Newark in the United States, was particularly adept at getting his message across. A charming and handsome man, he was so often speaking to the media about the ordination of women and homosexuality that he was invisible as far as the Conference itself was concerned. The Bishop of London, Graham Leonard, was equally determined to promote his opposition to the ordination of women. Richard Holloway, the Bishop of Edinburgh, was the other media star turn of the Conference. But while all three were successful in getting the ear of the wider public, they gave a misleading impression of what was happening within the Conference itself. In the background was an awareness that Provinces such as England were preparing to introduce legislation to ordain women as priests, and that others such as the United States were already thinking beyond this, to the ordination of practising homosexuals.

Cultural divisions between First and Third World Bishops became apparent at the Conference. These were brought to a head in an absorbing debate between David Jenkins of Durham and David Gitari of Nairobi. Both speakers were excellent, but the evening belonged to the developing world, as David Gitari spoke with real fire and passion, whereas, as I wrote in my diary that evening: 'David Jenkins' address was brilliant but had no cutting edge or call to discipleship.' To me, it simply lacked Christian conviction.

Lambeth '88 will always be remembered as the Conference at which Bishops of the developing countries 'came of age' and spoke with confidence and authority. They were no longer prepared simply to make up the numbers, or to take orders from white Bishops. They were the ones bearing the heat of persecution or the cost of poverty, and this gave them an authority that others lacked. It was largely the Bishops from the developing countries who gave impetus to one of the few Resolutions that was to have significance in the days ahead. Arising from the Pope's call to make the 1990s a Decade of Evangelisation, the motion that the Anglican Communion should declare it a Decade of Evangelism won overwhelming support. Resolution 44 read: This Conference

> Calls for a shift to dynamic missionary emphasis going beyond care and nurture to proclamation and service; and therefore
>
> Accepts the challenge this presents to diocese and local church structures and patterns of worship and ministry, and looks to God for a fresh movement of the Spirit in prayer, outgoing love and evangelism in obedience to our Lord's command.

Inspiring and splendid as the Resolution undoubtedly was, I walked away from the conference hall rather uneasy. We had failed to ask how this could be achieved. Everyone can agree that the world ought to be a better place, but mere words will not make it so. Structured action is required, a budget has to be prepared, leaders have to be chosen. Nothing like that was done, and that remains the central failure of the Decade of Evangelism, even though it achieved a great deal through its implementation by too few people.

For those of us from the Church of England it was good to be reminded how others saw us. In the words of a former Free Church Moderator, Professor Elizabeth Templeton, 'the Church of England is a kind of ecclesiastical duck-billed platypus'. And yet, as one Third World Bishop observed, it was through this 'strange Church in the United Kingdom that missionaries came to tell my people about Jesus. I shall always be grateful to you.'

At the '88 Lambeth I had the great honour to present one of the most significant ecumenical motions ever put to an international Christian body: that 'This Conference recognises that the Agreed Statements of ARCIC 1 on "Eucharistic Doctrine, Ministry and Ordination" . . . offer a sufficient basis for taking the next step forward towards the reconciliation of our Churches [Roman Catholic and Anglican] grounded in agreement in faith.' I spoke briefly to the motion, offering the opinion that our ready acceptance of the work done by ARCIC (the Anglican–Roman Catholic International Commission) would not only encourage the ecumenical theologians in their continuing work, but would signal to the Roman Catholic Church that the Anglican Communion was ready to move into an even deeper reality of Communion. The motion was overwhelmingly accepted, with just one absention.

Tuesday, 17 July 1990 will forever remain etched in my memory. At the end of the staff meeting at the Bishop's Palace in Wells, one of my secretaries told me that Robin Catford, the Prime Minister's

Secretary for Senior Appointments, had phoned earlier. I was asked to call back as soon as possible.

I was intrigued. Why did he want to speak to me? The announcement of Robert Runcie's retirement as Archbishop of Canterbury had been made some months previously, and I knew that the Crown Appointments Commission was due to meet soon. Not for one moment did I think I would be a candidate, and assumed that my advice was being sought concerning possible contenders for this crucial appointment. As soon as lunch was over, I phoned.

'George, are you likely to be in London in the next few days?' Robin asked.

'No,' I replied. 'I was in London for a meeting yesterday, and the next time I'm due to be there is in September. Can it wait until then?'

'I'm afraid not,' came the reply. 'I need to see you very soon.'

I was even more intrigued. 'Well,' I said, 'I suppose I could make a special effort. My day off is Monday. I could see you next week. Is the matter so important that you would want to break into my day off?'

The answer was swift, and made me anxious. 'Yes. I need to see you as soon as possible.'

I decided to push him. 'If it's that important, you must come to me. I commence a Teaching Mission on Thursday. I'll be speaking at a school near Bath at 10 a.m., but I'm free for two hours after that. I'll meet you at Bath railway station.'

'Right,' said Robin. 'I'll look at the timetable, but I'll have to catch the next train back to London, because I must return for the Royal Garden Party.'

I reported this conversation to Eileen. What could be so important that Robin would come all the way to Bath to see me on Thursday, then rush straight back to London for the Royal Garden Party? Surely it couldn't be 'Canterbury'? The thought seemed laughable. I had been a Bishop for less than thirty months, and it was surely ridiculous that one of the newest Bishops could be considered for this great office. We reasoned that Robin must be coming for some other reason – perhaps it was to seek my advice about another person who was under consideration. But then again, it might have nothing to do with 'Canterbury'. Even so, we were unsettled. We agreed that after seeing Robin I would meet up with Eileen at the most convenient spot for us both, which happened to be a pub on the outskirts of Bath.

I got to Bath about thirty minutes before Robin's train arrived. I went straight away to Pratt's Hotel near the station, and explained to the manager that I required a room to discuss some private matters with a friend from London.

I met Robin, and escorted him to the hotel. The manager was in the foyer, and came across to meet us. With no knowledge of the identity of my visitor, but possibly with a nose for intrigue, he said, 'You're not coming to take our Bishop away, are you? Is it Canterbury?'

'Come on,' I laughed. 'I'm one of the newest Bishops on the bench. Of course not.'

Robin and I went to the room I had reserved, and after a few minutes of desultory conversation he said, 'Well, I suppose we had better get down to business. I have a letter here from the Prime Minister.'

My blood ran cold. I opened the white envelope and read Mrs Thatcher's invitation to accept the Crown's offer of the See of Canterbury.

I laid the envelope on the table, looked up and stared into Robin's face. 'Robin,' I said, 'I need to ask you one question. Am I the first name, or the second name? I must have the answer to that question before we go any further.'

He replied in a level voice, looking at me steadily, 'I can confirm that you are the Commission's choice. You are the first name.'

I explained to him that I needed to know this, and that had it been otherwise I would not have accepted, because I was so inexperienced as a Bishop that the call had to be clear.

To say that I was shocked by the letter would be an understatement. I was deeply troubled. My work at Bath and Wells had just begun, and there were so many things I wanted to do. Eileen and I loved the diocese, and had expected to spend the rest of our working life in Somerset. I explained my turmoil to Robin, and said there were so many other good men in the House of Bishops who should have been considered. What about John Habgood, the Archbishop of York? Or David Sheppard, and other able men like them?

Robin agreed that they were able, and said they had been considered, but that the Commission felt a younger person, who could give at least ten full years to the role, ought to be invited. Furthermore, a different approach was felt to be necessary, and they had wanted an Archbishop with a yearning to put mission at the very top of his agenda. In short, the Commission believed that I was the person with the gifts required.

For nearly an hour we discussed the issues. I told Robin that I had never made a momentous decision without prayer and a full discussion with Eileen, but under pressure from him I promised I would get back to him as soon as possible. I warned him, however, that I was in the middle of a Teaching Mission which would not end until Sunday evening. I walked with him to the station, then returned to the Teaching Mission in Midsomer Norton with this staggering question: Should I accept the Prime Minister's offer?

In a daze I drove to the pub where Eileen was waiting. It was a lovely sunny day and we sat outside in the grounds overlooking the beautiful city of Bath, hardly appreciating the food before us. Eileen read the Prime Minister's letter, and we looked at one another with disbelief and astonishment. What were we to do? It would not be too much to say that we were both petrified and dismayed. One thing was clear, however. I had never sought a post in the Church, but equally I had never turned anything down. I have always had a high doctrine of obedience to the Church, and believed that if, after due processes and much prayer, it had decided to call me, I could scarcely refuse.

With a hurried farewell to Eileen I rushed away to resume the Teaching Mission, and the whirl of activities put this momentous matter almost out of my mind. But in between the various events – a Mothers' Union service, a young people's event and an evening speaking engagement in a marquee at Radstock – the terrifying invitation kept leaping into my mind. What was I to make of it?

I phoned Eileen late in the evening and we talked again at great length. There seemed only one answer we could give: it had to be 'yes'. I asked Eileen to phone Robin to say that I was prepared to accept the Prime Minister's invitation. My private diary takes up the story: 'Had a terrible night and simply could not sleep. Fear was present. Will I be ridiculed and mocked for my lack of experience? . . . What an awesome responsibility!'

The next day, there was another bombshell. The Prime Minister wished to see me on Tuesday. Could we go to Downing Street to meet her? We accepted, and following the final Teaching Mission event on Sunday evening we travelled to London to stay with our son Andrew.

On the Tuesday the Prime Minister was engaged in a reshuffle of Ministers, and I was asked not to go to 10 Downing Street, where the press would immediately put two and two together, but instead to go to Number 11, wearing an ordinary shirt and tie. We walked through a rabbit warren of corridors into Number 10, where in Robin's office I changed into my clerical shirt and dog-collar. Eileen and I met Margaret Thatcher in the famous Green Room. She greeted us warmly and then, to our astonishment, proceeded to speak at inordinate length. I glanced at my watch at one point and realised that she had scarcely drawn breath for eight minutes. I asked myself in desperation, 'How on earth do I get a word in edgeways? I must say something!'

My chance came when she mentioned John Wesley. 'Yes,' I said, more loudly than I would usually have done, 'that great Christian socialist.'

She bristled. 'What do you mean? Socialist, indeed!'

It was just the opening I wanted, and I replied that I was using the word not in the way she meant, but in the sense of one whose faith led him to engage with the whole of society. John Wesley's concerns, I went on to say, were for all people. He wanted everyone to know Christ and His love. But he also desired that each person should benefit as fully as possible from life's blessings. Following that interjection, we managed to engage in a real conversation. Mrs Thatcher was forceful and clear-minded. She was candid in her criticism of the Church of England and its focus on politics, to the detriment of spiritual concerns. I made it clear that I was committed to the *Faith in the City* report, which had been slammed by one of her Ministers as 'Marxist', and the Church's social witness, as well as wanting my Church to be less reticent about spiritual values. I noticed that not once did she glance in Eileen's direction or ask her a question. She was very much a person who preferred male company. Although she was out of office when I became Archbishop, I would have loved to have got to know her well as Prime Minister. I am sure we would have clashed at times, but her strengths were undeniable. She was in my opinion the right person in that historic office at the right time.

8

Archbishop-in-Waiting

'I received your Grace's letter in the midst of company just
going to dinner with me, and have but a moment's time to say
that I am quite terrified at the unexpected contents of it, that
I shall have great cause to be pleased if His Majesty thinks of
some worthier person, that if he should pitch on me I must
endeavour through God's help to appear as little unworthy as
I can.'

Thomas Secker to the Duke of Newcastle,
accepting the nomination to be Archbishop of Canterbury

THE PRESS CONFERENCE on Tuesday, 17 July 1990 in the Guard
Room of Lambeth Palace brought our entire family together to meet
the assembled journalists. The news had broken that morning, and
the media turned out in force. It was a bright and sunny day, and
with the addition of the television lights the medieval Guard Room
was almost too brilliantly lit. I glanced at my family to my left and
right, and smiled encouragingly at them, aware how nervous they
were to be in the spotlight. Eileen was looking composed, but I knew
she had butterflies too. Rachel with her husband Andy and their two
young boys, Simon and David, were on one side, and to the other I
could see Mark and his wife Penny, Andrew and his first wife Jane,
and our youngest daughter Lizzie, just nineteen years of age and a
student nurse at Bart's Hospital. I was proud of each of them, and
hoped that it wasn't proving too much of an ordeal.

Philip Mawer, Secretary General of General Synod, skilfully

chaired the press conference. It had been agreed that I would speak, and would then answer questions. In my opening remarks I expressed my opinion that the Church of England was at a crossroads; it had to shift its priorities from maintenance to mission, and it had to recover its confidence in the good news at the heart of its message. I made no secret of the fact that I was an evangelical – but I was a person who had grown from encountering other traditions. So much so, that I was actually unhappy with labels. I was first and foremost an Anglican. I could never deny all that the evangelical tradition had given me, but I was not prepared to de-Church other traditions either, or to deny their contribution to my intellectual and spiritual formation.

The questions that followed focused on the role of the Church in the nation, and especially on the ordination of women. I found I was able to be robust and confident in my answers to well-put questions, and felt that the press had given me a decent opportunity to introduce myself and my priorities. Indeed, the television and newspaper coverage that followed was very positive.

Perhaps that warm and constructive press conference lulled me into assuming that all would be well with the media – that they would see that I meant what I said, and would continue to report me as objectively as they had on that first encounter. But it was not to be – at least, not for a very long time. At that stage I was not fully aware of the way in which public figures are vulnerable to attack from the media. Exposure to public scrutiny would come as a painful shock. What I was totally unprepared for was the implications of my appointment for my family.

On Saturday, 28 July, Rachel's picture was displayed on the front page of the *Daily Mail* with the headline 'The Archbishop's Deep Sorrow'. There was nothing factually wrong with the article, which described Rachel's divorce from her first husband, who had left her with Simon still a baby. But for Rachel it, and the photograph of her which accompanied it, was an intrusion into her private life. She was now very happily married to Andy Day, and they were in their third year of marriage. A few days later, however, on the eve of a much-needed holiday, our son Andrew, who was working for the *Church of England Newspaper*, phoned in dismay to say that the *Sun* was going to run an article the following day on Rachel. According to John Little, the Archbishop of Canterbury's Public Affairs Officer, the article was likely to be entitled: 'The Sexy Secrets of the Archbishop's Daughter'.

I was appalled. I was confident that I could cope with any amount of personal criticism, but the thought that my family would be the victims of intrusive reporting was simply too hard to bear. We were and remain a close and loving family, and Rachel was a sensitive girl who would find this very difficult. She was devastated by the *Sun*'s intentions. We were determined to stop this. I phoned John Little to seek his advice. After conferring further with Andrew and a friend, Philip Crowe, both of whom had contacts in the media, the conclusion was reached that only Rupert Murdoch, the proprietor of the *Sun*, could stop the story running. I was told that the only two people who could influence Murdoch to persuade Kelvin Mackenzie, the paper's editor, to drop such a tempting story were Margaret Thatcher and Billy Graham. John Little volunteered to phone Number 10, and Philip contacted Billy Graham. By the end of that day, 31 July, the story was dead. However, that night sleep did not come easily, and it was only the appearance of the *Sun* the following day, devoid of any story relating to Rachel, that brought relief to mind and spirit.

I decided to phone Kelvin MacKenzie to soothe any ruffled feathers. His first reaction was very cool, but then he commented, 'You owe me one, Archbishop.' I suddenly saw an opportunity to make some capital out of the problem which had caused us so much distress, and replied that I would be very happy to write an exclusive for the *Sun*, which I duly did, entitling it 'The Church I'd Like to See'.

Understandably, some of the staff at Lambeth Palace were very concerned that to give the *Sun*, of all papers, such an exclusive, setting forth the contours of my new ministry, was strange at the very least.

My response was that to do so to four million readers, most of whom were out of touch with the Church's message, was no bad thing, however unusual it might seem.

Looking back on that affair, I can see it now as part of a sequence of problems in the interval between the announcement of my appointment and my enthronement eight months later. Not only was the period far too long, but I felt there was insufficient support for an inexperienced Bishop suddenly thrown into a strange new world of a national and an international ministry. It was short-sighted of the Church of England at the time to fail to recognise this problem.

Almost immediately I fell into another trap, this time of my own making, and one that would follow me through my entire period as Archbishop. In September 1990 I agreed to give an interview to the *Reader's Digest*, believing it to be a harmless magazine that would, at least, introduce me to millions of people around the world. The editor, Russell Twisk, who later became a good friend, conducted the interview personally, and did so in a sensitive and informed manner. He explained that for the sake of the style of this popular magazine it would help if I could keep my responses as brief and as focused as possible. I agreed to do so. He asked me first of all to describe how I saw the Church today. I decided to answer this by recourse to an image very popular in the infancy of Christianity – that of the Church growing progressively younger. Developing this analogy, I said that the Church today seemed to me rather like a very old grandmother who sat by the chimney breast muttering to herself, ignored by the rest of the family and out of touch with its culture. I honestly did not think that this historical analogy would cause any problems, believing that it would resonate with people's experience. Continuing the image, I said that it was my hope that this Church would become progressively younger as it was re-evangelised by the gospel.

Of course, this was grist to the press's mill. The context was ignored and the image used destructively. Many Church people were upset by the implied criticism, and a number of elderly people wrote protesting letters wondering what I had against old ladies.

If that was damaging, the second issue focused upon by Russell Twisk was far more serious and long-lasting. He raised the question of the ordination of women, and the criticism offered by Graham Leonard, then Bishop of London, that a woman cannot represent Christ at the altar – known in Catholic theology as '*in persona Christi*'. Even though I have theological reservations about this concept in itself, for men as for women, I met this objection to women's ordination with great passion, asserting that 'The idea that a woman cannot represent Christ at the altar is a very serious heresy.' The theological argument behind my statement was the classical incarnational principle outlined in the early fifth century by three Eastern theologians known as the Cappadocian Fathers. According to them, 'That which Christ did not assume remains unhealed.' They meant that if Christ was not fully human, humanity remains unsaved. By extension, if humanity is not female as well as male, then women are unsaved. The idea that women were somehow excluded from ministry because of gender was and remains, in my opinion, a serious mistake, and had to be met strongly and definitely.

I was quite unprepared for the explosion that ensued. The reaction was angry, and Catholics in the Church of England clearly feared the worst from this new Archbishop. The Archbishop of York, Dr John Habgood, and Philip Mawer urged me to put out a press statement explaining what lay behind the statement, and that I had actually intended to say 'theological differences' rather than 'heresy'. I did this reluctantly, and by doing so may have fuelled later claims by some sections of the press that I was prone to 'gaffes'. Looking back, I regret apologising for the phrase 'serious heresy'. With all my heart I was convinced, then as I am now, that it is a profound error to embrace a theology that makes it impossible for women to stand '*in persona Christi*'. Although condemnation arrived from many sides, I also received much support from theologians and teachers of all Churches and traditions, including a sturdy defence from Professor

Thomas Torrance, the most eminent theologian of the Church of Scotland, and several from Roman Catholic theologians who did not wish to be named publicly.

In the aftermath of the explosion it was clear that my misjudgement had been to choose the wrong organ for a profound theological argument which needed further exploration. The *Reader's Digest*, for all its merits, is not the place to discuss the erudite and arcane theology of the Cappadocian Fathers.

My greatest regret, as a pastor and as a student of Catholicism, was that the remark alienated me from those I wished to support. I was only too well aware from dealing with Catholic clergy in the diocese of Bath and Wells that morale among them was very low, and that they were worried about the consequences should women be ordained to the priesthood. It took several years for the trust to be restored, friendships renewed and my leadership accepted by Catholics in the Church.

Melanie Phillips in the *Guardian* expressed my situation perceptively: 'So before he has even passed "go" he has managed seriously to offend all who support homosexual priests; all those who oppose the ordination of women; all those who have tried to keep the show on the road until now; and all those who believe that the Archbishop of Canterbury should know the meaning of the word "heresy".'

The demands from the media for scrutiny and analysis of my personality and background continued. One opportunity that fascinated me, because it promised greater depth than the usual speculation, was an interview with the well-known broadcaster and psychiatrist Anthony Clare for the BBC television series *In the Psychiatrist's Chair*. I felt that talking to him would give me an opportunity to counter some of the ill-informed comments that had been made, and also to reassure people that my instincts were wholly positive. The interview took several sessions to film, and I learned a great deal from the thoroughness of Professor Clare's techniques. Not for him a glib and superficial approach, but a deep exploration of arguments and feelings. He rightly concluded that I was a person who does not easily reveal himself. I was determined not to be led down avenues where I was not keen to go, or to admit to weaknesses that might harm me or damage the Church. Nevertheless, this interview helpfully highlighted for me some areas of my new ministry with which I would have to come to terms.

One of them was an awareness that the office of Archbishop gave all my comments a Delphic significance: 'The Archbishop has spoken.' This meant, I told Clare, that I had to watch every word; my worry was that this would contain and curtail the very spontaneity that was an essential part of my character. 'I want to be free to speak out and to be myself,' I said, recognising that the gift of a historic office also meant being prisoner, to some degree, of that same office. He asked me about criticism: how did I handle it? Did it get under my skin? Did I lie awake at night wounded by criticism I regarded as unfair? I responded that I had been surprised that some commentators had already made up their minds about me before my ministry had begun. But I felt that I had the depth of faith and moral courage to rise above negative criticism, even though I was sure that I would need to develop a thicker skin. I believed I already had the ability to laugh at myself and to bounce back quickly from disappointment. I remember thinking as I said these words that I only hoped this would prove to be true.

My greatest fear was the enormous expectations of me as the 103rd Archbishop of Canterbury, but Anthony Clare did not explore this. It seemed to me that the demands were such that no human being could possibly fulfil them: leading a Church with no great enthusiasm for mission towards becoming a confident and growing Church; being a spokesman for the Church on all matters of faith and social witness; holding together a Church already deeply divided by entrenched views on the ordination of women, sexuality and faith. I could only offer myself as I was, and trust God for the rest.

It was suggested to me in January 1991 that, in line with an offer made to all Bishops, I might consider some radio and TV training. I leapt at the opportunity, because I was aware that there was much to learn. A consultant, Lucy Parker, soon took me in hand. For my third session she asked me to go to a studio close to St Paul's. As I emerged from the taxi a familiar figure approached me with a microphone in his hand, accompanied by another holding a television camera. 'Dr Carey,' he demanded, hammering out his words in an abrasive fashion, 'why are you having this training? Is it true that you are so useless with the media that you need to improve?' I was rattled, but attempted to answer his question. I had no sooner got into my stride than Lucy appeared and stopped me. It was all a put-up job. The interviewer was John Humphrys, famous for an inquisitorial approach that has unnerved many a politician. The lesson from that encounter was not to allow myself to be 'doorstepped' in such a way.

I met John Humphrys on several subsequent occasions in radio studios, which made me aware not only of some of the problems I was likely to meet in the days ahead, but also of the ephemeral and superficial nature of 'soundbite' techniques. It was a shock to discover that my whole approach, developed over nearly thirty years, to examine ideas, to live with questions, to be free to air doubts and difficulties, was anathema to the world of contemporary communication. John liked my bluntness and freshness, but said several times, 'You are going to be eaten alive! You are far too honest. You must do what politicians do – lie through your back teeth, man! Don't, for God's sake, answer questions so directly. Indeed, don't answer the questions at all. Know what you want to say, and say it. Use the question as a jumping-off point for what you want to get across.'

Although I learned a great deal from such advice, I was determined not to lie through my back teeth, nor was I going to avoid questions. Come what may, I decided, I was determined to be myself – even if it meant being 'eaten alive'. I was confident that I could handle criticism, even cruel and biased criticism. While that was true for me throughout my period of office, my family were sometimes incensed by unfair or even contemptuous reporting. In reality, of course, every public figure is seen as fair game. For better or for worse, the Church of England as the Established Church often takes the flak for negative criticism directed at the Christian faith in general. Furthermore, the Archbishop of Canterbury is obviously the prime target as the main representative of faith in the nation. In my first few years in office Eileen and I, together with my press officer, Lesley Perry, set up breakfast meetings with the senior staff of national papers which went some way towards creating a better relationship, but this never really moved beyond an agreed state of truce between two great institutions. Yet even unfair criticism never undermined my conviction that a free press is essential to a democratic society, and that all public figures should be held to account. A responsible, intelligent, critical yet unbiased press is central to the health of a nation.

A few weeks prior to the enthronement, journalists learned that I had arranged for singers and musicians from All Souls, Langham Place, under the direction of their Musical Director Noel Tredinneck, to lead some singing during the service. I was quite amazed by the furore this caused, and the conclusions drawn from it by many. It was assumed that the style of music would be charismatic and ultra-modern. According to much of the comment, I was about to betray the traditions of the Church of England. Dr Donald Webster, a Fellow of the Royal College of Organists, was quoted as saying: 'When you have popular music in the service it lowers the tone and atmosphere of the ceremony. So much of the idiom of popular music has unsavoury associations with drugs, unbridled sex and things of this kind.' I was both amused and astonished that my three innocuous choices of modern Church music were deemed to have such power. In fact all three were chosen from well-known Christian contexts – a song from South Africa, associated with Archbishop Desmond Tutu; a song from Taizé, an important ecumenical centre in southern France; and a third from the World Council of Churches. Neverthe-less, from that moment on I was promptly dubbed the 'tambourine-playing Archbishop' – with a *Spitting Image* puppet to ram home the point. I was confident, however, that the enthronement service would show that my choice was tastefully made.

The day of my enthronement, Friday, 19 April 1991, was a blustery one, with the sun appearing from time to time. Tight security had been maintained around the cathedral for several days. The Prime Minister, together with much of the Cabinet and the leaders of the opposition parties, was expected, as well as the Princess of Wales and Princess Margaret.

It was a memorable and moving service, starting with three traditional knocks on the great West Door with my pastoral staff. The doors slowly opened onto what seemed like thousands of faces gazing with expectancy in my direction. Then came the almost endless procession through the congregation to the front of the nave, where the Dean produced the sixth-century Italian gospels that had been given by Pope Gregory the Great to Augustine to bring to England. It was an emotional moment as I swore the oath on this priceless and ancient book and then kissed it. This enduring and precious element linked my ministry to that of the first Archbishop of Canterbury. As the 103rd Archbishop in that line I was determined to make Christ known to my contemporaries as each of my predecessors had in his day.

The music that had caused such controversy gained a round of applause. The songs laced together prayers led by leaders of the Anglican Communion and other Churches. During the Peace people of all backgrounds greeted one another. For at least ten minutes I exchanged the sign of peace with dignitaries from the worldwide Church and representatives of other faiths, who in many cases had made long journeys to be present at my enthronement.

In fact there are not one but two enthronements. First I was seated as Bishop of the diocese of Canterbury in the diocesan chair, and then, as Archbishop, in the ninth-century stone throne at the top of the steps overlooking the entire choir and nave. It was not until I sat on that great chair that I became aware of its size. Although I am above average height, my feet hardly touched the ground. The throne could easily have squeezed in another adult. It seemed to symbolise the awesome responsibilities of the office I was about to assume, and sent out a clear message: no one is worthy to sit in this seat, it is too big for one person. And yet in a way I found that not a discouragement, but a relaxing and important discovery – of course I was unworthy, I told myself. We are all in God's hands.

I had worked hard on the text of my address, knowing that it would be studied as much for what it omitted as for what it said. I was determined that it should reveal, however implicitly, my priorities and values, and decided on the theme of 'witness', quoting first from T.S. Eliot's description of a martyr in his play *Murder in the Cathedral*, and then from St Paul's words, 'Woe if I do not preach the gospel.' It would be my priority, I said, to proclaim that same gospel and witness to the same hope and values. But it was my hope to do so constructively and sensitively. I welcomed to the service those from other Churches, reminding them that the succession in which I stood went back to the one undivided Church of Jesus Christ: 'We cannot rest content with our scandalous divisions.' Next I welcomed those from the wider community, such as the Prime Minister and members of his government, adding that 'no Church can or should avoid political comment when freedom, dignity and worth are threatened'. I welcomed those of other faiths, saying that my desire to witness to Jesus Christ demanded that I had a responsibility to listen to their story of faith. I quoted the words of Bill Shankly, former manager of Liverpool Football Club: 'Football is not a matter of life and death – it's far more important than that.' That, I said, summed up the Christian faith. It is far more important than life and even death. I called on the many thousands, even millions, watching the service on television or listening to it on their radios, to join me in a fresh step towards faith or a willingness to explore the claims of the Christian faith again.

After the magnificent service, Eileen and I mingled with the crowds outside, delighted to be part of the pageantry and pomp of the occasion. Many of the people I spoke with had had little contact with the institutional Church, but just felt it was natural to be there. I was now their Archbishop, and they were welcoming me enthusiastically and sincerely. The press coverage was largely respect-ful of the event and positive about my sermon. There was not the slightest criticism of the music that a few weeks earlier had so excited the media.

Later I received letters from all around the world from people who were clearly touched by having seen or heard the enthronement on television or radio. One was from Peter Rowe, who lived in the diocese of Canterbury. He had been a Benedictine monk in the Roman Catholic Church, but had left fifteen years ago to become a successful lawyer. He said that listening to the service had marked a turning point in his life, and that he felt the moment had come to turn to God again. Seven years later I ordained Peter in Canterbury Cathedral.

More celebrations and introductions were to follow over the next few days. That same evening the Nikaean Club, an ecumenical dining club founded by Archbishop Randall Davidson in 1925, hosted a dinner for four hundred people at which Cardinal Cassidy and other ecumenical leaders proposed toasts, to which I responded. I presented a live broadcast of the BBC television programme *Songs of Praise* from outside the cathedral on Sunday evening, and also spoke at a diocesan celebration for all clergy, Readers and representatives of the many churches in the diocese of Canterbury.

Eileen and I began a visiting programme to meet every clergy family in the diocese over the next nine months. We felt it was our pastoral duty to get to know them, to make ourselves accessible and to share in their work. It turned out to be time well spent. On the whole we found the clergy were very able and dedicated men. There was realism about the problems facing the contemporary Church, and an enormous desire to be more effective. The clergy of the diocese were mainly from the Catholic and middle sections of the Church, and some were very resistant to the approaching debate on the ordination of women. One priest told me frankly that should it happen, he would leave the Church for the Roman Catholic Church. I said that I sympathised with his dilemma, but asked him, 'Do you really think that all that separates us from the Roman Catholic Church is the matter of the ordination of women? Don't you feel that that Church requires more from you than merely your opposition to the ordination of women?' I was anxious to get the clergy to see the matter not as a single issue, but as one tied up with mission and the role of women in the Church.

There were a number of parish churches where some very exciting things were happening, and where real growth was resulting, but many of the clergy said that they felt undervalued and unappreciated. I began to see with some shock that part of the malaise and low morale was due to successive Archbishops trying to be 'hands-on' in a way they clearly could not be on a day-to-day basis. This ideal may have been understandable, but it is impossible in the light of the national and international demands on an Archbishop of Canterbury.

Frank discussions with the two suffragan Bishops, Dick Third, the Bishop of Dover, and David Smith, Bishop of Maidstone, revealed their frustrations. Dick, the senior Bishop, was very supportive of Robert Runcie's ministry before me, and of Robert's desire to get out and about, but explained that no Archbishop could really get on top of the diocese, because he would be at best a part-timer. He fully understood my desire to be similarly involved, but what I had discovered made me resolve to give greater responsibility for the diocese to these concerned and energetic suffragan Bishops. I therefore appointed Dick as a quasi-diocesan Bishop, legally entrusting to him the powers of actually leading the diocese.

This raised a real question about the role of the Archbishop in the diocese. What could I do that might make a real difference, whilst accepting the time-limited nature of my role there? The answer was to continue to lead Teaching Missions similar to those I had started in Bath and Wells, with the aim of supporting clergy by using my teaching gifts in their parishes. In addition we were able to share in the pastoral care of clergy, and to host all ordination retreats at the Old Palace.

As the Archbishop of Canterbury has a time-honoured position

in the city of Canterbury, it was also crucial to be a real Bishop
to its people and its many organisations. Over the years valuable
relationships have been built up with the Rotary Club, the Lions, the
Citizens' Advice Bureau, Umbrella and other important clubs and
charities. Friendship with successive Lord Mayors and other Kentish
dignitaries became an essential way of getting to know the city and
county. Canterbury became a wonderful home for us as a family and
we always looked forward to the times we were able to leave the cares
of London to stay at the Old Palace. We had the special joy of having
Rachel, our eldest daughter, as steward of the Old Palace, a role for
which she was eminently qualified and which she exercised with
distinction during my entire time as Archbishop. Lambeth Palace,
however, was our principal place of residence and work. The three-
bedroom flat at the top of the building provided us with adequate
accommodation, although it meant there was no getting away from
the demands and pressures of the job.

It was this feeling of pressure that predominated during my early
years at Lambeth Palace. I entered another world, from being a very
busy diocesan Bishop to attempting to embrace all the demands
of being Archbishop of Canterbury and President of the Anglican
Communion. Every day I was learning something new and having
to make decisions on grave and momentous issues that needed more
time for exploration. Robert Runcie had left a good staff to assist
me, and I was impressed by the quality of each person and their
deep devotion to the office of Archbishop and to its incumbent. I
knew I would be able to rely on their expertise and advice. Bishop
Ronald Gordon, the former Bishop of Portsmouth, was Chief of Staff
and 'Bishop-at-Lambeth'; he would prove to be an invaluable support
and friend. John Little was entrusted with public affairs, but was
spending most of his time trying to secure the release of Robert
Runcie's former envoy Terry Waite, who had disappeared in Beirut in
January 1987, and was believed to be being held hostage by Hezbollah
militants. Sadly, John passed away just a few months after my arrival,
and did not live to see the fruits of his remarkable work. Roger

Symon, Officer for the Anglican Communion, had been asked by Robert Runcie to stand in for Terry temporarily five years earlier, and was still on loan from USPG. Stephen Platten was the Senior Ecumenical Officer, and Graham James the resourceful and efficient Chaplain. Eleanor Phillips was my excellent secretary and 'major-domo' of a small band of efficient secretaries who supported my principal officers. Brian Pearson joined the staff to assist me in matters to do with the mission of the Church and to be my Chaplain in Canterbury.

Nevertheless, however able its individual members, it was a tiny staff, and woefully inadequate for an office that comprised five great areas of responsibility: the diocese of Canterbury, the Church of England, state and Crown responsibilities, the Presidency of the Anglican Communion, and Senior Ecumenical Representative for the Communion. A sixth area was dimly discernible, inter-faith relations, but this was not in 1991 a clear and discrete area of responsibility. The five areas represented huge responsibilities, beyond the capacity of any single person. Indeed, as has been noted, well before the demands of the Anglican Communion were to impinge on the workload of his successors, Archbishop Cosmo Lang expressed it crisply and candidly: 'The work is impossible for any one man to do – but only one man can do it.'

Working with a team built by someone else is never easy, and I had to carve out my own way of doing things. One of the shocks was the huge number of speeches, sermons and talks I was required to give. Whatever I did, and wherever I went, it was assumed that the Archbishop would offer a contribution that ranged from a homily, to an after-dinner speech, to a full lecture. Robert had relied on a number of staff and outsiders to assist him in speech preparation, and this had worked well for him, but it was not my style. I was very happy to work with others, but I did not want anybody ever to think that any speech I delivered was the work of another person. From the first day I told the staff that the first draft of all addresses would be prepared by myself, and that I would share that draft with them all and get their comments, criticisms and suggestions. This became my invariable rule, and never became a chore. I loved preparing speeches, and was never happier than when I was starting on the creative responsibility of a new talk or address. It meant that I had to work hard at finding time for reading, and I set myself the target of fifty pages every day – a target that I was able to meet for most of my time as Archbishop. My technique was always to have the book I was reading visible in my study, so that in between appointments and meetings I could pick it up. This had also been the policy of one of my predecessors, Michael Ramsey. When asked how he managed to read so much during his busy life, he replied with a twinkle in his eye, 'I read as an alcoholic drinks, little but often!'

With my new colleagues I sought to work out a policy to make sense of my awesome new role. It soon became obvious that three things had to come clearly through my work as Archbishop: unity, mission and confidence. Unity, because the tensions within the Church and our seeming inability to see Christ in one another meant that too much energy was going into supporting 'my tradition' instead of strengthening 'my Church'. Mission, because Anglicanism is not generally noted for its evangelistic endeavour or its success in making disciples. Over the years I have often gone back to the words of George Borrow in his novel *Lavengro*:

> 'The Church of England is a fine Church,' said I: 'I would not advise anyone to speak ill of the Church of England before me.'
> 'I have nothing to say against the Church,' said Peter. 'All I wish is that it would fling itself a little more open, and that its priests would a little more bestir themselves; in a word, that it would shoulder the cross and become a missionary Church.'

What was true in 1851, when Borrow wrote these words, is of course even more urgent today in our secular culture. However, my understanding of the Church being missionary in its essential nature could not be reduced to a basic ABC of gospel preaching, but rather involved the taking of the radical message of good news into the heart and mind of the Church. It meant and still means for me an openness to society, a concern for life in all its dimensions and a willingness to work with others in seeking to change society and our communities.

The third word, 'confidence', was important to me, because the Church of England seemed too timid, often doubtful and reluctant to speak clearly of its convictions and faith. An Archbishop cannot change the hearts of unconfident people, but he can influence the culture of Church life and help to make it more aware of the riches of its message and the hope that it espouses. In the world of sport, winning teams are confident teams, brimming with belief in their ability to overcome all opposition. Similarly in the military sphere, lack of confidence is often at the heart of failure to take risks, and therefore to win battles.

I realised that if I was going to make a real difference as Archbishop of Canterbury I would require additional resources, particularly financial ones. I knew that extra support would not come from the Church Commissioners, and that I therefore had to raise independent funding. I saw a way forward shortly before taking up my new responsibilities when I met the Trustees of the Lambeth Fund under its Chairman, Lord Laing of Dunphail. Hector Laing, then Chairman of United Biscuits, had been a fellow tank commander with Robert Runcie during the war. When Robert became Archbishop, Hector, as a business leader, had been so shocked by what he viewed as the inadequacy of the support for the Archbishop that together with some friends he had raised substantial funds for Robert, his office and his home. Together with Hector and his wife Marion, I met other key members of the Fund, including Ewan Harper, who was its Secretary. I was encouraged by their unanimous support of my office and their desire to be of assistance. I was particularly impressed by the leadership given by Hector and Ewan, whose partnership meant that things got done. Out of that relationship the Lambeth Partnership was later to be born; it would make a significant contribution to awakening the Church of England to the urgency of mission.

In those early days, then, as Archbishop of Canterbury I was only too keenly aware of the enormous workload and expectations laid upon me. Daily, letters poured in, encouraging me but in many cases adding to the burden by the contradictory claims and advice they contained. I was under no illusion that the road ahead would be lonely and burdensome. I was equally sure that the Lord of Hosts was with me.

II

9

Women Shake the Church

'The Kingdom of God isn't there for the sake of the Church. The Church is there for the sake of the Kingdom.'

Jurgen Moltmann, God for a Secular Society *(1997)*

MY VERY FIRST HOUSE OF BISHOPS as Archbishop in June 1991 was dominated by two agenda items – money and the ordination of women. The issue of money and the role of the Church Commissioners will be discussed later, but the ordination of women, with its capacity to split the Church down the middle, was arguably the greater crisis unless the House of Bishops handled the matter responsibly.

The great majority of Bishops supported the ordination of women, as I did quite unequivocally. The two most vociferous opponents were Graham Leonard, the Bishop of London, and Eric Kemp, the Bishop of Chichester. Two more different men could not be found. Graham Leonard was a bombastic campaigner on this issue, with an acute political instinct and an uncompromising opposition to the ordination of women on the grounds that women *qua* women were barred from exercising a priestly role, as both scripture and tradition were against it. This was the principle that I had resisted strongly in my *Reader's Digest* interview, and that I found reprehensible in its view of women and simplistic in its interpretation of theology.

Eric Kemp's position was no less deeply held than Dr Leonard's, but it was far more scholarly, nuanced and sympathetic to women. For Eric, to depart from the teaching and tradition of the universal Church, found essentially in the Roman Catholic Church and the Orthodox Churches in communion with the Ecumenical Patriarch, would set back all that had been achieved ecumenically. He was in no doubt of the importance of tackling the issue, but to do so on our own was, in his opinion, mistaken. This was a view I respected and sympathised with. The only problem was that there was in fact no such being as the 'universal Church', and to limit one's interpretation to the Catholic and Orthodox worlds was an implied criticism of Protestant Churches, and indeed a significant number of Provinces of the Anglican Communion, where the experience of women in ministry was a reality.

As Chairman of the House of Bishops, I felt it was my task to help focus our attention on the key issues so that we could lead the Church forward responsibly when the ordination of women came before the General Synod for debate. There were, however, two problems that I had to face. The first was my relative inexperience as a Bishop, let alone Archbishop. How could I express my leadership of so many experienced colleagues, with so much ability among them? I had no worries about my competence as a Chairman of the House, but the days when an Archbishop could insist on his own way were over – if indeed there had ever been such a time. Our times required a consensual approach in which I would need to harness all the skills of the Bishops to hold the Church together, whilst endeavouring to keep the focus on mission. This meant drawing above all on the aid of John Habgood, Archbishop of York, and Philip Mawer, Secretary General of General Synod.

My predecessor had not drawn John Habgood into equal leadership, but I was determined to rectify this by making him Joint Chairman of the House of Bishops. John was one of the most incisive and able of the Bishops, bringing a cool, analytical, scientific mind to the theology and business of the Church. Similarly, I felt that Philip

Mawer's impressive ability to summarise ideas and to draw out the inchoate aspirations of others should be encouraged. I was delighted when, with their help, ways were found of moving our meetings on with coherent policies.

My second concern was that the House of Bishops was not truly a united body, but rather a loose collection of strong individuals who came together three times a year to agree policies that some, within days, chose to ignore. We had to conquer this tendency, and truly be a united body of Bishops, for the good of the Church. I cannot claim that we ever achieved it fully, but we did get a long way towards deepening our corporate sense of responsibility and working more closely together.

The first major step towards the ordination of women came from an unlikely source: the Vatican. On 16 August 1991, whilst on holiday, I received a memo from Stephen Platten, my Officer for Ecumenism, that the Sacred Congregation for the Defence of the Faith had issued its judgement on the final report of ARCIC 1, and it was negative. I was shocked by this news. As I had led the Lambeth Conference resolution welcoming the final report, this was not only a blow that I felt personally, but far more importantly, it was a severe blow to ecumenical hopes. Scholars on both sides had worked for twenty years on the three documents that comprised the final report, and the Pontifical Council for Christian Unity had kept the Congregation fully informed. What could have gone wrong?

The report was sent to me, and I could see at once that the Congregation had totally misunderstood the rationale of ARCIC. Whereas ARCIC's intention was to hold both Catholic and Anglican doctrines together, seeing points of unity and bringing them into a new consensus of faith that underscored the essential teaching of both, the Congregation's standpoint was very different: the final report had to conform to Roman Catholic teaching. I studied the Congregation's concerns carefully. On the Eucharist, the Congregation wanted ARCIC to make explicit that 'the sacrifice of Christ is made present with all its effects, thus affirming the propitiatory nature of the Eucharistic sacrifice which can be applied to the deceased'. This undigested Tridentine teaching was unacceptable to both Catholic and Anglican theologians of ARCIC 1. On the Ministry, the Congregation wanted clarification on the role of the Pope, asserting that 'The dogmatic definition of the First Vatican Council declares that the primacy of the Bishop of Rome belongs to the divine structure of the Church; the Bishop of Rome inherits the primacy from Peter who received it "immediately and directly" from Christ.'

It was clear from such language that we were in a wholly different world from the affirming tones of the final report. I wrote immediately to Cardinal Ratzinger, Head of the Congregation and undoubtedly the author of its report, expressing my dismay and firmly rebutting a theology that put ecumenism back thirty years. Also very profoundly dismayed were the two Co-Chairmen of ARCIC 1, Bishop Cormac Murphy-O'Connor (Roman Catholic) and Bishop Mark Santer (Anglican).

I remain convinced that this severe blow to hopes that we might see unity with Rome in our lifetime led many, including myself, to look at women's ordination in a new light. If the Congregation had given the green light to the final report I may have found it difficult to resist arguments that called for debate on the ordination of women to be delayed, in order to include the Roman Catholic Church on that substantive issue. Not, I must emphasise, with the intention that the crucial issue of the ordination of women should play second fiddle to ecumenism, but so that it might be considered in a new context. The possibility of a reconciliation of two world Churches was too rich a prize to be neglected. However, the Congregation's call for yet more 'clarifications' led many, including myself, to conclude that it was pointless to wait any longer. Indeed, it is my firm belief that the present low state of ecumenism, at the theological level, is mainly due to the appearance of that report in August 1991.

The way was therefore open to press on with the debate on the ordination of women, scheduled for November of the following year. Rival groups within the Church prepared for battle, and periodically the area outside Lambeth Palace's gates was filled with banner-waving factions. It became my task to try to keep all relationships deeply Christian, however strongly I and others felt about the issue. I remember arriving home one evening when two rival groups were outside, both naming me as a 'traitor' to their cause. The House of Bishops gave a magnificent example of maintaining deeply held theologies in an encompassing unity. Without doubt we were deeply divided, but the friendships were genuine too, giving refreshing evidence that Christians could remain in the same Church whilst disagreeing profoundly.

David Hope, the new Bishop of London, was a great source of strength and vision. Although a traditional Catholic, it was not on the grounds held so dogmatically by his predecessor that he opposed the ordination of women, but rather for reasons similar to Eric Kemp's, that we were going ahead without consulting the 'universal Church'. David had fears also that the consensus for ordination was not strong or deep enough. I was rather puzzled by that fear, because the only way that the ordination of women could go forward was by a two-thirds majority in the Houses of Bishops, Clergy and Laity. Two-thirds is, in any voting system, an extremely difficult proportion to reach. If that was not a consensus, I did not know what was.

A few days before the historic debate in Synod, Cardinal Hume called in person to hand me a long letter that he said he would be making public within a few days. In it he conveyed his deep unhappiness at the possibility that Synod might consent to the ordination of women. Such a decision, he averred, would 'adversely affect ecumenical relations' and 'raise disturbing questions about the identity and self-understanding of the Church of England'. He appealed to the writings of both Pope Paul VI and John Paul II, who had stated that women's ordination would cause a 'major obstacle' to 'achieving visible and organic unity'. He went on to say that arguments in the Church of England had not gone far enough, and there was not sufficient agreement within the Anglican Communion or the wider

Church, so 'caution and prudence are required'. The Church of England needed to ask 'what is meant by ordination', and whether its 'priests' were ministers in the Reformed sense, or priests in the iconic sense as understood by the Roman Catholic, Orthodox and Eastern Churches. If, Cardinal Hume continued, one believes that the bread and wine become truly and substantially present as the Body and Blood of Christ, and that the priest is acting not only on behalf of the congregation, but also for Jesus Christ, a woman cannot be a priest in this sense. Finally, he touched on the matter of authority: 'By what means and on what grounds has the majority within the Synod reached certainty that such ordination of women is in accordance with the mind and will of the Lord?'

Although my first reaction on reading this letter was of some irritation, as this was the first time the Cardinal had ever raised his objections with me, in spite of the many meetings we had had together, I realised that his concerns came from a deep personal commitment to the unity of the Churches. He ended the letter by saying that he was 'awaiting the outcome with considerable anxiety and I realise the large burden you personally are carrying'.

Four days later I replied, thanking him for his courtesy in writing such a substantial and thought-provoking letter, and affirming my own commitment to the same quest for visible unity. However, I went on to say:

> You speak three times of the 'certainty' of knowing God's will. Where is that certainty to be found? Doctrinal definitions do not work quite like that – if we were to take the Early Church disputes for example, both sides considered they had truth on their side. Within the Anglican tradition we maintain that 'very few decisions are ever made on the basis of certainty'. Certainty often comes at the end of a process, rarely at the beginning.
>
> If women's ordination is accepted it will begin with a period of reception as has happened in many other issues in the life of the Church (disputes about Christology and the Trinity, for

example). Thus if Synod makes the decision by a two-thirds majority in each House, that too will be part of the process of reception pointing towards the consent of the people.

As to authority, the Church of England has always believed it to have the authority to legislate for changes in doctrine and practice and this parallels a similar understanding in the Roman Catholic Church.

Here are some of the arguments I find compelling for taking this step now:

- The New Testament shows that the Spirit of God falls on women as well as men.
- Jesus gives women an unprecedented place in the context of His ministry – associating with them and counting them as valuable to His ministry.
- Even if women were not part of the apostolic group this certainly has something to do with the fact that as women they did not have the freedom to move about in society which suggests that cultural factors should not be excluded.
- All the first apostles were Jews; nobody would now argue that all priests should first be Jews.
- The distinction between women in the Reformed traditions being able to represent Christ but not within the Catholic tradition was inconclusive – there is no solid evidence that the gender of the priest was of theological interest to early Christians.
- I believe in a 'real presence' in the Eucharist but this does not require a male as Celebrant to make it valid – if maleness is definitive, what does this say about women in the role of God's economy of salvation?
- These, of course, are not new arguments but ones met in both of our Churches.
- Anglicans are disappointed by the 'cool response of the Vatican to ARCIC', and this has undermined the position of those arguing against the ordination of women on ecumenical grounds.

I concluded my letter by saying that 'despite these disagreements I remain committed to dialogue and eventual union with your Church.

I am sorry we are in disagreement over this issue but I too am determined to continue in our work together as Churches.'

This frank exchange did not damage our relationship – indeed, it had the opposite effect; we became more determined to maintain a good working relationship. Basil Hume was an easy man to like, and as with all truly holy people he wore his spirituality lightly, and with a deep humility. I had no difficulty in seeing Christ in him, and accepting him as a brother Christian and a fellow leader. We were able to talk about ordinary things as well as the deeper matters that drew us together. We joked at times about our different football allegiances – he was a Newcastle United supporter and I was solidly for Arsenal. The only time we attended a match between our rival teams together was when Arsenal beat Newcastle in the 1998 FA Cup Final. I enjoyed his company very much.

Wednesday, 11 November 1992 was the day set aside in General Synod for the debate on the ordination of women to the priesthood. I was up very early, feeling curiously relaxed and buoyant. Somehow I knew it was going to be a good day. It was also, I knew, a day of reckoning for the Church – so much hung on today's decision for us all, not least for me. I knew that I would be putting myself on the line by making a strong speech in favour of the ordination of women – indeed, there were those who felt that if I did not carry Synod with me, my authority and credibility would be suspect. Frankly, I did not accept that line of argument. Leadership is not about sitting on fences, but about giving a clear lead. If Synod chose to disregard my advice, that was not in my opinion a vote against me, so much as a rejection of the arguments that I and others had marshalled.

However, I knew one thing that many others did not know at the time; that the strong evangelical group in General Synod – known as EGGS – was now largely in favour of the ordination of women. A few days before, Mark Birchall, Chairman of EGGS and a leading layman, had phoned me: 'I believe I can persuade at least twenty-five of the waverers to vote for the ordination of women, but what worries many of them is a fear that this will open the floodgates to liberalism, and that the next item on the agenda will be the ordination of practising homosexuals. If you were able to reassure them, through me, that this is not the case, I'm sure they will be behind the motion.'

I was astonished to hear these issues juxtaposed like that, and had no difficulty in assuring Mark that they were two entirely different matters. There was in my opinion no scriptural or theological warrant for the ordination of practising homosexuals, but a great deal for the ordination of women. He could be sure that, in my time as Archbishop at least, I would resist a drift from the ordination of women to homosexuals. Mark put down the phone happily, and I was thrilled to have the support of that strong tradition.

When Eileen and I, together with Graham James, my Chaplain, arrived at Church House we found a huge crowd awaiting the historic decision; amongst them were a group of theological students from St John's, Nottingham, including our son Mark, who was in his first year of training for the ministry. Banners representing the shades of opinion made a colourful display, and a few television crews were visible. Cheers and catcalls greeted us as we emerged from the car and disappeared into the building. In the debating chamber the tension was almost tangible. The BBC was covering the entire day's debate, and the white lights of the TV cameras, together with the packed benches of delegates already in their seats long before the start of business, plus a crowded gallery, heightened the atmosphere and gave it a great sense of theatre.

The Archbishop of York chaired the morning session, which was designed to explore the scriptural and theological arguments on both sides of the debate. He called on the Bishop of Guildford, Michael Adie, to argue his case for the ordination of women. Michael did this very sensitively, acknowledging that there were good people on both sides of the argument and calling for us to handle disagreement in a loving and prayerful way. 'Scripture', he declared, 'is conclusive that women as much as men are created in the image of God. But scripture is inconclusive as far as women's ordination is concerned.

Women's role in Church and society has been circumscribed historic-ally. We now see women not as "inferior" to men but complementary. Women's ministry was a necessary development to stop ministry becoming "lopsided". We need to look at "development" not as some-thing to resist, not as something which has not happened before, but rather as something which is accepted in the light of contemporary truth.'

The Venerable David Silk, Archdeacon of Leicester, well known for his formidable debating skills, had been asked to put the case against ordination. He made it clear that he was speaking for many traditionalists, all of whom were agreed that what was not in question was the undisputed value of the pastoral and preaching ministry of women. He felt that ordination was so serious an issue that it should be decided by the universal Church in an ecumenical council, and feared that the legislation proposed could lead to divisions between Bishops. The Bishop of London, Dr David Hope, later developed this point, saying that although he wanted to support women's ministry, he was not convinced that the ordination of women as priests was the right way forward. He also believed that the legislation could lead to great discord in the Church.

When it came to my turn to speak, I reminded Synod that they had been debating this issue as far back as 1975, when they had concluded that there were no theological issues barring women from being ordained. I drew a parallel from Acts 10, where the early Church had to decide whether or not to baptise Gentiles. I contended that St Peter was led to see that the inclusion of Gentiles was not a departure from the tradition but a widening of it, as the first believers began to understand that Christianity was about 'God liberating, renewing and drawing out what has been there implicitly from the beginning'. I concluded by appealing to Synod to be bold and to begin the process that would lead to the full integration of women in the ministry of the Church.

The contribution of women to the debate was mature and impressive. Dr Christina Baxter, a well-known evangelical theologian, attacked the emphasis on priesthood, reminding Synod that a theology of ordination comes from two reference points – in relation to sacraments and in relation to the Word of God. Where was the logic in allowing women to preach, but not to celebrate the sacraments? The Reverend June Osborne spoke movingly of a call to priesthood that had developed over many years. Dr Ruth Etchells took us back to the theme of God's grace – no one is worthy to serve God. All ministry is a gift and flows from the gift of salvation. Were we really saying that God could redeem Gentiles, but not gender? Sister Carol, a nun from the Community of the Holy Name, suggested that one of the most important elements to consider was whether the time was right to ordain women. She believed it was, but it was important to advance together. The Reverend Susan Hope indirectly answered this by emphasising that today's culture already accepted women in most areas of work, and she was convinced it was time to act.

Following lunch I took the chair, and the debate continued. The speakers were impressive, and the tone of all speeches was dignified, courteous and compassionate. I felt the Church could be proud of the way Synod conducted itself, and I later received many letters from people who viewed or listened to the debate on their televisions and radios, and were thrilled by its character. At about 4.20 p.m. Synod accepted my guidance that the time for talk was over, and that we should spend a few moments in silent prayer. I then called for a division by Houses, and as Synod divided I sat in the President's chair, numbed and exhausted. For perhaps the first time I became fully aware how emotionally committed I was to the ordination of women, but at the same time how torn I was because I knew how difficult the road ahead for us would be.

Having cast their votes Synod returned to their seats, and members sat in subdued silence waiting for the decision. A sheet of paper was passed to me by Brian Hanson, Senior Registrar. The figures before me were:

	Bishops	Clergy	Laity
For	39	176	169
Against	13	74	82

I took in the significance of it. The motion for the ordination of women to the priesthood had been carried in all three Houses. Knowing that the cameras were on me, I tried as far as possible to control the emotion I felt. I was astonished and jubilant. Slowly, amidst a silence that seemed overwhelming, I read out the figures and then added: 'The motion has been carried in all three Houses.' A tiny squeak came from a lady on my left. Quickly I reminded Synod of my earlier request that we received the news in silence, aware that joy for some would be deep sadness for others. I then led Synod in a prayer and vacated the chair for John Habgood to take us through the rest of the legislation.

My request for dignified behaviour and compassionate awareness of the distress the decision would cause many traditionalists on both wings of the Church was certainly followed in the chamber. Understandably yet sadly, it was ignored outside. The great crowd outside, largely in favour of the decision, celebrated with abandonment and with singing and dancing. The noise was tumultuous, and penetrated the building. I could see the distress this was causing some of the Catholics; one man had his head in his hands, very obviously upset.

Following the end of Synod I did several radio and television interviews, then went home with Eileen for a quiet supper and a review of the day. I was in no doubt that 11 November 1992 would go down in history as one of the most significant events in the life of the Church of England since the Reformation. I could only hope and pray that God would use our decision to advance His Kingdom and glory.

I did not sleep well that night – my mind was too full for rest and my emotions too tangled to be at peace. I was up early to go to the BBC studios to be interviewed by Brian Redhead on the *Today* programme, and then back to Synod. The distress of traditionalist Catholics was palpable and raw. A few cut me dead in the corridor, and Dorothy Chatterley accosted me and said rather rudely, 'Archbishop, cut out the love stuff – we're fed up with that. We find ourselves no longer in our own Church.'

Knowing Dorothy as a forceful person of integrity, I replied, 'No, Dorothy, you must consider how others would feel today if the vote had gone the other way. Love and respect are the words we must employ now to settle the Church and move forward.' Dorothy was unconvinced. She went on to say that some of 'her troops' were suicidal, and in deep shock.

My foreboding that the historic breakthrough would give rise to a fierce backlash was not long in coming true. The *Sunday Telegraph* carried an editorial the following Sunday comparing the Prime Minister and me unfavourably with Douglas Hurd and John Habgood. Its conclusion was that having two commoners like George Carey and John Major leading such historic bodies as Church and state had not worked. Two Etonians would have done a better job. Perhaps that was true, but I was not going to let such elitism get me down.

More worrying was the view being spun by some traditionalists that the Church of England was now finished – that priests would leave in droves. One national paper suggested that as many as four thousand priests might leave. What seemed extraordinary to me was that the historic and triumphant moment of the ordination of women was being greeted in many quarters with breastbeating and sorrow. I believed that we now had an opportunity to put this enervating matter behind us, and unite in one common service to Jesus Christ.

There were of course a number of high-profile 'conversions' to Rome that seemed to underscore a perception among the chattering classes that the Church was finished. The first to declare herself at odds with the Church of England was the government Minister Ann Widdecombe, who announced her decision to leave the Church immediately, claiming that this was one more proof of its liberalism. I wrote to her at once, expressing my regret and saying: 'I wish we had the chance to chat as I would have liked to hear how you can justify your acceptance of women's leadership in society but not in the Church. I would have enjoyed explaining how theological arguments for [the ordination of women] are so overwhelming and that, one day, the Roman Catholic Church will accept women priests. However, what caused me more distress was your reference to liberalism in the C of E. In the light of the Decade of Evangelism and my personal initiatives in proclaiming the gospel of Christ as well as speaking out on issues of morals and spirituality I found your comments quite inexplicable.'

Ann replied two weeks later, thanking me for my letter, but saying that she had said she would resign if the Synod voted in favour of women's ordination, and that she had no intention of going back on that. She expressed regret that I had described her action as 'hasty' in public, but added that she was not referring specifically to me when she criticised the liberalism of the Church of England. She did not retract that criticism, however, and went on to question the appointment of Bishops who did not believe in the resurrection of Christ; Bishops who lectured the government, rather than individuals, on their responsibility; and the Church's equivocation on issues including abortion, divorce and homosexuality. She said that as I was not Archbishop of Canterbury when many of the things she referred to took place, I should not take her comments personally, and concluded her letter by expressing the hope that we would meet on good terms in the future.

This was a sad exchange, but rather typical of Ann Widdecombe's blunt and uncompromising style. I was truly sorry to see her depart on this issue.

John Gummer, the then Environment Minister, made a more courteous exit from the Church of England than Ann, and we have remained in touch. There was an amusing element to his departure, however. I knew of his sadness over the outcome of the vote, so it was not wholly surprising when he phoned and asked to come and see me. He came straight away, and handed me a letter that he wished to make public. In brief, it declared his sadness at leaving a Church that meant so much to him, but said that he was sure Church leaders like Thomas Cranmer, Jeremy Taylor, Edward Pusey and Michael Ramsey would not have agreed with the ordination of women.

I read it carefully and said: 'I can't speak for Thomas Cranmer, Jeremy Taylor or Edward Pusey, John, but I do know that Michael Ramsey would have approved of our decision.' John looked at me with astonishment and, grabbing the letter from my hands, scored out Michael's name. Michael Ramsey had said at the Lambeth Conference of 1968 that he supported the ordination of women, and Joan Ramsey told me in a private conversation that he had considered it 'only a matter of time'.

Although Synod had declared its intention to ordain women, there was a great deal to do in preparing the legislation and making pastoral arrangements for those clergy who could not in conscience remain in the Church or who could not accept their Bishop's authority in ordaining women. The measure of a great Church must surely lie in the care it takes in dealing with its priests and with people who find themselves conscientiously at loggerheads with it in such situations. It is my view that the Church of England, and the House of Bishops in particular, cannot be faulted for the thoroughness of the plans that flowed from the decision. I have to say, however, that I regret the financial arrangements made long before I came on the scene, which in essence gave resigning priests a lump sum and a pension on top of it. I was all in favour of pensions for service within the Church, but paying a lump sum seemed a dangerous precedent to set. Nevertheless, it had been agreed and we were stuck with it. Although comparatively few priests did eventually leave the Church, and though a minority of them returned, the cost was in the millions.

The work of the House of Bishops in the months following the decision focused on the necessity of providing a theological basis to allow both sides to live together in communion. In this regard David Hope's contribution proved to be significant and timely, and the

London Plans that he had devised to help traditional Catholics in the diocese of London were an important model for our national strategy. Two major documents followed, paving the way for the Episcopal Ministry Act of Synod that would be agreed by Synod a year later, in November 1993. These were the Manchester Statement of January 1993, and a document entitled *Bonds of Peace*. Both gave the theoretical grounds for those opposed to the ordination of women to remain within the Church in good standing.

The Bishops felt it crucial to make two points. First, there had to be no denial that, once ordained, women were lawfully and canonically members of the priesthood, however much some might question their validity. In the eyes of the Church, women would be part of its ministerial priesthood. Second, those who for various reasons could not accept Synod's decision would continue to hold a legitimate and recognised position within the Church. This would be protected by the appointment of three Provincial Episcopal Visitors (known later as flying Bishops), whose responsibility under the two Archbishops was to minister to those parishes which had voted for resolutions seeking the extended ministry of the Visitor.

It must be said that the success of these arrangements has been largely due to the thoroughness of the work done by the House of Bishops. Faced with the possibility of a meltdown in the Church, it applied itself to the task in hand and achieved a unity that gave us all joy. I recall the meeting of the House on 13 January 1993 when, as we worked on a draft document that would see the light later as *Bonds of Peace*, Stephen Sykes, Bishop of Ely, formerly Lady Margaret Professor of Theology at Cambridge, complained that it lacked theological coherency. Sensing danger, I intervened and said that we would continue after coffee, then instructed Stephen and a few other heavyweights to work on the text and come up with a satisfactory wording. Following the break, David Hope read out a statement on communion that everyone accepted. That was such a breakthrough that for a moment there was stunned silence; then Simon Barrington-Ward, Bishop of Coventry, started singing the doxology 'Praise God

Left On holiday with my parents as a teenager. Mine was a typical East End upbringing – happy and loving but very poor. Like many other families we migrated to Dagenham in Essex shortly before the war.

Above My father at the age of about sixty-five, on holiday in the Lake District. He worked for many years at Ford's motor company in Dagenham, and later became a hospital porter.

Left Dreaming of travelling the ocean waves, I broke the rules by applying to be a Sea Cadet at the age of twelve, when the entry level was thirteen (I am on the right). I was a tall, strapping lad, and they believed me.

Left National Service as a signals operator in the RAF. I was stationed in Egypt, and then at a quiet base in Iraq, where the one major incident was to nurse a transport plane with an engine on fire to safety at the airbase at Shaibah.

Right I was told I was to be pitied when my posting came to Shaibah, near Basra in Iraq. But I fell in love with the desert and the people, and began a lifelong interest in Islam. There were also moments of leisure – I am the top diver.

Below Married to the love of my life, my greatest supporter and critic, Eileen on 25 June 1960. She was training to be a nurse when we began to fall in love after I completed my National Service. It was an early sign of the busy life that would engulf us in the years ahead when I had to sit an exam during our honeymoon in Scotland.

Right After training for the priesthood I became Curate of St Mary's, Islington. In the summer our holiday camps for children always had a fun theme to draw in the kids. In 1964 it was a Wild West Week. I managed to track down a wagon and horse – no mean feat in Islington – but the owner would only hire them to us if we employed his pet monkey as well.

Below By 1966 we had three children – Rachel (three and a quarter), Mark (eighteen months) and Andrew (six months). But our family was not complete until 1972, when our younger daughter Lizzie was born.

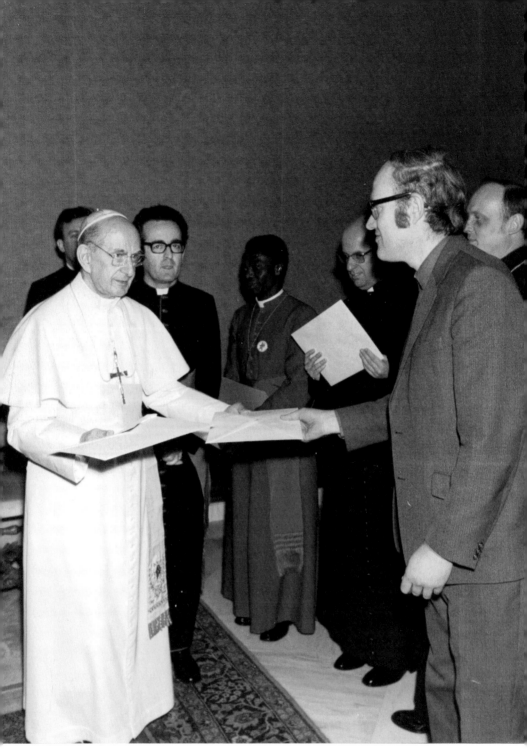

In 1977 I went to the Vatican for the first time, to study Roman Catholicism. There with a group of other Anglican leaders I met Pope Paul VI.

Left A rare picture of me actually teaching as Principal of Trinity Theological College in Bristol. After teaching at two previous colleges and then serving as a parish priest in Durham, I had many questions about whether the Church of England's methods of training for the priesthood were the best ones for our age.

Right My consecration as Bishop of Bath and Wells by Robert Runcie on 3 December 1987. The occasion was over-shadowed by the controversy that had broken out over the traditionally anonymous Preface to the new edition of *Crockford's Clerical Directory*, in which Archbishop Runcie was vilified for favouring 'liberals' as Bishops. The author of that Preface committed suicide shortly afterwards.

Left As Bishop of Bath and Wells with our beloved King Charles spaniel, Buccleuch. The cathedral dominated the small city of Wells, and we lived in the wing of a moated palace – perhaps the most beautiful Bishop's residence in England.

Ordeal by photocall in Wells on the day of the announcement of my nomination as Archbishop of Canterbury in 1990. Even the unexpected interest in my appointment could not prepare me for the media scrutiny of every word I spoke from that day forward.

With John Major in January 1991, when we were both new to our respective roles. Much of the criticism of John was unfair. Far from being a 'grey' man, he had a fund of good humour, and shared a love of football with me – leading to banter about the fortunes of my team, Arsenal, and his, Chelsea.

Above My first overseas trip as Archbishop was to Papua New Guinea in 1991. It was an eye-opening visit, revealing to me the vast cultural differences among Anglicans, but also our essential unity. Visiting the most remote parts of the islands, on one occasion we were presented with a pig which I was expected to slaughter. I was able to escape the task by donating the pig to the local theological college.

Above With John Habgood, the Archbishop of York. John's gifts were great, and I needed his experience when I became Archbishop of Canterbury, especially with the vote for women's ordination looming.

Left Meeting Nelson Mandela for the first time in January 1993, when he came to address the leaders of the Anglican Communion in Cape Town. At our private meeting I was left in no doubt that I was talking with one of the most impressive public figures of our time.

In December 1993 Yasser Arafat paid his first visit to Lambeth Palace. He and Prime Minister Ariel Sharon were later to support the Alexandria Declaration which brought together the key Muslim, Jewish and Christian leaders to call for a 'religious ceasefire' in 2000. Dr Mohammed Sayed Tantawi (pictured below), Grand Imam of Al-Azhar, hosted the gathering of faith leaders which led to the declaration. It was the toughest meeting I have ever chaired.

from Whom all Blessings Flow', and everyone joined in. It was a historic and moving moment.

But was such an attempt to hold people together theologically defensible? It points to the genius of Anglicanism in its endeavour to combine generosity of spirit, fairness of treatment and toleration of differences. Nevertheless, the pragmatism that this smacks of continues to be questioned for its 'apparent' indifference to clear doctrine and for putting unity before truth. Certainly Bishop John Baker, Bishop of Salisbury, thought so, and found it increasingly difficult to accept a proposal which suggested that the Church of England had two doctrines on the matter. How was it possible, he argued, for men to be ordained or consecrated who did not believe women priests were real priests? He thought a mixed message was being sent to women about the validity of their ordination which was not fair to them and could undermine their ministries.

This view was widely held, both within and without the Church. Graham Leonard, the retired Bishop of London, was dismissive of the idea and contemptuous of my leadership. He attracted considerable publicity for promoting the idea of a Uniate Church, that is a separate Church of England in communion with Rome. Indeed, Cardinal Hume phoned me on Sunday, 10 January 1993 to say that although he personally discounted the idea of a Uniate Church, the idea would be put before the Pope. He also stressed that in his view it was important that people or groups who turned to his Church because they opposed the ordination of women needed to accept the entire body of Catholic beliefs, not just its position on that issue. He also commented gratuitously that the idea of Episcopal oversight being given by an alternative Bishop was theological nonsense. I politely disagreed. One may and must agree that the concept of extending Episcopal oversight to another when a congregation is in such clear disagreement with its Bishop is less than one might desire for the good ordering of any Church. It was a matter of deep regret to me that proposals for Provincial Episcopal Visitors and talk of varying degrees of community had become the reality for our Church, at least in the short term. But that was, in my opinion, the price one had to pay – and should pay – for a Church prepared to live with differences and not drive people away. I am unable to agree that the House of Bishops put unity before truth. Glib talk about 'ecclesiastic joinery' missed the point. We were not trying to keep things together for the sake of order, but because at the heart of the gospel is love. Love is central to the good news of Jesus Christ, and I was as upbeat as I possibly could be about the coherence and faithfulness of the journey we had made together.

But Cardinal Hume did make an unguarded statement that strained relationships between our two Churches. Immediately following Synod's momentous decision I wrote to him suggesting that a joint Pastoral Consultative Group be formed to handle the transition of priests who wished to join the Roman Catholic Church following Synod's commitment to ordain women. Basil wrote back on 15 December saying that he was attracted by the idea, and would consult. Some weeks passed, and the issue became rather tangled when he gave an address in which he spoke of the 'reconversion of England'. All hell broke loose. The press worked themselves up into a lather, sensing that a critical moment had arrived in the history of the Church. Damian Thompson wrote in the *Daily Telegraph* on 11 March 1994 that relations between Cardinal Hume and the Archbishop of Canterbury had deteriorated, and that he could back this up with highly placed sources. I was staggered by such comments, but on the same day Basil wrote to me that he was 'very annoyed' with articles in the *Telegraph* and the *Catholic Herald*. He remarked that his misunderstood comment about the 'reconversion' of England referred to a 'metanoia [conversion] which includes us all . . . so absorption by one group was automatically excluded'. He also made it clear that relations between us had not deteriorated – rather that we got on well and were able to speak to each other frankly. Mark Santer, Bishop of Birmingham and Co-Chair of ARCIC, wrote a typically trenchant letter to me:

Basil's foolish remark about 'reconversion' of England did not help. It has angered the evangelical end and horrified many of the middle. Crispin Hollis [Roman Catholic Bishop of Portsmouth] has been excellent in making clear the RC perspective. But I am getting worried that the press preoccupation is on the minority position. The other side of the message is not getting through. Like you, I can report terrific things happening. For example, my visit to Liverpool showed a purposeful Anglican diocese. The general public is not aware that the RC ministry in this land is under strain with lack of vocations. We may be helping them to the tune of 250 plus – but some of the people they will receive will be among those we shall be thankful to see go!

Soon afterwards, I heard that the Roman Catholic Bishops' Conference had agreed to the formation of a Pastoral Commission, and Basil Hume and I had pleasure in establishing a group which did excellent work in advising both sets of Bishops on guidelines they could offer to Anglican clergy making the unfamiliar journey to another Church. Thankfully, compared with the number of women we would be ordaining over the coming years, the numbers of those leaving were very small – and quite a few of them were elderly. Nonetheless, it was regrettable that any felt they had to leave a Church which they had loved and served.

Looking back, was it all worth it? Yes, a thousand times over. Throughout this period I had Doreen Bergernie, with whom I had served in Islington, in mind. A capable, clever and spiritual person, she had no opportunity to share her gifts as a minister and priest, because she was a woman. How many Doreens in the land were in the same situation? It will always be a privilege to be identified as the Archbishop of Canterbury in whose time women were ordained to the priesthood. It was right to do so, and I hope to be around when the first woman Bishop is ordained. It will happen.

I personally was not to come out of this period unscathed. Two things occurred which badly jolted my self-confidence and taught me valuable lessons. The first arose incidentally from the controversy associated with the Lincoln Report on theological colleges. Named after the Bishop of Lincoln, Bob Hardy, Chairman of the report, it sought to address the worrying downturn in numbers going forward into theological training. The trend had started a few years earlier, before my archiepiscopate. The bleak view of the Ministry department was that it was necessary to close a number of colleges – Chichester, Salisbury/Wells, Lincoln, Oak Hill and Mirfield. This seemed to many of us a draconian measure, but the statistics convinced the House of Bishops that the Church could not go on supporting small, struggling colleges. The proposal for their closure came before the February 1993 General Synod. As each college had fierce supporters in Synod, and agreement to the proposal was going to be hard to achieve, there was obviously going to be a great deal of unpleasantness around.

The backlash came when I was being questioned as Chairman of the House of Bishops. I was frankly in no state to answer questions of any kind, and ought to have been in bed. The previous weekend Eileen and I had visited the European Institutions, starting with a visit to Strasbourg and then going on to Brussels. The whirlwind five-day visit was one of the most gruelling in my eleven years as Archbishop. I had given at least ten different addresses on varying subjects, from ecumenism to political matters. During the early hours of Sunday morning I had been violently sick, and was in poor shape for the service at Holy Trinity, Brussels, at which I was to preach. I managed to struggle through the address, then returned immediately to bed at the Ambassador's residence. Eileen had to stand in for me at lunch and at an engagement afterwards. A few hours in bed saw me greatly recovered, but not at all well. I staggered through another dinner and another address in the evening. The following day, Monday, I had meetings with Jacques Delors, Secretary General of the European Parliament, and Dr Woenner, Secretary General of NATO.

Following a press conference we flew home that evening, and the next morning I was at my place in Synod, looking only slightly better than I felt. My downfall came at Question Time that evening. For some years I had had trouble with my hearing, following a virus contracted in Durham that had left me unable to detect high frequencies. I should have done something about it years before, but I had always put it off. As I stood there, feeling physically sick, I realised that I could not hear the supplementary questions from delegates who were demanding to know why the House of Bishops was about to axe Chichester, Salisbury/Wells, Oak Hill, etc. The noise boomed around me. I tried to get the speakers to repeat their questions, but it was no good, I could not hear.

Mercifully, the misery was short-lived, and I returned to my place dejected and determined to do something about the problem as soon as time allowed. Eileen, who was in the gallery, knew immediately what was going on, and was furious that no official attempted to help me, believing that it was clear to all that I was having difficulty hearing the questions. She returned home very distressed for me, and I arrived an hour later, exhausted and vowing that never again would I take on commitments that close to General Synod.

The ongoing controversy over the ordination of women, and the uproar that the Lincoln Report had triggered, gave ammunition to some critics who claimed that the Church of England was in crisis, and that responsibility for a great deal of the damage could be laid at my feet. A week or two following that depressing Synod, an interview for the *Sunday Times* turned out to be an absolute disaster. I am afraid I was duped by a pretty young face and a friendly approach which fooled me into believing that the reporter was on my side. She took my relaxed attitude, as I showed her around the Palace and talked about the work and my family, as evidence that I was dazzled and overawed by the position I was in, and was not up to the job. Ironically, her final sentences struck me as a reflection of the world she inhabited, and which I felt needed redeeming: 'Political cunning, business acumen, effortless charm, sharp intellect and unfailing faith is a difficult combination. It is being suggested, as the crisis deepens, the divisions widen and the finances bleed away that Carey has made the ultimate error of putting his faith in God alone.' Well, I said to myself, I am content with that.

Friends, of course, leapt to my defence. The following morning Lord Laing phoned me, hopping mad about that 'bloody article which was so unfair ... disgraceful ...' I was grateful for David Sheppard's letter to the paper: 'Her research seems to have been highly selective, each of the attributable criticisms comes from within the group which [was] understandably hurt by the General Synod decision to ordain women to the priesthood ... George Carey stands in an honourable tradition, human, spirited, scholarly, charitable ... it takes great moral and spiritual strength to steer a steady course in such a turbulent world. I believe George Carey is already finding that strength.' These affirming and affectionate words meant a lot to me at a difficult time.

But worse was to come. Easter 1993 will always remain Black Easter for me, as sections of the press, acting like a pack, pounced on their victim – the Church of England in general and the Archbishop of Canterbury in particular. On Good Friday *The Times* carried articles on the Church of England in crisis, but it was clear to me that this 'crisis' was created by relatively few dissidents, who were briefing the press at every opportunity, and claiming that thousands would leave the Church when the first ordinations of women took place. Some journalists swallowed these briefings with very few questions about the actual numbers.

The following day *The Times* carried the headline: 'Easter Crisis – Heat on Carey'. The contents of the story however offered nothing new, amounting to little more than recycled nonsense about thousands leaving the Church. According to this and other articles, my leadership was to blame for the defections and the low morale in the Church. Cruel and malicious personal criticism does wound, and I had to face up to the charges, seeking spiritual and mental ways to prevent the barbs from leading to bitterness and self-pity. I found my way of dealing with the hurt by, first of all, facing the criticism, 'hearing it' and seeking to learn from it. There were times when I would walk around the Palace garden questioning myself: 'What is going on? What is causing the distress in the Church, and why am I being blamed for it? Am I really that bad? If I really were, is it conceivable that the Lord I serve would have allowed me to serve as Archbishop? Wasn't I chosen by the Church because I had the qualities necessary for this moment in time, and the spiritual, mental and moral resilience to cope?'

I knew that real spiritual strength would not come from myself, but from drawing upon God's grace. I began to consider that this was likely to be the cross I would have to bear, and that I should bear it gladly for my Lord. After all, I meditated, it was a very light burden compared with Christ's, or for that matter with the sufferings of fellow Christians abroad who died for their faith. A particular verse from the scriptures was of great help to me. One morning in chapel a passage from St Paul was read out, and seven words hit home: 'It is the Lord that judges me.' St Paul too was defending himself from adversaries who had been challenging his authority and questioning the validity of his leadership. I felt I was being told that 'those who exercise any apostolic role for me are bound to be criticised, dissected, analysed and wounded. You must bear it for me as I bore my wounds for you.' Those seven words became my motto in days to come. But, it has to be said, those closest to me found the criticisms hard to bear. Eileen and our children were often incensed by the personal attacks on me.

Through this battering I became more and more convinced that the Church would win through. It was my job, I believed, to help the Church keep its eyes on the bigger picture, and not on the squabbles which were distractions from the more serious and demanding task of relating the Christian faith to the world around. It was my unwavering understanding that the Church's concern should not be its own mere survival, but the Kingdom of God. 'The Kingdom of God', declared Jurgen Moltmann, 'isn't there for the sake of the Church. The Church is there for the sake of the Kingdom.' As

I saw it, the health of our Church must be assessed according to the degree to which it looks away from its own interests, and towards God's concern for the flourishing of His Kingdom in the lives of men and women. I was sure that the decision to ordain women to the priesthood was a Kingdom-moment. Time would confirm it.

10

Forced to Change

'The great problem of the Church of England is that no one,
I repeat no one, is in charge . . . Just a series of power centres,
all floating around . . . I found that terribly frustrating.'

Sir Douglas Lovelock, First Church Estates Commissioner

No.1 MILLBANK IS AN IMPRESSIVE ADDRESS. Almost directly
opposite the House of Lords, it is the home of the Church Commissioners, whose stake in the Church of England has been at many
times extremely important, and at other times deeply ambiguous.
To most people, including regular members of Anglican congregations, the Church Commissioners are an unknown and mysterious
body. The vast majority of clergy probably only know the Commissioners as the body that pays their salary monthly, and does so
regularly and conscientiously. It is the job of the Commissioners to
manage the money of the Church of England – funds collected and
accumulated from the gifts of generations of Anglicans down the
centuries.

This has not always been so. From before the Norman Conquest
secular clergy had to find a 'living' from the income of their parish.
Often they had to till the land and graze their own sheep to sustain
their ministries as priests. From their income, taxes were paid to the
Pope. The break with Rome in 1534 changed little as far as clergy
stipends were concerned, except that tax was now paid to the Crown.

Thus, King Henry VIII and his successors found the clergy a convenient and welcome source of income.

The situation remained unchanged until the beginning of the eighteenth century, when Queen Anne, a devout and sensitive Christian sovereign, became aware of the poverty-stricken plight of many clergy, and from tax revenue created Queen Anne's Bounty (1704) 'for the maintenance of poor clergy'. Matters remained largely unchanged as far as remuneration of clergy was concerned until 1948, when the Ecclesiastical Commissioners, established in 1836 for the reorganisation of English dioceses, were merged with Queen Anne's Bounty, to form the Church Commissioners. It is thus a relatively new body, entrusted on behalf of the Church as a whole to manage its historic endowments, to assist poor clergy, to provide for the housing of clergy and to do everything in its power to further the mission of the Church. And it has to be said that on the whole it has served its parent body rather well.

The danger, however, with any limb of a parent body, is that by the very nature of its specialist activity it may become so separate that it begins to possess an independent life. Upon becoming Archbishop, the moment I first came into contact with the Commissioners I sensed that this was beginning to happen. Although the staff were anxious to assist the Church in its ministry and life, they seemed to me to be out of touch with the reality of the Church's role today. The evidence was indirect and sometimes anecdotal. Bishops and clergy from inner-city parishes would sometimes mention their concerns about the Commissioners to me. They described an inability on the part of the Commissioners to comprehend the desire of many dioceses for reform. There were reports of Commissioners' staff travelling first class on trains to adjudicate in matters where diocesan and Commissioners' responsibilities clashed; Bishops would complain to me that sometimes junior members of the Commissioners' staff would intervene in a high-handed manner in the management of their residences, and other matters in which the purse strings were tightly controlled by No.1 Millbank.

Sir Douglas Lovelock, the First Church Estates Commissioner, was a burly man with a shock of white hair and a confident, bullish manner. I liked him a lot – he was easy to deal with and easy to understand. General Synod, however, was often irritated by his manner. In his breezy presentations, he annually told Synod how well the Commissioners were handling the Church's affairs, but he failed to satisfy everyone. Nevertheless, Douglas seemed equal to any objector, and his ear-piercing cough, rather than suggesting nervousness, seemed rather to say, 'Let me make it clear: I'm in charge.'

And I thought he was. As Archbishop I chaired the Board of Governors, but my duties made it difficult for me to be present at every meeting. I therefore followed my predecessor's tradition by appointing a deputy to chair the regular meetings of the Commissioners. I could not have chosen a better person than the Bishop of Chelmsford, John Waine. As a senior Bishop, John was greatly respected for his wisdom and caution. I had every confidence in him.

By right every diocesan Bishop is a Commissioner. A number of senior officers of state (including the Prime Minister and the Lord Chancellor) are also Commissioners, along with clergy and lay representatives elected by the General Synod. Other Commissioners are appointed by the Crown, the Lord Mayors of London and York, and the Universities of Oxford and Cambridge. From among this number, who meet annually, the Board of Governors – responsible for the day-to-day oversight of the Commissioners' activities and staff – was drawn. The Board was large, unwieldy, and had no expertise in investment management.

Unbeknown to John, myself and most people in the Church, the Commissioners were in deep trouble. The problems were manifold but had begun in the 1980s, when the British economy was booming. The underlying causes were, on the whole, driven by an honourable desire to serve the Church's mission. But the result was that excessive commitments were driven by a reliance upon high-income investments and lucrative returns through property development. New commitments made by the Church Commissioners, including additional assistance for poorer dioceses, better pensions and an annual £1 million grant to the Church Urban Fund, were in themselves admirable and, in the case of clergy pensions, absolutely essential. However, the Commissioners were not acting independently – General Synod was insistent that funds should be made available for all these objectives, even though very few members were aware of the fragile state of the Commissioners' funds. This massive increase in commitments was augmented yet further by a decision to neutralise the effect upon clergy of the Community Charge (at an initial cost of £8 million a year).

Put under pressure to give tangible and rapid returns to the Church, the Commissioners crossed that fatal line from prudent to imprudent management of their funds. The decision of the Assets Committee, the body that had control of policy, was to invest in commercial property. At first these investments, especially the Metro Centre in Newcastle, were highly profitable for the Church. But they left the Commissioners dangerously exposed to the vagaries of the market. When the property bubble burst, the Commissioners found their stocks significantly reduced in value. For the Church the implications were shocking, and there were other factors that suggested that the investments were not managed as wisely as Synod had been told.

On Saturday, 11 July 1992, in the middle of the annual meeting of General Synod at York, a leading article in that day's *Financial Times* dropped like a bombshell on the assembly. The article, by John Plender, was entitled 'Unholy Saga of the Church's Missing Millions', and the picture it painted was an alarming one.

I recall that morning well. I was about to go over my speech for the debate on 'stewardship' the following day. It was my intention to urge parishes to give more for the ministry of the Church. Although myth has it that the Church of England is very rich, the facts are otherwise. The largest part of income goes on clergy salaries and pensions: in 1991, 61 per cent of those costs came from the Commissioners, and the rest was raised through the parishes and dioceses. My Press Officer handed me the cutting from the *FT*. 'You're not going to like this very much,' he observed. I was astounded and horrified. That evening, in a serious mood I remarked to Eileen, 'When I took up office I thought that the ordination of women would be the toughest challenge I had to face. I was wrong – this is it.'

John Plender's article made several accusations: that over the past two years no less than £500 million (the figure was said later to be £800 million) had slipped through the Commissioners' fingers, increased by a controversial decision to finance speculative property developments with borrowings, mainly from the National Westminster Bank. In reply to the defence that there had been no real loss of £500 million plus, since this was merely the result of re-evaluation of the Commissioners' assets in the light of market conditions, Plender quoted Matthew Oakeshott, an independent fund manager, who expressed his surprise that 'the Commissioners attributed their faltering income to recession, since the property of most long-term funds continues to rise'. Among the most speculative developments, Plender claimed, was one at Ashford in Kent, where the Commissioners had made some serious blunders.

What I held in my hand was not a sensational and inaccurate story dreamed up by a writer on a tabloid, but a report by a responsible and well-known journalist writing for the *Financial Times*, no less – an organ respected the world over. This was all news to me. No one from the Church Commissioners had hinted at any difficulty. Just a few weeks earlier I had chaired the AGM of the Commissioners, and under severe questioning by John Smallwood, Chairman of the Board of Finance of the Southwark Diocese, Sir Douglas had stated categorically his belief that there were no major problems; indeed, he said, the Commissioners had outperformed many of their competitors. The only admission of difficulty was mentioned in the minutes in the following way: 'The First Commissioner explained the current state of finances and that there was a tension between the increasing expenditure commitments of the Commissioners and the yield on income-producing assets. This was leading to a need to consider how to best deal with this shortfall.'

But now, with John Plender's article in front of me, I knew that the Church was in serious trouble. This posed the immediate personal dilemma of how I could give a robust speech on the need for parishioners to give more generously, when those entrusted with the management of our funds had been found wanting. Sir Douglas was contacted immediately and asked to respond at Synod the following Monday.

In typically robust style, he made his defence in a speech I would summarise thus: 'This is my last speech on finance, as I shall be retiring in the course of this year. In the eighties income grew. We did rather well. The new money allowed us to do extra things. Expectations rose, but the recession hit ... The recession is deeper and more persistent than expected, particularly affecting property. Too much property? Yes, but that is not easily altered. Mistakes? No doubt, but some spectacular ones we did not make: viz. Docklands investment and central London offices. This same portfolio produced the "fat" years and raised expectations. As for the immediate future, investment income will remain flat; the pension bill will go on rising by at least £5 million per annum. Giving needs to be increased to be at least 5 per cent of take-home pay. This is not a crisis; it is a manageable problem, though serious. It is true that the Commissioners will not be able to give as much to clergy stipends, and that is why parishes have to give more. The recession will end. The aim of the Commissioners will be to balance today's and tomorrow's needs. We have not lost £500 million – valuation rises and falls. We have had a difficult year. We have had to maintain income while reducing borrowing. Overall the Commissioners have done well compared to many other companies, but there is a problem, and it would be no service to the Church to deny it. I believe that if we get the message across to Church members that giving must increase significantly, they will respond as they have done before. As for the Commissioners, we will learn from our experience and will report on this debate to the Board.'

It was an impressive and reassuring defence – as far as it went. But it was hardly likely to convince the experts, or to reduce the level of dismay in the parishes. Nor did it contain any admission that the Commissioners might have made mistakes. I felt I had to reassure the Church that the matter would be addressed firmly. I therefore told Synod: 'Serious accusations have been made about the management of funds and about judgements on investments. I want to assure Synod that these will be examined closely by the Church Commissioners and others concerned.'

There were, it seemed to me, three separate matters that had to be addressed: the claim that the Commissioners had let more than £500 million 'slip through their fingers' was essentially an accusation of poor management of investments; the accusation that the Commissioners had borrowed inappropriately for property development – Plender's article claimed that 'Even for a contributory pension cash inflow, borrowing is usually regarded as a questionable practice'; and the allegation that millions of pounds had been lost at Ashford in Kent through imprudence. I was astonished to learn about this last claim. Ashford was in my diocese, but neither I nor anyone on the Diocesan Board of Finance had been kept in the picture about development projects there.

My worries were compounded a few days later when a senior member of the Commissioners' staff phoned me and pleaded that an internal investigation be set up. 'There is no need for an independent Commission,' he said. 'The Commissioners can be trusted to handle this wisely. Furthermore, it would only alarm Church members if outsiders were entrusted with this responsibility.'

I was staggered. It seemed to me that the vast majority of Church members would be more alarmed if the investigation were internal only. I dismissed the suggestion at once, and by October, with the help of John Habgood and Philip Mawer, and following consultations with the Board of the Commissioners and the Governor of the Bank of England, two decisions were taken. First, that the accountants Coopers & Lybrand should be asked to examine and report on the Commissioners' borrowings and management of assets. Second, that a group, known later as the Lambeth Group, should be established to consider the Coopers & Lybrand report, and to make recommendations for reform. The nine-man group, chaired by John Waine, included leading figures from the worlds of finance and business, as well as from the Church.

In my opinion, and in that of the experts whose advice I had sought, this group was very strong, well informed and trustworthy, and would not fudge or duck the issues. There was, of course, a question about the Chairman, John Waine. As he was the current Deputy Chairman of the Board of Governors of the Commissioners, there was a risk that, to some, his appointment would suggest a whitewash. I did not think this would be the case, because it was clear that the Board had itself been kept in the dark, and was largely unaware of decisions taken by those most closely involved in investments. There was another reason why I thought John should be involved. He was a highly respected Bishop, a man of the deepest honour, and his participation would be absolutely vital for the implementation of whatever might come from the Group's proposals. I was confident that he could be trusted to chair this body well. However, to press home the point, I met him shortly before the Group began its work and affirmed my commitment to an objective review, in which I for one would not flinch from root and branch changes if they were found to be desirable.

Deep down I was excited by what was taking place, although the news was desperate and discouraging. I was committed to a more enterprising and effective Church of England, and this review was a God-given opportunity to consider the organisation of the Church as a whole. It had always seemed to me that our Church was an essentially dysfunctional body, with centres of power at national level residing in the Archbishops and Bishops, General Synod and the

Commissioners. As the Commissioners were the financial engine room of the Church, there was a structural fissure between policy and funding; between vision and money. Indeed, Sir Douglas Lovelock himself was later to say: 'The great problem of the Church of England is that no one, I repeat no one, is in charge. There are a number of power centres – Lambeth, with the Archbishop, the Synod, the dioceses, the Bishops in their splendour, the Church Commissioners and all those other bodies, some of which I was on. But there is no single person who can do as we were accustomed to do at Whitehall, who can say: "OK, I've listened to everything you've said. I've weighed up all the objections and this is what we're going to do." No one at all. Just a series of power centres, all floating around. I found that very, very odd indeed, I found that terribly frustrating.'

It seemed to me that, at last, we had a golden opportunity to bring the disparate centres together for the good of the Church. However, it was crucial that the longer-term issues about governance and integration of policy and funding should be considered calmly and objectively in their own right, and not get caught up in the heat and fury generated by the events of the recent past.

While Coopers & Lybrand and the Lambeth Group were doing their work, it is not an exaggeration to say that the mood in the Church was very dark indeed. Bishops, clergy and lay people were appalled by the accusations of negligence levelled at the Commissioners. I was concerned that our eyes were being taken off the issue of mission and focused, inevitably but too narrowly, on that of money. Again and again I urged that we bore in mind that when any organisation – be it religious or secular – has clear focus and objectives, the issue of funding usually takes care of itself. We should not allow money to dictate our policy on ministry.

I was particularly worried by meetings of the House of Bishops, at which some of the more senior Bishops poured out their fears about the ability of their dioceses to pay the quota and therefore pay the stipends of the clergy. The tones of gloom and doom seemed out of place, when our role as Bishops was surely to give expression to a faith which trusted in the power of prayer and in the living God. I personally did not regard this pessimism as justified, and said so repeatedly. In particular I and a few others emphasised the importance of stewardship. Giving was very poor in the Church as a whole: less than 3 per cent of take-home pay. It was surely not unreasonable to ask for a greater commitment from churchgoers to the work of mission and ministry of the Church. That message had to come from the top, and had to be taken into every area of Church life with conviction and confidence.

Within a few months I had Coopers & Lybrand's report, together with the conclusions and recommendations of the Lambeth Group. The documents constituted a damning indictment of key judgements made over the years by the Commissioners, and of the systems of control, accounting and accountability within the various departments. The performance of certain individuals was criticised, and the Assets Committee was singled out for indiscipline: 'They frequently amended development projects and succumbed to pressure to make quick decisions to take advantage of short-term opportunities but failed to take "full account" of their cumulative effect on the portfolio.' The overall performance had been poor – largely because of the lopsided commitment to property investment, exacerbated by imprudent borrowing. What I found particularly revealing was that the report dismissed the myth that if the Commissioners had not 'lost' £800 million, everything would have been all right. While the report was critical of the Commissioners, it made it very clear that the investment losses simply shortened the fuse on a bomb that was bound to explode in the near future. In short, the Commissioners' funds were too small for the commitments they were required to finance.

The report also addressed the complicated and sorry tale of the extent of borrowing. It seems that falling income had forced the Assets Committee to borrow to fund property developed at floating rates of interest. The intention was that the interest on those loans would be rolled up until the developments were completed, in the expectation that rent would cover both interest and development costs. However, as interest rates soared into double-digit figures in the early nineties, and the letting market collapsed, the Commissioners incurred heavy losses in repayments for the borrowing. Borrowing at that level – it reached £500 million at its peak – was quite usual for a property company which could cut or drop its dividend when the market was difficult, but was most unusual and indeed very unwise for an institution like the Church Commissioners which had heavy obligations to finance and very little manoeuvrability.

What was reassuring to me was that no individual was found to be culpable of criminal conduct or of seeking personal gain. Rather, the documents told a story of an organisation that needed drastic reform very quickly to ensure that it was more accountable to its Board, and to have financial experts in key positions. The most charitable thing that could be said about the Commissioners' performance – and it is important to say so – is that some of the misjudgements were caused by enthusiastic determination to go for ambitious targets in order to meet the strong wishes of Synod to fuel the mission of the Church.

I felt particularly sad for Sir Douglas, then on the point of retirement, when all he had fought for and stood for over many years was being questioned, criticised and damned. On the public record he has said: 'I don't see the criticism that has been made in the later years, or the praise that was heaped on me in the early years, being of me personally ... Of course, where I was complacent or not assiduous enough at looking into something, I regret that ... But over a period you do some things better than others.' Yet much had been achieved during his period in office. Parts of the portfolio were managed well, and returns had not always been bad. Not the least of his many contributions was an initiative that has enabled clergy to borrow or rent without the nightmare of fluctuating interest rates and the costs of renting privately. Many clergy will be grateful for that, among many other things.

The implication of the reports was that at last we had an objective review of the Commissioners' financial position and of their ability to provide salaries, pensions and housing for the clergy. The truth was revealed in all its alarming clarity: the three historic commitments could not be maintained at their present level. Indeed, pension provision alone would consume the entire Fund unless something was done. In summary, the Lambeth Group recommended:

- The creation of a separately constituted fund for pension liabilities
- Sweeping changes to the Assets Committee
- Closer liaison between the Board and Assets Committee
- The creation of an Audit Committee
- Investment portfolio should be gradually changed away from excessive commitment in property to a portfolio not markedly different from that of other major bodies with comparable responsibilities
- Advice from external fund managers was necessary
- The Commissioners should normally avoid borrowing
- A new post of Finance Director should be created

The appointment of Sir Michael Colman as First Church Estates Commissioner gave impetus to the reforms. This appointment was in the gift of the Crown, but both the Archbishop of York and I, together with Philip Mawer, were closely involved in it. Michael, coming from a successful business and being a committed Anglican Christian, was an ideal choice. His general ignorance of the bureaucracy of the Church allowed him to approach issues with freshness and innocence. He was therefore able to charm – and at times infuriate – the House of Bishops and Synod by his candid opinions.

The difference in style between Sir Douglas and Sir Michael was noteworthy. Whereas Douglas Lovelock would always seek to suggest that the Commissioners could find a way out of a particular problem confronting the Church, Sir Michael could be devastatingly brutal in his assessment – insisting, for example, that unless the Church as a whole was prepared to tackle the issue of finance, dioceses would go bankrupt. As a businessman he would insist on clear thinking; as a practising Christian, however, he knew that when faith and works came together, you had the right chemistry for change. Sir Michael thus set about reforming the Commissioners in the light of the reports. This he did in an atmosphere of fear and plummeting morale, as staff feared redundancy.

While changes at the Commissioners were going on, a great deal of energy was focused on how to enable the whole Church to address this crisis together. In essence, the problems that the Commissioners had been grappling with posed a challenge to virtually every part of the Church. It was impossible to limit the pain to just one part of the body. Nobody could fail to be aware that the shift in responsibility for funding the Church's ministry from central funding to local was going to be dramatic and traumatic. It was going to ask a great deal from us all in terms of leadership and teamwork.

It was therefore necessary to take the dioceses carefully through the need for change, and to involve them closely in the painful decision-making that would inevitably follow. In this the Bishops had to set a positive tone, and challenge any retreat into parochialism and defeatism. But another group of people were essential for creating a climate of hope: the Chairmen of diocesan boards of finances and the Secretaries of dioceses. This involved Philip Mawer of General Synod, Sir Michael Colman, of the Commissioners, Alan McLintock of the Central Board of Finance, Howard Gracey of the Pensions Board, and other staff. Gradually the message was getting across: we must change and live, or remain as we are and wither away. It was heartening for me to note how the two bodies – those at the centre and those in the dioceses – united and in many significant ways invigorated an embattled Church.

I was disappointed by the defensiveness, myopia and instinct for self-preservation which followed the disclosure of the Commissioners' losses. Some diocesan spokespersons viewed the matter in local terms only, expressing fears such as: 'We shall be bankrupt. We will have to lay off clergy. The lay people can't be expected to give any more.' The same mentality prevailed at the centre, where there was resistance to the logic of change, and arguments that further change could not be absorbed, and low morale made it impossible to take on fresh responsibilities. Philip Mawer, commenting on this period, remarked that he knew how Sisyphus must have felt when the boulder kept driving him down the hill. Nevertheless, we were definitely winning. The consultations were paying off, and our steady resolve to involve the entire Church in understanding the problems as well as contributing towards the answers was, increasingly, being met by faith and commitment.

Another result of the reports, particularly the Lambeth Group report, was that the House of Commons Select Committee on Social Security decided to investigate the matter, as part of a wider review it had been undertaking on the funding of pensions. On 26 April 1994 I had the dubious honour of being the first Archbishop of Canterbury to face public questioning in such a forum. Chaired by Frank Field MP, the Committee subjected a number of us to searching and fierce interrogation. The appointment of Coopers & Lybrand was questioned. The Chairman offered the view that 'some of us felt that Coopers & Lybrand ought to be investigated, not just the Commissioners'. John Waine agreed to some extent that, as auditors of the Commissioners, Coopers & Lybrand should have raised the alarm much earlier. I took a different approach, telling the Committee that 'soundings from a wide circle of friends, colleagues and professionals in the City gave me confidence in appointing them'. However, the important thing was not to dwell on past mistakes, but to learn from them and build a better future for the Church and the Commissioners.

The Select Committee was most helpful in terms of urging the Church to provide adequate pensions for its servants. Frank Field was pessimistic about the ability of ordinary churchgoers to take on the extra burden of providing funds for pensions. In a bleak aside, he prophesied that the Commissioners would prove to have done more damage to the Church of England than Oliver Cromwell ever did. Philip Mawer, John Waine and I disagreed. John replied that 'The Church Commissioners are not the Church of England. The Commissioners have been major contributors to the ministry of the Church of England, but increasingly over the years parishioners have given more. It is within our competence to manage this. After all, other denominations have had to do so, and we have been somewhat cosseted.' I agreed with this assessment: 'Three-quarters of all giving comes from the parishes. I am quite confident that the Church can find more money. We are looking at in the region of £2.70 per church member to close the gap. It is not a large amount.'

The meeting with the Select Committee ended on an amusing note. As we stood up to leave, Frank Field gratuitously offered me some advice concerning press criticism: 'Don't let the buggers get you down!'

Feeling that this ought to be played with a straight bat but with a smile, I replied, 'Thank you very much indeed, I shall bear that in mind' – as I have endeavoured to do ever since.

The Lambeth Group report and its accompanying document, the Coopers & Lybrand analysis, dealt with the immediate problems but could not be concerned with the future. The nettle had to be grasped. As it was presently structured, the Church was dysfunctional – it had to undergo a drastic reform.

First of all, the issue of pensions had to be addressed with the utmost urgency. Actuaries were appointed to examine critically the ability of the Commissioners to maintain their present level of giving to those retired. Within a few months their report confirmed all we had feared – that pensions alone would soon gobble up all the Commissioners' resources. This survey was to lead to the creation of two pension funds. The first, still funded by the Church Com-missioners, for pensionable service before 1 January 1998. A second fund, for service thereafter, was administered by the Pensions Board and paid for by the dioceses (and ultimately the parishes). The impli-cation of this was that, at a stroke, roughly half of the Commissioners' assets were committed to being spent over at least the next five decades to pay for pensions earned before January 1998. The remaining funds, comprising some £2 billion, were earmarked as investment for the Church's present and future ministry. This meant that the Church of England would continue to be endowed by the giving of past generations but at a greatly reduced level, with far more of the responsibility for funding the Church's mission and ministry resting on the Church of today.

By the end of the 1990s the Commissioners' contribution to clergy stipends had reduced from 45 per cent to 22 per cent, and their overall contribution to stipends and pensions from 61 per cent to 42 per cent. Over that period, dioceses and parishes took over the £75 million per year's worth of funding ministry which was formerly the responsibility of the Commissioners. Such a change was a remarkable testimony to the commitment of the average churchgoer. Indeed, it represented a historic shift not only in responsibility for the funding of the Church, but in the centre of gravity of the Church, from national to diocesan and parochial level. The day on which the *Financial Times* broke the story of the Commissioners' losses may in time come to be seen as the day the Church of England grew up.

There was one final matter to be examined, and that was the matter of Ashford Great Park, in the diocese of Canterbury. The background to this sorry saga was that in 1988 the Commissioners bought three fields for the tidy sum of £3 million with development in mind, although planning permission had not been given. The site was next to the railway station serving Eurostar, and, not unreasonably, the Commissioners had concluded that property in Ashford was likely to be a splendid investment for the Church. There were numerous attempts to gain planning permission in 1988, 1989 and 1992. By 1992 nearly £90 million had been spent in professional fees, interest and management fees with no development in sight, and without planning permission the investment appeared doomed to fail.

The newly formed Audit Committee was given the task of examining the matter in detail, and commissioned Sven Tester, formerly a partner at KPMG, to investigate the failure, which he duly did in 1996 with professional thoroughness. His report revealed that although there was no question of activity that could be classed as criminal, there was plenty of evidence that mistakes had been made. I found it difficult not to agree with the forthright comments of Norman Baker MP in his questioning of the Second Church Estates Commissioner in the House of Commons on Monday, 16 March 1998: 'Will the hon. gentleman confirm that as a consequence of this fiasco, the Church Commissioners have lost an absolute fortune, not least because they acted as guarantors for unsecured loans of £87 million, against agricultural land valued at £3 million? Does not this represent excessive incompetence, and can he guarantee that such a fiasco can never again occur?'

I mentioned earlier that this entire episode highlighted the fragmentation of responsibility and authority in the Church, particularly at national level. The Lambeth Group had recommended that the wider organisational issues raised by the affair should be examined. But what kind of reforms did the Church require? That could only be decided by a thorough investigation of the issues involved.

On 16 February 1994 the Archbishop of York and I established the Turnbull Commission, with the aim to 'review the machinery for central policy and resource management in the Church of England, and to make recommendations for improving its effectiveness in supporting the ministry and mission of the Church to the nation as a whole'. Chaired with great distinction by the Bishop of Durham, Michael Turnbull, the Commission did not disappoint the Church with the thoroughness of its report, *Working as One Body*, which appeared the following autumn.

I was kept closely informed of the work of the Commission, and supported its fundamental recommendations, which addressed the endemic problem of dispersed leadership in the Church. The main proposal was the establishment of a seventeen-member National Council chaired by the Archbishop of Canterbury with the Archbishop of York as Vice-Chair. The National Council would bring together the Church Commissioners, Synod and House of Bishops, so that important decisions could be made together. The Council would replace a number of existing committees and bodies, such as the General Synod Standing Committee and Policy Committee and the Central Board of Finance. The aim, in short, was to move away from a culture of committees to an environment more conducive to deciding priorities and focusing vision. One of the Turnbull Commission's most radical recommendations was the appointment of eight members who would be drawn from the vast numbers of skilled and experienced lay people outside the ranks of General Synod. They would be appointed by the Archbishops. The aim of this was to bring in fresh ideas and expert opinion to help the Church in its task. It was a step in the right direction.

When the Turnbull report, *Working as One Body*, was published, steps had to be taken to get the reaction of the Church as a whole before the final step of legal ratification. Reaction to the report was generally positive, although I was amazed that some chose to call it 'bureaucratic', and that this was picked up in the press and regurgitated for years to come. If by 'bureaucratic' our critics assumed the Council would be a 'talking shop' or concerned with management only, the report itself nailed these criticisms firmly. It reduced rather than increased the number of separate bodies. My aim, and that of the Archbishop of York, was to lead the Church, not merely to manage its affairs or deal with its committees. Our common desire for the Council was that it would relate very closely to the House of Bishops and General Synod, but would be a creature of neither.

In February 1998 *Working as One Body* metamorphosed into the National Institutions Measure, and was agreed by General Synod and later by Parliament. The National Council was renamed the Archbishops' Council and given its specific remit to help the Church at the national level to work more effectively as one body. Philip Mawer was appointed Secretary General of the Council, a well-deserved recognition of his crucial role in helping to shape the proposals into a workable whole.

I was very keen that the Archbishop of York and I would be joint Presidents of the Council and share the leadership of this fledgling body. Inevitably there was a price to be paid. Synod wanted to be more involved, and after some tense debates the Council ended up containing more Synod representatives than either I or the Archbishop of York would have liked. I say this not because of an animus against Synod, but purely on the grounds that more Synod representatives on the Council meant fewer people from outside the ranks of the Church establishment. As Anthony Trollope once observed of an Archbishop of his time: 'We hate an evil and we hate a change. Hating the evil most, we make the change but we make it as small as possible.' In my judgement, whilst the National Institutions Measure captured the spirit of *Working as One Body*, I regretted Synod's unwillingness to go the whole way with it.

Looking back on the ferment of the 1990s and all the changes which were introduced, I have no regrets about any decisions I made. The mission of the Church always came first. It had been evident for years that its structures impeded its mission. It was crucial to make the Commissioners once again part of the Church of England and subject to the whole. It was also necessary to find ways to bring the central organisations of the Church together in common service to the gospel, Church and nation.

I can take some satisfaction in the creation of the Archbishops' Council. Of course the journey will continue, with further change and evolution in the Church's institutions. I would be very disappointed and alarmed if that were not so. But the essential shape of what was achieved will continue to serve the Church well for decades to come.

11

Bishop in Mission

'Tell all the Truth but tell it slant –
Success in Circuit lies
Too bright for our infirm Delight
The Truth's superb surprise
As Lightning to the Children eased
With explanation kind
The Truth must dazzle gradually
Or every man be blind –'

Emily Dickinson, 'Tell all the Truth but tell it slant'

ON BECOMING ARCHBISHOP I had to face up to a stark reality. The statistics of long-term decline mocked the Church's claim that it possessed good news. Judged by any standard of growth the Church of England had failed, and was continuing to fail to win the hearts and minds of the English people. Whatever 'good news' the Church believed, we were failing to touch the hearts and minds of our contemporaries.

The emphasis I placed on evangelism in my enthronement address was in fact inspired by the ministry of St Augustine, the first Archbishop of Canterbury. Although there is much that we do not know about Augustine, the timid missionary monk sent by Pope Gregory to re-establish the Church in England, one thing we do know is that he was obedient to the command, in spite of his weakness and fears. As I considered the impressive list of men who had followed Augustine as Archbishop, I was surprised by how few of them appeared to have seen their priority as reaching out to others. Theologians, teachers, administrators, leaders and statesmen they may have been – but none, as far as I could discover, consciously viewed himself as a missionary following the example of St Augustine. Yet this, above all, was my goal. With all my heart I desired to communicate the claims of Jesus Christ to ordinary men and women.

The overwhelming nature of the challenge was obvious, and it was clear that no single person – however senior – could possibly attempt it alone. The entire Church had to be mobilised. As I saw it there were many complex reasons for the failures of the past, for some of which the Church was blameless. There was the impact of the eighteenth-century Enlightenment on modern thought, with its implicit denial of the supernatural. Thinkers such as David Hume were particularly critical of Deism, which was the main expression of European Christianity in the eighteenth century – a vision of God which saw Him as the expert watchmaker and absentee landlord rather than the Creator, omnipresent in His creation – and this scepticism became rooted in the intellectual life of our nation. Despite the efforts of the evangelical revival and its Catholic equivalent, the Oxford Movement, scepticism became embedded in British culture. While the Enlightenment ignited this mood, Charles Darwin's great work *On the Origin of Species*, published in 1859, swept it aside and destroyed the faith of many.

Matthew Arnold, a devout yet unorthodox Christian to the end of his life, viewed Darwin's theories as a shocking challenge to belief in God. His magnificent poem *Dover Beach*, written on his honeymoon, points pessimistically to some of the implications of Darwin's discoveries. Can the Church claim with confidence that God loves and cares for humanity, when the new world view suggests a cruel and uncaring universe? Where is God in all of this? How secure is our reading of scripture? Arnold reached into the security of human love for solace and meaning:

Ah, love, let us be true
To one another! For the world, which seems
To lie before us like a land of dreams,
So various, so beautiful, so new,
Hath really neither joy, nor love, nor light,
Nor certitude, nor peace, nor help for pain;
And we are here as on a darkling plain
Swept with confused alarms of struggle and flight,
Where ignorant armies clash by night.

This is scarcely the stuff that honeymoon poetry is meant to be about; Arnold was sensing that something profound and disturbing was happening to the 'Sea of Faith', which had hitherto seemed so comforting and secure. All that he could now hear was 'its melancholy, long withdrawing roar'.

While the Church struggled with these questions, others, in the tradition of Thomas Huxley, found no place for God in their concept of life. Typical of their generation in the 1920s, the philosophy of the Bloomsbury set had little sympathy for faith and Church. Virginia Woolf's reaction to the news that T.S. Eliot had become a Christian was one of profound horror: 'He has become an Anglo-Catholic believer in God and immortality and goes to Church ... there's something obscene in a living person sitting by the fire and believing in God.'

It cannot be said that, in the eighty or so years since then, the challenges that the natural sciences offer an intelligent faith have lessened. Indeed, the amazing discoveries humankind has made in recent years make the issues far more complex, and yet more exciting. This has become the most interesting era for Christians and believers to explore the authenticity of faith, and it is clear now that science and faith are no longer on opposite sides of the argument. There are many scientists who are fervent believers in a personal God, and who would want to say with Albert Einstein that 'Religion without science is blind; science without religion is lame.' What unites all searchers for truth is the incomprehensible mystery of all things. 'Why does the universe go to all the bother of existing?' asked Stephen Hawking.

'What is it that breathes fire into the equations and makes a universe for them to describe?'

That wondering metaphysical question, asked by those of us who have taken the trouble to consider the heavens on a clear evening, is the very same one that the philosopher Spinoza asked two centuries ago: 'Why does this exist rather than that?' We might want to put the question another way round, to face directly the problem of God: 'Why do we have such incredible order that allows us to talk of "laws of the universe", suggesting that an intelligent Mind is behind all things? Yet is this contradicted by the universe's chilling indifference to the fate of its inhabitants?' That there are no easy resolutions to such questions is not an argument against belief. However, when the questions emerge from an agnostic culture, people are robbed of the chance to consider them without bias. As I saw it, the role of the Church, through its ministers and members, must be to confront the issues in a spirit of enquiry and eagerness to impart what we have learned about God and His revelation to us. As Michael Ramsey put it so evocatively: 'We state and commend the faith only insofar as we put ourselves with loving sympathy inside the doubts of the doubter, the questions of the questioner, and the loneliness of those who have lost the way.'

This intellectual and apologetic task was not the only challenge to be addressed; there was also the issue of culture. As someone who had become a Christian on the housing estates of Dagenham, I knew all too well that the Church was estranged from the culture and life of the vast majority of the people it served. Nevertheless, as Grace Davie has shown in her book *Religion in Britain Since 1945* (subtitled 'Believing Without Belonging'), decline in institutional belonging is not limited to religious communities. Many groups in our society – including trade unions, political parties and voluntary organisations – have seen their memberships drop since the last world war. In a later book, *Europe: The Exceptional Case* (2001), Davie argues that the decline in church attendance has not been as dramatic as that of other groups – in fact, the churches have fared reasonably well.

Yet it is hardly good news to be told that your organisation is 'dying, but not as fast as the trade unions'. One could not, and should not, infer from the decline in church attendance that people lack interest in spiritual things. I knew from my own experience of life in the East End of London that people prayed and had 'religious' yearnings that institutional faith had not satisfied.

I decided as a missionary Archbishop to exercise my leadership in two focused ways – first by example, and then by encouraging the wider Church to be more confident and effective in its role as a missionary organisation. The personal side of this was relatively easy, in that I continued the Teaching Missions I had developed as Bishop of Bath and Wells. The traditional role of a Bishop did not satisfy me, within its main work of confirmation and the instituting of vicars. While many Bishops did a superb job of working in the wider community and representing the Church in secular organisations, that did not go far enough in making the connection between the Church's faith and the general public. Clergy and congregations, in my opinion, needed their Bishops to lead mission directly, and to help parishes engage with their communities.

I found the Teaching Missions deeply satisfying and challenging. For a start, they earthed me in a way that few other forms of a Bishop's ministry can. To go into a sixth-form class and face the searching questions of young people is not the usual comfortable pastoral area for a Bishop to be. Sixth-formers are noted for their indifference to titles and status, and once encouragement is given to ask any question they like, they do so with vigour and deep intelligence. I remember one school near Bearsted in Kent where a boy of seventeen kept pursuing me with questions about the problem of pain, to the extent that the headmaster eventually had to silence him because he was hogging the questions. I enjoyed his persistent and intelligent questioning. Following the discussion it became clear that the boy's interest was sparked by his mother's plight – she was dying of cancer, and he wanted reassurance for her. Nothing it seems is ever only intellectual.

During the course of Teaching Mission weekends the small team supporting me would visit schools, nursing homes and clubs. We would go to pubs and have a drink with local residents. Breakfast meetings also always formed part of the weekends. Normally, however, the purpose of such 'teaching' weekends was to provide me with an opportunity to share my faith and to encourage it in others. Invariably they would lead to new believers and strengthened congregations. Eileen and I would usually return to work on Monday shattered but curiously refreshed by the opportunity to have met others in such an intense and personal way.

While this personal ministry was useful, and was something I was anxious that other Bishops should develop in their own way, clearly something more radical was needed as far as the national Church was concerned. The question puzzled me deeply. How on earth could this sleeping giant of the Church of England get on its feet and declare itself to the world? To hand, of course, was the commanding mandate from the Lambeth Conference of 1988 encouraging the Anglican Communion to make that 'shift from maintenance to mission'. Endorsed by General Synod, the Church of England had committed itself to the Decade of Evangelism. The problem was that no resources were committed to bringing this change of culture in the Church about, and not once during the next ten years did the Church's Parliament, General Synod, move beyond talk to action, and allocate funds to this clear need. Alternative means had to be found to discharge this mission. The means came in two surprising forms – through the human gifts of three able men, and through financial resources raised with the help of the Lambeth Fund.

The men concerned were Bishop Michael Marshall, Canon Dr Michael Green, and Martin Cavender. The 'two Michaels' as they were called were well-known and effective communicators working in America and Canada at the time. I knew both of them well, and respected them hugely. When I learned that they were eager to return to their mother Church and use their gifts I met them individually and offered them the opportunity to work with me in spearheading an initiative that became known as 'Springboard'. Bishop Michael Marshall, formerly Bishop of Woolwich, rooted in the Anglo-Catholic tradition, was a gifted preacher and evangelist who was at the time leading the Anglican Institute in the United States. Canon Michael Green, my former teacher, and my Principal at St John's, Nottingham, was teaching at Regent College, Vancouver. Michael Green, also a brilliant communicator and scholar, represented the evangelical tradition with its emphasis on conversion and mission. Inseparable from his ministry was his wife Rosemary, whose shrewdness and teaching ability made her an important part of the team. My aim in bringing together such able teachers and evangelists from quite different traditions was to signal the importance of those traditions – often seen as bitter rivals – working with each other for the sake of the Church. But evangelists are notoriously difficult to direct and organise, however willing and enthusiastic they may be. To make fullest use of the two Michaels' gifts I invited Martin Cavender, Legal Registrar to the diocese of Bath and Wells, to be Executive Director of Springboard, a role that he was to exercise with distinction for the next twelve years.

Springboard was launched with great publicity in St Paul's Cathedral on 23 September 1992. In my charge to the evangelists I stressed the need to stay in touch with the needs of ordinary clergy – to affirm and support them in their ministry. I offered the view that no special gift of evangelism could replace the quiet mission going on in every parish and church up and down the land. Their job must be to work alongside the many thousands of Christians who longed for a more dynamic and relevant Church. My charge to the Church took a different form – it was our task to value and cherish these gifted men whose task would often be lonely and at times controversial.

Indeed, the initiative was not launched without controversy. In the House of Bishops some of the more senior Bishops greeted it with scepticism or even apathy. 'It's all been tried before and failed,' was the muttered comment of one elderly Bishop who left the room early after a presentation by the Springboard team. John Habgood, the Archbishop of York, although from the liberal tradition of the Church, entered fully into the vision and was a great supporter in 'selling' Springboard to many of the Bishops.

As I saw it, evangelism was not divorced from the wider mission of God's love in action in the world. It is the timeless task of sharing what one knows and has discovered. In the words of the Indian theologian D.T. Niles, evangelism is simply 'one beggar telling another beggar where to find bread'. That means evangelism can never be divorced from social justice. What my predecessor had started with *Faith in the City* I was committed to carrying forward. That too was a vital part of the Church's outreach to society. Nigel McCulloch, newly appointed Bishop of Wakefield, was a sparkling and encouraging presence in the House of Bishops. Although from the Catholic end of the Church, he was in no doubt about the need to present the Christian faith with conviction, zeal and love. He had already declared Wakefield a 'missionary diocese', and had warned that unless mission was taken deeply into the heart of every Anglican Christian in it, there would be no Wakefield diocese in twenty-five years' time. Although the House of Bishops was by no means totally convinced that my initiative was necessary, the majority were prepared to lend support.

There was controversy outside the Church as well. Leaders of other faiths were alarmed that this emphasis on mission meant that their communities would be specifically targeted. When Sheikh Zaki Badawi, the foremost Muslim leader in Britain, voiced his concern in a radio interview, I arranged to meet him. Zaki, as he was known to all his friends, was an alert and articulate spokesman for Islam. I reassured him that other faith groups were not the principal target of Springboard. He acknowledged that Islam was also a missionary religion, and that 'mission' itself was not the issue – it is how that mission is conducted. I explained to him my understanding of mission: it is about God's gift of Jesus in sharing our human condition; it means that no one is outside the range of God's love. I went on to develop a point I had made in my enthronement address, that evangelism for me is not thrusting the message down the throats of unsuspecting people, but God's invitation to all to consider His message made through Jesus Christ. This involves a risk, because if I want to invite non-Christians to consider the Christian faith, I must not avoid the challenge that other faiths offer me. We agreed that deepening such dialogue was essential. But, I added, 'Let me reassure you that Christianity's appeal is to all. Springboard's primary attention is not on minority non-Christians who live amongst us, but on the twenty-five million baptised Anglicans in England whose commitment to institutional faith is slight.' Zaki went away satisfied, and a friendship began that day that would deepen in the years to come.

For myself, the questions raised then about mission suggested a particularly relevant question: In a multicultural world such as ours, is it any longer possible to present a plausible case for evangelism? Yet mission is the heart of the Christian faith, and proceeds from our theology of God. It is His mission that the Church shares, and by word and deed we are compelled to enter into the movement of God's love and 'witness' to it. Indeed, 'witness', in my opinion, is the most important and basic element in the life of any disciple, and is the least controversial form that evangelism can take.

The horrors some associate with evangelism usually stem from crude, arrogant and ignorant attempts that do more harm than good to the Church's witness. I was able to give Zaki an example from his own faith. Just two days before he came to see me, a group of Muslim students accosted me outside a conference centre where I was going to give an address on inter-faith matters. I was told in no uncertain terms that 'There is no God but Allah and Mohammed is His faithful prophet. Islam is on the increase throughout the world and it is only a matter of time before Christianity is evicted from this country.' I endeavoured to make this a conversation in which differences could be aired, but their minds were already made up that Islam is superior to Christianity. Zaki saw the point: true sharing of faith emerges from honest dialogue, and we have to confront intolerance and bigotry wherever they appear in civil society.

But was changing the culture of Anglicanism equally necessary? Compared with Pentecostalism, Anglicanism can seem cold and lifeless – not least in terms of worship – but in fact the same passion for God is found within it. The difference may be that the missionary impulse of Anglicanism has never allowed it to separate evangelism from the broader mission of God in caring for others and showing that love in medical care, education and social witness.

Over the next decade the Springboard team made a magnificent contribution to the life of the Church of England. After four years the two Michaels moved on to other work, and Martin Cavender gathered other teachers and evangelists around him. The work broadened, and became overwhelmingly popular and accepted by all the Bishops. But funding Springboard was a critical preoccupation throughout my time as Archbishop. It was my desire that, at a time when the Church was under great financial pressure, I should offer Springboard as a gift to it. Over the next ten years, through supper parties at Lambeth Palace and the generosity of many friends, some £7 million was raised to keep Springboard and other personal projects going.

Apart from myself, the initiative was almost entirely lay-led. Lay people who were willing to support Eileen and me in our personal ministry – by prayer, by offering their gifts on occasions and by financial assistance – became members of the Lambeth Partnership. On my retirement in 2002 the partners numbered well over 350, and had been a great and generous source of support. At the heart of the Partnership was Ewan Harper, later Sir Ewan, whose encouragement and enterprise was outstanding.

Inspiring support and unfailing co-operation came from the Chairmen of the Fund and Partnership, Lord Hector Laing and Lord Brian Griffiths. Hector, who had built United Biscuits into an internationally successful firm, was shocked by what he considered the amateur and inefficient management of the Church by the Church

Commissioners, and became a great supporter of my attempts to reform the central structures. The office of Archbishop of Canterbury he believed to be 'disgracefully under-resourced'. From the beginning of Robert Runcie's time and throughout my own Hector endeavoured to raise funds to improve facilities at Lambeth Palace and enable the Archbishops to do their work. His favourite saying about the art of leadership was: 'Only do what YOU have to do.' I learned a great deal from that principle of focusing sharply on one's role and delegating what was unnecessary to it. Brian Griffiths' leadership was also deeply appreciated. Formerly the head of Margaret Thatcher's Policy Unit and a Professor at the London School of Economics before becoming a partner at Goldman Sachs, Brian had humble roots. Brought up in Forestfach, in north Swansea, he had come to Anglicanism from the Chapel tradition. Whenever Brian chaired a Partners' evening his Welsh enthusiasm proved to be a galvanising force. Behind the scenes of the Partnership was Rachel Mallows, our remarkable secretary, whose calm efficiency and attractive personality made sure that the growing body of 'partners' was cared for and managed.

Springboard was not the only initiative developing in the Church. I had always been interested in alternative forms of worship, believing that contemporary idioms had to be found for the substance of faith. In the 1980s I had got to know Robert Warren, who had led St Thomas's Crookes into astonishing growth through new forms of worship. No one could dispute the fact that St Thomas's was touching the roots of modern culture in an impressive form. Sometime in 1989, when I was still Bishop of Bath and Wells, Robert asked if he could see me with some of his staff. It was an encouraging meeting, in which Robert told me of the impact his church was making on the area and the significant results arising from experiments in what was later to be called the 'Nine O'Clock Service' (NOS). I was introduced to Chris Brain, who was being groomed to take over the experiment. He seemed to me a capable and interesting young man with a real desire to communicate a living faith.

Robert described the way a new service was developing after the evening service at St Thomas's. A group of young Christians, interested in influencing the many nightclubbing young people who found church life totally meaningless and irrelevant, started to explore worship in multimedia forms. Worship therefore flowed from the way young people had experienced or thought about God. There was no mistaking the radical form in which their worship was being developed. An NOS pamphlet described the atmosphere as 'a sea of paradox – high tech, but with the ambience of a crypt. It is designed to be a place where beat, meditation, dance and light can reconnect people with God, transforming their vision of the world.' Robert was excited about the way the experiment was going, and as I had every confidence in him and a reference group which included Graham Cray, the Principal of Ridley Hall, Cambridge, and John Rogerson, Professor of Biblical Studies at Sheffield University, I was happy to give it my blessing.

I watched with interest as the Nine O'Clock Service developed a life of its own, eventually outgrowing St Thomas's and moving to separate premises. Central to the experiment was a commitment to living in community. This was quite a common feature of charismatic life in the 1970s and eighties, and often drew single and sometimes lonely people into an extended family life.

In August 1995 I was shocked to learn that NOS had collapsed after serious allegations had been made, and the diocese under its Bishop, David Lunn, was dealing with the pastoral, legal and religious implications. It was clear that this was a major calamity for the Church, but any possible damage to vulnerable human beings was my principal concern. Where were the structures of accountability one would expect in any Church of England parish, through churchwardens or equivalent leaders? It was a humiliating blow to the Church's attempt to communicate its faith in a contemporary mode. In several interviews I was asked if this amounted to a condemnation of the Church. My reply was that that would be like blaming the Stock Exchange for the collapse that same year of Baring's Bank.

'One failure', I declared, 'does not make the whole movement invalid.'

I met several of the individuals involved, and was disappointed by their failure to acknowledge that to some degree they were culpable of misbehaviour too. They blamed the Church for their plight, and were seeking compensation. I was unable to accept this, and made myself unpopular with them by strongly challenging their assertions. They were, I said, intelligent and articulate people. How could they say that they were misled and duped by the Church? They were responsible adults. If Christian morality had any part to play in their faith, surely they too must share some of the blame? There seemed no willingness to hear this. Nevertheless, I was determined that lessons should be learned from the affair and that any other experiments in the Church of England should be properly supervised.

Despite the failure of NOS, all was not lost. Many other churches up and down the country were quietly learning to connect with modern culture. As for St Thomas's Crookes, it is now one of the largest churches in the United Kingdom, with an impressive ministry to young and old.

A more impressive, lasting and honourable initiative that I was anxious to support was 'Alpha', which originated in Holy Trinity, Brompton – like St Thomas's Crookes an evangelical church with a charismatic style. Led by the Reverend Sandy Miller, whom I first met when he was a theological student at Cranmer Hall, Durham, HTB, as it is widely known, has become a significant world church. The Reverend Nicky Gumbel, Sandy's colleague, is the author of Alpha, which has caught the imagination of thousands of churches and influenced thousands of lives. The idea itself is very simple, and startlingly similar to the meal that Jesus taught his disciples to keep in memory of him. Alpha is a course designed to help people understand the Christian faith, and its genius lies in the fusing of a home, a meal and attractive and well-led teaching. It continues to be a remarkable tool for the Christian faith, and is now used by all traditions. As Springboard developed, a strong partnership emerged between it and Alpha.

Springboard was not the only initiative that flowed from the Lambeth Partnership. A close friend, Dr John Ledger, was asked to lead a project encouraging parishes to develop imaginative ways of connecting with local communities through supper parties. The extra money available allowed me to send a Chaplain, the Reverend Philip Warner, to Belgrade to facilitate relations between the Church of England and the Serbian Orthodox Church, which had been weakened through the Kosovo war. We were able to create a Millennium Youth Choir, led by the Royal School of Church Music. Martin Cavender, a lawyer before he was asked to lead Springboard, agreed to go to Rwanda as my emissary to help the Church there through a constitutional crisis following the genocide. A tape of the Turnbull recommendations concerning the reform of Church structures was sent to all parishes. Funding for an officer, Stephen Lyanas, to liaise with the government regarding plans for the millennium and events at the Dome was largely provided by the Partnership. All these projects were fully backed by this loyal band of lay people, whose contribution was considerable.

Another critical initiative of Springboard was to help the Church face the crisis in children and youth work. The phrase often used in Anglican circles that 'The Church is one generation away from extinction' clearly expressed a reality. The statistics revealed the staggering crisis in the Church, and report after report had been earnestly debated in Synod, then quietly shelved. Gavin Reid, whom I appointed as suffragan Bishop of Maidstone, drew attention repeatedly to the fact that barely one in three churches had any viable youth work to speak of, but his words went unheeded, as had those of too many before him.

I wondered how I could set an example to stress the importance of young people in the Church, and Eileen and I decided that one visible symbol would be to take a thousand of them to Taizé, in southern France. Taizé is known the world over for its deep commitment to unity, and especially to the role of young people in the Church. It was founded after the war by a young Swiss man, Roger

Schutz-Marsauch – known to millions as Brother Roger – who yearned for reconciliation between Christians. He had seen what war could do to human beings: not just the broken bodies, but the broken dreams of a new world order and the shattered hopes of peace. He had personally helped many Jews escape death by providing them with a hiding place. At Taizé he had gathered together a few like-minded friends who began to live as a community of prayer and worship.

With my small staff taking the lead, we decided to invite each of the forty-four dioceses in the Church of England to nominate twenty young people between the ages of sixteen and twenty-three to accompany us. This seemingly simple objective itself made me aware of the crisis at the heart of the Church, as a significant number of dioceses reported that they could not raise twenty young people. I was appalled by this, and made my disappointment public. It seemed beyond belief that dioceses with hundreds of churches were so short of young people.

In the end we did gather together a thousand young people, and had an inspiring week. What came across through speaking with so many of the youngsters was the way our churches were alienating them – through inhospitable services, through lack of pastoral care, through the inability of many parish priests to relate to them and through the sheer loneliness of being young in a predominantly elderly environment. One girl of seventeen said: 'I'm the only young person in my church, and I have no one of my own age to talk with. I'm glad to have come to Taizé and see with joy that I'm not alone!'

Following Taizé I decided to ask Pete Ward, a former member of my congregation at St Nic's, Durham, now leader of Oxford Youth Works, if he would consider becoming my Officer for Young People. Pete was overjoyed to take on this responsibility, and a creative partnership commenced between him and the national network of Youth Officers. His unorthodox approach had made Oxford Youth Works a great success in reaching out to young people, and he had huge respect in the professional world of youth workers. He shared my concern that there were alarming conceptual and cultural gaps between the world of the Church and that of young people. We agreed that his task was to draw attention energetically to the needs of young people among youth workers and leaders of the Church. Over the next five years Pete did this with great ability in a variety of different ways. Not only did he promote the work of young people at many church events, he also promoted courses in youth training and education that eventually led to a full degree course affiliated to King's College London. In 2000 I had the pleasure of awarding the first degrees in youth ministry and education to thirty young people from a variety of Anglican and Baptist colleges from all over the country.

But the event that did most to raise the profile of young people's work was 'Time of Our Lives' in 1999. The aim was to invite one hundred young people from each of the dioceses to London for a four-day Celebration of Young People over the spring bank-holiday weekend. It was not my desire to charge them what might be beyond their means, so £400,000 was required to cover all costs apart from travel. Again the Lambeth Fund and Partnership rallied round, and the money was raised.

The weekend began with a rock concert on the Friday evening in the Royal Albert Hall, followed by almost a hundred seminars the following day in such august centres as the Houses of Parliament, Methodist Central Hall and Lambeth Palace. Saturday evening was time off, with various leisure options available in Lambeth Palace. In the gardens Courtney Pine and his jazz group held a concert for several thousand, while in the main building contemporary films were shown. The evening culminated with a quiet, meditative service in the chapel. On Sunday the young people, staying in the homes of churchgoers in nearby parishes, attended the churches of their hosts, and that evening special services took place at St Paul's Cathedral, Southwark Cathedral and Westminster Abbey. On the final day, a warm and sunny bank-holiday Monday, the Archbishop of York and

I led a communion service in the grounds of the Palace. In my address I urged the many young people present to take the news of the weekend back to their parishes, and to encourage their clergy to be more adventurous in reaching out to young people in all sections of their communities.

Although Time of Our Lives was generally a spectacular success, there were two disappointments. Again we were let down by some dioceses failing to support the event with total enthusiasm, with the result that our initial aim of five thousand young people was not achieved. The excuses they offered variously concerned distance, or imminent examinations, or the view that 'people do not like London-based events'. Consequently fewer than four thousand booked in advance, though many young members of London churches swelled the numbers. I felt disappointed for the young people that, once again, they had been let down by the institution.

There was a pitiable sequel to this a few months later. At the 1999 July Sessions of General Synod at York the delegates applauded Time of Our Lives, and urged that I should mount a similar event in a few years' time. I agreed, on condition that the dioceses should cover the cost entirely, which would work out at a mere £5000 per diocese. I then wrote to each Bishop and diocese asking for a commitment to pay the amount in two instalments – the first within that calendar year, and the remainder shortly before the event. It was no surprise to me when the response from half the dioceses was that they could not afford it. Once more, vision was blunted by short-sightedness.

Another disappointment related to press coverage. I was well aware that in many parts of the land the Church was getting on with its work with joy and vision, but it was difficult to get positive stories in the national press. I and the organisers therefore worked hard to attract the interest of the papers to Time of Our Lives, and the initial response was very positive. Here at last was a story worth celebrating, as so many young people showed their commitment to the Christian faith. But on the first evening of the celebration a bomb was planted in a Soho pub, killing three people and injuring dozens more, so our event was well below press radar that weekend. I certainly had opportunities to speak to TV and radio channels, but they were to do with the Soho bombing rather than Time of Our Lives. Later we would find out that a young man of twenty-two had committed that terrible crime, as well as two other bombings – the same age as many of those attending our Celebration; perhaps in its own way this signposted the importance of the Church's work among the young.

Throughout my time as Archbishop, and indeed, before it too, the press focused on the theme of decline, by which they meant numerical decline. This was entirely understandable, and was one of the principal reasons why I was putting so much effort into finding ways of promoting mission. As I saw it, the real issue related to how one measured growth. Numerical increase is only one way of measuring an effective organisation. This is where things got interesting, because through the 1990s ordination figures rose steadily, and congregations valiantly met the rising costs of supporting the ministry of the Church. As has been seen, the loss of up to £800 million in the early nineties led to a shift of financial support from the Church Commissioners to the parishes, and they rose to the challenge. The facts are hardly indicative of a declining institution; indeed they show that there is a depth and a resilience in the Church that many did not perceive.

This led the newly formed Archbishops' Council to ask questions about the way statistics were collected, and about the changing pattern of church attendance and worshipping life. Relevant to this was the way in which society itself was changing. The – to my mind regrettable – deregulation of restrictions on trading on Sunday under John Major's government led, as some of us feared it would, to that day becoming just another day of the week, which had an inevitable impact on Sunday attendance.

Gradually, however, statistics began to emerge that indicated that more and more congregations were responding to the challenges to be 'seven-day-a-week' churches. The research showed that although at the end of the twentieth century people were attending church less frequently on Sundays, weekly and monthly attendance figures presented a more encouraging picture of Christianity in England. Statistical analysis in July 2000 revealed that mid-week attendance added 16 per cent to the numbers of those who attended church on Sundays. Just as significantly, a picture of strength in depth emerged, as local ministry teams involving considerable numbers of lay people grew throughout the nineties. At least half of the dioceses now have ordination schemes focusing on local ministry, known as 'Ordained Local Ministry'. My experience of those entering this form of ministry in the diocese of Canterbury has left me in no doubt about the impressive quality of a goodly number of men and women.

The wider picture also challenges the received opinion that the Christian faith is on the way out in this country. The 2001 government census disclosed that 72 per cent of the population call themselves Christian, and Church research has revealed that one in two adults consider themselves Anglican. A quarter say they attend church once a month whilst 60 per cent say they pray regularly. Whatever we may deduce from these figures, they certainly do not suggest that Britain is now a post-Christian or secular nation, even if they do show that the Church still has an enormous task in making faith relevant to life.

12

Power and Politicians

'Those who become Prince . . . by virtuous means . . . achieve
their princedom with difficulty.'

Machiavelli, Il Principe

THE WORD 'ESTABLISHMENT' has many different meanings. To
the average person it represents the ordering of society, in which
certain classes possess institutional authority. For some it is the vestige
of a bygone age, and the sooner it is gone the better. For others it
is a benign way of conveying order and status alongside the level
playing-field of parliamentary democracy.

'Establishment' also refers to the peculiar role of the Church of
England, and originated in the medieval period when the Catholic
Church, under the authority of the Pope, played a central role in the
nation. At the Reformation the Church in England, breaking from
the yoke of Rome, became the Church of England, in a special
relationship with the sovereign and Parliament. By virtue of its
establishment, the Church of England ministers to all in the land
through its parish system, is governed nominally by the sovereign
and Parliament, has its Bishops and key appointments made by the
Prime Minister, and has seats for twenty-six Bishops in the House
of Lords. There were groups in society, of course, who refused to
accept the religious uniformity that was considered essential for
nation-building. Many Catholics, now called 'Roman' Catholics,

bravely continued to worship according to their conscience, as did Anabaptists and others from the more Protestant end of the spectrum. The Toleration Act of 1689 relaxed the expectation of uniformity for Protestants, but Roman Catholics were only given equal freedom in the nineteenth century. It is hardly surprising that resentment and bitterness tainted Church relationships well into the twentieth century.

On becoming Archbishop I was not able to accept the view of some that the time had come for the disestablishment of the Church of England. My friend and former colleague Bishop Colin Buchanan was the leading proponent of the campaign for disestablishment. Four particular arguments guided the disestablishment agenda which he and others put forward. They were: that dependency on the state restricted the Church's freedom to elect its own leaders, hindered ecumenism, choked the Church with too many legal restrictions, and confused its mission by an obligation to be the servant of all. In short, it appeared to a growing number in the Church, as well as to many outside it, that disestablishment was the only honourable, indeed moral, option for our Church.

Although I was committed to share fully with other Christian leaders in service to the nation, I was not convinced by these arguments, or persuaded that the time had come to lead the Church of England into separation from the nation – not least because I felt that it would not be in the best interests of the country. Establishment, if seen merely as a privilege, is a contemptible idea. But establishment as a service and mission to the whole community, in maintaining a Christian presence in every part of the country, is an entirely honourable policy, and I was determined to use the relationship for the benefit of all.

One aspect of establishment which immediately became apparent to me on taking up office was the unrivalled access I had to those with political power and authority in the nation. Margaret Thatcher was the Prime Minister at the time the Church Appointments Commissioner offered my name to the Crown, and it was she who invited me to accept the office of Archbishop. However, by the time I took up office she had been replaced by John Major, with whom I enjoyed a warm and positive relationship. It is well-known that my predecessor as Archbishop, Robert Runcie, had a troubled relationship with Mrs Thatcher's government during the 1980s. It is possible that this may have continued had she remained at Number 10 after I became Archbishop, because I could not agree with many of her social policies; yet her approach attracted me. She was thoroughly committed to the nation, and tough and uncompromising in her determination to get it back on its feet again. With that sterling desire to give the country back its sense of pride I could readily agree, but I was less than happy with policies that threatened, it seemed to me, to split the nation into 'haves' and 'have nots'. The poverty of my early years convinced me of the danger of such an approach. Norman Tebbit's call to unemployed people to 'get on your bikes' aroused the fury of many by its explicit assumption that people in need could easily uproot themselves and their families and travel to find work. The harsh reality was far different.

Several months after I had taken up office as Archbishop, the government announced its intention to cut aid for people in the inner cities, and to give central government the prime responsibility for apportioning grants and aid. The irony was that the Church of England through the Church Urban Fund, one of the direct results of the groundbreaking 1980s report *Faith in the City*, was already directing new money into inner cities. I was immediately concerned by the implication of the cutbacks, and the implicit assumption that inner cities are only beneficiaries of wealth, and never creators of it. Not only was this clearly wrong, it demeaned those who lived in poverty-stricken areas of our large cities, who for the most part were not responsible for their lot. In a speech I argued that those who suffer the trauma of unemployment, homelessness and inadequate facilities are our fellow citizens. They suffer because we have yet to recover a vision for our society that includes them.

In speaking out on many matters that concerned the Church –

housing, homelessness, inner-city squalor, poverty, unemployment, consumerism and welfare – I was inevitably criticised for putting my head above the parapet. I was accused of interfering with politics and neglecting my primary responsibility, which was for moral and spiritual matters. The logic of this separation defied me. You simply cannot split the Church's concerns off from issues of poverty, homelessness and need.

The criticism that most saddened me came from within the Church itself, from fellow Anglican leaders who refused to be identified but who complained about me in the press. Reports reached me of a 'senior Bishop' who was said to be 'disappointed with George who is in danger of splitting the Church'. Although I had a very good idea who my 'senior' colleague was, I was rather saddened that he lacked the courage to tell me to my face what he believed I was doing wrong.

Yet there were many moments of encouragement which convinced me that I was right to identify with social concerns. I recall going to Birmingham in 1993 and visiting an area where poverty and unemployment had blighted many lives. Vandals were wrecking schools, clinics, the post office and homes. Oddly, the local church had been almost the only building to escape their attentions. A local black leader told me that the reason had to do with the faithful witness of the vicar and the congregation. Even though I had grown up in a working-class culture I was shocked by the conditions of these people, whose homes seemed closer to Soweto than Solihull.

The following year I was required to speak at Church House, Westminster, for the Churches' Housing Coalition, a group of homelessness charities. I was introduced to a young woman in her twenties who until very recently had been a prostitute. Hers was a story of deprivation, destitution and drugs, which led her eventually to a life on the streets. Then she met some Christians who, she said, did not take advantage of her. 'They treated me as if I were a person and very special,' she said. She and her two children had been rehoused with the help of the Church, and she was determined never to return to her old life. I kept in touch with her, and will never forget the day she wrote to say she was going forward to ordination. Her story showed the power of local Christian community to bring the grace of Almighty God to others. I was delighted to see the way that *Faith in the City* was paying off.

Following Margaret Thatcher's resignation in November 1990 I had more contact with her personally, and began to appreciate her significant gifts and her personality. Certainly her period in office was one in which pride was restored to our country. That sense of a nation proud of its history, values and ability will be her lasting legacy.

Curiously, it was in opposition to Mrs Thatcher's social beliefs that my own thinking began to evolve around the concept of a moral vision for our world and society. It was possible to agree with her that more and more people in Britain were enjoying the benefits of being part of an increasingly prosperous nation, even though there were worrying signs of an 'underclass' of very poor people emerging. The agendas of all three main political parties seemed united in their pursuit of economic blessing for all, and apparently oblivious to an underlying moral purpose that transcended it and gave it meaning. *Faith in the City*, which angered some Conservative politicians, seemed to me to go to the heart of the issue – that policies had to emerge from a concept of humanity which included the spiritual and moral as well as the economic. I was especially alarmed to note that morality was increasingly seen as a private matter. This resulted in a prevailing assumption that 'right and wrong' was a matter for the individual alone. Morality is in fact for the whole of life. In a correspondence with Professor Peter Hennessy, one of the country's leading authorities on the theory of government, I argued that political systems cut off from ideologies are like compasses which cannot locate magnetic north – the pointer ends up waving all over the place. Politicians who lack a moral imperative (which should be the lodestar of their profession) will soon find their 'idealism' transmuting into cynicism, disillusionment and self-serving policies. Politics

– at its best – is an honourable profession, and requires the very best men and women to represent us.

John Major, Mrs Thatcher's successor, shared many of her ideals and aims, but was a warmer and less combative person. He enjoyed meeting people, and had a remarkable gift for making them feel special. He was in politics for the very best of reasons – he wanted to make a difference to the lives of others. In this I felt that his conservative ideology was more supple and inventive than the more rudimentary and doctrinaire spirit of Margaret. John was equally convinced of the importance of the market economy and the urgent need to use private enterprise to boost employment and create growth, but he was not afraid of compromise if circumstances dictated it. And circumstances were certainly pointing in that direction.

John's first Cabinet on being appointed Prime Minister was a carefully-thought-out balance of 'doves' and 'hawks' – possibly he had concluded that a 'broad church' approach was required. I found people like Douglas Hurd, Geoffrey Howe and Virginia Bottomley very easy to do business with, whereas Michael Howard, Ann Widdecombe and Kenneth Baker were less easy to get on with, mainly because a certain right-wing triumphalism framed and focused their political vision.

I encountered this in a painful form when I addressed Church school heads at Chester College in September 1991, barely six months after taking up office. My aim was to affirm the vital role of head teachers and staff, and particularly the role of Church schools in state education. Just a week or two earlier, riots had erupted at the Meadow Well estate in Newcastle, causing much damage and social disturbance. The government were clearly rattled, and condemned the irresponsible behaviour that had caused the rioting. As it happened I knew Meadow Well very well from my seven years in Durham. It was a notoriously deprived area – a social dustbin, some called it. One Geordie said tersely to me: 'You don't go to Meadow Well, you're sentenced to Meadow Well.' I became very concerned by the comments of politicians and Church leaders who claimed that the riots were caused by delinquents who had abandoned moral principles. There was insufficient recognition that many people in Meadow Well were trapped in a vicious cycle of poverty, unemployment, broken relationships and poor education, as well as crime. In my address I referred to the Bishop of Chester who wrote in 1785 that on Sundays the town's inhabitants were apt 'to be idle, mischievous and vicious'. I then observed: 'The Bishop was right to recognise the presence of our sinfulness, but he no doubt ignored the fact that human wrongdoing is inextricably linked to social deprivation, poverty, poor housing and illiteracy. The story has a familiar ring about it – the events we saw on our televisions of the riots in Newcastle last week occurred where people are socially deprived.'

Before I gave the address, certain members of my staff were worried by my comment that such disruptions were 'inextricably' linked to issues like unemployment and social deprivation. The more I thought about it, however, the more convinced I became that my words were accurate. It is a fact that desperation drives people to act desperately. I did not want the speech watered down. It went ahead unamended, and was greatly appreciated by the intelligent and critical audience, who heard my comments in context. However, the media were there in force, and that part of the speech was milked for its implied criticism of government policy. Some sections of the print media and representatives of the government sought to rubbish my comment, stating that it was another of 'Carey's gaffes'. Others sought to rebuke me as a Christian leader for having chosen to comment politically instead of condemning the behaviour of the rioters.

It was clear that some sections of the media saw this as an opportunity to drive another wedge between the Church and the government. My response was to point out that a 'gaffe' means a mistake, and I was quite clear I had not made one. I was convinced that social ills are inextricably linked to social problems. Clearly one's morality plays a key part in how one deals with the inequalities of life, but to expect Christian leaders to criticise the moral deficiencies of others when other factors were evidently in play was quite wrong.

I wrote to John Major to assure him that it had not been my intention to attack the government, but that it was my perception that morality was 'all of a piece'. Politics, in terms of one's commitment to the betterment of society, could not be kept out of Christianity, any more than a politician could keep his values and beliefs out of the public domain. John phoned me the following Monday evening and said that he fully understood the point I was making; he also believed that a pluralistic approach to such serious social problems was required.

Following the uproar, I decided to visit Meadow Well to spend a day listening to the people of the area. Together with Eileen and my new Press Officer, Lesley Perry – whose first day at work with me it was – we flew to Newcastle and saw for ourselves the grim situation of this neglected estate. We listened to the despairing cries of single parents; we heard the harsh, angry tones of men who had been out of work for over five years with no prospect of a job; we saw some of the squalid buildings that people lived in. We returned home quite convinced that my comments were not gaffes, but were an appropriate response to a serious reality of life that politicians ignored at their peril.

From time to time some journalists enjoyed commenting on the fact that John Major and myself had attained such prominent places in British society, having both started out from such inauspicious beginnings. We were pilloried for being 'ordinary'. I think John found such criticism harder to bear than I did. In our regular meetings he often shared with me his anger at unfair criticism and personal attacks on him and his family. I saw part of my responsibility towards him and other political leaders as being to support them, and to assure them that they could always depend upon my encouragement and prayers.

Much of the criticism of the Prime Minister was deeply unfair and untrue. John had a sharp critical intelligence, and was easily capable of holding his own with his colleagues. The accusations of 'greyness' also wounded him, and were also, in my opinion, thoroughly undeserved. In John there was a fund of good humour and interest in many things, including cricket and Chelsea Football Club. There was much banter between us regarding the respective fortunes of my team, Arsenal, and Chelsea. But he could talk with the same ease about art and music as he could about matters of popular culture. In addition, there were few politicians better than John at the impromptu speech or the off-the-cuff remark. 'Grey' was the last colour to describe him – he was a man of distinction.

But John Major's position as Prime Minister was precarious. There were many who did not expect him to win the general election of April 1992, but he fought an honest and intelligent campaign that earned him a narrow victory. It seemed to me, however, that it was only a matter of time before his party blew itself apart through factions and divisions over Europe, the economy and the 'Back to Basics' campaign. The Prime Minister's placing of basic morality at the heart of a decent society and culture was one that I and many could gladly support. It was self-evident that as a liberal democracy Britain was in danger of losing the very values and virtues that had made it great. A so-called post-modern and post-Christian Britain was possibly post-ethical as well. Anything that put moral education and decent citizenship at the heart of community life was surely welcome. But the condition of the Conservative Party as scandal after scandal involving its Members of Parliament hit the front pages made a mockery of the 'Back to Basics' campaign and sentenced it to oblivion.

The 1990s were also a period of rising crime, and the public demanded that something be done about law and order. Perhaps the same moral self-righteousness that drove some politicians to attack my remarks about Meadow Well was behind the desire to respond to crime with much tougher prison policies. I watched this trend with anxiety, and seized the earliest opportunity to state my views in the 1996 Prison Reform Trust Lecture. I knew I would be at odds with the Home Secretary's stance, so I went to see Michael Howard to share my perspective with him and to elicit his response.

Michael was well known to me, not least because his constituency was in the diocese of Canterbury, and I knew him as a conscientious and dedicated MP who spent as much time in his constituency as his ministerial duties allowed. But he was undoubtedly a hardliner when it came to prison reform. In his opinion, 'prison worked'. I was suspicious of how he could be so dogmatic, since statistics for recidivism showed that an alarming number of prisoners reoffended. As a former prison Chaplain I was personally aware of the effects of long sentences on the families of prisoners; it was urgent, in my view, that alternative forms of punishment should be found. It is likely that Michael found my position as unconvincing as I found his. I got the strong impression that his desire to be seen as a tough Home Secretary who was not afraid to 'bang people up' and show society's displeasure at criminal behaviour was leading him to dismiss more humane and potentially more successful forms of restoring men and women to society. Certainly, as successive Home Secretaries have found, tough policies which hit criminals hard are greater vote-winners than soft policies.

In my address I said: 'From the point of view of restoring relationships, I believe we need to invest in a more satisfactory range of community-based forms of punishment, rehabilitation and reintegration into society.' I went on to say that where such provision is compatible with the safety of the public, it seems to have a number of powerful advantages over custody. Community options seem to be roughly comparable to prison in preventing reoffending, but at a much smaller cost. Moreover, research shows that some kinds of community supervision can reduce reconviction rates by between 20 and 50 per cent. These include programmes that confront offending behaviour and attitudes, teach people to restrain aggression and provide them with skills training and employment. I criticised the penal policy of the government as being too heavily weighted in favour of imprisonment, to the detriment of other forms of correction which offer more hope in the long term. Referring to experiments in other countries, I appealed for a 'more intensive investment of resources in making these kinds of programmes more consistently and more generously available to the courts in all parts of the country. Not only will such forms of sentencing take some of the strain off the Prison Service, but the prospects for restoring relationships are better.' Those words seem to me still relevant today.

Curiously enough, Michael Howard saw me a few days later at the FA Cup Final when Manchester United beat his team, Liverpool, in a scrappy game, and thanked me for my address. But in the following weeks he showed he had every intention of ignoring it. I was heartened that a few years later Douglas Hurd gave the same lecture, and made the same appeal for alternatives to prison.

The access that the establishment of the Church of England gave me to the Prime Minister and his Ministers came in very useful when Robin Eames, Archbishop of Armagh and a greatly respected leader in Ireland, phoned me late one evening to ask if I could secure a private meeting for him with the Prime Minister. As the matter was urgent and secret I met Robin the following day, and he told me that he had had meetings with Loyalist paramilitary leaders who were prepared to start talking unconditionally with the government. A condition, however, was attached – they had to have access to the Prime Minister personally from the beginning.

I contacted the Prime Minister at once, and took Robin to see him. Robin did indeed have important information to share, which has to remain confidential to this day, and I was struck by the way the Prime Minister handled the meeting, with exceedingly shrewd observations and an alertness and acuity of judgement that was impressive. I believe that this meeting, and several others the Prime Minister had with Robin and other Church leaders, including Cardinal Daly, who played an important role in talking to IRA spokesmen, paved the way for fruitful dialogue with the protagonists that Tony Blair was able to build upon a few years later.

But the end was in sight for John Major's government. After his defeat in the 1992 general election the Labour leader, Neil Kinnock, had given way to John Smith, whom I also got to know well. John Smith was a considerable man, with one of the sharpest minds in Parliament. He could be devastating in his witty critiques of political opponents, but there was nothing cruel or personal about his comments. He had a high regard for John Major, even though he had no time for his policies. John Smith was a socialist through and through, and to this day I often wonder what kind of Prime Minister he would have turned out to be. I doubt very much that he would have been as eager to sweep away the Labour Party's socialist roots as Tony Blair has been. His untimely death on 12 May 1994 deprived the nation of a gifted leader whose contribution could have been immense. A few weeks later I was honoured to receive Elizabeth Smith's invitation to preach at John's memorial service in Westminster Abbey. The large congregation was testimony to his place in people's hearts. In my tribute to him, I spoke of his love of people and his desire for all to have the opportunities to develop their full potential:

> Social justice was his cause, rooted in his fierce and instinctive commitment to the worth of every living person made in the image of God . . . We find a typical expression of this respect for others in his essay 'Reclaiming the Ground': 'An ethical approach to life and politics can be held as firmly by people of other faiths and by those who hold no religious convictions. Nor should Christian socialists ever seek to suggest that Christians must be socialists. Because we, like Tawney, see our Christian faith as leading towards democratic socialist convictions, we must always recognise that fellow Christians might properly arrive at different conclusions from ourselves.'

It was a moving occasion in which political differences were laid aside as we thanked God for an outstanding leader.

It was not long before I had the opportunity to meet Tony Blair, soon after his election as leader of the Labour Party. On 13 October 1994 Eileen and I invited him and his wife Cherie and three of his senior colleagues, Alun Michael, Donald Dewar and Jack Straw, to dinner at Lambeth Palace. I was immensely impressed by the idealism and intellectual vigour of the quartet. Eileen, as a Scot, got on very well with Donald, and I could hear them and Cherie reminiscing about Scotland and arguing about Scottish politics at the other end of the table. Alun Michael was in typically combative mood, and it was not long before our guests and I were engaged in a conversation about the country's current political malaise, which in their opinion was caused by a Conservative Party in its death throes. Although appreciative of John Major's honesty and integrity, they were contemptuous of the government's record, and anxious to get the country on its feet again.

'What makes you think after your election defeat under Neil Kinnock that you are now electable?' I asked them.

I glanced across at Tony Blair, who was sitting opposite me. He looked almost absurdly young for a man who might one day soon be Prime Minister. It was Tony himself who answered the question: 'We believe we have strong policies underpinned by a socialist philosophy that offers room for all, but gives priority to the disadvantaged. We know we can bring down the appalling unemployment figures, and we shall aim to reform state education and the National Health Service.'

I was in no doubt about Tony Blair's steel and authority, yet he had appeared to me a rather reticent and shy person, even lacking in fluency of speech. As I got to know him better it became clear that my first impressions were only half-correct. He was at times reticent, not because of any conversational shortcomings so much as an inner quietness that did not require him to dominate a conversation or force his views on others. In short, there was a stillness about him suggesting that he was at peace with himself and at home with other people.

His shyness we saw at first hand when Eileen and I met up with him outside Buckingham Palace in May 1995 at the celebrations marking the fiftieth anniversary of VE-Day. I had the great privilege to lead the service. Following lunch in the Palace with leaders from around the world, we were all bussed to Regent's Park to have tea with members of voluntary societies associated with the life of our nation. It was a happy occasion as the great and the good, celebrities and public figures, mingled with the dedicated people who form the backbone of the country. Shorn of staff personnel to shepherd, protect and advise them, not all the politicians and celebrities could cope with the pawing and 'mateyness' of the occasion. I could see Margaret Thatcher, with Denis in tow, enjoying the adulation greatly. John and Norma Major, likewise, were lapping it up. We bumped into Tony several times, and felt he was less at ease. Was it, I asked myself, because Cherie was not with him? Or could it be that he did not enjoy such social moments because they did not rate highly on the scale of political significance? Buses were laid on to take us to various destinations, and we saw Tony on his own, looking rather lonely. We invited him to join us, and shared some animated minutes with a crowd of ladies who had recognised us. As I glanced at Tony joining in the laughter, I could not help but wonder if in a short while this young man would be our next Prime Minister, and what kind of Premier he would be.

Now, seven years into his premiership, many would agree with me that he is proving to be an outstanding leader with real authority. He swept into office in May 1997, winning a landslide victory. I did not feel that John Major's premiership deserved such a humiliating defeat, but the country was giving its verdict on more than seventeen years of Conservative rule. It is possible that John did not really enjoy his six and a half years as Prime Minister, but he served his country well and led his divided party with ability. History, I believe, will judge him kindly.

There was more to the 1997 election campaign than a rejection of Thatcherism. The freshness and intelligence of Labour's young leader struck a chord with many longing for a new political vision. Tony Blair had perceived that some intellectual modernisation of socialist principles was required to make it a convincing alternative to a conservative agenda. His appeal to a 'Third Way', which transcended the old ideologies of the past, seemed to many to lift the debate into a new order of political realities. The way he almost single-handedly removed Clause 4 from the Labour Party's constitution helped to make it electable. The party's new embrace of the market economy and partnership with the private sector was another significant factor in its electoral success. To be sure, he had the great advantage of entering office on the back of a strong economy – surely the legacy of the previous regime. But with a first-class Chancellor in Gordon Brown, the economy continued to be managed prudently and with some imagination. The jury must still be out on whether Tony Blair destroyed the historic Labour Party in the process, but John Major is in no doubt about it. In his autobiography he describes Tony Blair as sounding 'like a middle-of-the-road Tory', and continues: 'I did not, at the time, appreciate the extent to which he would appropriate Conservative language and steal our policies. The attractive candidate turned out to be a political kleptomaniac.' Whether this is true or not, Tony Blair has certainly redefined socialism politically, making it more acceptable in a changing world.

He and I had several conversations which touched on these issues. In our first meeting after his election victory I asked him to name the thinkers who had had the greatest influence on his political and intellectual development. Without hesitation he mentioned William Temple and R.H. Tawney – together with the New Testament. He went on to say that his form of socialism owed more to Christian thought, particularly Methodism in the north-east of England, than to Communism. As we continued to discuss the ways that ideas affect people and their actions, it was clear that his thinking about the Third Way was still being formulated. What was deeply important to him was a socialist vision that all people should have access to learning and opportunities to develop their God-given capacities.

During our private meetings, my respect grew for Tony Blair personally, and for his deft awareness of what appealed to the public. He is able to draw out the emotions of his audience in a manner that few can. We found ourselves, however, on opposite sides when we were invited to address the Trades Union Congress on the same day, 9 September 1997. It was the first time that an Archbishop of Canterbury had received such an honour, and it was one I took very seriously. I spoke in the morning, and Tony in the afternoon. I began my address with a piece of information of which I was sure very few delegates were aware – that I had been a member of two unions in the past, ETU and NALGO, when I was a teenage employee of the London Electricity Board. That amused them greatly, as both unions were involved in some dispute at that time. Unlike my father, whose experience of unions had been negative, mine had been positive, and I was well aware from the history of working people how much the nation owes to the unions. My affirmation of them, based upon Christian principles, received a very warm response. Tony Blair however went to the Congress with a stern warning that the TUC had to change. The following day the papers contrasted our speeches, saying that the Prime Minister had preached the sermon, and I had given the political address.

The very personal way Tony exercised his office was echoed by his senior colleagues. With the exception of John Major and just a few members of his Cabinet, the Conservative government presented an image that was uncaring and at times arrogant. In contrast, I was able to develop very close relationships with a number of New Labour leaders quickly, easily and positively. I saw Robin Cook on many occasions, not only in the United Kingdom but often abroad when we met at international gatherings. In spite of giving the impression to some that he didn't listen to others, I found him to be a most intelligent and discerning politician, who loved it when people stood up to him and argued their case. Gordon Brown and Clare Short were, and continue to be, among my favourite politicians – no doubt because our common interest in combating poverty brought us together frequently. Gordon did not limit the office of Chancellor to the interests of his own nation. His passion, no doubt fed from the wellsprings of a faith honed in a Scottish manse, was to make this world a better place for the majority of its inhabitants. Clare was no less committed. I invited her to address General Synod on her work, and she gave an electrifying speech which earned her two standing ovations. Her challenge to Synod to get more involved in the fight against poverty was well targeted, and energised the Church's already considerable contribution. Strong relationships with other leaders also developed – with Jack Straw, David Blunkett, Alun Michael, Estelle Morris, Patricia Hewitt, Alan Milburn and Charles Clarke. All were very able, and well chosen for their different responsibilities.

In addition to my own contact with the government and public figures, other Church leaders were also involved at senior levels. The contribution of Bishops in the House of Lords grew in significance through the nineties as the 'Lords Spiritual', as they were denoted, led by Richard Harries, Bishop of Oxford, and Tom Butler, Bishop of Southwark, made major contributions on subjects ranging from the closure of pits to the campaign against Section 28 of the Local Government Act, which banned the 'promotion' of homosexuality in schools. They too spoke out on matters that affected the Church's mission, often in collaboration with other Christian leaders, as well as with the Chief Rabbi Jonathan Sacks. I was proud of our involvement, and at times perplexed that some people in our Church did not regard this as mission. In my view it was an important part of the Bishops' role to speak out on social issues and to represent their communities. They, more than most members of the House of Lords, were in touch with the people of the nation.

However, dealing with political leaders at such close quarters and having easy access to express my concerns and represent my own Church and other faith communities sometimes involved a degree of discomfort, misunderstanding and controversy. Such was the case in relation to the invasion of Iraq by American and British forces in the spring of 2003. A year before, I had written a strictly private letter to the Prime Minister shortly before he had an important meeting with President Bush at the White House. In the course of the letter I wrote:

May I raise with you the issue of Iraq? I am not alone in having considerable anxiety about American policy with respect to that country. Of course, I recognise Saddam Hussein as a detestable man and his regime as odious. The world would certainly be a better place without him. But moral communities should not lapse into aping the odious behaviour of evil people. As no clear links have been proved between the events of 11 September and Iraq we must not use the present uncertainties as an opportunity to settle old scores . . . My greatest fear is that the US might unleash its crushing might on Iraq and not only intensify the misery, poverty and suffering of millions of ordinary Iraqis but destabilise the entire Middle East.

A week later I received a four-page letter from the Prime Minister in his own handwriting, in which he set out his position with great clarity. It was evident that he believed that getting rid of Saddam Hussein would be highly desirable, not least for the Iraqi people. Furthermore, he argued that whether or not we undertook any military action depended on both our ability to do so without causing undue suffering, and on whether Saddam allowed the weapons inspectors back into Iraq unconditionally, as United Nations resolutions required him to do. He indicated that should we take such a step, we would have to ensure that the situation in the Middle East was radically changed: there could be no strategy for Iraq without a strategy for the Middle East in general, including a kick-start to the peace process between Israel and the Palestinian Authority. He also made it clear that he was the only Western leader the United States would listen to on such issues. This meant that he couldn't grandstand publicly, but had to negotiate privately. He had a very difficult and delicate line to tread.

I agreed with the Prime Minister that a regime change in Iraq was necessary, but only under the right conditions, and preferably with the support of the UN. Of great interest, especially in the light of later statements from the Prime Minister and President Bush, is the fact that in his long personal letter to me there was no mention of the significance of 'weapons of mass destruction', apart from the implications of allowing UN weapons inspectors back into Iraq. In my opinion it was a major mistake to allow the issue of weapons of mass destruction to dominate the policy of the British government.

The Prime Minister's public statements on Iraq worried me a little because they seemed more gung-ho than his private letter to me. They suggested that a certain amount of sabre-rattling was going on, and President Bush's policies were dominating the agenda. In a private meeting following his visit to the White House I mentioned to the Prime Minister that a perception was growing in the Churches that British foreign policy was now being decided by America. He laughed at that suggestion, and sought to reassure me that his views had not changed, and that Britain would never surrender its foreign policy to others. He repeated his determination to ensure that if Iraq was attacked it would be on moral grounds, and with the strongest coalition possible.

My experience has convinced me that Britain is served by politicians of integrity and ability. Compared to most other countries, the levels of corruption and duplicity are low. Machiavelli may well have been right when he wrote that no leading figure ever gets to the top without difficulty, and we should support and salute those who do. Nevertheless, it is essential that a free press, the Churches and other groups should encourage and expect those elected to live up to the highest standards of their offices. I watched with alarm in the late nineties as unelected people from outside the Civil Service were employed at Number 10 and in key ministries, seemingly undermining the authority of Parliament as they, rather than Members themselves, wielded power and authority. Democracy is a fragile and precious flower, and will only flourish in the soil of accountability and openness.

No single political party can claim the moral high ground for honesty or religious authority. George Lansbury, a great Labour leader in the 1930s, once claimed that 'My reading and my prayers have all united to confirm my faith that socialism ... is the only outward expression of a Christian faith.' I honour his magnificent achievements in working out his political philosophy from the Christian faith in that way. Others however have also asserted the compatibility between their Christian faith and their political beliefs. There are Christians and good people of all faiths and none in different political parties, and all are charged with the same goal – to make our nation good, prosperous, decent and fair. If any child goes hungry, or does not have access to proper education and health provision, we are all diminished. If our great nation ever shrinks from a courageous commitment to an ethic based on the Judaeo-Christian moral tradition we shall reap the whirlwind of cynicism, bad behaviour, violence and corruption.

The Church has a vital part to play in the rejuvenation of our land, because it is at the local level that the Christian faith is most authentic and most characteristic. Does establishment matter these days? I think it does, and it is at the local level that it is worked out. The Church of England alone among the religious groupings has a comprehensive network of parishes and priests covering the entire country. Some thirteen thousand parishes offer a ministry that is available to every member of our communities. The strength and the value of that undertaking was well demonstrated during the foot-and-mouth crisis in 1999, when local networks based around churches and parishes in rural areas provided a vital lifeline to suffering farming communities, breathing into them a vision of new life and fresh possibilities. Sometimes the parish priest is the only professional person living in the area he or she serves. It was at the critical period in the early nineties when BSE was at its height and the farmers at their lowest ebb that the Archbishop of York and myself launched a national appeal for the farming community that was well supported and appreciated.

In my opinion therefore the establishment of the Church of England does matter – both to the nation and for the Church's mission. But would the Church's commitment to the nation cease were it to be no longer 'by law established'? I can say from experience that it is inconceivable that the Church of England would walk away from its service to the nation. But inevitably over a period of time the open and inclusive culture of the Church, the range of its partnerships with other stakeholders in society, would tend to become diluted, narrower and more remote. There would be the likelihood of a greater focus on looking after its own; a tendency to become congregational in attitude that would lead to it becoming more closed and self-contained. Were that to happen, this Church, my Church, would no longer be at the historic centre of the nation in the way that it has been since Archbishop Dunstan crowned King Edgar in Bath in 973.

13

Clash of Cultures

'Culture! I have always agreed with our poet Hans Johst who used to say "When I hear the word culture, I unlock my revolver's safety catch."'

Hermann Goering

TYRANTS AND DICTATORS are not the only ones who abhor differences. It is also a trait associated with those who love tidiness and uniformity, and cannot abide the richness of variety, colour and limitless expression that go with diversity. In biology it is called ecology, whereby infinite varieties of species co-exist and complement each other in a lived environment where each is necessary for the survival of the whole. The same is true of human civilisation, where a form of ecology exists which allows different cultures to flourish in an environment common to all. However, just as in the world of biology not all species get on happily, so in human groupings cultures may clash and collide; they may irritate and sometimes express anger towards each other; they may fight and sometimes go to war. But a cultureless society is a contradiction in terms. Culture is the dress in which local traditions, epics, sorrow and rejoicing find expression, and the garment which makes visible the particularities of 'my' culture against 'yours'.

Those who belong to Churches live in two cultures. They inhabit the culture into which they were born and whose imprint they bear, for better or worse. I am English, and I cannot escape the implications of being born into a working-class London culture. As I grew older I was able to add to this inheritance wider learning and experiences. I am rightly proud of my culture, as you should be of yours, but to claim that mine is better than yours would be difficult to substantiate.

There is another culture I belong to, and that is to one of the many cultures of Christianity. But can one talk of the culture of the Church in the same way that one talks of the groupings of human society? I believe so, because the Church is a social organisation which embraces its members in a living community expressed in a shared faith, a common liturgy and agreed moral principles. A Church has its traditions, songs and time-honoured ways of worship. Indeed, for many Christians their faith is more important than issues of race, nation and even family – although no one would wish to be put in the invidious position of having to choose between them. As Richard Niebuhr makes clear in his book *Christ and Culture* (first published in 1951, but still relevant), we cannot avoid the implications of working out how we relate the culture of faith to the world around us. To accept our human cultures unquestioningly is to make the Christian faith a servant to the world; however, to assume that these cultures are alien and sinful ends in the collision of cultures and rejection of the world. Between these two extremes Christians, or anyone else for that matter, cannot avoid the fact that their beliefs are conditioned by their cultural setting, and that same culture must be constantly evaluated.

In my time as Archbishop the issue of culture was one of the most important affecting the mission and unity of the Church, but insufficient attention was paid to its significance and how it impacted on the Christian faith. It is impossible in this memoir to record all of the many visits I made to different parts of the Anglican Communion, but in this chapter I want to reflect on three Provinces where the issue of culture plays a significant role in the life of the Church – for good and ill. The three Provinces are the Episcopal

Church of the United States, the Province of the Church of Kenya and the Province of the Church of Nigeria.

I paid at least a dozen visits to America and to the Episcopal Church of the United States as Archbishop. My first visit was in the spring of 1992, when the Primates of the Communion met at Kanuga, a retreat and holiday centre in a majestic mountain landscape in North Carolina. Over the years the resourceful and energetic President of Kanuga, Albert Kooch, had developed it into a popular meeting place for groups of all kinds to gather for rest and refreshment. This proved abundantly to be the case for us all, especially some of the Primates who had arrived extremely tired and worn out. I was very concerned for Desmond Tutu, who in spite of his usual exuberance was looking shattered from the effects of several demanding rallies in South Africa.

In addition to the usefulness of the meeting at Kanuga this visit to the United States enabled me to experience my first Episcopal service, when the Primates worshipped at St James', Hendersonville. I was struck by the beauty and dignity of the service, enhanced by an American heartiness and vigour which made it an enjoyable act of worship. Billy and Ruth Graham came across for coffee, looking very well in spite of advancing years.

My first official visit to the Episcopal Church was in September 1992. Its primary purpose was for me to meet the American House of Bishops in Baltimore, Maryland. To some degree I was uneasy about this meeting, because I knew that a minority of American Bishops had some reservations about my approach on a number of issues. It was my task, I believed, to establish a firm foundation of friendship in order for a fruitful dialogue to emerge in the days to come. Ed Browning, the Presiding Bishop of the House, I knew reasonably well. Ed and his wife Patti had been missionaries in Japan some years earlier, and carried forward in their lives and work many of the qualities that make fine missionaries: a genuine interest in people, warmth of personality and a great desire to express an inclusive gospel. Ed led with his heart. Although I disagreed vehemently with some of his concerns, a nicer and more caring person would be difficult to find. Ed welcomed me on behalf of the House of Bishops and I greatly enjoyed the twenty-four hours I spent with them.

It was impossible not to compare the American House of Bishops with their English counterparts. It seemed to me that in two respects the English Bishops had the edge: first, in terms of theological ability and intellectual vigour, and second in their ability to work as a united body, in spite of differences of outlook and theology. The former is possibly a result of the way American Bishops are appointed, which places little emphasis on academic attainment or learning, even though there is a considerable tradition of scholarship in the American Church. The democratic process of appointment places a premium on success in building up impressive congregations, business management and preaching ability. Very few, if any American Bishops come from academic institutions, either seminaries or university faculties. This is not a criticism of individual Bishops, but of the system. Although many of the Bishops were gifted and able people, very few had been formed by academic scholarship. The consequence is that when confronting intellectual and theological issues the American House of Bishops was inclined to deal with them pastorally and experientially.

Jack Spong, then Bishop of Newark, was a typical case. He could not in my opinion be ranked highly as a biblical scholar. Yet his unorthodox and controversial views on the Resurrection, the Virgin Birth and scripture gave him a certain scholarly renown, and he had become recognised as a spokesman for those members of the American Episcopal Church who shared his position. Jack and I sparred playfully on my first morning with them when I gave a short address on the authority of scripture. Jack, a tall, handsome man, advanced to the microphone and very quietly asked if orthodoxy amounted to fundamentalism. As he knew perfectly well that it does not, I assumed that the purpose of the question was to flush out where I drew the line. I replied that if by fundamentalism he meant biblical literalism, then it certainly did not. I was not a literalist, but I did take scripture as the fundamental authority for the Church. Orthodoxy, I said, challenging him in turn, is the formulation of the Church's teaching on given dogmas and doctrines. As Bishops of the Church we were committed to interpreting those doctrines and obeying them. Did he not agree? Jack paused for a moment and then, with a straight face, agreed, and offered the view that as Bishops were also required to be teachers who challenged others to think, sometimes this meant walking on the frontier between unbelief and faith. This remark raised some suppressed laughter from a number of his colleagues, as it was my opinion, which I think was shared by others, that he himself had strayed well beyond the frontier of belief. Nevertheless, Jack would remain an influential figure in the continuing debate. The following year the Koinonia Statement, largely written by him, was endorsed by the majority of American Bishops. This report was a strong appeal for the acceptance of homosexuals in loving, committed relationships, alongside traditional marriage.

In another respect I felt that the American House of Bishops was a less united and less integrated body than its English counterpart. Beneath the friendliness and courtesy of the way the Americans worked, it became clear to me that there were deep divisions. A small but significant number of Bishops were disenfranchised from the rest. Some felt alienated because they were traditional Catholics who, because they opposed the ordination of women, believed that they were being forced out of the Church. Others felt estranged from the House of Bishops because they challenged the strong liberal agenda that prevailed there. It saddened me that there did not appear to be an overarching unity that held them together. Even though in England we had strongly-held and divergent beliefs we seemed far more united. This may stem from the fact that England is a much smaller nation, offering many more opportunities for Bishops to meet regularly and share together. But that only partly explains the differences. It was my conclusion that the theological differences between

American Bishops were very deep indeed, and there seemed to be no common desire to find a rapprochement.

From many other points of view I felt – and later experience did nothing to shake this firm conclusion – that the American House of Bishops and the Episcopal Church itself had many wonderful strengths and gifts. There was a warmth and sense of fun about the meetings of the American Bishops that made a refreshing change from English starchiness and over-seriousness. They took more earnestly than we did then the importance of group dynamics and working in small groups. Starting from that first official visit I began to appreciate the American character, perhaps honed from those early days of being a frontier people, that challenges and difficulties were there to be overcome – even though it was odd that they did not put it to work in the case of their divisions. I learned a great deal from the American 'Why not?' attitude, so different from the European tendency to multiply problems rather than find answers. Later, when I was compelled to raise considerable sums for the Anglican Communion, I learned the lesson not to be embarrassed about asking for money. Money is the currency of action, and if I believed the cause to be right and just, then I had to develop confidence in sharing that need with others and ask in a straightforward way for financial support from those able to give it. The Anglican Communion continues to owe much to the generous and lively American Church.

On that first visit I took part in a Trinity Lay Institute Conference led by Trinity Church, Wall Street, New York. Trinity is the wealthiest endowed church in the Episcopal Church of the United States. Its wealth is almost entirely due in the first instance to a gift of land given by Queen Anne in 1697, when Trinity was but an outpost of the Church of England in the American colonies. Through careful management of that land, on which several considerable buildings and skyscrapers now rest, Trinity Church has become a major source of help for the Communion. Eileen and I had met Dr Dan Matthews, the Rector of Trinity, and his wife Deener at the World Council of Churches in Canberra in 1991. They were warm, outgoing and attractive people with a huge love of life and a faith that reached out to others. We immediately became firm friends. Under Dan's leadership Trinity's potential was being unlocked and used in a variety of ways for the good of the Communion – ranging from direct funding for scores of projects around the world to 'hands-on' initiatives designed to empower people.

One such initiative was to challenge lay people to exercise their gifts in the service of the gospel. I was delighted to agree to take part in Trinity's conference for lay people. However, I was unprepared for the size of the enterprise. I knew that I was to give a major speech, but it dwarfed anything I had ever been involved in before. Not only was one of the smartest hotels in Washington DC taken over for the event, to which 350 lay leaders were invited, but the session was beamed to fifty-six audiences in other parts of the country in an interactive event which meant a two-way consultation between myself and my far-flung audience. The costs involved must have been quite staggering. Equally impressive was the thoroughness of the preparations, which led me to encounter for the first time the mysteries of the autocue – forgoing the security of a hard script in one's hand.

My address explored the role of lay people in the Church. Why is it, I asked, that so many able lay leaders are de-professionalised by the Church? Why is it that people who are so professional in their lay jobs are willing to settle for less in their Church? How may the gifts of lay leaders be properly affirmed and expressed in the ministry of the Church, and how may the wider Church support and encourage lay gifts in the world? The following debate, in which I answered questions from some of the fifty-six distant audiences, was entertaining and very helpful.

The *Washington Post* the following day gave the event a very positive write-up, although it added the questionable comment that my remarks reflected my 'roots in the evangelical wing of the Church'. In subsequent addresses I sought to challenge that mistaken view – if it is only the evangelical wing that emphasises the role of lay people in the Church and in the world, then the Church is in deep trouble.

The truth lies elsewhere. Evangelicals are more prone than other traditions to limit the role of lay people in the Church, and hardly take an interest in their work in the world. Catholics, on the other hand, are more likely to affirm the role of lay people in the world, but are unlikely to use them in the Church unless they are officially recognised as liturgical assistants. The challenge facing all Churches is to welcome the rich gifts of lay people in both secular and religious forms and to allow them to influence and shape their own ministry and mission.

From Washington Eileen and I set out on a crowded, busy but very enjoyable journey which took us to Cincinnati, Seattle, Albuquerque and New York. The visit to Cincinnati took us to the diocese of Southern Ohio, where we were welcomed by Bishop Herb Thompson and his wife Russelle. Herb, an outstanding black leader, had invited me to give the Charles Taft Memorial Lecture, which I entitled 'Tolerating Christianity in a Pluralist Society'. In the lecture I endeavoured to explore how one can hold on to the distinctiveness of Christianity in a pluralist world. The reaction of the audience was surprising. A number of my questioners assumed that the acceptance of pluralism meant the acknowledgement that one's faith was culturally conditioned, that 'we had to accept that Christianity was just one faith among others'. I rebutted this idea vigorously, saying that the pluralism of a society such as the United States is no different from the position of the early Church, when fledgling Christians had to work out their principles in a context of cultural differences. Why should pluralism neutralise and modify strong beliefs? Herb later offered the view that mainstream Churches such as Episcopal, Methodist and Presbyterian were more likely to modify faith claims in the cause of liberal conformity to culture, whereas the Roman Catholic, Baptist and new Churches were more inclined and more prepared to be distinctive groups in society. He agreed with my opinion that clarity of belief and distinctiveness in society were crucial ingredients in Church growth, and it is hardly surprising that such faith groups were flourishing whilst others were declining.

From that lecture in the evening of 15 September 1992 we flew to Seattle, where we were welcomed by Vincent Warner, Bishop of the diocese of Olympia, and taken immediately to the Marriott Hotel, where I was to address fifteen hundred people at a 'Business of God Banquet'. The title of my address was 'Evangelism: Religious Longing in an Irreligious Age'. By this time we were feeling very tired. There was a three-hour time difference between Seattle and Cincinnati, and our body clocks were now at 3 a.m. However, so warm was the reception of the people and the eagerness of the Church to make us feel at home that we were revived by their enthusiasm. While my speech seemed to be well received, I was struck once again by the number of questions which focused more on making Christianity acceptable to the world and in tune with its philosophy than on working from a rootedness in Christian faith and morals that offered an alternative to secular thought and life.

It was in Seattle that we were to see the Episcopal Church at perhaps its most compassionate and inspiring, at least on this visit. The following day we were taken to refuge homes for Cambodian and other Asian peoples, and night shelters for the homeless. The most poignant of the visits was to Three Cedars AIDS Clinic, where a dozen terminally ill young men were being cared for by a dedicated staff. The home had been started five years earlier by a man who had lost his partner to the AIDS/HIV virus, and had since become one of the most important clinics caring for those dying of this dreadful disease. One of the dying men, Tom, was anxious to meet me. A young man of no more than twenty-five whose family had rejected him, Tom was very emaciated, with ugly lesions disfiguring his face and upper body, but he greeted me with a warm smile. I gave him a Canterbury cross, which thrilled him, and he held it lovingly as I took his other hand and prayed with him. Sadly, within two days Tom was dead.

Bishop Vincent Warner explained that the diocesan philosophy towards those suffering from AIDS was one of unconditional love and acceptance, whatever their lifestyle had been. Although many in the diocese disapproved of explicit homosexual lifestyles, all were united in fighting the virus and caring for those suffering from its effects. I was very impressed by Vincent's leadership, and considered his policy wholly admirable. But it did seem to me that the issue of homosexuality was not being tackled head-on by the diocese. Instead, it was reacting to cultural trends which assumed that active homosexuality was an acceptable lifestyle.

This was certainly not the case in the next diocese we visited, that of Rio Grande in New Mexico, under Bishop Terrence Kelshaw. As it happened, we arrived in Albuquerque at the same time that Bill Clinton hit town on his election campaign, and there was a frenzied police presence for the three days we were there. Terry and Hazel Kelshaw, ex-Brits, had settled happily in the States but were deeply at odds with the widespread acceptance of practising homosexuality in the Episcopal Church. Terry, as an evangelical, saw the issue – as it clearly is – as one of authority, and was an outspoken critic of the Presiding Bishop's liberal views. As a consequence the diocese had withheld funds from the national Church, in line with similar action from other dioceses. Although my views on the issue of homosexuality were in line with Terry's, I was disturbed by his unilateral action in withholding funds, and by his tendency to withdraw from participation in the House of Bishops' meetings. When we were alone I questioned his approach, suggesting that it weakened the mission of both the national Church and his own diocese. But there was no gainsaying the vigorous life in the diocese of Rio Grande, and the appreciation of Terry's leadership. I spoke at a huge rally which itself was testimony to the enthusiasm of the clergy and the people, and to the encouraging numbers of young people coming into the life of the Church.

The final leg of our trip took us to New York, and once again to many different and tiring events. I was particularly impressed by the extensive social witness of the Cathedral of St John the Divine. So well known is its work that when one day I caught a taxi and told the cabbie my destination, he said unthinkingly but genuinely, 'St John's? Oh, that place is absolutely divine!'

Under the then Dean Jim Morton, the crypt of St John's was used for a great variety of activities, including childcare, housing needs, fostering children, employment issues, environmental concerns and political activity, to name but a few. The diocese, under Bishop Dick Grein, was also involved in many significant social initiatives. I was particularly impressed with the Nehemiah Housing Project, funded to a considerable degree by Trinity, Wall Street. The Nehemiah Project sought to provide good social housing for very poor, largely black people, and was an impressive gift to the community.

So it was that on my first official visit to the United States I formed a strong impression of a significant Church reaching out into its community with confidence and hope. Later visits did nothing to shake this view. But on reflection I had a distinct impression that the Episcopal Church had been infiltrated by its culture more profoundly than its leaders and members realised. Instead of sustaining a creative spiritual and intellectual critique of culture, the Church was inclined to accept the prevailing therapeutic 'feel-goodism' and pragmatic indices of success as gifts of the Spirit. Whilst some adaptation to culture has to happen in order for mission to be successful, to be relevant culturally also means being different – otherwise 'conversion', 'repentance', and 'forgiveness' have lost their meanings.

In May 1996 I paid official visits to the dioceses of Chicago and Los Angeles. Bishop Frank Griswold and his wife Phoebe welcomed us warmly to Chicago and to a frantic round of activities that revealed the variety of ministries in that great city. The opening service in the cathedral took an unexpected turn at the beginning, when a liturgical experiment went wrong with amusing consequences. As we lined up for the procession two senior clergymen joined the procession, armed with large buckets of water. I was informed that Bishop Griswold and I would bring up the rear of the procession and would sprinkle holy water on the congregation. We were given palm branches for this purpose. All went well until we entered the sanctuary, where the fun really began. Richard the Archdeacon, my assistant and water-carrier, tripped and lost his balance, and water from his bucket flooded the sanctuary. Struggling frantically to keep upright he slipped on the now treacherous surface, fell over and slid across the floor. With great difficulty I managed to keep my footing and avoid the prostrate Archdeacon. The entire sanctuary was now looking like a children's paddling pool. And then, in a manner which could only happen in America, with hardly a pause four young female liturgical assistants emerged from the vestry with towels over their arms, and with a calmness and dignity that suggested the whole thing had been planned from the beginning dried the floor within seconds.

That episode was the start of a most enjoyable visit in which we got to know Frank and Phoebe Griswold well. Frank was later to succeed Ed Browning as Presiding Bishop. A wise, tolerant man with a wry sense of humour, he presided over a diocese in which practising homosexuals were accepted in the priesthood. This worried me, and in a private conversation with him I wondered how Bishops could justify the ordination of practising homosexuals when it went against the moral tradition of Anglicanism and was likely to provoke major controversy in his own Church and the wider Communion. Frank acknowledged the problem, and in defence cited the experience in his diocese, where very few people had objected. Some of his finest priests, he said, were in committed same-sex relationships. I was troubled by the pragmatic and decidedly narrow preference this implied. The canons of the Church and the consensus of the wider Anglican Communion were clearly of secondary importance to the needs of the homosexual community. Although I respected Frank's pastoral care and sensitivity, it seemed to me that he and others sympathetic to this trend were ignoring the catholicity of truth.

I met several homosexual priests during the following days, and listened to their concerns carefully. I was impressed by their dedication and love of the work. Nevertheless, I felt that the diocese was on a slippery slope, as expediency, heavily influenced by a liberal, middle-class culture, was dictating the policy. Indeed, Frank's acceptance of practising homosexuals, whilst attractive to those who approved of this lifestyle, made him immediately suspect in the eyes of conservative and orthodox Anglicans when he became Presiding Bishop.

A few days later we were in Los Angeles as guests of Fred and Barbara Borsch. Fred's fine teaching ministry and the couple's love of people had enabled the diocese to grow steadily. I was not surprised to find that LA's huge diversity of faiths and cultures had altered the Episcopal Church profoundly. Fred was straightforward about the inclusive character of the diocese, and I heard a whole range of opinions about the place of homosexuals in the life of the Church.

I was taken aback by the way this matter was raised in my presence again and again. It was not on my agenda as an issue, but whether I liked it or not I was challenged to explain my position and substantiate my opposition to practising homosexuality. One memory stands out vividly. I had just finished giving a presentation on the mission of the Church at a luncheon, and had fielded a few questions on homosexual priests when a young priest came across to thank me and said with a great deal of emotion, 'I trust, Archbishop, that you will not shut your ears to our needs, and the desire of so many of us homosexuals to serve in our Church.' I was touched by his boldness, and assured him of my great desire to include all in our Church but said I would be failing in my duty if I did not speak the truth as I saw it. I told him that, without any desire to condemn him or others like him – which I truly did not – I saw heterosexual marriage as the rightful context for sexual relationships, and celibacy as the only option for those who could not choose that way. Could he not see that it was not I who was trying to revise the moral tradition of our Church? We parted with a firm handshake. I was greatly moved by his openness and candour in talking to me.

Two other incidents stood out on that visit to Los Angeles. The first was a trip to a magnificent Episcopal social project at Pueblo Nuevo started by a young priest, Philip Lance. The Bishop introduced him as a 'gay' priest who was at that time not in a relationship with another man. Philip's work was nothing short of breathtaking. The

Bishop had asked him to work among poor Mexicans in a very tough part of the city. There was no church building, and no support whatsoever. How could he possibly achieve anything in an area known to be highly dangerous, without any resources or support? Philip told me that after some thought and not a little prayer he decided to begin with the generosity and grace of the gospel – he would take Holy Communion to the Mexican people where they were. In fear and trembling, at noon each day he set up a rickety card table in the local park, a notorious place where drugs and guns were sold openly, and where prostitutes gathered in the evening. Bread and wine were placed on the table and a simple order of service was given to the very few people who gathered around. Gradually Philip began to be trusted as someone who had no ulterior motive other than wanting to help poor Mexican families. A regular congregation eventually gathered around him each day in the park. The breakthrough came when he started to counsel some families who were in great distress, and was able to give aid to them.

Months passed, and Philip managed to find some rather dingy premises, in which he began a school. An enterprising janitorial service to help provide employment followed. A thrift store, a clinic and then a small church were added to the centre. At the time of my visit the venture was a roaring success, and had attracted sufficient funds from the city to make the Pueblo Nuevo project a significant social achievement.

At the same time, the lives of individual Mexicans were being influenced by Philip's sacrificial work. Alex Escobar, whom I met during my visit, had been a gang member selling drugs in the same park where Philip had first set up his card table. Through the Pueblo Nuevo project he had been reunited with his wife and baby, brought to a deep personal faith, and at the time of my visit was employed by the church. A few days later I baptised several Mexican babies in the diocesan celebration. I was profoundly moved to see such evidence of authentic Christianity.

*   *   *

If the Episcopal Church of the United States has tended to be seduced by the prevailing culture of its society, with no overarching strategy for discerning where the lines should be drawn, my visit to some African countries revealed that other Provinces were consciously, and often unconsciously, struggling to work out the implications of the Christian faith in cultures that were not entirely inimical to it.

I paid three visits to Kenya, but the most interesting and important was just before Christmas 1994, when as part of the visit President Daniel arap Moi invited me to lead the prayers at the National Day of Independence in Jamhuri Park, Nairobi. The trip was at the invitation of Archbishop Manesses Kuria, who was about to retire, and was intended to share in the life of one of Africa's most vigorous Anglican Churches and to celebrate its 150 years of history. Under the dedicated ministry of Manesses the Bishops were united, and I sensed that the mission of the Church was going well. Manesses had a wonderful, beaming smile and was a great influence in his nation. The Bishop most likely to succeed him was David Gitari, a fearless leader who had made himself unpopular with President Moi and other leading members of the government for his prophetic preaching. Several attempts had been made on his life, but he scorned them all and carried on attacking corruption in civic life and the misuse of political power.

My first port of call, to All Saints' Church, Limuru, was to a site closely associated with historic mission of the Church. I was pleased to meet three very elderly white sisters who were descendants of the missionary who founded the church, although I was rather taken aback when one introduced herself with the words: 'I am the eldest son of my father.' I blinked and attempted to correct her. However, she repeated her statement, then explained that according to law, only sons could inherit, but a legal fiction had developed that allowed her as the eldest to be counted as a son. She was clearly proud of this casuistical interpretation of the law that had worked in her favour.

This episode may have had its amusing side, but I feared that if Kenya's laws could be so casually manipulated, it had serious problems. Indeed, corruption was rife, and this potentially great country was riddled with injustice and greed. As I had been encouraged by Kenyans to address this issue before my arrival, I decided to touch upon it in my prayers at the National Day of Independence. This was obviously not without risk, as I was there as a guest of the President, who had invited me to contribute a ten-minute address prior to his 'State of the Nation' speech.

It turned out to be a splendid occasion, with fifty thousand people present and the usual march-past of soldiers, sailors and airmen, with dozens of ancient tanks and armoured carriers and a fly-past of ten aircraft or so. My turn came. After thanking the President warmly and making some sincere remarks of praise about his nation, I expressed my concern at the high level of corruption in Kenyan society which had been reported to me. I suggested that the only way to combat this was to harness the values of the Christian faith to the ideals of democracy and to see them lived out in public life by all who have authority, especially politicians.

This gentle admonition did not go down well. The President began his own speech clearly riled by my remarks, however diplomatically they had been expressed. After welcoming me and other guests to the National Day of Independence, he turned on me and more or less said that I had a nerve to talk about corruption – that was a sermon that the West in general and Britain in particular needed to heed. His criticism was greeted with much applause, but according to Kenyan journalists who spoke to me later my comments were widely appreciated because they were so palpably true. Every Kenyan knew, they said, that the President had only retained power all these years by selling power and privileges to unelected people. A culture of dishonesty had been established which had trickled down to affect every level of society.

Two days later, with Archbishop Kuria and Bishop David Gitari I had a personal audience with President Moi. He seemed to go overboard in his praise of the Church of the Province of Kenya and the ministry of both Manesses and David. He was also generous about my speech, and not an objection was raised to my attacks on the widespread corruption and dishonesty in his society. What this conversation revealed was his opinion about how faith related to the world around. Although a churchgoer, the President saw the Christian faith as hermetically sealed off from the real lives of people and their social and political aspirations. He believed that religion had no right to interfere with the way governments and communities were governed. This, of course, was the fundamental reason why David Gitari clashed with him so sharply. David's forthright and bold teaching and preaching originated in a view of the Christian faith that saw no distinction between personal and corporate existence. The Kingdom of God introduced by Jesus related to the whole of life, and culture itself had to be assessed and criticised in the light of the gospel.

The President went on to express his fear of Islam sweeping down from Sudan to invade East Africa. His foreboding was that unless it was stopped, Kenya might find itself in danger of being swamped by terrorism and fanaticism. He seemed oblivious of the fact that among the reasons for the growth of Islam in East Africa are the region's pervasive corruption and dishonesty, and a desire on the part of ordinary people for a strong community ethic around which all could unite. In spite of many personal strengths, the sad reality was that in all his years of office President Moi had done very little to offer an example of selfless service that could make his nation great and provide a bulwark against the extremism he feared. Regrettably, what he did offer was little more than tribal leadership at a national level.

For many years I had wished to visit Nigeria, where one of the greatest African leaders, Bishop Samuel 'Ajahi' Crowther, had lived and died. Ajahi, born in 1810 of a pagan family, was taken at the age of ten by Arab slave traders, sold to the Portuguese and put on a ship bound for Brazil. Rescued by the Royal Navy, young Ajahi and his fellow slaves where taken to Sierra Leone, where the Church Missionary Society educated the boy and led him to faith. His brightness impressed the missionaries, and he was sent to Britain for further study. On returning to Nigeria he became a missionary, and in 1864 was consecrated Bishop of Nigeria in Canterbury Cathedral, the very first African Bishop. His contribution to Nigerian Christianity cannot be underestimated.

Ever since I had read about him, Samuel Crowther had become one of my heroes, and I was keen to visit the land that had produced him. The first date offered for a visit, in 1993, had to be cancelled because of the Nigerian presidential elections, then a second visit was aborted at the last minute because of the unpreparedness of the Church. Finally, in February 2001, the long-awaited visit came about. It was the most spectacular of all our foreign trips, as well as the most gruelling. We were greeted at Abuja airport by Archbishop Peter Akinola, a lively, outgoing man who had just taken over from Archbishop Joseph Adetiloye, who had originally issued the invitation. Peter was now presiding over the largest Church in the Anglican Communion. The welcoming crowd at the airport was huge, and in the mêlée my Press Officer had his computer and camera stolen – a costly reminder that dishonesty and corruption were problems in Nigeria too.

The first part of the visit focused on the north of the country, where Christianity and Islam lived side by side, not always in an easy relationship. We went to Ikka village, fifty miles north of Abuja, to see a typical rural church. Leaving the teeming urban sprawl of the city, and changing into four-wheel-drive vehicles as we left the roads behind, we journeyed along uncomfortable, bumpy tracks. As we had found on earlier trips, this is the only way to appreciate the beauty, wildness and life of Africa. Stone buildings gave way reluctantly to simple mud and straw huts; children on their way to school wearing shoes and carrying satchels gave way to children with hardly any clothing; women in smart clothing gave way to women in simple traditional dress.

Ikka village eventually came into sight – a straggling community of about two hundred houses. A band of youngsters led us into a square where the Mothers' Union had gathered, easily identified by their smart white dresses and blue sashes. On this and other occasions we were able to appreciate the strength of the Mothers' Union and its formidable contribution to Church and the nation. There were the inevitable speeches, followed by the exchange of gifts. The visit to the overcrowded clinic, filled with screaming children and harassed mothers, revealed the dedication of the tiny staff and the important work of the Church in caring for the very poor. I noticed with interest that the village's population was made up of Muslims as well as Christians, and was told that the two religions got on extremely well in this area. The Church's social care, so appreciated by the Muslim community, was central to the harmony that had been established.

But there was no doubt about the extreme poverty in the village, and a number of children showed serious signs of malnutrition. The doctor explained that he was only able to visit this clinic once a week, and expressed his irritation at the hypocrisy of government claims that full medical care was available to all. The reality fell far short of that. In his opinion the Churches played a vital part in the life of Nigeria, and without them medical cover would be unsustainable in many rural areas.

After an hour at Ikka village we drove on for forty miles until we reached the main highway, where we changed into fresh cars to take us to the city of Kaduna, which struck us with its great untidiness yet startling dynamism. The streets teemed with people, mainly teenagers, going about their business. We met Bishop Josiah Al Fearon, one of the most intellectually able Bishops in the Church of Nigeria. Josiah spoke of the dire situation in Kaduna which has a dominant Muslim population but a significant Christian presence. Over the last eleven months many hundreds of people had been killed in riots, the majority of the victims being Christian. An uneasy calm now lay over the city. Josiah had built up a strong relationship with the new Muslim Governor, Alhaji Ahmed Muhammed Makarfi, and this friendship was at the heart of the peace between the two sides.

Following lunch I met the Governor. After a private interview we followed Nigerian custom by moving into a conference room for an exchange of gifts and speeches. The room was filled with about a hundred people, including the press and TV cameramen. I spoke first about the need for respect and tolerance, deploring the recent violence, which shamed, I said, both great religions. The Governor spoke of Muslims honouring Jesus – a remark I have often heard – and respecting the place of the Church: 'No good Muslim burns churches down or kills a Christian.' With almost unveiled contempt he alluded to the Governor of the neighbouring state of Zamfara, who had recently introduced Sharia law, and insisted that the introduction of religious law alongside civil law was bound to confuse the people, and could lead to civil law being seen as inferior to Sharia.

Following this visit we made another long journey, to Wusasa, known as 'the cradle of Christianity in northern Nigeria', where we had the most vibrant reception of the day. We were first greeted by the youthful Bishop of Wusasa, Ali Buba Lamido, and his wife Mary. Behind a number of bands we entered a huge square next to the old cathedral. Typically, we found that the programme sheet given to us bore no relation whatsoever to what had been worked out by the national committee. But the worship was lively, vibrant and joyful. I remember wistfully thinking to myself that the Nigerian Church could teach us in Britain a thing or two.

Deep poverty existed alongside this robust faith, and I was delighted to see that the Church was fully involved in social programmes to help the poor. We were taken to St Luke's Hospital, which has 230 beds and only two full-time doctors. Here Eileen was in her element, and with a more discerning eye than mine was able to tell me later of the serious shortage of trained personnel, to say nothing of the acute shortage of drugs and equipment. Bishop Ali shared with me his anxiety about encroaching Muslim groups, whose practice was to burn churches down in order to weaken the resolve of Christians to stay in the areas concerned.

The following day we were in the notorious state of Zamfara, now under Sharia law. It was noticeable as we entered Zamfara how few women were about; those who were wore either traditional Islamic head covering or were covered entirely. Even more noticeable was the poverty. Gasau, the capital, was a sprawl of huts and buildings in advanced stages of decay, many of them derelict. We were met by a cavalcade as we entered the town, and slowly drove behind a few youth bands to the cathedral, where Bishop Simon Bala and his wife Talatu greeted us.

We found ourselves in what can only be described as a religious/ political meeting. There were well over a thousand people crammed into the square, with TV crews including a BBC team, emotional hymn-singing and speeches charged with complaints about mistreatment, injustice and lack of freedom. An impressive young Roman Catholic priest, Father Linus, the Chairman of the local branch of CAN (the Christian Association of Nigeria), was introduced to me. He expressed his fears about the plight of Christians under Sharia, and warned me to be on my guard against the Governor, who he said would try to persuade me that Sharia law did not affect Christians. In fact, said Linus, the reverse was true: since the imposition of Sharia the previous year, Christians no longer had freedom, they could not broadcast on radio or television, they could not build new churches or establish schools, and women felt under pressure to assume the veil. The Governor, claimed Linus, was trying to eliminate Christianity from Zamfara, after the pattern of Saudi Arabia.

The rally over, it was time to meet the Governor, Ahmed Sanni Yerima, at his residence a short drive away. Together with Archbishop Peter and Bishop Simon I was introduced to him in a small waiting room, whilst the rest of the party was ushered away. We were led into a large public room where two hundred people were gathered, and as I was led to the dais I noticed to my dismay that the crowd was segregated. To the right were a large phalanx of Muslims, with some venerable Imams among them. To the left had been placed all the Christians, including some Anglican Bishops and leaders of other Churches. The tension was palpable.

I was called upon to speak first, and decided to play down the friction as much as possible, as the potential for conflict seemed high. But I was determined not to squander this opportunity to raise important issues in a direct but diplomatic manner. I began by thanking the Governor for his gracious welcome, and applauded him as a man of faith and courage with laudable intentions to build unity in his state. A round of applause greeted this tribute. Then, deliberately echoing the Koran, I said: 'I come as a man of peace and bring a message of peace from friends in the United Kingdom and around the world. Peace is at the heart of Islam and peace is central to the Christian faith. Peace be upon this house and the state of Zamfara.' Shouts of 'Amen!' and a great round of applause was the response. I then proceeded to my main point: 'I know it is your intention to make this state a united one. Yet we all know the problems are huge. You yourself told me so before this public meeting that you are concerned about high levels of illiteracy and the worrying extent of poverty and unemployment. It is vital to have a united state to combat these terrible social problems. However, a large number of your citizens who are Christians believe themselves to be marginalised, even excluded and second-class citizens.'

I then read out from a document Father Linus had given me earlier: 'The Church in Zamfara is plagued by hardship, marginalisation and religious segregation. Here in Zamfara we are treated as second-class citizens, with little or no attention paid to the protection of our rights. Our children are not allowed to receive Christian moral education in schools; we are not allowed to make Christian broadcasts on radio and we are not represented in government.' At this point the Christians to my left broke into applause.

It was the Governor's turn to speak, and he did so at great length, thanking me for coming and for putting my concerns in such a way that Muslims as well as Christians could understand and sympathise. He said it was his concern to involve everyone, then launched into a defence of Sharia – which I had not even mentioned. He remarked that Sharia was central to Muslim self-understanding: 'Sharia is Islam: Sharia is a way of life for Muslims,' then went on to say that punishments such as flogging and amputation were only enforced after careful evidence, and that at least four witnesses must give evidence in the case of adultery. Then, almost unbelievably, he cited the example of a thief whose hand had been amputated six months before, and who also received a prison sentence, who now rejoiced in his amputation because he knew it was just and because it meant he would now go to Paradise.

There was simply no meeting of minds. The Governor was convinced that the imposition of Sharia would make his state just, and that Christians had nothing to fear. The reality was of course that they had every reason to fear the menace of a faith promoted with such zeal. My final exchange with the Governor following the public meeting took the form of arguing for Christians' right to build churches and to have Christian education in schools. 'If new churches are needed, tell the Bishops to contact me,' he said cheerfully. Five years on, the situation remains the same – empty promises and vain words.

The second half of our visit to Nigeria took us to the southern half of the country, which is predominantly Christian. There we were able to glean a better idea of the great influence of Christianity and the growth of the Anglican Church. The sheer diversity of Nigerian society seemed to have its mirror image in the different forms of Christianity. The Roman Catholic and Anglican Churches stood out everywhere, but equally prominent was the bewildering range of alternative Protestant churches and assemblies, predominantly Pentecostal, that expressed so colourfully the religious enthusiasm of Nigerians. I attempted to scribble down the names of the different churches, but when I reached 250 I gave up. The huge crowds that came out into the streets to greet us dwarfed anything we had experienced before, and their joy and enthusiasm sometimes alarmed us as they surged around seeking a hand to shake. Frequently the police had to break up the crowds, sometimes with truncheons and rifle-butts.

During the seven-hour drive from Abuja to Akwa through the

rich heartland of Nigeria our cavalcade of a dozen cars with a police escort was cheered as we swept through the villages. Beyond the roadside young children herded cattle and men were burning the fields to eradicate weeds – an environmental tragedy seemed to be unfolding before our eyes as field after field was ablaze.

I had deliberately refrained from preparing addresses before coming to Nigeria, believing that this critical visit demanded a more spontaneous style. It seemed to me that the messages the Church needed to hear were that it should build on the truly remarkable work it was doing for the poor, but also confront its own weaknesses. I was uncomfortably aware that the Nigerian Church had adopted some of the worst features of English Church life. Bishops referred to one another as 'My Lord Bishop', or addressed their three Arch-bishops as 'Your Grace' – terms that seem anachronistic in England but are positively ridiculous in Nigeria. In a few speeches I encouraged the Church to think of power and wealth in terms of the message of the gospel, and not, as I feared some Bishops and people were doing, in terms of hierarchical structures and worldly power. To judge by the evident wealth of those in the front rows of the cathedrals I preached in, it was a message the Church in Nigeria needed to hear. I was dismayed too that Bishops seemed to display a tribal attitude towards their people, and expected instant obedience. In the vestry of one cathedral a clergyman who had been expected to be present at the 8 a.m. service for a minor role but had not showed up was publicly berated by the Bishop, and made to kneel before him as the verbal chastisement went on.

The ways in which the Church touched all levels of society were also apparent. On one occasion, in response to a plea from Bishop Cyril Okorocha, we made an unscheduled stop at the town of Owerri. This was against Archbishop Peter's judgement, because the huge crowds were making us late by at least three hours every day. To our surprise we were met by fifty thousand people in a stadium as large as an English football ground. Cyril informed us that the service was being beamed to another stadium, where an equally large crowd was gathered. It was a staggering example of the depth of faith in the south, and the devotion of the people.

The final act of this remarkable visit was a twenty-four-hour Retreat with all the Bishops, during which I tried to put before them my hopes for their great Church. It was a Church that had been very profoundly influenced by the evangelical tradition, and it saw its authority in biblical terms. I meditated on the way all our traditions and customs must be evaluated according to the way of Christ. I was aware that this Church was critical of the way in which cultural trends influenced the Western Church, but from Archbishop Peter I was also aware that many Nigerian Bishops turned a blind eye to the prevalence of polygamy, for pastoral reasons. I was sympathetic to this, knowing that in some African societies when polygamous marriages were broken up it was the women who suffered. Certainly this was Bishop Crowther's view a hundred years ago. I felt the Church needed to return to its roots. Even so, I returned home humbled and inspired by this large and growing Church. Embattled in the north by a resurgent Islam, and encumbered in the south by worldliness and corruption, the Anglican Church in Nigeria seemed to be very well led under Archbishop Peter Akinola and his colleagues.

Margaret Mead, the renowned anthropologist, once observed: 'As the traveller who has once been from home is wiser than he who has never left his own doorstep, so a knowledge of one other culture should sharpen our ability to scrutinise more steadily, to appreciate more lovingly, our own' (Coming of Age in Samoa). My reflections on the three quite different cultures of the United States, Kenya and Nigeria led me not only to appreciate the great difficulty of relating the Christian faith authentically to the world around us, but also to have greater sympathy with those who had attempted this and had failed. Where it seemed we had the greatest success was where the Christian faith was lived courageously in situations of great challenge, such as those experienced by Father Philip Lance and the Pueblo

Nuevo project, or by David Gitari and those who sought to change a culture of corruption, or by the many Christians in Nigeria whose faith led them to struggle for the freedom of all religions.

14

Empty Stomachs Have no Ears

'You see, Archbishop, there is an African saying: "Empty stomachs have no ears."'

Sudanese Bishop

ON 29 DECEMBER 1993 EILEEN AND I, with Roger Symon, my Officer for the Anglican Communion, and Jim Rosenthal, Press Officer for the Anglican Communion Office, entered Sudan illegally.

The background to this unprecedented act lay in a worsening relationship between the United Kingdom and the Islamic Republic of Sudan. The UK and other Western nations had accused Sudan of breaching the United Nations Declaration on Human Rights, and the British Ambassador in Khartoum, Peter Streams, had been active in protesting at Sudan's actions against civilians in the Nuba mountains. Our visit had been planned for well over a year. We were going as guests of the Episcopal Church of Sudan, and we had been informed by the Sudanese Embassy in London that no restrictions would be imposed, and we could visit anywhere freely.

On Christmas Eve I was in Canterbury preparing to join many thousands in the town square for carols when Roger phoned with the news that the Sudanese government had made a significant change to the visit. They now wished me to go as a guest of the government, rather than of the Church, and assured me that in spite of this change a warm welcome awaited our party. On the surface this seemed an entirely hospitable act. What could possibly be suspicious about a government offering facilities such as transport and hotel accommodation to a visiting Christian leader, and so releasing the Episcopal Church from a burden it could hardly afford?

However, I was not at all happy with the sudden change of plan, and asked Roger to get advice from the Sudanese Church and the Foreign Office. Archbishop Benjamina, Primate of the Episcopal Church of Sudan, was indignant, believing that the Khartoum government would use my visit to try to persuade the world that religious liberty was alive and well in the Sudan. The Foreign Office also believed that the Sudanese government was trying to hijack the visit. Both urged me not to go.

I made my decision within an hour. To go as the guest of an Islamic government would suggest to the Sudanese Church that I had been bought. It was crucial to maintain objectivity. I therefore asked Roger to reply courteously to the Embassy that I had already accepted the invitation from the Church, and would stick with this agreement even if it meant cancelling the planned visit to the north of the country. It was, however, still my intention to visit the rebel-held south. The reaction from the Sudanese government was unexpected and swift. I was told that I was not welcome, and my visa was cancelled. But by this time my mind was made up – we would visit our Church in the south, which was controlled by the SPLA (Sudanese People's Liberation Army).

The media's reaction was frenzied, sensing a major diplomatic event as well as an unprecedented snub by a Church leader to a host government. Roger Symon gave interviews to BBC Radio 4's *Today* programme, BBC 1 news and ITV news. I did not make any statement, apart from a press release which simply stated that it was my intention to visit suffering Christians in the south, and that I regretted the Sudanese government's unilateral takeover of my programme, leading to the cancellation of the visit to Khartoum.

The following day we flew to Nairobi, where we were met by the British High Commissioner, Sir Kieran Prendergast, Bishop Karibe

Taban, the Roman Catholic Bishop of Torit and Chairman of the New Sudan Council of Churches, and a host of journalists. I was most impressed by Bishop Taban, who gave us an excellent briefing on the suffering of the people in the area we were going to visit.

Within a few hours we had exchanged the comfort of a BA flight for an eight-seater Cessna piloted by Heather Stuart, a South African in her forties who had been flying in and out of southern Sudan for several years delivering aid. A highly intelligent and 'no-nonsense' woman, she made it clear that once we were in her plane, she was in charge. 'If any of you gentlemen', she declared, 'has any trouble about being flown by a woman', then now is the moment to walk away.' She relaxed when no one moved, and explained that my intention to enter the south had infuriated the Sudanese government greatly. She did not expect trouble as the Sudanese had so few aircraft, but there could be some bombing of places we intended to go to – indeed, she reported, there had been a bombing raid the day before.

The flight took ninety minutes. We left behind the rolling hills of Kenya, with grand views of the Rift Valley, as well as the rugged mountain scenery of northern Uganda. We flew in low over southern Sudan, observing scattered villages before bouncing along some very rough grass on the airstrip at Nimule, where we were welcomed by a contingent of SPLA forces in their jungle uniforms, and by Nathaniel Garang, the Bishop of Bor. Bishop Nathaniel, a tall, distinguished-looking man with an attractive open face and a wispy grey beard, was dressed in a shabby but brilliant red cassock. He introduced Eileen and me to the people present, and we were taken to the church compound at Nimule where many thousands of Dinkas were gathered to receive us, each one waving a Dinka cross, made from the dark wood common to the country and held together by discarded cartridge shells, sadly easily available in the country.

After a short service in which I gave an impromptu address I met a remarkable American Episcopal missionary, Marc Nikkel, whose lifelong service to Sudan had been outstanding. Marc gave us a brief introduction to the Church in the south, and the way that –

together with the Roman Catholic Church – it was now the only lifeline for the people. Every other national network had collapsed, and the Churches were providing education, health care and social ministries.

From Nimule we drove to Ashwa camp, a long journey over very dry, bumpy roads, passing the sad ruins of General Gordon's house and along the remains of a road laid by the British in the days when Sudan was under British rule. We were greeted at the camp by another crowd of thousands, with many clergy in shabby, dirty surplices and Mothers' Union members in long, white, beautifully clean dresses with the distinctive blue sash of the MU. After the inevitable speeches and singing I encountered thirty or so young men who had been crippled by war, with banners proclaiming 'We need help', 'We don't want to be Arabised, Mohammedised', 'The world no longer cares for us', 'We are the forgotten people'.

We went immediately to Ashwa hospital, which has 240 beds and a mere handful of medically trained personnel to deal with a seemingly impossible situation. Sick and wounded people lay everywhere, packed into dirty, badly lit wards, crowded together in the corridors and in the compound outside. The hospital was clearly unhygienic, and the operating theatre, far from being spotlessly clean, looked positively lethal. A short meeting with several doctors and senior nurses followed, in which they expressed their concerns. A picture emerged of outstanding medical care in spite of great difficulties. There was a serious shortage of drugs, and the overburdened staff desperately needed more trained personnel. Lives would be saved, one doctor told us, if they had even one ambulance to bring seriously sick people in for treatment. There was no doubt that Ashwa hospital was doing an amazing job in the most terrible of situations.

We left for the long journey back to Nimule and a delicious meal as sunset fell, embracing us in the velvety darkness of Africa, with the increasing racket of the crickets, the sound of drumbeats coming from every direction and the glow of many campfires around.

The following day, New Year's Eve, Eileen and I were awoken in our tent at 5.30 a.m. not only by the local cockerel, but with the sensational news brought to us by journalists that Peter Streams, British Ambassador to Sudan, had been expelled as a result of my visit. This was amazing and disturbing news. I issued a statement immediately, expressing my regret that Sudan was losing a distinguished diplomat who cared deeply for its people. I made it clear that he was not responsible for my decision to enter the country.

A brief breakfast, and away we went in battered Land Cruisers to Lowa, north of Nimule, over trails that had been churned up by lorries during the wet season, making the journey uncomfortable and at times very painful. The caravan of vehicles churned up the red dust, which choked our lungs and burned our eyes. Our first visit was to the Catholic Mission and its hospitable Sudanese priest, Father Julian. In my speech I reiterated my statement about Peter Streams, adding that the Sudanese government's refusal to welcome our visit would inevitably further isolate it internationally.

After prayers in the Catholic church, in which I was able to affirm the great co-operation between all the Churches in Sudan, we took to the dusty trail again, bound for Arati and the local headquarters of the Sudan Relief and Rehabilitation Association. The flamboyant and genial Secretary General, Mr Mario Mor Mor, gave us a description of its work caring for the 125,000 displaced people in the area. Rather extraordinarily, he digressed from his speech about the urgent need for aid to the importance of using English. He said that he was proud to speak the language because 'the English preserved our culture', and saluted the work of generations of missionaries in translating the Bible and worship into the languages of the Sudanese people. This, he remarked, had been a crucial factor in preserving local tribal customs.

I was about to make my response when a note was handed to him with the news that people were starting to leave Kotobi camp, which housed thirty-five thousand people, twenty miles away because the camp had run out of food. This brought home to us the stark reality of the 'forgotten war'.

Then we were on the move once more, this time to Akote, a camp of twenty-five thousand displaced people. The crowds that greeted us were enormous. We left our vehicles and walked with the dancing, swaying crowd as they led us into the camp. We were greeted by Archdeacon Peter Boll, who had done an impressive job building up many of the churches in the area. After a moving service in a straw-covered church, in which a dove was frantically flying around seeking escape, we were led outside for lunch. And then, in a way that could never be stage-managed, just as the Archdeacon had presented me with my own Dinka cross, the dove that had been trying to find its way out of the Church appeared, calmly landed on the cross in my hand and posed for a picture. We were all greatly moved by this wonderful sight, which gave me the most perfect sermon aid. I commented that the cross, made of dark wood and cartridge shells, represented the pain and hopelessness of the people of Sudan, but that one day the country would be transfigured. The dove, the symbol of peace, was a sign of God's promise to reconcile all things.

Before leaving Akote we visited the Therapeutic Feeding Centre for children who needed extra care. There we saw tiny, emaciated children being cared for by young Irishwomen from the Irish charity 'Goal'. We were thrilled to see such dedicated young people. Eileen sat on the ground with toddlers who were revelling in the pleasure of being loved and cuddled by someone. More speeches followed, in which I urged the clergy to stay with their people. The other speakers included a venerable Dinka teacher called 'Uncle' who asked me to take his greetings to the Queen – a duty I duly carried out a few weeks later.

When we finally arrived back at our base at Nimule after a long, taxing journey, our clothes were saturated with sweat and covered in dust. After a lifesaving wash from a bucket of water as well as a lifesaving drink of duty-free, which even Eileen succumbed to, we enjoyed a meeting with Bishop Nathaniel and some members of the clergy. Nathaniel took the opportunity to give a surprising and impassioned speech, in which he appealed for aid for his Church, which was bearing the brunt of the deteriorating conditions. He spoke accusingly of the intention of the Khartoum government to 'Islamicise' the south, which, he said, 'we shall fight to the death to stop'. 'So many young men have been killed that the population is declining, and our women are so weak that they cannot bear children,' he declared. His speech brought home to us all the fact that politics cannot be kept separate from faith. We toppled into bed exhausted by the heat, the crowds, the journeys and the emotional intensity of all we had witnessed.

About two hours later, at 12.15 a.m. on New Year's Day 1994, I was seized with terrible griping pains. I crept out of my bed carefully, not wanting to disturb Eileen in the adjacent bed, fumbled for a torch and headed off to the loo – a mere hole in the ground – about ten yards away in the darkness. As I walked towards it I could see rats scampering out of my way. In all I had to pay five visits that night, and was sick twice. My last 'call' to the toilet was at 4.45 a.m., and I felt so spent that I decided there was no point in even trying to get back to sleep. My compensation was to see the dawn break and Africa come to life as animals, children, women and men stirred and greeted the new day.

At 7 a.m. we left for the airstrip, and Heather took us on our next flight to Akot. I was feeling increasingly poorly as we approached our destination. Jim Rosenthal gave me a tablet, which helped, but the pains were racking, and there was no toilet in Heather's tiny plane. I gritted my teeth and instructed Roger to ensure that as soon as we landed I must find one, and also have some peace for a few hours. However, as we approached Akot from the air we could see many thousands of people gathered to welcome us. I realised with alarm that it was not going to be easy to have a break.

It is amazing, however, how the human spirit responds when buoyed up by the challenge of a new situation. The genuine warmth of the welcome, and the sad condition of the people who had walked many miles to greet us, gave me the strength to cope with the speeches. Here at Akot I was in the diocese of Rumbek, nominally under the notorious and absentee Bishop Gabriel Roric. Gabriel was now State Minister at the Ministry of Foreign Relations in the Islamic Sudanese government, and a great grief and embarrassment to the Church. The diocese was meanwhile led by two faithful priests, Archdeacon Reuben and Father Abraham. I was more than a little taken aback when Father Abraham greeted me with the memorable words, 'Thanks be to God that He has sent His son incarnate in the Archbishop of Canterbury.' It was clear that he did not realise how unorthodox his statement was, but it inspired me nevertheless to make a strong impromptu address linking the incarnation of Christ to the life of the people here at Akot, in that Christ had been a displaced person too. I think I may have been upstaged by Eileen, who was taken to a chair labelled 'Mother of Christ'.

Much to my relief, Eileen and I were taken to a beautiful conical hut specially erected for us, where we were able to relax and rest for a short while. It was yet another illustration of the fact that people in the most terrible conditions are more wont to be generous and caring than those from richer backgrounds. One hour later we emerged from our hut much refreshed, and I was feeling a more 'integrated' Archbishop. We were soon on our way to Thiau Kei, about an hour's drive away. We left Akot with much singing, led by a Catholic choir conducted by the Vicar General. I noticed that their banner was also innocently heretical. It read: 'Blessed is he that comes in the Name of the Lord'.

Thiau Kei, although off the beaten track, is of great significance to Dinka people because here, twenty years ago, a revival began that continues to this day. In 1982 Reuben, now the Archdeacon, and one other priest were the only clergy in the diocese of Rumbek. They established a small church at Thiau Kei, and two illiterate men approached them asking to be taught the Christian faith. Reuben used the Bible to teach them to read, and prepared them for baptism. He then encouraged them to go and tell others. They did so, and an astonishing number of people followed the example of the two new believers, leading to thousands seeking baptism. Reuben, in telling me the story, added a sentence that made authentic theological sense: 'We didn't go out to preach Christ as though He wasn't there before. He was there in the hearts of the people and they then received His word.' I cannot think of a better description of 'grace in action'.

The crowds on this visit surpassed anything we had seen thus far; indeed, there were far too many people even to estimate their number. As our open truck entered the village thousands of people on all sides accompanied us, waving their crosses and singing. We were preceded by two trucks full of heavily armed SPLA troops, and another military vehicle with a menacing anti-aircraft gun for our protection. We stopped at a huge cross, where I made a short speech. There were many banners, including one that read 'For Christ's sake – we face death – all day long'.

We went on to a new Bible Institute, where 182 people were already in training, with the same number on a waiting list. Half of those in training were women and half of the total were illiterate, but were on their way to literacy. I laid the foundation of the Institute and opened a Mothers' Union hut for work among the women. We were due next at the 'Conference Hall', which we found was an open space under some large trees where one day a building would stand. More speeches followed, including a moving one by Reuben setting out his vision for the growth of the Church. The local SPLA commander took advantage of my presence and that of the journalists to appeal to the international community to give aid to the suffering people of Sudan, and to make more of an effort to bring peace to the south. When the platform was finally mine I used the few minutes available to express my profound admiration of such heroic Christians as Reuben and Abraham, and to encourage Christians and Muslims to seek peace together.

Then we were off again, suddenly realising that although we had been supplied with plenty of water to drink, we had not had time for lunch. On arrival at the airstrip we were able to witness the arrival of a huge Hercules plane bearing food supplies given to the Christian south by the Lutheran World Federation.

Heather then flew us to Yambio in the south-west of Sudan, about an hour's flight away. We were greeted by Bishop Daniel Zindo. Yambio was not only more peaceful than the other places we had visited on this trip, but the countryside was very different. Instead of dry brown bush and scrub, we were driven through avenues of trees and tropical vegetation. Although Yambio showed signs of poverty and neglect caused by the long war, it was still possible to see that it had once been a busy and prosperous town. We received another excited and generous welcome as jubilant Anglicans and other Christians thronged the streets to greet their visitors from England. Once more I noticed that distinctions between religion and politics were blurred. Banners proclaiming 'Freedom from oppression' and 'NO! to Arabisation' jostled with others stating that 'Jesus is Lord' and 'Jesus offers peace'. We were taken to the cathedral, built by Australians in 1925; apart from the surprising bareness of its interior and the absence of symbols, it could easily have been a church in Kent.

Glancing at the order of service, my heart sank as I saw that it included thirteen items and five speeches. We steeled ourselves to endure it, but the sheer delight of the people who had made long journeys to get to Yambio gave us pleasure. Once again the members of the wonderful Mothers' Union, swaying and dancing, gave us a great welcome, and garlanded Eileen with flowers greeting her as 'big Momma'.

The celebration over, we were able to get to the Bishop's house for a welcome rest. To our great joy we noticed that a makeshift shower had been erected specially for us, consisting of a bucket of water dangling from a tree, and a man on the other side of a curtain whose job was to pull on a rope once commanded to do so. This was certainly not to Eileen's liking, and the man was politely asked to leave us. We managed to improvise ourselves. The cold water was instantly refreshing, and perked us up for another round of talks and discussion. As we sat on the veranda of the Bishop's house we watched another beautiful African sunset, with the background hum of the crickets, the spirited laughter of children at play, the clatter of women preparing the meal and sometimes breaking into song, the drumming from many different directions – all combined with the warmth of the dying sun and the rich smell of Africa.

Over supper the local SPLA commander praised the inspiring example of our Sudanese clergy. But then came a sting in the tail. He spoke reproachfully of the wider Church's neglect of Sudan, and compared Anglican support with that of the Roman Catholic Church, which gave far more in aid to their Church in Sudan than did the Anglican Communion. I myself had noticed that there were many more expatriate Roman priests than Anglicans in Sudan, which inevitably resulted in their gathering more support for their Church. The result, continued the soldier, was that the dedicated clergy of the Sudan Episcopal Church, including the Bishop, existed on next to nothing, 'while the Roman Catholic clergy have cars and houses that mark them out as more important'.

Although I was not sympathetic to the language of status, I could not but agree with his assessment. Salaries paid to our clergy were very inadequate, and sometimes not paid at all. Sudanese Bishops often had to travel to America or England to raise support, although generous help did come from the English dioceses of Salisbury and Bradford, which had formal links with the Sudan. I was also uncomfortably aware that there was a perception in the Sudanese Church that the Church of England gave nothing towards development and aid. I had to challenge this several times, pointing out that Christian Aid and Tearfund were arms of the Church of England in partnership with other Churches in the United Kingdom. Nonetheless, I was horrified at the level of poverty in Sudan and vowed to do something on my return to Britain.

Over supper Bishop Daniel dropped a bombshell: would I conduct his marriage to his wife Grace tomorrow morning? I had been warned that Daniel might ask me to bless his marriage, but to marry him was an entirely different proposition. Besides, he and Grace had several adult children – surely they were already married? Daniel explained that they were married years ago according to traditional custom, and now they wanted a Christian marriage. Although I was unconvinced by Daniel's logic, I felt it was important to go as far as possible in acceding to his request without denying the legitimacy of the traditional ceremony which had made him and Grace man and wife.

The following morning, however, revealed their determination to make this a true marriage ceremony, when Grace appeared in white with several bridesmaids, looking as radiant as a young bride. A hundred guests witnessed a solemn reaffirmation of vows as two devoted people gave themselves to one another again. Tragically, such is the violence of Sudan that a few years later Grace and her eldest daughter were shot dead by her deranged son-in-law, who then committed suicide.

Immediately after this ceremony another huge open-air service took place outside the cathedral, attended by many thousands. It was an extraordinary mix of piety and politics as the traditional Sudanese service was punctuated by speeches, testimonies and protest songs. When it was my turn to speak I was moved when a very old priest sitting near me pulled a Bible wrapped in plastic from his dirty surplice. As I preached from the gospel passage I could see him writing notes in the margin of his beloved Bible, and thought how much he could teach us in the West about devotion and commitment to learning.

We were then driven to Nzara airstrip, where Heather was waiting to take us on the four-hour flight back to Nairobi. What a visit it had been, and what scenes of hope and despair we had witnessed. How thankful to God we were for His goodness and for allowing us to see our Church, of which we felt so proud, in such good heart and bearing suffering so patiently.

But it wasn't completely over. The following day at the residence of the High Commissioner in Nairobi I met Colonel John Garang, leader of the mainstream SPLA. He was knowledgeable and realistic about the course of the war, and believed that the two armies were evenly matched. He did not think the Sudanese government could defeat the SPLA, but on the other hand, he did not think he had the resources to take Khartoum. He was contemptuous of Riek Machah's United Party, which was also fighting the government. Machah arrived shortly after Garang left, and was equally dismissive of Garang, stating that he had no confidence in him as either a military commander or a politician. Divided and weakened, the two armies of the south continue to fight the north and one another.

On 4 January 1994 we returned to London after what could only be described as a truly momentous visit. I immediately issued a press statement which, while describing the impressive, brave and inspiring witness of the Episcopal Church, also expressed the mood of Christians in southern Sudan who felt abandoned by the world. My visit as Archbishop of Canterbury had been a visible sign that they were not forgotten. I thanked the media for covering it so thoroughly and for giving such prominence to the country's appalling problems. In order to placate the Sudanese government just a little, I expressed my regret at the unfortunate fracas surrounding my visit, and my hope that it might be possible to visit the north of the country in due course.

To maximise the impact of my visit, I decided that Roger Symon should go to New York to report our impressions to the United Nations, as they had requested. The account he took was of a suffering people who after thirty years of war and carnage were pleading for help. It was a picture of desperation, because it was the most vulnerable who suffered most. Thousands of destitute orphans and widows lacked basic human provisions. Hundreds of thousands existed, rather than lived, in camps in the south and north. The network of Churches – particularly Anglican and Roman Catholic – provided the only viable social structure, including health care and education. I had returned home so burdened by the plight of the Sudanese people and the weight falling on the Churches that I immediately mounted an appeal for the witness and mission of all the Churches. Within a very short period over £400,000 was sent to the New

Sudanese Council of Churches to help them with their many social programmes.

Two years later, in 1995, I paid my second visit to Sudan, this time to the north. I had been concerned that my well-publicised and controversial earlier visit had led to very bad relations between the Islamic government and the Episcopal Church, and I wanted to help repair bridges. I therefore decided to extend a planned visit to Egypt to take in Khartoum as well.

Egypt is one of the most enlightened Muslim countries, where Christianity may be practised, but not without some restrictions: any attempt to convert Muslims is strictly forbidden, and approval for new church buildings is very difficult to obtain. Indeed, the Cathedral of All Saints, Cairo, was still not registered as belonging to the Episcopal Church of Egypt after many years of applying. Bishop Ghais Malek was hoping to use my visit to help with this. I decided to raise the matter with the Governor of Cairo, and was rather alarmed when, as we waited to be introduced, the senior adviser to the Governor remarked that registration could easily be achieved if the Church paid a fee – and an exorbitant one at that. The Governor, however, a distinguished elderly man, could not have been more co-operative, and when I mentioned that the Episcopal Church had been waiting a dozen years for registration of ownership, ever since the new cathedral had replaced the earlier one at the request of the government to make more room for housing and traffic, he waived the fee and said that registration would be completed instantly.

This visit gave me an opportunity to establish warm relationships with the Islamic authorities in Egypt, especially with the Grand Imam of Al-Azhar. Al-Azhar is the leading Sunni place of learning in the world, and the Grand Imam its leading authority. I was delighted to meet Dr Mohammed Sayed Tantawi, the Grand Mufti of Cairo, who a few months later took over as Grand Imam of Al-Azhar. A warm, gentle man, Dr Tantawi was anxious to develop strong relationships with the Western Church, and saw my visit as an opportunity to do so. However, I was advised that the present Grand Imam would be less co-operative. David Blatherwick, the British Ambassador, described him as rigid and unhelpful to Christians, and cautioned me to measure my words carefully.

Thus warned, I was delighted when in fact we received a cordial welcome and settled into a good discussion around two questions I posed: What did the Grand Imam hope for in Christian–Muslim relations, and how did he see the West? He was constructive regarding the first issue – he desired good, open relationships based on respect and co-operation. The second drew from him indignation about the way Islam was perceived in the West, and he accused the West of hypocrisy concerning Bosnia. When I replied that American and British forces were at that moment protecting Muslims in Bosnia and fighting against the forces of Christian Serbia and Croatia, he was unconvinced although unable to contradict the facts. However, our discussion was a good beginning, and I was anxious to establish the strongest possible links with this important centre of Islam. It was at this meeting that tentative steps were taken towards a formal dialogue between the Anglican Communion and Al-Azhar.

Following the meeting with the Grand Imam I gave a lecture to the Al-Azhar University entitled 'The Challenge Facing Christian–Muslim Dialogue'. I appealed for 'repricocity' for Christians in Muslim countries. I stated that, very properly, Muslims expected to have freedom to worship and to build their mosques in the West. Human rights, surely, demanded that Christians should possess equal freedom in Muslim countries. With some trepidation I touched upon another thorny issue as far as Christian–Muslim relations were concerned, that of conversion. Muslims saw no problem in people of other faiths accepting the Islamic faith, but often meted out severe penalties to Muslims who converted to Christianity. Following the lecture, this point was strongly endorsed by the diminutive Pope Shenouda, leader of the Coptic Church in Egypt. Pope Shenouda, a lively, irrepressible man whose dynamism and strong faith was behind the growth of his Church, had complained bitterly and often that Christians were victimised in his own country.

The next day I had an instructive meeting with Father Mattu, who had also been of great importance for the growth of the Coptic Church. I made a long journey into the desert to the fifth-century monastery of St Macarius. It surprised me by its size, with a community of over 130 monks. Twenty or so years ago, however, it had fallen on hard times, with only seven monks in residence. The revival of Coptic Christianity since then is largely the work of Pope Shenouda, the great teacher and leader, and Father Mattu, the spiritual director, contemplative and healer. Father Mattu, now seventy-six and quite frail, lives in a retirement home (a 'cell') in Alexandria, but had returned to his monastery to greet me. I was astonished by his spiritual alertness and sharpness of mind. He urged me to see good relations between Islam and Christianity as central to world peace. He felt that the Church had failed God by neglecting wholesome links with the Muslim world: 'We have failed Muslims by not loving them. Love is a matter of the will, not of the heart. Muslims recognise love.'

I asked him, 'Isn't that all very well for a monk to say? What about the fact that even in Egypt, a modern Islamic state, there is victimisation of Christians, great difficulty in building churches and persecution of people who convert to Christianity?'

He replied equally directly, 'Although I am a monk, my entire life has been lived in the context of Islam. Love eventually conquers. The trouble with Christians is that we trust more in our intellect than our hearts. Love wins. As for churches, we don't need them. Church buildings are not necessary.'

I don't think I have ever been in the presence of a more radical person.

As diplomatic relations between Egypt and Sudan had broken down, the only way to enter Sudan was through Saudi Arabia. This presented me with a personal dilemma. Should I insist on going in as a priest and Bishop, and hide the insignia of office, my clerical collar and Episcopal cross? The fact that Saudi Arabia does not allow Christian worship or welcome ministers or priests in their official capacity is in my view deeply offensive, but I was told that I risked not being able to get to Sudan if I did not conform to Saudi Arabia's regulations. It was therefore with great reluctance that I allowed myself to be persuaded to enter Saudi without collar or cross, although it was clear from the way I was received by Saudi officials that they were aware of who I was.

Laurie Green, the Consul General and a warm and genial Christian, was on hand to deal with all practical matters. Eileen had a far scarier time. As the only woman in the party she was segregated from the men on arrival, and had to go through a special 'ladies' reception area' with only black-robed Arab women as companions. She was more than relieved when Olive, wife of Laurie Green, appeared to escort her out of the customs area to rejoin the main party.

Jeddah was very hot and sticky, and we were glad to arrive in the British Compound and be whisked into the cool home of the Consul General. There then followed one of the most extraordinary and unforgettable experiences of my life. I had agreed to take a service for Christians of all denominations from the embassies around, but I had no idea of the complications this had caused. Because Christianity was not recognised and worship forbidden, the service was advertised as a meeting of the 'Welfare Committee (P & C)' – with the 'P & C' standing for Protestants and Catholics. The hall was packed, with all denominations represented. I led Evening Prayer and preached spontaneously, moved by the feeling that this act of worship had many parallels with the early Church. This was confirmed when immediately following the service the convener of the 'Welfare Committee' urged everyone to go straight to their cars, so as not to raise suspicions. Within ten minutes everyone had left this meeting of an 'underground church'. Laurie Green informed us that in spite of the restrictions and the penalties imposed by the authorities when the religious police discovered that Christianity was being practised, the faith was flourishing in the Kingdom.

We left for Sudan the following day, 7 October, and arrived in Khartoum to be met by a huge crowd of Christians waving banners, beating drums, swaying and dancing in the warm sunshine. There to greet us was Alan Goulty, British Ambassador to Sudan, and his wife Dr Lillian Craig-Harris, together with the Minister for Social Housing, representing the government. At the press conference I made it clear that the intention of my visit was to establish warm relations with the government, as well as to support the work of the Episcopal Church of Sudan. I made no reference to my earlier visit to the south in case that soured the beginning of this trip. I especially praised the faithful work of Archbishop Benjamina Yugosuk, who was coming to the end of a long haul as senior Bishop of the Church. Benjamina and his wife Miriama had suffered a great deal in their long ministry, and could look forward only to a hard and pensionless retirement.

Following lunch, we met Benjamina and eleven of his Bishops to talk about the problems of the Church and the country. They spoke feelingly about the needs of the many refugee camps around Khartoum, where Dinka tribespeople, scooped up in the conflict, lived in very bad conditions. 'You see, Archbishop,' offered one senior Bishop, 'we have an African saying: "Empty stomachs have no ears." We are embarrassed when we enter the camps, because the people need food, clothing and medical help. Of course they love us to speak of Jesus and His love for them. It gives them great hope and strength – but they need food too.'

It was clear also that Bishop Gabriel Roric, who had scandalously made himself absent from his diocese in the south and taken a post in government, was not trusted by any of them, and that his presence inhibited frank speech. In my response I addressed Gabriel, better-dressed and looking considerably better-fed than any of the other Bishops, and said he must choose between being a minister in an Islamic government and a Bishop in the Episcopal Church. He couldn't be both. I made reference to the fact that he had absented himself from his own diocese of Rumbek, and said that although it was in SPLA hands, that should not stop him being with his people. Sadly, I had to put Gabriel's exploitation of the situation down to Benjamina's weakness in allowing the younger and better-educated man to manipulate him.

A visit a little later to the Sudan Council of Churches led to introductions to the leaders of the main Churches. The Roman Catholic Archbishop of Khartoum was an impressive, well-educated man. The Council does a great deal of effective work in the refugee camps, and receives support from most Western donors including Christian Aid. We then embarked on a long journey outside Khartoum to Mayo camp for displaced persons. We were first taken to a Sudan Council of Churches clinic swarming with hundreds of desperate people, mainly young mothers with crying children on their laps, many of them suffering from malnutrition. The staff were run off their feet. When she had a brief interval between dealing with patients, I asked the senior nurse on duty what was the greatest problem facing the clinic. She looked at me in astonishment. 'I can't think of *one* great problem! We have many problems, and they are all great. We need food for the children. We need medicines in abundance. We need more staff – doctors and nurses – to deal with ill patients.'

It was almost certainly this that prompted the government official with us to change our programme, because our next visit was to a Muslim school in the camp, which we observed was very well equipped, and then on to a large Islamic agency by the name of Mufawaq, which was totally empty of people. We were shown huge banks of drugs, ranging from codeine and aspirin through to medicines for TB and malaria. The official solemnly declared that such drugs were freely available in the camp, and that those who could not pay were given them free.

The Ambassador and others told me that this was all a sham put on hastily to impress us, and possibly to counter the impression we had gained earlier that the SCC clinic was chronically short of medical supplies. If so, the attempted deception was bound to fail, because the camp was obviously in bad condition, with the majority of its inhabitants undernourished and in dire straits. I was particularly moved when a group of tall Dinka women pushed excitedly towards us, and one of them with two young children in her arms pleaded: 'Please help me get back to my people, Archbishop. Please help me.' It was a harrowing cry, but there was nothing I could do but seek to ease the conditions that victimise people like her. Nevertheless, although Mayo camp was a terrible place, the positive attitude of the people, with their smiles and joyful singing, wakened a feeling of optimism that better times would arrive for the Dinka people. One day they will be able to go home.

A few hours later we were in Khartoum's Green Square in the blazing sunshine for a long service that attracted well over ten thousand people. I had decided that political realities had to be addressed, and I spoke about the need for freedom for Christians in the north: 'I trust I will be understood by my Muslim brothers and sisters for speaking out for Christians. They are not treated as equals. They feel persecuted by the laws of this land. The list of grievances which Christians feel is long and heavy. Religious tolerance, which should be at the heart of any civilised nation, is not being granted to them.' The address went well, punctuated by applause and shouts of affirmation as I spoke of injustice.

Immediately following the service Alan Goulty and Lillian Craig-Harris hosted a reception so that we might meet some of the senior people of Khartoum. I was profoundly impressed by Alan and Lillian's commitment and dedication to Sudan, which continues to this day. At the reception I met Dr Hassan Al-Turabi, the key Islamic intellectual behind the Republic of Sudan, and because of that sometimes called the Sudanese Lenin. He had received part of his education at the London School of Economics and the Sorbonne, and was well known as an impressive speaker and Muslim apologist. We greeted one another politely but briefly, as we would be meeting the following day. Another important guest was Dr Mustapha Osman Ismail, Secretary General of the Council for International Peoples' Friendship and

Co-Ordinator of the Council for Inter-Religious Dialogue. A friendly, slight man, Dr Ismail had trained as a doctor at Bristol University, and had appreciated the hospitality and generosity of Britain. That experience, enjoyed by so many foreigners, is a clear statement of the value of offering university education on generous terms to those from abroad. Dr Ismail would eventually climb up the ministerial ladder to become Foreign Minister for Sudan – a role he would fulfil with distinction.

It was necessary on this second trip to Sudan to visit Juba, the historic centre of the Episcopal Church, two hours south by plane, close to the SPLA-controlled territory. Eileen and I with my senior colleagues and Mustapha Ismail travelled comfortably in the President's private jet. Two of my other colleagues made the journey in a transport plane, with two hundred troops and no seats, that left at 4 a.m. It was, in their words, 'a dreadful and uncomfortable experience'.

A huge welcoming party greeted us, and we were hoisted into the back of a truck and travelled through Juba, waving to jubilant crowds as we made our way to the cathedral for the service. The crowd was far too large to fit in the building, so an open-air stage had been erected in the square outside, and ninety thousand people had gathered for the ecumenical service. The Roman Catholic Archbishop of Juba was present, a fine, articulate man who greeted me warmly. He was another example of the Roman Catholic Church's attention to education and theology. Although our Sudanese clergy lacked nothing in their desire to serve Christ and in the wholeheartedness of their faith, they did lack depth in education and training.

The service itself was a tremendous celebration of faith, witness and the solidarity of all Christians in resisting common enemies – oppression and fundamentalist Islam. The devotion of ordinary people and the tenacity of their faith made a deep impression on us all, and perhaps showed up the untested nature of the faith of so many of us in the West. Then it was back on the plane for two further events that evening in Khartoum.

It was now that the talks with representatives of the government could really begin. I took the opportunity to press Mustapha Osman Ismail on the issue of dialogue, as he was clearly an open and educated man. He said that Christians had nothing to fear from the programme of Islamicisation going on in the country, which simply aimed to apply Sharia laws at every level of family and community living. This was for Muslims only, he contended. When I pointed out that Christians, even clergy, had been sentenced under Sharia law, I could sense his unease. He insisted likewise that the repeal of the Missionary Act of 1962 (which had given the missionary societies a role in Sudanese society) and the registration of all Churches and church buildings was not discriminatory against Christians. I could tell by his face that he found this unconvincing. I reminded him that the government had confiscated Church property that had formerly belonged to the Church Missionary Society and that now belonged to the Episcopal Church, on the pretext that CMS was no longer functioning, and therefore its property could be commandeered by the government. As for Sharia laws, the application of Islamic law to non-Muslims was in my opinion an infringement of human rights. My strong impression was that Mustapha found his loyalty to his government's religious and political policies clashing with his own sense of right and wrong.

A few hours later I was raising the same questions with Dr Turabi at a dinner for the Council for Inter-Religious Dialogue. He was dressed in a white Arab robe with the traditional *keffeyeh* headdress. A laughing, highly articulate man, he hardly looked the type to be associated with terrorism and fanaticism – indeed, a more charming and engaging companion one could hardly wish to meet. Our conversation had been set up as an opportunity for Dr Turabi to argue for the reasonableness of the Sudanese programme, and the country's desire to be a friend rather than an enemy to the West. I raised the question of the well-equipped Muslim-run camps we had seen, and the many other enticements to Christians to convert to Islam. That, I said, was a most questionable form of Islamicisation. I also mentioned the deliberate attempt to give us a misleading impression of life in the camps. This was greeted with great astonishment and an assurance that the government would do nothing to influence people unfairly.

I pressed Dr Turabi about Islamic terrorism, and he replied that good Muslims are against violence in any shape or form. I then shifted the topic to theology, and questioned him on the application of Sharia law to non-Muslims. He agreed that the tradition of Islam restricted Sharia to the faithful, but argued that in certain cases it could be applied to non-Muslims. I then put forward a hypothesis that Islam, unlike Christianity and Judaism, was a profoundly political and social phenomenon which, once it had acquired a critical mass in any society, was likely to impose its life and laws upon the rest of the community. Turabi did not dispute my analysis, although he added that people had nothing to fear from Islam. It was a religion of peace, he said, and Christians had lived for centuries in Muslim countries, under Muslim protection and Muslim laws.

Following the dinner, Dr Turabi was present for my lecture, in which I argued once again for freedom for Christians to live fully as citizens in Muslim countries, with the right to worship freely and to share the faith with others. We parted cordially, and I was in no doubt that I had just spent a few hours in the company of one of the most fascinating of Muslim thinkers.

We spent the following day in Jabarone, another displacement camp, and like Mayo many miles away from Khartoum in the desert. Unlike at Mayo, the press were present in large numbers. Alan Goulty told me that the government was not happy with the way my visit was being reported in the West. It was likely, he said, that they would do all in their power to try to contradict me at every available opportunity.

This happened as soon as we reached the camp. I noticed that there were many men around me in blue overalls, the uniform of camp officials. Their leader welcomed me and told me that people were well treated and well cared for at Jabarone, and that I should not listen to outside propaganda. My blood boiled at such blatant lying. 'In that case,' I asked, 'why is it that camps like this are pushed into the desert far from human habitation, and people treated like animals?'

He replied, 'Such camps are temporary. Very soon refugees will be living near Khartoum in homes with gardens.'

'In that case I will send a representative in two years' time to see this miracle,' I said.

His confident assertion was, 'Why wait two years? Come back next year. You will see a transformation.'

Needless to say, the camps still exist around Khartoum, as wretched now as they were in 1995.

Towards the end of my visit I met the President of Sudan, who greeted me reasonably warmly, although it was obvious from some of the things he said that aspects of my visit had irritated him. I thanked him for the considerable lengths he and his government had gone to offer me hospitality, and said that I wanted good relationships with Muslim leaders, because I respected Islam. I told him I had established exceedingly good friendships with Muslim leaders in Great Britain. I then went on to question the record of human rights in Sudan, mentioning in particular the report of the UN Special Envoy, Dr Gaspar Biro, which was severely critical of the abuse of people in the Nuba mountains and in the camps. The President reacted angrily to this, and stated that the report was flawed, and agencies like Amnesty International were not to be trusted. They were simply political parties and tools of America. Then came a statement that made my blood boil: the President said that Sudan's record on human rights was not inferior to the United Kingdom's. Indeed, he said, Christians were better treated in Sudan than Muslims were in Britain.

This was so ludicrous that I interrupted his long discourse. 'Could you tell me, Mr President,' I asked, 'how many churches have been built and opened in Sudan? I can tell you – none. But in the UK there are now over 1500 mosques and Islamic cultural centres.' He was not pleased to be interrupted with such a firm denial of his assertion, but when we parted I received an open invitation to return to Sudan. I said I would be back.

The return journey to Britain via Saudi Arabia was not without its comical side. Once more I had to change into lay attire, despite my feelings of rebellion. But just as the plane door was closing, in shot a Sudanese Bishop who placed in my hands an enormous crucifix. I realised that no pretence could possibly hide this cross when we landed at Jeddah. I did not feel it fair to ask a staff member to carry this obvious and glaring symbol into the airport – I had to do it myself. To my astonishment I received not a single objection. I too needed to be reminded that one should never be ashamed of the cross.

My third visit to the Sudan followed the tragic and untimely death of Archbishop Daniel Zindo, the former Bishop of Yambio whose 'marriage' I had conducted in 1994. Daniel, who had already suffered the murder of his beloved wife Grace and one of his daughters, was fully prepared to take on the difficult responsibility of leading his Church, but he was sadly killed in a road accident in Kenya shortly after the Lambeth Conference of 1998.

The man chosen to follow him was Joseph Marona, Bishop of Maridi. Joseph had been a headmaster before his ordination, and his appointment surprised no one. It would be difficult to find a wiser and more spiritual man. There was however a difficult problem with his appointment, not only because his diocese was in the south, and therefore in a rebel-held area, but he had been very critical of the government of Sudan's policies. We were worried that the government might try to prevent him from living in Khartoum or travelling freely in the south of the country. I raised this with the Sudanese authorities, and was satisfied that they would not imprison Joseph or restrict his ministry.

It was important to show solidarity with Joseph and to give international support to his installation as Archbishop in Juba. So with a few staff I flew to Sudan at the end of April 2000. The brief visit confirmed our impression that there had been no significant improvement since we were there five years before. At Mandela Camp we had lengthy discussions with displaced people and staff, and a sense of hopelessness and weariness seemed to affect everyone. Indeed, I came away sharing the same sense of hopelessness.

This was the mood that I took into my meeting with Dr Mustapha Osman Ismail, now Foreign Minister, who was extremely friendly and constructive. Mustapha had grown in stature and authority, and was very influential in the nation. He was frank about the matter of human rights, and agreed that there were serious questions to be addressed. He assured me that the government would take the issue forward, but he was critical of the fact that the West continued to favour the SPLA, without listening to the position of the Sudanese government. It was clear to me after the meeting that America, with its pivotal role in world affairs, had to be at the centre of the peace process for it to work.

One of the most promising highlights of the visit was an ecumenical service at St Matthew's Roman Catholic Church. The Archbishop of Khartoum, Gabriel Zubeir Wako, presided over a large open-air gathering at which I preached. In my address I referred to the agreement that Pope John Paul II and I had reached concerning closer working between the two Churches in Sudan. 'We have agreed,' I said, 'that we would share more deeply together, and when one Church is under attack the other Church would support and encourage it.' This was greeted with rapturous applause.

Then came the long flight to Juba for Joseph's installation. Once again we were met by a huge crowd, and led with much singing into Juba itself. Our convoy was made up of about forty vehicles, and Eileen and I were positioned precariously on the top of an open-top truck, waving to delighted Sudanese whose joy was overwhelming. Arriving at the cathedral compound, we were disappointed to learn that it had been decided that Joseph's installation would take place in the cathedral, which could only accommodate just over six hundred people. Unfortunately, those responsible for planning the service had not taken into account the many thousands who wanted to be there with their new Archbishop. There was nothing we could do at this point, but I was disappointed that the service was not in the open as it had been the last time we had come, because despite the warmth of our greeting, the general mood of the people was very depressed. The entire feel of the place, in fact, was very different from five years ago. The war was taking its toll on the lives of so many people that it was bound to affect adversely a Church on the frontline of caring for the very poor.

In my address I attempted to rally everyone, encouraging them to support Joseph in his lonely ministry. 'The message of hope that was at the heart of the Christian gospel', I said, 'must once again be re-ignited by love and devotion, by prayer and by renewed commitment to the service of others. Without that hope, the spirit of pessimism and negativity will only feed the spirit of conflict, oppression and violence.'

Sudan is now written on the hearts of both Eileen and myself. One lasting memory I have of the country is the wonderful Dinka singing, the legacy of a remarkable, charismatic Dinka woman called Mary, who wrote many of the songs of renewal at the heart of the growth of the Church. 'When Sudan stops singing,' said one Bishop, 'that will be the time when Sudan will die.' I am confident it will not. A new Sudan will one day appear, in which Christians and Muslims will be free to live with one another in peace. I am not alone in longing for that day. Sudan needs it; Sudan deserves it; Sudan longs for it.

15

The Rosewood Tree

'When the missionaries came to Africa they had the Bible and
we had the land. They said, "Let us pray." We closed our eyes.
When we opened them, we had the Bible and they had the
land.'

Desmond Tutu

THE ANGLICAN COMMUNION is one of the very few branches of
world Christianity to have an international structure, a common
doctrinal basis and a common liturgical tradition. Although
Methodism, the World Lutheran Fellowship, the Baptist tradition,
the Orthodox Churches of West and East and other great Churches
have also spread throughout the world, unlike the Roman Catholic
Church and the Anglican Communion, they lack an accepted and
visible focal point of leadership. That is to say, Catholic and Anglican
forms of Church life have in common visible and personal leadership,
exercised through the Bishop of Rome and the Archbishop of
Canterbury.

Needless to say, great differences exist when these two offices
are compared. The Pope has immediate, juridical and commanding
authority over all Catholics throughout the world. He takes pre-
cedence over all other Bishops, and his word is final in matters of
faith and morals. The reach of his authority extends through the
Curia, which consists of numerous 'dicasteries', or departments, that
serve the personal ministry of the Holy Father. Compared to the

Roman Catholic Church, with its billion members, the Anglican Communion is tiny, with a mere seventy or so million members, and structures far less organised and hierarchical. As for the Archbishop of Canterbury, he neither rules nor governs the Communion or the Primates of its thirty-eight Provinces, but leads as 'primus inter pares', first among equals. He has no authority to intervene in the affairs of another Province, although his office clearly commands respect as a defining ministry. An Anglican is defined as someone 'in communion with the See of Canterbury'.

The somewhat untidy and loose structure of Anglicanism is partially explained by the rather accidental way in which it came about. The Church of England never intentionally and consciously planted congregations in other countries in order to create worshipping bodies in its own image. The missionary movement within the Church sprang from gifted individuals whose concern for the welfare of others abroad was greater than that of the hierarchy of the Church. Firstly, Thomas Bray (1656–1730), Rector of Sheldon in Warwickshire, founded the oldest Anglican missionary societies, SPCK (the Society for Promoting Christian Knowledge, founded in 1698) and SPG (the Society for the Propagation of the Gospel, founded in 1701). SPG received the Royal Charter of William III to 'supply the want of learned and orthodox ministers in the plantations, colonies and factories beyond the seas'. Its dual responsibility was to 'settle the state of religion as well as may be for *our own people* . . . and then to proceed in the best methods they can to the *conversion of the natives*'.

The second great missionary drive emanated from the formation of an evangelical society that became the Church Missionary Society. Whereas SPG was limited by its royal patronage and charter, CMS was a voluntary society with few limitations on the scope of its work. Its genius can be traced to a meeting in 1796 when Charles Simeon, Rector of Holy Trinity Church, Cambridge, and a great luminary among evangelicals, asked: 'With what propriety and in what mode can a mission be established to the Heathen from the Established Church?' The question had long been on the minds of a group of wealthy evangelicals who lived mainly in Clapham and were known as the 'Clapham Sect'. Their most famous member was William Wilberforce, but around him was gathered a talented group of individuals including the Reverend John Venn; Henry Thornton, a banker; Charles Grant, a Director of the East India Company; and James Stephen, a leading barrister. The formation of a society for 'Missions to Africa and the East' followed in 1799. From these modest beginnings the worldwide Anglican Communion grew, and to this day increases in number.

A few months after my installation as Archbishop I paid my first visit to an overseas Anglican Province. I could not have chosen a more picturesque and moving trip than to the Province of Papua New Guinea. The reason for the visit was the centenary of the founding of the first Anglican church in 1891 by two young Australian missionaries, McClaren and Copland King. Their story is a remarkable and moving one of courage and sacrifice. Although quite different in churchmanship – McClaren was an evangelical and Copland King an Anglo-Catholic – they were united in their desire to bring the fruits of Christianity to peoples of a primitive culture. They came ashore on 10 August 1891 at Kaieta beach, on the northern coast of Milne Bay. Within a short while they were followed by two carpenters, Lehmann and Carroll, and then a month later by a remarkable couple, the Tomlinsons.

McClaren and King's first task on landing was the building of a small chapel from a Modawa tree, known to us as rosewood. They established cordial relationships with local tribes, who were interested by such different people with white skins. Then tragedy struck. King contracted malaria, and died within three weeks of the landing. He was buried alongside the chapel. McClaren lingered on for almost a year before having to return to Australia, seriously ill. Only the Tomlinsons endured to see the Church established. When, a few years later, carpenters came to dismantle the chapel and adjacent buildings, with the intention of rebuilding them with more durable materials, they found that one of the corner posts of the chapel had taken root.

It was left to grow undisturbed, and it still stands today, a living symbol of the successful planting of the gospel.

Exactly one hundred years later thousands of Papua New Guineans, together with myself, government officials and many former missionaries, gathered in Dogura to celebrate the fragile beginnings of the Anglican Church in Papua New Guinea. I found it very moving to shake hands with an elderly man, Andrew Balona, whose mother had watched King and McClaren come ashore by canoe from a whaling boat a century ago.

That celebration was the climax of our visit. Before it we had shared in the life, mission and joy of the Church. Although there are hundreds of different tribes in PNG, with an equal number of languages, people communicate through 'pidgin English', a dialect evolved through the interaction of immigrants and tribes. Before leaving England I had received a few lessons in pidgin from an ex-missionary. They enabled me to offer greetings to people, and on one occasion I took an entire service in pidgin – not without giving some amusement to those present.

However, nothing can ever prepare one for the amazing experience of a PNG welcome. Wherever we went, scores of native people in elaborate headdresses made of cassowary feathers, with beaded decorations incorporating boars' tusks, grass armlets and loincloths, beating thin, hour-glass-shaped *kundu* drums, would emerge to greet us. Bare-breasted women waved painted *tapa* barkshaws which matched their long skirts, into which the Mothers' Union badge was woven. The joy of their welcome was heartwarming, and their enthusiasm in greeting their visitors was sincere and deeply touching.

The first leg of our journey after being welcomed to the capital, Port Moresby, was to Popondetta, a great centre of Anglicanism. On disembarking from our plane we were greeted by a great crowd of tribespeople, with a welcoming party of fierce-looking warriors and splendidly attired women who arranged dozens of woven flowers around our necks. Together with Bishop Walter and his wife Nellie we clambered aboard our own 'Popemobile' and were taken to the cathedral compound, where tens of thousands of people had gathered to greet us and share in the acts of celebration. Services, speeches, cultural events followed in quick succession, with occasional visits for rest to a nearby hotel, where we were given the best suite in the building. It could have done with a proper clean, however. As I lay on the bed with a fan droning away overhead, feeling very hot and tired, I became aware of an uncomfortable feeling that started at my left foot. I scratched vigorously, but nothing seemed to stop the strange itching. The 'itch' travelled up my leg, then continued to advance further. Suddenly the awful truth dawned: 'This thing is alive!' By this time it had reached my chest. I leapt from the bed, and reaching into my shirt withdrew a huge cockroach, which I flung to the floor. There it lay, wriggling upside down as I recovered from the shock and tried in vain to beat it into submission. It was not to be my last encounter with cockroaches during my visit to PNG, and later to other parts of the Communion.

Returning to the celebration after this short break, we were introduced to the cultural life of the area through dance and drumming, storytelling and mock combat. Students from Newton Theological College enacted the story of the coming of Christianity to PNG, and children on colourful floats sang gospel songs. It was a spectacular portrayal of the tribal life that had gone on since time immemorial, with the addition of Christianity which was now firmly embedded in its culture.

I was not expecting the finale. Suddenly a large, black, squealing boar was presented to me, trussed up, upside down and very much alive. A sharp knife was handed to me, whether in earnest or in jest, and Graeme James, my former Chaplain and now Bishop of Norwich, whispered in my ear, 'Archbishop, I believe you're expected to cut its throat!'

I whispered back, 'Surely not! I'm Vice President of the RSPCA!' I then said in my speech that I was honoured to be presented with such a fine boar, however, I would be delighted if the students would accept it as a gift. I am glad to say that an international diplomatic incident was avoided, and the gift accepted happily.

If Popondetta was spectacular, our next trip, to Simbai in the Highlands, equalled it in terms of scenery and cultural life. We flew first to Mount Hagen in the diocese of Aipo Rongo, where we were the guests of the dedicated and charming Anglo-Catholic Bishop Paul Richardson. Paul was a missionary Bishop of the old rugged kind. A celibate priest, he loved to be with his people, and long distances formed no barrier to his personal ministry of supporting and tending his flock. His practice was to train catechists whose role it was to prepare people for baptism, and he would travel from village to village, baptising and teaching. As a result his diocese grew rapidly.

Paul informed us that Simbai was totally inaccessible except by plane. He also warned us that conditions would be very basic, as the area had only been opened up to the wider world forty years earlier. To our astonishment, at this point the government official detailed by the Prime Minister to look after us flatly refused to go to Simbai. 'They are savages there!' he exclaimed, and flounced out of the room. We never saw him again. That solved one problem, because the small MAF (Missionary Aviation Fellowship) Cessna plane could only take five passengers, and our party was five in all.

As the plane approached Simbai we were able to make out the tiny landing strip and a huge number of people awaiting our arrival. Paul instructed me: 'A fierce warrior will approach you with a lethal spear in his hand. Do not flinch or seem afraid.' I thought this was an extraordinary warning to give an Archbishop, and wondered what kind of welcome it might herald. I was soon to learn. On landing, a large number of excited tribespeople were there to welcome us, dressed in traditional costume, the men carrying savage spears and knives that seemed alarmingly real.

Suddenly a man burst out of a group of dancers and ran towards me, brandishing a spear as if he was about to throw it. The spear stopped a few inches from my nose. There was a silence as his eyes, unblinking, gazed into mine. I attempted to match his coolness and disdain. Then, breaking into a broad grin, he said in perfect English, 'Welcome to Simbai. I am the churchwarden of All Saints, Simbai, and you are most welcome, dear Archbishop.' This was surely the most unusual greeting I have ever had from a churchwarden.

Singing recommenced, followed by a welcome speech from the churchwarden, then we processed up a narrow pathway, with the deep forest stretching on both sides, climbing steadily until we came to a clearing with a few dozen huts made of mud and wood. More speeches followed, then we were shown to our hut. A special hut had been erected for Eileen and me, in which we found two beds – brought up from a village far below, we found out later, by some of the tribespeople. An additional kindness was that they also erected a simple privy twenty yards from our hut. If I had been in any doubt that we were sharing the jungle life of the Simbai people, they would have been removed shortly afterwards when, as I approached the privy, a wild boar shot by, only a few feet away, before disappearing into the thick wood. The women and girls found Eileen particularly interesting, and gathered around her, touching her white skin and feeling her hair without any embarrassment. Although divided by culture, language and experience, the women communicated with another female from a completely different culture with gentle touch, smiles and laughter.

As dusk descended we gathered around a central fire, and joined the people in a meal cooked in a time-honoured way known as 'Mau-mau'. Earlier in the day a long, narrow trench had been dug and lined with banana leaves. Hot stones were laid on the thick leaves, food placed on top of the stones, and more leaves laid on top. Water was then sprinkled regularly on the leaves, and the process of heating stones, laying them on top and constant sprinkling with water continued throughout the day. The result was a delicious meal that we enjoyed as much as all present. Then came the presentation of gifts – including stone axes which I was told had killed 'many enemies'. Eileen caused much amusement as she allowed herself to be dressed in a grass skirt, a possum-fur hat and a *bilum*, a straw bag, and was then declared the senior wife of a 'great chief'. Then singing, storytelling and speeches continued for an hour or two until the people dispersed to their huts, or – as many had travelled for days to be with us – slept on the ground in the open air.

The following day, refreshed by a delightful night spent on the mountains we gathered with several thousand people for the communion service and, in the middle of it, the commissioning of fifty or so catechists who had been trained by Bishop Paul to go into the villages around to teach the faith and prepare people for baptism. It was a moving event as I blessed each one individually and saw in their eyes the devotion they had to our Lord and His faith.

Alongside the ministry of the Church in catechising new converts went the work of education and healing. Criticism is often expressed in developed countries of the so-called 'harmful' influence of missionaries in destroying native cultures and languages. While there have certainly been examples of cultural damage and Christian imperialism, mainstream missionary influence has undoubtedly been positive and affirming of local cultures and languages. This is certainly so of Anglican mission in PNG, particularly in mountainous regions like Simbai, through missionaries like Bishop David Hand, who was the first to open up Simbai to the world when he established a small church there a mere thirty-three years ago. Anglican and mainstream denominations despise such underhand practices as the so-called 'cargo cults', which use parachute drops of foods to precede evangelisation. When David Hand and his colleagues brought education and medical care to the tribespeople, rather than destroying what they found and calling it 'paganism', they respected local traditions and belief structures, even when they viewed them as less than desirable.

What I found particularly interesting about Anglican mission in PNG was the serious endeavour to fuse the gospel with local culture. David Bosch, the well-known missiologist, wrote, 'There is no such thing as a cultureless gospel.' That is to say, Western missionaries will either pack their understanding of the gospel with their own cultural baggage, or they will endeavour to fill it with ideas, images and forms from the culture that they are seeking to influence. The success of PNG Anglicanism is due in no small measure to the influence of indigenous clergy from the earliest days of the founding of the Church, and liturgies fully grounded in the life of the people. We were glad that our first overseas trip to a member Province of the Anglican Communion was to such a rich culture as Papua New Guinea.

My first encounter with the Province of South Africa, at the beginning of 1993, introduced me to a different set of problems, and to a mission no less rooted in the life of people and nation. The ostensible reason for the visit was a meeting of Primates together with a gathering of the Anglican Consultative Council, consisting of 120 or so delegates from the different Provinces of the Communion.

Our host was Desmond Tutu, Archbishop of Cape Town and Primate of the Province. Desmond and his wife Leah were at the airport to meet us, together with the British Ambassador, Tony Reeves. Desmond was in typically good humour, piercing the air with whoops of delight and quick repartee. Leah was more restrained, and helped to keep her incorrigible husband under control – if it were ever possible to contain a man whose exuberant joy in living flowed from a profound spirituality, earthed in daily worship, prayer and contemplation. Deeply anchored as he was in the Anglo-Catholic tradition, Desmond's outgoing temperament, and his love of God and his fellow human beings, made it easy for him to connect with most people.

The following day gave us an example of this when we drove to Malmesbury, north of Cape Town, to share in a special open-air Eucharist. Desmond and I processed in front of a Church Lads' Brigade band through crowds of black people who were weaving and swaying to the hymns played by the band. Desmond was rhythmically and uninhibitedly dancing, while I in my restrained English way attempted to appear perfectly at ease and at home. The service was a wonderful blend of Anglo-Catholic worship that would have graced

All Saints', Margaret Street, enhanced with African chants, dancing and movement. My address seemed to go down very well, especially when I mentioned the role of the Church in confronting oppression and racism. I commended the prophetic role of the Church of the Province of Southern Africa, that had given such outstanding service to black people over the years. I singled out three people whose contribution to freedom and social justice had been exceptional – Oliver Tambo, Nelson Mandela and Desmond Tutu. Oliver Tambo had been Mandela's friend, senior partner and mentor. Tambo held the reins of the African National Congress when Mandela was in jail, and the ANC's debt to him remains incalculable. Desmond's great contribution was in being the visible and articulate spokesperson for his people. Nelson Mandela's enormous legacy is the clear and authoritative leadership which in time would help make South Africa's transition from oppression to democracy so seamless. The simple mention of these names was greeted with an enormous cheer and whoops of joy.

A few days later I met the President of South Africa, F.W. de Klerk, at his office, together with Tony Reeves, Desmond, Ed Browning, the Presiding Bishop of the Episcopal Church of the United States, and Archbishop Paul Reeves, the former Governor General of New Zealand and at that time the Anglican Communion's representative at the United Nations. Mr de Klerk greeted us warmly. He struck me as an intelligent and friendly man, with whom one could have a good discussion. I decided to test this impression, knowing that our time with him was limited. After a short while I found an opening that led me to say, 'Mr President, would you not agree with me that apartheid is an evil thing?'

I don't think he expected such a full-frontal attack, and his reaction was angry: 'My father was a Dutch Reformed minister, and was one of the many in his Church who believed that separation of black from white was the best way to organise our new country. Are you telling me that he was evil?' Before I could explain what I meant, he continued, his voice softening and relaxing. 'Yes, I agree. What has developed from the attempt to separate two peoples has led to something completely unintended. I guess one must agree that it is evil, to some extent.'

This was an extraordinary and unexpected confession that surprised even Desmond, who had never heard such a direct admission before. Desmond himself spoke up feelingly for the majority black community: 'Mr President, I call you my President, but I have no vote because I am a black person. When are you going to allow black people like me to live in dignity in my own land and share in democratic rights which are at present limited to white people?' The point hit home. President de Klerk could not deny that injustice was the daily lot of black people. His reply was that white and black people must address the problem together.

It was a most constructive meeting which made me more aware of the crisis confronting South Africa, but not even that revealing remark by the President could have led anybody to suspect that within eighteen months the dreadful system of apartheid would be dismantled. History has since recorded that de Klerk played a vital role in its destruction, and thus in avoiding a civil war that would have led to many deaths. Notwithstanding Nelson Mandela's outstanding leadership, authority and demeanour, it required a very big man to see the writing on the wall, and to take the steps that led to the transference of power. President de Klerk was such a person. Quite properly he and Nelson Mandela were jointly awarded the 1993 Nobel Peace Prize.

Six days later I was able to see for myself something of the grim conditions that many black people lived in. The papers were full of the murder of eleven people in Khayelitsha, a township close to Cape Town. Desmond asked me to go there with him to help calm things down. I was glad to accompany him, but nothing could have prepared me for the appalling conditions that some 800,000 people lived in, squashed together in a relatively small area, with whole families living in tiny huts with no sanitation or running water. I was filled with a sense of outrage as I saw the evidence of how apartheid deprived human beings of basic human rights and even dignity itself.

Several hundred people had gathered at the spot where the murders had occurred, and were singing moving African laments. As Desmond and I stepped onto a rickety platform with several ANC leaders, a huge crowd gathered around us. Desmond spoke first, urging the people to be quiet and restrained in their response to the violence. I then addressed the crowd and, speaking quite freely, said that I felt ashamed to be a white person in a place like this where it was so apparent that white rule was responsible for the conditions which created violence and the deaths of innocent people. It was clear that I had touched a raw nerve, and my comments were greeted with enthusiasm and not a few tears. Desmond said later that my spontaneous remarks had helped to defuse a potentially volatile situation, although the Afrikaans press the following day carried acerbic criticism of the visit, and attacked my views of apartheid.

However, not all the problems of Africa can be put down to white tyranny and superiority. Tribalism is also a terrible blight that holds back African development, and there was plenty of evidence of it in the hostility between the Zulu leader, Chief Mangosuthu Buthelezi, and Nelson Mandela. Chief Buthelezi came to see me, accompanied by his senior advisers. Rather to my surprise, after the introductions he proceeded to read out a speech which lasted fifteen minutes. In it he argued his right to speak on behalf of Africans as leader of the Zulu people, the most powerful black group in the nation. It was clear that this tall, dignified leader felt humiliated and sidelined by the more articulate and popular Nelson Mandela. Although there was obviously a personality clash between the two leaders, the more serious issue was a deep-rooted enmity between ethnic groups, fostered, some say, by the Nationalist Party government. However, I liked Chief Buthelezi a lot, and in later meetings with him came to understand his position more, as well as his deep unhappiness that Mandela did not seem to appreciate the need of the Zulus to be affirmed and acknowledged. I believe it is to the credit of Chief

Buthelezi that he put the unity of black people before tribal loyalty, and thus helped to integrate the nation following the collapse of apartheid.

A few days later Nelson Mandela came to our Conference to address the Primates and the Anglican Consultative Council. He arrived in a white BMW followed by several other cars which swept into the parking lot outside the conference centre. His bodyguard of six tough, silent black men surrounded him as he entered the building. Desmond and I greeted him and took him into a side room for a private conversation which included Robin Eames, Archbishop of Armagh. Nelson Mandela was taller than I had expected him to be, but I was struck much more by his impressive bearing and courtesy of manner. I particularly noticed his attentiveness to people – a quality he shared with Diana, Princess of Wales, who also had the ability to make a perfect stranger seem the most special and important person in the world.

He seemed at first to be slow in movement, thought and speech, but this was not so. In our private meeting, during which we were able to share some of our concerns about South Africa and hear his reflections, we were left in no doubt that we were talking with one of the most impressive public figures of our time. We then entered the Great Hall, where I introduced him to the Conference and invited him to address us. He had been well briefed. He thanked us all for coming to South Africa, and for siding with 'his people'. He congratulated me on my address earlier in the week, and spoke with real warmth of Desmond's outstanding role in the country. He expressed his appreciation of the role of the Churches in fighting apartheid, and especially of remarkable individuals like Oliver Tambo and Father Trevor Huddleston, who for many years had been a leading figure in the struggle. He was quite candid in his conviction that the present regime in South Africa was moribund, and desperate to find a solution to the divisions in its society.

I listened attentively to his description of the place of the Church in his own formation as an individual, and the pastoral care of some clergy during his twenty-eight-year captivity on Robben Island. Nonetheless, I formed the impression from that speech and from private conversations later that his personal faith in God was not deep, although no doubt real. His speech was received with a standing ovation as the entire conference expressed its admiration of a courageous leader. And then it was time for him to depart, and with a screech of tyres the cavalcade disappeared, leaving us all with a still greater desire to see peace and justice come to the lovely land of South Africa, but with a foreboding that it might all end in bloodshed and tragedy.

However, the end of apartheid came surprisingly quickly in the following months, and in a landslide election victory in April 1994 the ANC came to power and Nelson Mandela was elected President of a new South Africa. I was fortunate to be invited to his inauguration on 10 May 1994 in Pretoria, and flew to Johannesburg with my staff member for the Anglican Communion, Canon Roger Symon. We decided as a prelude to the inauguration to visit the Voortrekker Monument, a symbol of Afrikaner pride and self-esteem, to help us appreciate the magnitude of the historic event we were about to witness. To our surprise we met Neil Kinnock, the former leader of the Labour Party, who had the same intention. As we surveyed the panels depicting the story of the Afrikaner people it was not difficult to appreciate their bravery as they sought to build a new life for themselves and to establish a great nation. But their policies were misconceived, exclusive and ultimately destructive. Christianity did not emerge from this story entirely on the side of right. To be sure, many mainline Churches stood on the side of black people, and churchmen like Trevor Huddleston, Desmond Tutu and many others were significant in their brave opposition to the evil of apartheid. However, the Dutch Reformed Church gave a theological legitimation to apartheid that hindered the development of black people – equally loved, of course, by Almighty God – created the appalling shanty towns and led to millions being deprived of their basic human rights. It was yet another example of the Church being seduced by a political system, leading to a betrayal of its own teaching and principles.

On the morning of the inauguration I went for coffee at the British Ambassador's home in Pretoria, where other British guests attending the ceremony were gathered. I was delighted to meet Archbishop Trevor Huddleston again. Although in a wheelchair and looking frail, he was the centre of attention as he spoke of the importance of this day – a day, he said, he never believed would come in his lifetime. Then, his voice breaking and trailing off in tears, he said: 'If only Oliver Tambo were here! Oh, if only Oliver were here. This day belongs to him as much as to Nelson.' He was right, of course, to lament the fact that Oliver Tambo, who had died the previous year, did not live to see this momentous event. But the day also belonged to the many thousands, departed and living, whose sheer guts, determination and faith had caused apartheid to crumble.

The inauguration ceremony was a dignified yet emotional event. I had been given a seat just a few rows away from Prince Philip, representing Her Majesty, and the Foreign Secretary Douglas Hurd, representing the Prime Minister and the British government. Desmond led some prayers, and the South African Attorney General administered the oaths, which Nelson Mandela swore in a clear voice. The applause that followed was raw with emotion. A voice behind me remarked: 'Ironic, isn't it, that it's the same office of the law that sentenced Mandela to twenty-eight years on Robben Island that is now declaring him our President.' Ironic or not, Nelson Mandela was now the rightful President of a united South Africa with a promising future, and which although it had many difficulties still ahead, at least now gave equality to black and coloured people. In a dignified speech President Mandela said: 'Never, never and never again shall it be that this beautiful land will again experience the oppression of one by another ... the sun shall never set on so glorious a human achievement. Let freedom reign. God bless Africa!'

It was understandable that the euphoria created by this un-precedented event undermined the well-laid plans to take large numbers of VIPs to the President's home for lunch. Every street for miles around was filled by colourful parades and bands that often lacked any musical merit but more than made up for it in enthusiasm and noise. Gradually the VIPs were taken away, but the British contin-gent – including Prince Philip, Douglas Hurd and myself – were among the last to leave. Prince Philip, with his inimitable sense of humour, was able to see the funny side of it, and looking out over the swinging, swaying crowds while police were trying to form VIP passengers in an order known only to themselves, remarked, 'You are seeing chaos theory being worked out before your very eyes!' The heat was by now quite intense, but Roger Symon managed to find a few cans of beer and soft drinks, which kept us all good-humoured. Eventually we got to the President's residence just in time to hear him thank the international community for their part in the downfall of apartheid.

If South Africa managed to avoid civil war through outstanding leadership, Rwanda failed to do so for the opposite reason – weak and dishonourable leaders. Rwanda had been colonised by Germany and then Belgium, and European influence had been significant in its past. French was the country's second language and Roman Catholicism was dominant, although the Episcopal Church of Rwanda was strong and growing. I was aware of the problems of the country through worrying reports from our Bishops in Rwanda, who had spoken in particular of the fraught relations between the two dominant tribes, Hutus and Tutsis. The Hutus were currently in power, and their strength was reflected in Church leadership too, with both Roman Catholic and Anglican leaderships predominantly Hutu.

In April 1994 the ruling party, the Hutus, launched a pre-emptive strike to kill all Tutsis. This mad, shocking and evil plan started at the very top, and involved senior religious figures. The genocide started on 6 April 1994 with a signal from the President, leading to the murder of at least 800,000 Tutsis over the following weeks, with many thousands of others maimed, raped and traumatised.

As soon as the Anglican Communion learned of the tragedy, aid poured in, particularly from the Canadian Church which, through its French-speaking ministries, had a good relationship with the Rwandan Church. I made plans to visit the country as soon as I could, but was held back by the civil war that saw the return of the Tutsis, who had formed an army in neighbouring Uganda under the resourceful General Paul Kagame. However, even if I could not enter the country I managed to meet up with eleven of the Rwandan Bishops in December, when I paid an official visit to the Province of Kenya.

We shared together the terrible situation and the dilemma that faced them in deciding whether or not to return to their country. I fully understood the danger of their position, but still had to ask them the question: 'Are you able, ready and willing to return to your dioceses and be with your people?'

There was a deathly hush, then one young Bishop replied, 'I don't mind returning with the Archbishop of Canterbury and dying as a martyr – but I don't fancy the idea of being found dead in a back alley.' The comment brought home to me the reality that faced them as Hutu Bishops, and the likelihood that they would be targeted by vengeful groups even if they were not implicated personally in the genocide.

Following the advice of the British Foreign Office, the earliest date I could visit was May 1995, and my party were among the very first Western leaders to see the condition of the country following the genocide. On arriving at the capital Kigale we were met by Dr Lillian Wong, the British Government Liaison Officer, and several of our Bishops, including Onesiphor Rwaje, the Dean of the Bishops, a burly and friendly Hutu. I made an immediate mistake at the press conference by saying 'I am not here to judge or condemn.' In the context of my opening statement, this made sense – my primary role was to speak to people and seek to understand the background to the genocide before anything else. But so raw was the emotional background, and so angry the Hutu mood, that the remark was bound to be misunderstood. How could I not condemn such an awful and obscene act? I was able to rectify that mistake in later press statements.

At the press conference I was able to meet Thacienne Karuhije, widow of Alphonse Karuhije, Dean of the Cathedral of Kigale. He had been murdered in his own cathedral and his body never found. Alphonse, a very bright young man, had been one of my students at Trinity College, Bristol, and had completed a master's degree before returning to Kigale as Dean. We were able to hold and hug her, and share her tears. It was becoming all too clear to us that this would be one of the most challenging visits of my ministry, as this Church – my Church – was not only victim of the genocide, but perpetrator as well.

I will always be haunted by what I saw on 10 May. We were taken by government and Church officials to Nyarubye, an isolated village fifty or so miles from Kigale. The journey by helicopter took just twenty minutes, but allowed us to appreciate the fertility and beauty of the country. From the air we could see a large Roman Catholic church and several buildings in the surrounding compound. Here in this place five thousand Tutsis, mainly women and children, had been murdered. Nothing could have prepared us for the horror that awaited us as we stepped from the helicopter. Skeletons were everywhere: ribcages, skulls, clothing. Most touching of all were the tiny skulls of very young children. There were so many human remains that it was only with great difficulty that one could walk without treading on bones. Although they had all been picked clean, there was a pervading rich smell of death, that I had never experienced before.

We entered the church, where most of the killing had taken place, although all but two of the bodies had been removed from the building, presumably by the government when it had decided to leave the remains as a monument to the genocide. There was one skeleton just inside the door, and another in front of the altar. Two stoles lay on the ground, as if the priests had run in terror from the aggressors. Our eyes were drawn to the remains of the woman in front of the altar. She wore a simple, colourful dress. Her feet had been hacked off. One arm was thrown out as if she were pleading with her attacker to let her go, and the other was across her body, as if she were warding off a blow.

It was a sight too awful for words and too grim even for tears. We stood numbed by the scene – such evil committed by the army, we were told, against defenceless women and children. Their only crime was that they belonged to a different tribe. I was asked to say a prayer, and it was only with difficulty – with a BBC camera trained on my face – that I could compose myself to do so, commending the souls of all the people around us who had died so terribly in this holy place. They had gathered there for refuge, believing that a Christian place of worship would be their protection, only to discover that not even a church was a sanctuary against such depths of evil. It was not difficult to visualise and even to hear in one's imagination the screams of the terrified people as they sought to escape the bullets and machetes of cruel men.

But where was God when this happened? This question was raised by the scene, although not of course for the first time. It is the question that the Holocaust raises, and Hiroshima too. In theology, the silence of God at times of such horror is called 'theodicy'. Christianity, perhaps more than any other religion, carries a story of abandon-ment at its very centre, in the loneliness and abandonment of Christ by God. 'My God, why have you forsaken me?' were the accusing words of Jesus – indeed, the very same words I was hearing in my imagination in that Catholic church in Nyarubye. I felt it important to take into my very heart the numbness of such a question, in order that the awfulness of the scene should not be trivialised by superficial answers.

That evening I met thirty or so ecumenical leaders, including five

Roman Catholic Bishops. One of the Bishops remarked, 'What has happened in Rwanda, a country profoundly influenced by Christianity, actually shows that the blood of tribalism is thicker than the water of baptism.'

I responded to that statement with a question that had been troubling me since even before my arrival in the country: 'Does this not represent the failure of Christianity in Rwanda?'

The response from the representatives present was that it was 'not a failure of the faith, but certainly a failure of the Church in not paying attention to the deep enmity and distrust which has riddled our society – so that both tribes were guilty of favouring their own people against the other'. The mood of the meeting was sober and depressing as they admitted that the Church had to acknowledge complicity in a genocide that made Rwanda a nation of widows and orphans.

The following day I celebrated Holy Communion in Kigale Cathedral, where Alphonse, my friend and former student, had been murdered. Thacienne was there with Jenny Green, another of my students and now a missionary in Uganda, and, supported by Eileen, embarked on the process of letting go and forgiving the people she knew had killed her husband. Two hundred people attended the service, which I endeavoured to make as much an act of repentance as of healing. I was especially worried by the witch-hunting that was going on. It was obvious that the spiral of violence had not ended. Tutsis were hunting down Hutus who had been accused of killing and raping, and impromptu justice was leading to summary executions. Silent groups of people stood outside the cathedral with banners naming a senior member of the Church, a Hutu, as being implicated in the genocide. He vehemently protested his innocence, and was clearly very frightened by the level of hatred directed at him.

A little later I had a private meeting with Prime Minister Faustin Twagiramunga, a Hutu – an impressive man, cultured and wise. The new government, although mainly Tutsi, had already decided that it must include Hutus, and the appointment of Prime Minister Twagira-munga was a step in the right direction. He was forthright in his criticism of the United Nations, whose forces were present in significant numbers in his country, yet did nothing to stop the genocide. Turning to the Church, he felt that both the Anglican and the Roman Catholic Churches, as the two strongest denominations in the land, bore a great deal of responsibility for their support of the former government. The leadership of the Church had failed the people, and there was little hope of departed Bishops returning without having to face prosecution.

My meeting with Vice-President Paul Kagame was if anything even more profitable. The Vice-President, who had commanded the Tutsi forces in the civil war, was the real power in the land. A tall, determined and authoritative man, Kagame was frank about the nation's difficulties and the awesome task of rebuilding that lay ahead. He felt that the future lay in a closer relationship with Britain, and was determined to make English, rather than French, the second language. He too was bitter about the UN's failure to stop the genocide and was critical of the huge numbers of non-governmental organisations (NGOs) pouring into Rwanda. 'They ride around in their white Land Rovers,' he said contemptuously, 'and attempt to justify their existence by making my country more dependent on their aid.' I felt this was a somewhat unfair criticism of the majority of NGO agencies in Rwanda who desperately wanted to help the thousands of needy people.

While I was meeting Paul Kagame (who has since become President of Rwanda), Eileen was seeing the Minister for Social Affairs – a striking woman whose job was to secure the peace and to get as many people housed as soon as possible. In her opinion the women had been most traumatised by the genocide and its sequel; not only had thousands been killed or widowed, but many more had been raped and then dreadfully injured. Rwanda, she declared, was now a land of 'widows and orphans'.

That same day we drove to Ruhange, a short distance outside the city, where several hundred Hutus and Tutsis had been murdered together in a church. This time the story was more heroic than at Nyarubye. The army had surrounded the church and ordered the Hutu Christians to leave. They refused to do so and, knowing what was about to happen, had decided to die with their Tutsi brothers and sisters. The army opened fire, then dragged the bodies out, some to an open grave and others to be burnt. In silence we walked through the abandoned church, observing the bloodstains and bulletholes that testified to the evil act that had taken place here not so long before.

The following day we flew south to Butare, where we visited a hospital where five thousand people had died following the signal given by the President on 6 April. Survivors told us that doctor had killed doctor and nurse had killed nurse. Those injured outside the hospital who came seeking medical attention were butchered as they entered. We walked through the wards and saw evidence of these terrible events: young women and children with machete wounds, some without feet and hands. The medical superintendent who showed us around told us he had lost four of his children. Everybody seemed to have tales to tell of relatives who had been victims of the tribalism.

Then it was on to Kigeme, near the Burundi border, where the UN had one of many refugee camps. Two and a half thousand people were crammed together in a small area on the slope of a hill, in appalling conditions – just simple huts with no sanitation apart from evil-smelling privies close by. Runny-nosed children with wonderful smiles were everywhere, and malnutrition was very much in evidence. The hospital, started by missionaries, had 160 beds but there was only one doctor. It was difficult to see how these poor people could ever be expatriated. They were Hutu refugees from Burundi, unable to return home, but unable to enter Rwanda. Their position was desperate.

Yet, there were signs of hope. Norman Kayumba, the Bishop of Kigeme, was a cheerful and enterprising Hutu whose Christian faith transcended the vicious rivalries of tribalism. He himself had rescued the only Tutsi Bishop in Rwanda, Alexis Bilindabagabo, and his family when they were about to be taken away for execution. Norman was uncompromising in his assessment of Rwanda's problems. The answers, he believed, lay in education, in the integration of both tribes in the life of the nation, and in law and order. Sadly, within two years Norman and his family were to be hounded out of Rwanda by fear of reprisals, and had to seek refuge in England, where they now live.

Our final day in Rwanda was a constructive yet inconclusive time with the Synod of Bishops. A host of others, priests and lay people, crowded in, as apparently was the custom. Bishop Onesiphore Rwaje chaired the meeting extremely well, though there were times when it came very close to breaking up in anger and even violence. At one point a senior member of the Church accused another of being behind the placards accusing him of killing Hutus. The latter responded with anger, but without directly denying the accusation. I attempted in my speech to get the Bishops to unite in a common mission to their people. They must stand together, I said, and work for the renewal of the Church. 'The Church has failed the people and it must learn the bitter lessons of failure. Above all, the Bishops must return to their dioceses and start on the process of renewal with their clergy and people.'

However, there was one last visit to make before I left Rwanda. Bishop Alexis Bilindabagabo and his beautiful wife Grace, a doctor, had started a string of orphanages which were now accommodating the staggering number of eight thousand children. We went with them to one of their homes, where we met four 'houseparents'. Each of them had been bereaved through the hostilities and was now looking after a family of orphans. One of them was a young girl of eighteen, who had been raped and had given birth to a baby. She was houseparent to twelve youngsters. An elderly lady of seventy who had lost her entire family was looking after seventeen children. A boy of seventeen was looking after eight, and a woman of fifty was looking after fifteen. Their hopefulness was inspiring, as was their dedication and determination to make a contribution to the youngsters of Rwanda.

16

The Challenge of Homosexuality

'If a Church were to let itself be pushed to the point where it
ceased to treat homosexual activity as a departure from the
biblical norm, and recognised homosexual unions as a personal
partnership of love equivalent to marriage, such a Church ...
would cease to be the one, holy, Catholic and apostolic Church.'

Wolfhart Pannenberg,
'Revelation and Homosexual Experience' (1996)

IN APRIL 1991 the very first House of Bishops document I signed
as Chairman was *Issues in Human Sexuality*, a report that was to
hold much significance for the future, particularly as it expressed
the House's pastoral mind on the fraught and sensitive issue of
homosexuality. In my Foreword I made it clear that it was not
intended to be the last word on the subject, although my private
opinion was that it would be difficult to find a stronger document
that commanded such agreement among the Bishops.

It is often forgotten that this report has never been debated by
General Synod, and has no more authority than the House of Bishops
itself – important of course though that is. Much more significant
as a statement of policy was the overwhelming vote recorded at
General Synod in November 1987, which affirmed 'biblical and
traditional teaching that sexual intercourse is an act of total commitment which belongs properly within a permanent married relationship', and that 'homosexual genital acts fall short of this ideal and

are likewise to be met by a call to repentance and the exercise of compassion'. This in fact was an amendment put forward by Michael Baughen, Bishop of Chester, modifying a tougher motion from Tony Higton that 'fornication, adultery and homosexual acts are sinful in all circumstances'.

However, when the House of Bishops reassembled in January 1988 following the debate there was clear dissatisfaction, and it was felt that a serious study of homosexuality was needed. Canon June Osborne was asked to chair a working party, which duly reported to the House; but much to the horror of the Bishops, the Osborne Report had swung so far in a permissive direction that it was hastily buried. A decision was taken under my predecessor that the House should study the issue itself first, and only when we ourselves had reached a common mind should we attempt to give a lead to the Church. Two prior defining matters were identified and agreed: that homosexuality had to be set in the context of human sexuality, and that the focus of the document should be pastoral. The work was entrusted to a small working party but such was the involvement of the House in scrutinising every sentence of *Issues* that the report may truly be considered as representing the mind of the Bishops.

Quite unusually for a report from the House of Bishops, *Issues in Human Sexuality* was well received by the vast majority of the Church of England and those beyond it. Its sympathetic consideration of the importance of sexuality, and the way we are all affected by it for good and ill, was accepted as the proper context for the study of homosexuality. Its strong commitment to limiting sexual practice to faithful, monogamous, heterosexual couples committed to one another for life received affirmation too. I was delighted with it, although I would have preferred a more consistent expectation of clergy and laity. The document implied that homosexual clergy were expected to be celibate, but that homosexual laity were not bound by the same discipline. This in fact was not so. The House had agreed this difference simply on the basis that clergy are office-holders, and by their ordination vows committed to a certain lifestyle, whereas lay people cannot be compelled in the same way. It seemed an understandable distinction within the discipline of the Church's ministry.

The publication of the report forced me to clarify my own thinking and approach on the matter, as it was increasingly obvious that homosexuality would be one of the most urgent and vexed issues in the Anglican Communion during my leadership. The actual questions were far from clear-cut. I first needed to remind myself that the subject was not academic, but about actual people. As a Christian leader, I had to avoid the temptation to distance myself from those people, who need love and friendship like any others. If the point of the debate was about people who happen to be homosexual, the question is rightly posed: 'Why can't I and others happily accept that some are created heterosexual and others are homosexual? If God made them like that and they are acceptable to Him, what is the problem?'

As I saw it, there were three problems that stood in the way of accepting practising homosexuality as on a plane with heterosexual relationships: the teaching of the Bible itself; the sacrament of marriage; and outstanding questions which had not yet been resolved by scientific research.

For the first of these, there is very little written in the Bible about sexual acts between people of the same sex, but what there is is uncompromisingly hostile to it. The most significant passage – Romans 1. 25–27 – is also the most critical and damning of homosexual activity. If it is objected that Paul's teaching in Romans 1 merely represents contemporary attitudes at the time, we could conclude that it may be discarded as belonging to the same genre as his teaching about women wearing hats. The weakness of this argument is that once it has been used with respect to that issue, it must surely apply to other areas of Paul's theology and thought too. Furthermore, the epistle to the Romans is Paul's most significant theological work, and his treatment of homosexual practice in Romans 1 is part and parcel of his teaching about the fallenness of humankind. But could it be that we are talking about two different things? Did Paul only have in mind the warped and depraved male prostitution that was characteristic in the ancient world – especially pederasty? However, there is nothing in the passage to suggest that this is what Paul is condemning. Unambiguously he speaks of 'women exchanging natural relations for unnatural ones', and men 'abandoning natural relations with women and . . . inflamed with lust for one another'. There seems to be a close relationship between what Paul – in line with the rest of scripture – condemns and contemporary experience. In any case, those who would reject such teaching must face the challenge that it is incoherent to dismiss one part of Paul's theology as culturally conditioned and therefore irrelevant for today, and yet to regard the remainder of it as valid and binding on Christians for all time. While a small fringe of theologians have entirely rejected the stern warnings of scripture regarding homosexual practice as no longer relevant, the consequence of that is to cut oneself off from the Bible. For myself, I could not be that cavalier.

The second issue, of the sacrament of marriage, poses a different set of questions to those seeking some degree of scriptural validation for practising homosexuality. It is sometimes averred that as Jesus Himself makes no mention of homosexuality, it was clearly unimportant to Him. He must have known about it, and His silence indicates that love is the essential quality in all relationships, including homosexual ones. Appeals are therefore made to the generous and inclusive nature of the gospel of Jesus – that 'His attitude of acceptance to women, slaves and all victims of oppression must surely apply to homosexuals.' It does, of course, up to a certain point. He welcomes all – but what we must not forget is that He does so on His terms, not ours. What is often conveniently overlooked is that though Jesus never refers to homosexual practice, He says a great deal about sexuality in general. There are no grounds for believing that He ever approved of sexual activity outside marriage. In brief, what Jesus said about sexual activity, building on teaching in the Book of Genesis and other parts of the Old Testament, is that it must be limited to those in a covenanted heterosexual relationship of love. May other forms of bonding be equally covenantal and sacramental? As I reflected on the matter, I could only conclude that Jesus's teaching gave no basis whatsoever for any form of bonding other than husband and wife committed to one another forever.

Finally, there were remaining questions that are still unresolved about the origin of homosexuality. Is there an unambiguous genetic basis for it? Is it innate and inherited? Is it a phase that many pass through, and therefore reversible? My pastoral experience and my study seemed to lead to different conclusions. From experience I could not deny that there were some – not a great many, but some – people who were definitely homosexual, and were happiest in the company of the same sex. Even so, the experience of homosexuals was not unambiguous. Some had gone through a homosexual phase and had later grown away from it, finding fulfilment in heterosexual marriage. A few of these now felt a strong bias against the homosexual community, which they claimed had influenced them negatively. Study of the issue indicated to me that there is no hard biological evidence for a genetic basis for homosexuality. The most that could be said is that some people are more predisposed towards homosexuality than others. It would be foolish for the Church to change its approach while scientific knowledge about the condition we describe as homosexual is still incomplete.

I was conscious that many outside the Christian Church would not necessarily find appeals to the Bible convincing, including liberal Christians for whom scripture is not always the last word. How does one find common ground with conscientious people for whom the Bible is not normative for truth? It seemed to me that one way of bridging the gulf is by reference to the purpose of scripture. The Bible does not simply stand on its own, in an intellectual vacuum. On the contrary, I believe that what it presents to us is more than simply what God wills; it also sets out what is good for us as human beings. In other words, God wills that which is truly fulfilling for us. This means that evidence, facts and consequences are all relevant parts of the process of discerning what it is that the moral life comprises. In the present case, when we see the Bible as holding up the model of lifelong marriage between a man and a woman as the only proper context for sexual expression, this should not be viewed as an arbitrary *diktat*. Rather, it points to a mode of life in which our human, social and sexual needs may find fulfilment. Other arrangements may therefore be expected to fall short in terms of the wellbeing they can make available. Transient or casual sexual encounters, incest, group marriage, polygamy or whatever other permutations come to be devised cannot, on this view, be expected to deliver corresponding wellbeing; indeed, many of them demean one party in gratifying the other. The Bible and Christian tradition are merely telling us that the fullness of happiness and wellbeing is a path best opened to us by the tradition of chastity on the one hand, and marriage between a man and a woman on the other. Anything else will fall short.

This perspective has a number of consequences, of which two are especially pertinent. Firstly, we are called to engage with facts and evidence about the impact on human happiness of different moral options. We cannot simply cut ourselves off from all enquiry and debate, and share our moral insights with a megaphone. We have to be morally engaged, and this will always be a challenging and continuing task.

Secondly, the Church has a very deep responsibility to uphold its historic moral insights and teaching, even while we continue to explore their fullness of meaning and their most adequate contemporary expression. The teachings of the Church are not arbitrary or frivolous, and may not be cast aside with misplaced presumption. The Church would be committing a profound wrong in offering models of how best to live that fall short of the truly good which God wills for us. In the case of same-sex relationships I think it would be a grievous error to offer some sort of 'blessing' that is a pretended substitute for a marriage, which such a union can never comprise. To do this is to harm the people involved by offering them a pretence and a deception. To borrow a telling American phrase, it is an 'act of pastoral violence'. But to perform such an act is also to mislead society at large. Offering such ceremonies seems to suggest that something resembling a marriage can exist where it does not. It is also a trivialisation of gender. If a shop pretends to sell goods and services it cannot in fact provide, we all know this to be wrong – and the Church is in this respect no different.

This is not in any sense to suggest that love, profound friendship or even commitment are not good, but it is to say that marriage is not simply a product of some combination of these things between assenting parties of any orientation and gender. Logic further entails that it cannot be right for the Church to hold up as a special example persons who adopt lifestyles that fall short of what the Church teaches.

While members of the clergy are human, and fallible in all kinds of ways, there is no warrant for consciously appointing as leaders those whose lifestyle is deficient in the eyes of the Church. This is why it cannot be right to make a Bishop of someone who expressly proclaims that he lives in violation of what the Church teaches. To do this would be to offer a false teaching, and to harm society at a time when contemporary culture finds it difficult to maintain, or even see, the necessity of shared moral standards. Again, it is necessary to emphasise that the voice of homosexuals is one to which we are called to listen and to offer a loving and welcoming response. But this welcome must have integrity. A true welcome, as with true love, is never false.

Even though my reflections led me to the conclusion that homosexual sexual intercourse fell short of God's intention, I felt, as did the entire House of Bishops, that the discussion had to be kept open. Personally I attempted to hold before me Robert Runcie's wonderful ending to his speech in General Synod in the debate on the issue in 1987. He said: 'In this earthly tabernacle of Christ's Kingdom there are many mansions, and all of them are made of glass.' Such a tolerant, sympathetic attitude, if held by all, had the potential to hold the Church together in spite of deep and strongly held differences.

If I was content with *Issues in Human Sexuality*, not everyone was. On 22 April 1991 I invited to lunch at Lambeth Palace a group of people who had expressed some unhappiness with it, and who desired a meeting with me. They included Professor Rowan Williams, Lady Margaret Professor of Divinity at Oxford University; Dr Jeffrey John, who later became well-known when he was forced to stand down from his appointment as Bishop of Reading over the issue of homosexuality; and the Bishop of Sheffield, Jack Nichols. I also invited Dr Elaine Storkey, a well-known evangelical scholar, and my Chief of Staff, Bishop John Yates.

The debate was lively and frank. I put the report in context: it was a discussion document, and the Bishops were anxious to get reactions to it. I encouraged my guests to speak freely, which they did. Jeffrey John, for example, was strongly of the opinion that *Issues in Human Sexuality* had not given sufficient attention to the experience of homosexuals and did not draw upon their insights. At the most it gave grudging hospitality to homosexuals in the Church. 'Do we have a place?' he asked. 'And if we do, on what basis is it? Is it merely of toleration but disapproval of our lifestyle? Why can't homosexuals, who are homosexuals by nature as much as heterosexuals are such by nature, be treated on the same basis?'

Rowan Williams raised perceptive questions concerning the issue of scriptural authority in making moral judgements. He felt that the patchy nature of statements about homosexuality in scripture demanded that we give prior authority to the nature of the gospel and the love of God. He also raised the issue of double standards for clergy and laity. For Bishop Jack Nichols a major issue was the pastoral care of homosexuals, and the message sent out to them that, once again, the Church had not advanced in its thinking or attitude.

The exchanges were direct and very useful, even though little in the views expressed was new. It was however a very important meeting in outlining the principal areas of discussion. Is homosexual practice between consenting adults sinful? Or, as some of the group were suggesting, is it not the case that homosexual relationships may be as rewarding and as holy as heterosexual marriages, and could therefore be dignified by a service of blessing? Is the authority of scripture so clear and certain on the matter that it may never be challenged or refuted? Is it not the case that the Church has changed its mind on other seemingly clear issues – slavery, the ordination of women and cosmology – making it conceivable that the Church's and society's attitude towards homosexuality will be reformed in the light of science and human experience?

As I have said, these questions were not new to me, nor was I unsympathetic to the situation of homosexuals in the Church and society. Eileen and I had friendships with homosexual people – some of whom were in relationships – and we respected their trust in us, even though they knew we did not approve of their lifestyle. Nevertheless, sympathy and understanding were not enough. The real question remained whether there was sufficient theological convergence and knowledge to lead to a revision of the Church's teaching allowing practising homosexuals to be ordained and their relationships to be honoured by services of blessing. I concluded that there was no such consensus in the Anglican Communion nor in the wider Church for this even to be considered, and on biblical and doctrinal grounds I felt there was no basis for change. As time went on my views were to be tested and challenged again and again.

The first salvoes came, predictably from the Bishop of Newark, New Jersey, Jack Spong, whose commitment to the cause of homosexuals was honourable even though in my view his spirited arguments lacked judgement and objectivity. In August 1994 he drafted his Koinonia Statement, which was signed by over thirty-five active American Bishops and more than twice that number of retired Bishops. There was no ambiguity about this statement: it began with an argument from 'collegiality' and purported to be a contribution to the Church's thinking on the subject of homosexuality, asserting that 'some of us are created heterosexual and some of us are created homosexual'. It insisted that both were 'morally neutral', and both could be lived out with 'beauty, honour, holiness and integrity'. The statement affirmed the contribution that homosexual clergy have made to the Church through the 'very witness of the committed nature of the lives they live with their partners', and concluded by pledging that the signing Bishops would not exclude homosexuals in committed relationships from the priesthood and full participation in the life of the Church. It was an honest statement of intent, and it raised the temperature considerably in the Anglican Communion.

To some degree the Koinonia Statement was doing little more than making explicit what had been going on in the American Church for many years. Along with a smaller number of Bishops in England – notably in the dioceses of London and Southwark – and in some other First World Churches, the American Bishops had been paying lip-service to the tradition of the Church by gradually allowing practising homosexuals to be admitted to the priesthood. But as this became known, alarm grew and opposition built up. The significance of the Koinonia Statement was its blatant commitment to a course of action which had neither been agreed by the entire House of Bishops nor had the consent of General Convention, which meets every three years. Among the signatories was the new American Presiding Bishop, Frank Griswold; I feared this would undermine his authority. The Koinonia Statement was a bombshell, and led to the formation of an opposition group known as the American Anglican Council (AAC), chaired by Jim Stanton, Bishop of Dallas, and later by Bob Duncan, Bishop of Pittsburgh.

It was not only in the States that opposition was building up to what many in the Anglican Communion feared was a drift away from a moral tradition shared with the Roman Catholic and Orthodox Churches. My travels indicated how much this development was worrying other parts of the Communion, particularly Christians living in Islamic cultures. The Bishop of Lahore, Alexander Malik, was quite certain that the mission of the Church in his country was undermined by an acceptance of homosexual practice in the West. My discussions with missionaries in such countries confirmed that such worries were well-founded and ought to be taken into account by those in the Western Churches who seemed determined to force through practices which other Christians deemed wrong. I became increasingly apprehensive as I saw a backlash forming among Third World Christian leaders to resist what they called the 'homosexualising' of America and the Western Church. Thus was born a coalition that would be called the 'South to South' movement.

In England, the backlash was taking a different form. 'Reform', representing conservative evangelical parishes under the leadership of a prominent Sheffield vicar, the Reverend Philip Hacking, began to flex its muscles against what it considered to be the liberalising of the Church of England. Although Reform did not represent mainstream evangelicalism, it was still a significant force and its views had to be taken seriously.

In December 1995 Philip Hacking wrote to me: 'We do feel that our position is not represented with the House of Bishops nor do we have a PEV [Provincial Episcopal Visitor] to represent us. I have been approached to see if I, or a group with me, could present our case . . .' I was surprised by the theology expressed in the letter, as if Bishops were appointed to represent interest groups. I replied accordingly, making it clear that, in spite of a shared position on the issue of homosexuality, I would not and could not countenance a PEV for conservative evangelicals only, as this was quite foreign to the Anglican theology of episcopacy. I went on to say that the three PEVs in the Church of England were appointed to minister with other Bishops to those congregations and priests who were opposed to the ordination of women, and that included evangelicals as well as Catholics. However, I agreed to see the group in due course.

I was disappointed but not wholly surprised when Reform issued a press statement which announced that the Archbishop of Canterbury had 'rejected' the evangelical group's request, but that the Reform council had 'mandated the Chairman to go again to Lambeth Palace to facilitate the appointment of three evangelical Bishops to minister to the fast-growing Reform constituency'.

A few months later I met the group, which included Wallace

Benn, a wise and effective preacher and teacher. A frank and helpful exchange of views took place. I listened to their concerns, but told them that I was not going to budge on the issue of appointing a Bishop, let alone three, for them alone. Furthermore, I told them directly, setting up a system of pastoral care would inevitably bring them into collision with diocesan Bishops. I attempted to address their higher motives, which were to bring the love of God to all. I argued that 'It would be madness for any group within the Church with a commitment to the gospel to walk off the pitch when the ball was at their feet.' In time, with the appointment of Wallace Benn as Bishop of Lewes, together with some wiser heads in the Reform council, I felt that the group began to understand that it was being taken seriously and had an important role to play.

In the meantime the Church was having trouble with Outrage!, an extreme 'gay rights' group led by the inveterate campaigner Peter Tatchell. I was appalled when prior to General Synod in November 1994 ten Bishops were 'outed' by Outrage!. The naming of these Bishops, who it was claimed had had homosexual relationships in the past, was deeply reprehensible and humiliating to them and their families. I contacted each one, and heard all too clearly the distress caused. In the majority of cases the Bishops were adamant that, despite Outrage!'s claims to the contrary, the information was inaccurate, and each one of them wanted redress but did not know how to clear his name.

However, Outrage! got its just deserts when it tried to take on the Bishop of London, David Hope. Just after Christmas 1994 Peter Tatchell wrote to David: 'As you are no doubt aware, it is widely understood by many lesbians and gay men . . . that you are gay. Although Outrage! has been passed a lot of detailed information about your personal life which would have enabled us to confidently name you at Synod on 3 November, we chose not to do so.' This appalling letter went on to say that Outrage! believed the Bishop capable of playing a very special role morally and historically: 'It is our sincere hope that you will find the inner strength and conviction to realise the importance of voluntarily coming out as gay and speaking out in defence of lesbian and gay human rights.' David showed me the letter, and said that he intended to address it directly. This he did very courageously by calling the press together and revealing its contents. He described it and other letters he had received as 'intimidatory', and went on to say, 'With regard to the question "Are you gay, Bishop?", the answer to this question is that I have from the beginning chosen to lead a single, celibate life.' It was an extraordinarily brave action to take, which shamed Peter Tatchell and his tactics of intimidation, and no doubt gave courage to others in similar situations.

The good news was that not all initiatives were being taken by those intent on destruction. Many were delighted when, at the request of the Church of England Evangelical Council, a group of well-known theologians chaired by Dr Timothy Bradshaw produced the St Andrew's Statement. It was a fine, scholarly piece of work, attempting to go deeper into the issue of sexuality, examining the principles and considering the application. This, I thought, was exactly what the Bishops wanted in the wake of *Issues in Human Sexuality* – solid, sensible reflections. The Statement argued, contrary to the 'gay' lobby, that our sexual affections no more define who we are than do our class, race or nationality. I was pleased to see in the Statement a defence of our report's distinction between clergy and lay people: 'The Bishops have scripture on their side in arguing that special considerations affect the behaviour of clergy who have a particular commission to expound and exemplify the teachings of the Church.' This was absolutely right, and was the real reason why *Issues* had made the distinction between clergy and lay people. Clergy, chosen for office, are expected to live the kind of life that exemplifies the Christian faith in a visible and public ministry. The ordination service demands of them: 'Will you accept the discipline of this Church and give due respect to those in authority?' And: 'Will you strive to fashion your own life and that of your household according to the way of Christ?' The idea that has crept into the Church that there is a homosexual alternative to marriage and celibacy is of course a departure from ministerial formation.

While a great deal of energy was going into the public controversy, as was reflected in the pages of the newspapers, many Bishops were concerned that not enough was going into calm reflection and moderate and dignified reflection. Church people were not interested in discussing the issue, which meant that extreme behaviour was grabbing the headlines and discouraging debate. The disturbing side-effect of the 'outing' of Bishops was that it tended to feed the expectation that the Church was about to give way on the issue of homosexuality. I was determined that this would not be the case, and in answer to many questions I made it clear that homosexuals were as much part of the Church as single men and women and married people. I wanted them to play a full part in the life of the Church. I saw nothing wrong in deep friendship, but no one should confuse this with marriage. Sexual relations, I repeated, echoing the moral tradition of the Church through the ages, are reserved for heterosexual couples bound together in marriage.

These statements brought me into contact with the Lesbian and Gay Christian Movement (LGCM), led for many years by Richard Kirker. I recognised and respected Kirker's commitment to the rights of homosexuals in the Church, but regretted the hard tone and language that characterised his public comments, which seemed the opposite of the friendly and mild-mannered man he actually is. In a television interview in 1997 I repeated my opposition to practising homosexuals in the ministry of the Church. My argument was that I saw no justification for the Church changing its stance on the issue: that homosexuals had the same rights as others in the Church; if they wished to be ordained then it was a matter of obeying the rules – either marry or remain celibate.

Richard Kirker issued a press statement claiming that 'George Carey is digging a bigger and bigger hole for himself . . . those he singles out most for his heartless and cruel condemnation are gay clergy . . . the Church of England is being turned into an object of ridicule by its own Archbishop because he shows so little understanding of human nature and the gospel of love. It is shameful to be associated with such bigotry. We challenge the Archbishop to meet us ... if he were to agree he might learn a great deal and become less homophobic.'

I was to get used to the style of rhetoric and language that LGCM employed in dialogue. To be called 'heartless', 'cruel', a 'bigot' and 'homophobic' in the course of a few sentences made me appear a monster. I replied that this was hardly the vocabulary of thoughtful dialogue, and that as for a public debate or a private meeting, the House of Bishops had agreed that the working party led by the Bishop of Oxford, Richard Harries, was the proper context for dialogue with the House of Bishops. I reminded Kirker that a meeting of LGCM and the Bishops had already been arranged, and that it was not my intention to undermine their role. In retrospect, I think I made a mistake by not seeing the group, because it might have helped relationships, and would have been time worth investing. However, at the time it had been agreed by all the Bishops that we would let Richard Harries' group lead on the issue and I felt it important to adhere to this principle.

The House of Bishops' intention to keep the debate on homosexuality open, which after all was the point of their report, and to inculcate a climate of listening and generosity of spirit, was not helped by the language and behaviour of some homosexuals, or, it must be said, by some of their adversaries in Reform. On Sunday, 20 April 1997 I and a number of guests became victims of Peter Tatchell's abusive tactics. It was a very important day in my calendar. Eileen and I were expected to entertain the Planning Group for the 1998 Lambeth Conference, led by Archbishop Keith Rayner, the Primate of Australia. In attendance were at least ten other Archbishops and theologians, including Rowan Williams, who was now the Bishop of Monmouth. I had just celebrated Holy Communion, and following coffee we wandered in the garden of Lambeth Palace to enjoy the beautiful summer morning and to have an official photograph taken of the group. Suddenly, from nowhere, there appeared six to eight people brandishing banners and screaming at the top of their voices. Peter Tatchell appeared before me, his face a few inches from mine, shouting, 'Why do you hate us so much, Archbishop? Why won't you talk to us? Why are you such a moral coward?' The entire group of us were dumbstruck, and the tirade seemed to go on for hours. I tried to reason with Tatchell, but to no avail. He was interested in maximum media exposure, and listening and dialogue were the least of his concerns. It was an unpleasant moment, and it particularly shocked some of my overseas guests. It was however a media coup for Tatchell, and the papers the following day recorded the occasion in detail.

The pressure was mounting, and on 14 July 1997 General Synod debated a motion presented by David Gerrard, Archdeacon of Wandsworth, who commended *Issues in Human Sexuality* for discussion in the dioceses, but called on Synod to 'acknowledge that it is not the last word on the subject'. There was little one could quarrel with in the motion itself, but I suspected that it was intended to give the Archdeacon an opportunity to raise the matter from a liberal viewpoint. It was a good but predictable debate, with a minority wishing the Church to change its stance towards homosexuals. My contribution was to put the debate in the context of the Anglican Communion.

I began by referring to the picture presented in the media of a Church hopelessly divided by a furious debate on homosexuality. In fact, I said, this was not the case. The Communion was in good heart, and a sense of mission and service prevailed. In the preparations for the forthcoming Lambeth Conference homosexuality was but one of many themes that would be considered. However, 'we know that in the Communion there is a strand of opinion challenging the traditional understanding of the Church, and that Desmond Tutu, a personal friend of mine, is an eloquent exponent of that opinion. But it remains a minority view.' I then laid my cards firmly on the table: 'Let me make clear my starting point. I do not find any justifi-

It was often my privilege to escort the Queen Mother at state banquets; so much so that one day as the line was forming, Prince Philip said to her, 'Come on, Mother – your taxi is waiting!'

With Dinka children in Sudan, 1993. This visit to the south of the country led to the expulsion of the British Ambassador. I was to visit the Anglican Church of Sudan three times during my period as Archbishop.

Above Uganda, 1994. A
typical cavalcade, with
crowds lining the road to
greet the Archbishop of
Canterbury.

Left With Patriarch Illya II
of Georgia on a river boat
on the Thames in June 1995.
It was on this cruise that he
asked me to supply a
Rottweiler bitch so he could
breed guard dogs. We man-
aged to ship a female puppy
to him, which he named
after me.

Right Perhaps our most harrowing overseas visit of all, to Rwanda in 1995, only months after the genocide in the country. Eileen and I are pictured in a church witnessing the grisly remains of the victims of the killings.

Above With United Nations Secretary General Kofi Annan in Uganda in 1995.

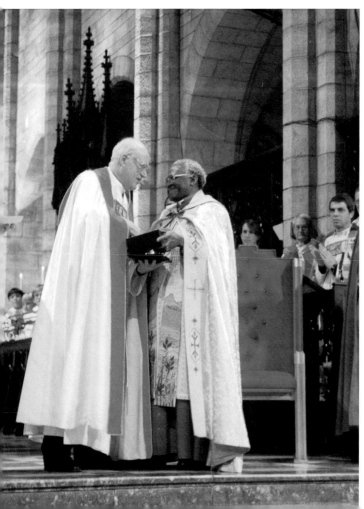

Left As Archbishop of Cape Town Desmond Tutu made an outstanding contribution to freedom and social justice. His retirement service in 1996 was a wonderful blend of Anglo-Catholic worship with uninhibited dancing and African chants.

Left With my second Prime Minister, Tony Blair at the TUC in 1997, when we both gave addresses. It was said by the papers the next day that the Prime Minister had preached the sermon while I had given the political address.

Below Eileen and I greet Princess Margaret when she came to celebrate Ash Wednesday in a community Eucharist at Lambeth Palace in 1999. She was nervous, never having come across the practice of marking the communicants with ash before, but later said it was meaningful and reassuring to be reminded of one's mortality and need for God's grace day by day.

Left In the summer of 1999 Christians and many others formed human chains as part of the Jubilee 2000 campaign to call for the cancellation of unpayable debt on behalf of the world's poorest economies. Chancellor Gordon Brown would later tell me of the impact of the campaign on G7 leaders meeting in Birmingham.

Right With a frail but still very alert Pope John Paul II in the Vatican in 2000. The Pope invited me and Metropolitan Athanasios, representing the Orthodox Churches' Ecumenical Patriarch, to attend while he opened the Holy Door of St Paul's in Rome, as a demonstration of our commitment to seek full, visible unity. It was impossible for the Pope to accomplish the task on his own, so we three leaders pushed together. For me this was a symbol that no Church can act alone – we have to work with each other.

Eileen and me with President George W. Bush at the White House on 24 April 2001.

On a rainy day in June 2002 the Queen came to a Lambeth Palace garden party to celebrate her Jubilee with children from many local schools.

With His Royal Highness Prince El Hassan bin Talal of Jordan (centre) and the Chief Rabbi Jonathan Sachs. Relations with other faiths received a distinct and growing emphasis in the ministry of the Archbishop of Canterbury during my time in office. Prince Hassan co-hosted the first 'Building Bridges' seminar with me at Lambeth Palace in 2002, drawing together Christian and Muslim scholars.

cation from the Bible or the entire Christian tradition for sexual activity outside marriage. Same-sex relationships, in my view, cannot be on a par with marriage, and the Church should resist any diminishing of the fundamental "*sacramentum*" of marriage. Clergy especially must model relationships that commend the faith of Christ. I know that this statement will distress some, and I understand the pastoral difficulties that come from working out the discipline of the Church in personal life, but I could not commend any significant departure from the principles and conclusions set out in the *Issues* Statement.'

I was pleased by the tenor of the debate, and that my appeal for a commitment to *Issues* was reported widely. I was however saddened that the *Guardian* called it my 'most uncompromising rejection of gay clergy reform to date', because rejection was hardly central to my theme. But at least that and other reports also recognised my insistence that more study was needed on the subject, and that an International Commission might be the way forward.

In the run-up to the 1998 Lambeth Conference two opposing trends were developing and heading towards a collision. The first blow was struck by the Kuala Lumpur Statement, originating from the second 'Anglican Encounter in the South', which drew together Bishops and lay leaders from Africa, Asia, Latin America and Oceania. I knew that the meeting had been convened, and that mission was central to it. But far more was going on than deliberating on mission: there was great anxiety about changing attitudes to homosexuality in the West, and a strong statement was issued that attacked fellow Anglican Churches in the northern hemisphere. Homosexual practices were called 'sinful', and the conference expressed its concern that 'the setting aside of biblical teaching in such actions as the ordination of practising homosexuals and the blessing of same-sex unions called into question the authority of Holy Scripture'.

Maurice Sinclair, Archbishop of what is called 'the Southern Cone' – that is, the southern part of South America – was a particular zealot in presenting the views of 'South to South'. Although I was sometimes irritated by Maurice's earnest and nitpicking manner, I admired his persistence and his willingness to put forward unfashionable views to fellow Primates whose theological position was diametrically opposed to his own.

The expression of the views of the South in such a public manner was enough to bring Bishop Jack Spong racing back into action with a message to the Anglican Communion attacking numerous targets: religious prejudice, the Archbishop of Canterbury, the Archbishop of the Southern Cone, General Synod and the Kuala Lumpur Statement. He poured contempt on those who endeavoured to 'use' the Bible against homosexuality. Such an approach, he claimed, had 'been used to oppose Copernicus and Galileo, to support slavery and oppose the use of vaccinations, the ideas of Charles Darwin, to undergird segregation, apartheid and the second-class status of women'. His arguments, I felt, signally failed to do justice to the very many people in the Church whose devotion to scripture had challenged evils such as slavery and apartheid.

Regrettably, Spong's passionate language raised the temperature of the debate in the Church. His excessive liberalism made dialogue with more conservative Bishops impossible. A few months later he published a text called *A New Reformation* that placed him outside orthodox Christianity in any meaningful form. This 'Reformation', he argued, would be 'far more radical than Christianity has ever before known and this Reformation must deal with the very substance of that faith'. In the reformation he called for, God talk was dead, Christology was bankrupt, the biblical story of the Fall was nonsense, the virgin birth was impossible, the miracle stories unbelievable, the cross as a sacrifice for sin was a barbaric idea, the physical resurrection of Jesus did not happen, the ascension was unbelievable, there was no external, objective revealed standard writ in scripture, and prayer does not effect change. It was an astonishing and sad credo that if followed would empty the Church of any meaning, and also empty it of followers. Oddly, Spong still found a place in his creed for hope for life after death, and for the belief that all human beings bear God's image – assuming, of course, that such an unknowable deity had any recognisable image to bear.

There was much about Jack Spong I liked and admired. I loved his passion for truth and justice; I liked him as a person, and admired his willingness to speak up for others and to walk the way of unpopularity. Oddly, he was the mirror image of the very people he despised – evangelicals – for their commitment to truth and passion for God, their willingness to stand up for unpopular ideas. Yet individuals like Jack Spong show that when liberalism loses its anchor in a revealed revelation it is doomed, and has nothing of importance to say to the Church or to the world.

My hopes of a calm, reflective Lambeth Conference were further damaged when Peter Tatchell struck again. Easter in any church or cathedral is always a big event, and Canterbury Cathedral is no exception. I loved celebrating the Holy Communion service in the cathedral, and valued the privilege of preaching on that most holy of days. Easter Day 1998 was a particularly sunny day, and the congregation was very large, with many families and young children.

No sooner had I entered the pulpit and said the opening prayer than six young men bounded into the pulpit with banners, shouting at the top of their voices. I was pushed to one side, and Peter Tatchell commandeered the pulpit and addressed the congregation to complain about the Church's attitude to homosexuals, objecting to my views on the age of consent, and asserting that I was against equal rights for homosexuals. The noise made by him and others shouting into a live microphone was deafening, and I was very concerned for the young children present, who could easily have been terrified by the commotion; I could see some mothers leading children out.

I tried to regain control of the situation by appealing to the better side of the interlopers, but this fell on deaf ears. To my right was a small Asian man holding a banner who appeared to me to be embarrassed and distressed. Periodically he would mutter, 'I am so sorry, Archbishop. I am so sorry.' While this was going on – and it seemed to go on for a lifetime – I sought to attract some attention so that someone might assist. I was amazed that the microphone system remained turned on, but I was relieved when I saw a senior police officer in the Lord Mayor's party getting police reinforcements to put a halt to the interruption. The problem was that although the pulpit can hold up to eight people, the stairs leading up to it are narrow, and can only be ascended by one person at a time. It took several minutes for the police to get the men out, and some, including Tatchell, were not going to go without a fight. He continued to shout as he was dragged away. His shouts, echoing and re-echoing around the cavernous building, gradually died away, allowing me to speak once more.

It was important to reassure the congregation that this bedlam bore no relationship to the loving theme of Easter, with its message of resolving conflict through suffering, death and renewal. I apologised for the interruption, and thanked everyone for their composure and their prayers. 'Let's now forget it and get back to a far more important theme,' I said, and my address commenced. After the service several homosexual men came up to me and apologised for the conduct of those who, in their name, had perpetrated that act of desecration on such a festival of the Church. I was grateful for their comments.

So, in the build-up to the Lambeth Conference it was obvious that the issue of homosexuality was going to be one of our greatest challenges. I had already reached the conclusion that acceptance of practising homosexuality and the blessing of same-sex marriages were unacceptable to many in the Communion, and that the best we could hope for was for further debate and discussion, perhaps in the hands of an International Commission to help Provinces deal with the underlying cultural and theological issues that had come to the surface.

Professor Wolfhart Pannenberg, one of the greatest living Protestant theologians, had already uttered his judgement a year or two earlier that 'If a Church were to let itself be pushed to the point where it ceased to treat homosexual activity as a departure from the biblical norm, and recognised homosexual unions as a personal partnership of love equivalent to marriage, such a Church would stand no longer on biblical ground but against the witness of scripture. A Church that took this step would cease to be the one, holy, Catholic and apostolic Church.' I was convinced he was right, and I was determined to resist any move that might make our great Communion take a step in that direction.

17

Lambeth '98

'For myself, I shall always look back on the Conference as an important era in my life and archiepiscopate. I trust that it has tended to bind the different branches of the Church in our Anglican Communion more closely together in the bonds of brotherly love.'

Archbishop Longley, 1867

THE FIRST LAMBETH CONFERENCE OF 1867 was a rather reluctant affair. Charles Longley was sixty-eight when he became Archbishop of Canterbury, and the last thing he wanted to do at that age was to call together all the Bishops of the Anglican Communion to resolve problems abroad. But it was an idea whose time had come. Although the Anglican Communion was still largely made up of Church of England Bishops working with English assumptions, it had reached the point where it needed to start out on a journey seeking an international identity and corporate integrity. The presenting issue was the interpretation of scripture at home as well as abroad.

At home, the publication in 1860 of *Essays and Reviews*, written by seven Church of England theologians, had caused an enormous upheaval by its challenge to traditional doctrine. Among the seven eminent writers was a future Archbishop of Canterbury, Frederick Temple. The volume raised the ire of Dr Edward Pusey, leader of the Oxford Movement, who collected eleven thousand signatures of protest, and the consequent uproar led to three sensational heresy trials. Abroad, the teaching of the Bishop of Natal, John Colenso, was also causing deep anxieties. Colenso was convinced that it was necessary to apply techniques of literary criticism to the scriptures, and this he did with missionary zeal but with, perhaps, little thought for the implications. Opposition grew, and little attention was paid to Colenso's deep concern for the African people, or to the fact that the Zulus in particular respected him as a trusted ally and champion. Colenso was arraigned before his superior, Archbishop Gray of Cape Town, and summarily deposed. He refused to leave his office, and appealed to the Privy Council in England. The issue was put before the Master of the Rolls, who ruled that whatever the theological issues, Colenso was still entitled to his salary from the Colonial Bishoprics' Fund. As a result he carried on teaching unperturbed.

Extremely disturbed by the South African problem, Bishops of the Church of Canada appealed to Archbishop Longley to call an urgent meeting of Bishops 'for brotherly love and conference', which he duly did in 1867. The Archbishop had his opponents, and the Bishops were divided between those who did not wish to attend the Conference unless it had full synodical powers, and those who did not wish to attend if it had. To add to his difficulties, the Archbishop of York did not approve and did not attend, while the Dean of Westminster Abbey, alarmed by the novelty of such a gathering, refused permission for the final service to be held there. Seventy-six Bishops attended this historic first international gathering, small enough for the Conference to be held at Lambeth Palace, from whence the name 'Lambeth Conference' has ever since designated the gathering of Bishops called by the Archbishop of Canterbury every ten years.

The first Conference would define subsequent ones in another significant manner. Longley was absolutely against it being anything other than consultative and spiritual. He assured the English bench of Bishops that it would have no power to make decisions binding on any branch of the Communion. Consequently, while the Conference considered the Colenso matter, it had no authority to resolve it. It issued two resolutions concerning the problem, giving the Archbishop of Canterbury a stronger hand in dealing with urgent issues as they emerged. Longley was satisfied with this; what he wanted to provide and what he felt was necessary was consultation and community among Bishops who shared the same leadership role in the Church, but who often had to conduct their work in lonely and adverse situations.

It fell to me to convene the Thirteenth Lambeth Conference in 1998, in entirely different circumstances. The world and the Church had changed in ways that Longley and his colleagues could hardly have dreamed of. The Communion had grown enormously, and there were now more than eight hundred Bishops. It was at the gathering of Primates in Newcastle, Northern Ireland in April 1991, just before my enthronement as Archbishop, that I had to begin the process of deciding whether or not to call the Bishops together for consultation. Canon Colin Craston, Chairman of the Anglican Consultative Council, assured me that Canon Sam van Culin, the able Secretary General of the Communion and his staff, would give me every assistance, but he told me frankly that I had to be in the driving seat. If I did not take on the Conference with enthusiasm and energy, it would very probably fail. The financial challenge alone was daunting. An amount in excess of £2 million had to be raised to pay for the Conference, and I could not count on the use of any profit from the 1988 gathering, which had ended in debt.

It was not a propitious start, and with the almost overwhelming challenges that always confront a new Archbishop of Canterbury, it was not an enviable moment to make such a momentous decision. However, a moment's reflection was enough to convince me that in spite of the obstacles, the Conference had to be called, for the very reasons that Archbishop Longley had invited the Bishops together in his day – for mutual consultation regarding the manifold problems which no Bishop could avoid: problems concerning the human family, poverty and exclusion from the global economic order; problems of international debt, war and civil unrest; problems concerning the individual, women and children, the issue of homosexuality; problems concerning mission, relations with Islam and other faiths; and problems to do with other Churches and the search for unity.

The list seemed endless, and spoke eloquently of the need for the Bishops of the Church to meet once more; and not only the Bishops, but their spouses as well. I knew from my experience of the Anglican Communion how crucial a role is played by the spouses of Bishops, and following the example of my predecessor, I was very keen for them to share in such an important Conference. At a conservative guess at least 650 spouses would come, resulting in total numbers well in excess of two thousand once staff, media and experts were included. Archbishop Keith Rayner, Primate of Australia, accepted my invitation to chair the Design Group, and Eileen, quite properly, decided that she should lead the Spouses' Design Group.

In the period between 1991 and 1998 I was assisted by two excellent staff members in Canon Roger Symon and Canon Andrew Deuchar, and by the generous financial assistance of the Church Commissioners, who seconded one of their senior staff, David Long, to act as Lambeth Conference Manager. The new Secretary General of the Anglican Consultative Council, Canon John Peterson, was Secretary to the Conference, and did his job thoroughly and well. As many of the African Bishops could not contribute anything towards Conference fees and travel, we decided to raise five hundred bursaries of £5,000 each in the run-up to the gathering, and this was achieved, principally through the generosity of English and American dioceses.

In my meetings with the Design Group I urged the importance of keeping the number of resolutions down. I was not alone in longing for a Conference shaped more by the character of its discussions and less by formal resolutions. The 1988 Conference had been dominated by resolutions which, apart from a few exceptions, proved to be an ineffective way for Bishops to express their concerns. I still recall a Scottish Bishop emerging from a Plenary in 1988 who, when asked by a visitor which issue was being debated, shrugged his shoulders and said, 'I don't know. The Lord gave me the blessed gift of sleep.' The group agreed to do their best, but warned that the matter ultimately lay in the hands of the Bishops themselves.

The other thing that concerned us was how to ensure that the issue of homosexuality did not dominate the agenda. Partly in order to prevent this from happening, Bishop Mark Dyer, Chairman of the Editorial Group, circulated a questionnaire to all Provinces. To our relief not one region designated the issue of homosexuality as a pressing matter, so as a result no Plenary was arranged on the subject. (In organising the Conference we had decided to split the Bishops into four Sections, which would do the basic work of the Conference, while the Plenaries would look at issues of particular concern.) With the benefit of hindsight, this was a great mistake, as we were lulled into believing that the issue could be settled in one Section, without a full Plenary being devoted to it. The Design Group concluded that it was sufficient for Section 1 to debate it thoroughly, and to bring forward a resolution to the Conference as a whole that might allow us to move on.

We should have heeded the signals in the build-up to the Conference, because there were plenty who wished to talk up the problem. Rather extraordinarily, the conservative faction were as determined as Jack Spong and his supporters to raise the temperature on the subject. Archbishop Maurice Sinclair of the Southern Cone and Archbishop Joseph Adetiloye of Nigeria, leaders of the 'South to South' coalition, wrote public letters, copied to me, urging the Lambeth Conference to send a strong signal to the Communion endorsing the Kuala Lumpur Statement which had taken such a strong line against practising homosexuality. On the other side, Jack Spong very unwisely insulted African Bishops in an interview in the *Church of England Newspaper*, contemptuously dismissing them as having moved 'out of animism into a very superstitious kind of Christianity. They've yet to face the intellectual revolution of Copernicus and Einstein that we've had to face. That's just not on their radar screen.' These were hurtful and untrue words that encouraged more than a few African

Bishops to approach the Lambeth Conference in a combative mood, determined to deal with what they saw as this Western obsession with homosexuality.

However, such unpleasant outbursts did not mar the great joy and excitement as over 750 Bishops and 650 spouses, together with support staff of all kinds, gathered in Canterbury Cathedral on Sunday, 19 July 1998 for the opening service. The day was bright with a gentle breeze as purple-cassocked Bishops, including eleven women, and other delegates processed into the mother church of the Anglican Communion. Hundreds of children outside waved blue and gold banners, while the cathedral's fourteen bells rang out their own welcome. His Royal Highness the Prince of Wales, our principal guest, was slightly delayed because of animal-rights demonstrators as well as a noisy group of homosexual activists. Their jeers were drowned out by the excited cries of a large body of children and their parents who welcomed our royal visitor and others, including the Lord Chancellor, Cardinal Cassidy of the Pontifical Council for Christian Unity and other ecumenical leaders, as well as my immediate predecessors Lord Coggan and Lord Runcie, and many Ambassadors.

My opening greeting in Swahili, 'Bwana akae nanyi' (The Lord be with you), set the tone for the truly international service that followed, as with trumpets, drums, dance and bells we weaved a colourful garland of worship from the rich diversity of many nations. The hundreds of spouses, especially the African wives, lit up the cathedral with their brightly coloured dresses and spectacular hats. Panamanian liturgical dancers dressed in white swept through the choir and into the nave with whirls of peach, gold, blue and green ribbons. John Sentamu, formerly a High Court judge in Uganda and now Bishop of Stepney, led a Kenyan version of the *Gloria*, beating on a huge drum with great energy and joy. African-American spirituals were sung alongside traditional English and American hymns. The service itself was expressed in French, Swahili, Spanish, Arabic, Portuguese and Japanese. In a masterful sermon, Bishop Simon Chiwanga, Chairman of the Anglican Consultative Council, challenged the entire Communion to be more Christ-like in its mission, and not to allow bitterness and anger to distort its 'image of a living gospel'. 'Evangelism', he said, 'must remain our guiding principle.' And then, responding to concerns that the Conference might be marred by sharp disagreements over homosexuality, he uttered some telling words about 'interpretive charity', defined as 'the ability to give the most loving interpretation to the actions and opinions of others'. 'Interpretive charity', he said, 'challenges us to avoid demeaning labels that we are eager to apply to our opponents.'

Relevant words, indeed, to the Conference. But there was much on which we could agree common views and common action. One such issue was that of unrepayable Third World debt, to which the Anglican Communion had already made a strong contribution and where it still had a role to play. Section 1's brief, 'Called to be Fully Human', under its leader Njongonkulu Ndungane, Archbishop of Cape Town, focused attention on the needs of the many millions whose lives are cut short by poverty. 'International debt', Njongonkulu said, 'is the new slavery of the twentieth century. The human cost of the international debt burden is intolerable. Its effects are evil and sinful.'

A high point came when Jim Wolfensohn, President of the World Bank, came at my invitation to address the entire Conference. Jim had flown in from America by Concorde that morning, and immediately following his address he was going to fly back to New York to address an important gathering at the UN. He knew of the Anglican Communion's commitment to the cause of eradicating poverty, but he was not expecting criticism of the World Bank. The Plenary on International Debt included the participation of many Bishops from Third World countries who had first-hand experience of the legacy of the debt problem. What took many by surprise was the screening of a Christian Aid film that was particularly stinging in its analysis of policies adopted by the World Bank and the International Monetary Fund. I was sitting next to Jim, and I could feel the temperature rising as he boiled with anger at assertions he believed to be false.

The film over, I invited him to address the Conference. Jim advanced to the podium and, departing completely from his prepared speech, gave an eloquent and powerful defence of the World Bank. 'I am not angry about the film,' he said. 'I am upset. I'm upset because it paints a picture of our institution which is quite simply wrong. We do not get up every morning and think about what we can do to ruin the world. I and my colleagues work to make the world a better place.' He went on to say that the film 'would have you believe that I rather like children dying, that I have no faith, that my interest is to collect debts, that I have no understanding of education or health, that I know nothing about the impact of payments imposed by governments'. He gave a moving description of the crippling burden of international debt, and of what the Bank was trying to do in co-operation with others, and concluded by appealing to the Bishops to work with the Bank by focusing on 'the kids that are dying, on the children who are not being educated and on the horrors of poverty together. Together we can do a lot. We have expertise. You have expertise. We know a lot about development. You know a lot about people and communities. You have the best distribution system of any NGO in the world.'

For that passionate and articulate speech Jim received a standing ovation, and he departed for his plane aware that the Conference was totally committed to the goals he had so clearly identified. Sadly, the time allowed did not give us sufficient opportunity to explore the huge differences in perception between our two completely different worlds – the Bank's top-down approach and the grassroots world of the Bishops. No one was in any doubt about Jim's deep concern and the way he was changing the Bank, but some African Bishops were disappointed that the video led him to defend the World Bank, while they wanted him to state ways in which a new partnership with the Bank could emerge in the service of the very poor.

As part of our work on the debt issue the following week at

Lambeth Palace, a selected group of Bishops aired their concerns to senior British politicians, representatives of the World Bank and the IMF, Chairmen of international banks and some Ambassadors. Among the politicians were the Chancellor of the Exchequer, Gordon Brown, and the Secretary of State for International Development, Clare Short. Baroness Chalker and I chaired the meeting at which Bishops, politicians and bankers engaged in thinking creatively about the urgent needs of the very poor. Bishop Peter Selby, one of the group that had written the report on international debt, said, 'We thought it critical to put a resolution before you that was not a moral free-lunch, nor an exhortation to other people to do something – but one that also affected our lives as Churches and as a Communion.' If the Bishops impressed their political and business colleagues by their experience of living with the very poor and their insights into the devastating effects of poverty, they themselves were equally impressed by the compassion and determination of Gordon Brown and Clare Short to move beyond sympathetic words to real action. It is my view that the work of Section 1, the visit of Jim Wolfensohn and that meeting at Lambeth Palace were important steps towards the setting-up of the Millennium Development Goals for reducing world poverty endorsed by the United Nations a few years later.

Whilst we were earnestly discussing the issue of international debt, forty-nine coaches were on their way from Canterbury to London for a day out – lunch at Lambeth Palace with the Prime Minister, a garden party with the Queen at Buckingham Palace, and a boat ride down the Thames, past the Tower and the emerging Millennium Dome. Eileen and I hosted two thousand people for lunch in the palace gardens with a huge tent which, we were told, covered an area of one acre.

The Prime Minister was our principal guest, and gave a superb address that commenced with a confession: 'I think this is the most terrifying audience I have ever set eyes on in my life! Are there really 750 Bishops here?' Tony Blair's speech on the role of religion in modern life, especially in resolving conflict and representing the interests of the very poor, echoed the theme of Jim Wolfensohn's address a few days earlier, but stressed the importance of new partnerships to make a real difference. As a Christian he was unreserved about the importance of the role that faith communities can play on the international scene and in Britain. He too received a standing ovation. Tea with the Queen, Prince Philip and the Duke of York was our next engagement, with our party of just over four thousand being the smallest Royal Garden Party that year. The Queen was in her element as she was introduced to people from many different countries and cultures that she knew well. She was able to engage knowledgeably with them, laughing and chatting away. Prince Philip, as always, was ready to comment on unusual happenings: approaching a new line of Bishops, he quipped, 'I've hit another purple wall!'

The Garden Party over, we boarded our boats for a cruise to the Dome, meeting on the way a substantial group of protesting homosexuals surrounded by a formidable police contingent. There was one rather touching moment on my boat to which later developments would add poignancy. With an excellent jazz band entertaining us in the background, the banter was animated and boisterous. I was in a group of Bishops which could not have been more diverse if we had chosen it deliberately. It included Richard Holloway, Jack Spong and Jack Iker (well-known for his conservative views on the ordination of women as well as sexuality). Richard, who is well-known for his sense of fun, had brought with him several mitres which he described as 'biologically friendly', and he invited the four of us to cast them on the waters as a sign of our rejection of 'pomp-fed' prelacy, which of course we were all happy to do. It was the last time we agreed on anything, and alas, within a few days we were to be separated by the deepest of divisions.

Recognising that the final week, which was devoted to reports from the Sections, would bring the possibility of controversy, the Design Group had invited Jean Vanier, a French-Canadian Roman Catholic layman, to lead a Vigil to which representatives of all

Anglican religious communities in Britain had been invited. Jean, founder of the L'Arche Community, which ministers among seriously disabled people, is a man one could easily term a 'saint'. Tall and rugged, with a shock of white hair, dressed in a scruffy jacket and an open-necked shirt, he stooped over the podium and held us spellbound by his stories of handicapped people. It was in the 'weakest and least presentable members of the Body of Christ', he remarked, 'that the beauty of Christ is revealed'. True unity, he suggested, is found when we begin to see Our Lord in the people furthest from us. Then, to capture the spirit of his words, we had a service of foot-washing in which everyone participated. It started with Jean washing my feet, then I washed Eileen's, and the act was repeated in the many circles of Bishops, spouses and other colleagues in the great conference hall. White hands washed black feet, male washed female, and in more than one instance I glimpsed people who disagreed passionately over issues such as women Bishops and homosexuality washing one another's feet. It was for us all an unforgettable evening in which the gospel became once again authentic. Could we replicate it in reality, I found myself wondering, or only symbolically?

In the meantime, other Sections were producing excellent work, resulting in some splendid Plenary presentations. Professor David Ford, Regius Professor of Theology at Cambridge University, gave a riveting presentation on 'The Bible, the World and the Church' with the help of Riding Lights Theatre Group. Rowan Williams, the Bishop of Monmouth, brought his considerable theological ability to bear on 'Making Moral Decisions', and his lecture was also a highlight of the Conference – although I would guess it was above the heads of many people present. The Plenary on Muslim–Christian relations brought together contributions from Bishops working in predominantly Islamic cultures. For some, relationships with Muslims were healthy, and the Church was given sufficient freedom to carry on its work. For others the situation was dire, and Church life was made very difficult, with harassment and persecution common experiences.

Bishop Josiah Idowa Fearon of Kaduna in Nigeria spoke with eloquence and passion about the alarming situation in the north of his
country and the possibility of several states imposing Sharia law on
all citizens. Bishop Alexander Malik of Pakistan spoke of the impact
of the 'Blasphemy Laws' on the tiny Christian Church there. The
Plenary on youth was among the highlights, and brought home to
us all the urgency of passing on a living faith to others, and of making
children and young people's work a top priority.

In the meantime the Spouses' Programme was popular not only
with the spouses, but also with the Bishops. For several years the
Steering Group under Eileen's leadership had worked hard to create
a balanced programme which, unlike the Bishops' programme, had
the great advantage of not being restricted to specific topics. For
their gatherings a huge marquee had been erected in the middle of
the campus, and it became a great draw for Bishops in need of a
break from their heavy programme. Although it was never designed
to be so, the spouses' marquee became a centre of real spiritual
encounter, where the real stories of the punishing ministries of
Bishops and their spouses were heard and prayed through.

As Eileen explained, the philosophy behind the Spouses' Programme was not only 'to provide a time of fellowship and building
up together, but to enable us all to go home with fresh insights,
better equipped to share with people at home'. Health and social
issues were crucial elements in a wide-ranging programme. Tessa
Jowell, the British Minister of State for Public Health, gave a major
speech, and WHO experts addressed the impact of HIV/AIDS on
Africa. Susan Howatch, the well-known novelist, gave an electrifying
address on 'Harassed Heroines and Healing Centres', packing the
huge marquee to capacity and attracting a great company of Bishops
among the audience. And there were many amazing women whose
testimony to the work of their husbands revealed that their own
contribution, though often underrated, was just as crucial: women
like Marion McCall, wife of the Bishop of Willochra in Australia,
who had learned to pilot a plane so that she could fly her husband

around his vast diocese; like Berta Singulane, wife of Dinis Singulane, Bishop of Lebombo, Mozambique, whose faithful ministry had helped to secure peace in a very poor and wartorn country (sadly, Berta was killed in a car accident shortly afterwards); like Madeleine Kayumba, wife of Norman Kayumba, Bishop of Kigeme in Rwanda, whose quietly-spoken description of the appalling genocide and of their attempts to rescue people fleeing their would-be killers gave her hearers a tiny glimpse of the terrors of life when everything falls apart; like Clavera Ntukamazima of Burundi, who had witnessed terrible atrocities in her native land and been involved in reconciling estranged communities, who led a workshop on 'practical reconciliation'.

As the Conference entered its third and final week the tension mounted regarding the resolution on homosexuality to be laid before the Bishops. Unfortunately, campaigning groups had infiltrated the Conference and were deepening the sense of Armageddon facing the Communion. Richard Holloway, one of the principal leaders seeking a change in Anglican attitudes to homosexuals, would later claim that conservative American Bishops were trying to buy the votes of African Bishops with 'chickens and sausages', referring to barbecues held at the Franciscan Study Centre. Such accusations infuriated African Bishops. Emmanuel Kolini, Archbishop of Rwanda, as conservative as Holloway was liberal, answered tartly, 'We have chicken back home in Africa, you know,' and added, 'Only one thing bought me and still buys me, and that is the cross – and nothing else.' One of the most distinguished Bishops, Dinis Singulane, added quietly that African Bishops had come to the Conference well aware of the views of their dioceses, and if anything 'had been bought by their own people'.

The opposite side was equally guilty of heightening the sense of conflict. Richard Holloway had invited individuals to the Conference who had no right to be there, and I was amazed when at the Scottish Celebration of Holy Communion some of the assistants offering the chalice were known to be practising homosexuals. A particularly embarrassing moment was captured on television when a Nigerian Bishop confronted Richard Kirker and offered to pray for him. Kirker replied that he did not need prayer, as God had made him homosexual. The Bishop nevertheless attempted to lay a hand on his head for prayer. Kirker intercepted it, and for a moment two hands, black and white, were caught on camera in a grip of conflict, perhaps symbolic of a cultural divide, although many Nigerian Bishops distanced themselves from the actions of their brother Bishop.

In the meantime, Section 1, under the chairmanship of Bishop Duncan Buchanan of South Africa, was endeavouring to hold the Conference together on the issue. The resolution that they hoped would secure the agreement of the Conference was a strong affirmation of the centrality of marriage, yet recognised the presence of homosexuals in the Church, requesting the Primates to establish a means of monitoring the work done on the subject of homosexuality. It was an impressive statement. Unfortunately, for many Bishops it did not go far enough. As a result other motions appeared, which were in my view extremely objectionable. Tension was visibly mounting, and many Bishops were distressed at the likelihood of an extremely happy Conference being wrecked by a matter which imperilled the unity of the Communion. I was conscious of the burden of my office, and the need to give a lead.

On the morning of the debate on the resolutions a number of African and Asian Archbishops came to see me. Among them were the Primate of Nigeria, Joseph Adetiloye; the Archbishop of Province III of Nigeria, Peter Akinola; the Archbishop of Kenya, David Gitari; the Archbishop of Tanzania, Donald Mtetemela; the Archbishop of Uganda, Livingstone Mpalanyi-Nkoyoyo; and the Archbishop of Rwanda, Emmanuel Kolini. They were frank in their assessment of the situation, and told me bluntly that they could not and would not vote for the Section's resolution, which they felt was conciliatory but weak, and was bound to send the wrong message to the Communion. But they were equally worried about the other motions on offer, such as a strong condemnation of homosexuals from West Africa.

Livingstone summed up their difficulty: 'Archbishop, we don't want to split the Conference, but what can we do? We are all quite clear that practising homosexuality is wrong. That is the orthodox Anglican position.' Donald Mtetemala echoed this cry: 'We are caught between two extremes. The Section resolution is too weak, and the motion from West Africa is too strong. But we shall have to vote for the stronger motion, unless a clearer expression is found.'

The discussion continued for some time, until I proposed the addition of eight additional words to one of the clauses of Section 1's resolution. 'Would it meet your concerns,' I said, 'if we added the words "While rejecting homosexual practice as incompatible with scripture" to clause (d), which calls on everyone in the Communion to minister pastorally to all?' The suggestion met with approval as being the best way through the impasse, and it was agreed that Donald should speak to this motion in his name.

The conference hall on the afternoon of 5 August was full to overflowing, with a strong media contingent present. Robin Eames, Archbishop of Armagh, chaired the meeting in his customary genial and authoritative manner. Even so, the tension was high, with speeches ranging from the measured to the wild and intemperate. Some very hurtful things were said about homosexuals that lowered the tone of the debate. As the discussion continued I was not alone in becoming concerned by the tone of some speeches, and by the anger that was being displayed.

I was on the platform to the left of the Chairman, and after Donald had spoken to the amendment I asked permission to speak. I was very conscious that this could be misunderstood, but I felt leadership had to be exercised. 'Allow me to express my own view on this difficult matter and the motion before us,' I began. 'I have long been persuaded that the entire Bible and Christian tradition gives us no permission to condone sexual practices of any sort outside the relationship of husband and wife in holy matrimony. Therefore, so far as I can see, physical homosexual acts fall within that restriction. With that in mind it is my hope that we shall affirm this motion gladly and expect the Provinces and dioceses of our Communion to heed our strong affirmation.'

Soon after, Robin called for a vote on the amendment. Five hundred and twenty-six Bishops voted in its favour, seventy voted against, and forty-five abstained. The huge majority surprised us all, and was a clear statement of the mind of the Conference across the Communion. Later comments that this was a victory for the African Bishops and that it expressed a rigid cultural divide were nonsense. The high figure indicated that a majority of Western Bishops had also voted for Donald's amendment.

Immediately following the announcement of the result, which was greeted by some with gasps of dismay and by others with broad smiles of elation, I felt it important to intervene once more. I said: 'I am aware that not everyone is comfortable with the revised motion, and it seems to me that we need to pledge ourselves to carry on listening to one another, especially with those who disagree with our point of view. The dialogue continues among us. But Mr Chairman, if this Conference is known and named by what we have said about homosexuality, we will have failed. International debt, world poverty, ministry to young people, our ministry and mission to a very needy world – these are the things we must take home with us. I implore forgiveness of the Conference for making these points, but as I sat there I became conscious that we could not at this point allow dis-agreement to become division.'

Alas, despite my hopeful words, division had truly set in, and the wide differences were clearly exposed for all to see. Richard Holloway described my intervention as a 'pathetic' example of leader-ship, and said that the vote left him feeling 'gutted, shafted and depressed'. I was amazed and saddened by such an immature outburst of anger, and have since wondered why a contribution from the Archbishop of Canterbury with a clear responsibility to guide should be called 'pathetic', when silence, the only other option, seemed a dereliction of responsibility. The Conference needed to be reminded that the issue of homosexuality could not compare in importance with the fact that two-thirds of the human family lived on less than $2 a day. But the vote was an overwhelming statement of where the Anglican Communion stood on the issue of practising homosexuality.

On the next day, 6 August – the penultimate day of the Conference and, in the Anglican liturgical calendar, the day of the Transfiguration of Our Lord – two events occurred which transfigured the Conference. The first was a moving Eucharist led by the Church of Japan on the fifty-third anniversary of the atomic bomb dropped on Hiroshima on 6 August 1945. As we entered the hall we received copies of an apology from the Japanese Church for its complicity in wartime aggression. The Japanese Archbishop had invited a woman priest, the Reverend Susan Cole-King, daughter of the former Bishop of Singapore, Leonard Wilson, who had been imprisoned and tortured by the Japanese military in 1943. Susan spoke of how the Church's apology had brought her a deep sense of reconciliation with Japan, because she had never truly forgotten or forgiven the way her father and other British soldiers and civilians had been treated. She also reminded the West of our complicity in the devastation of Hiroshima and Nagasaki. Her words illustrated the power of forgiveness in the same way that one of her father's torturers had been so impressed by the Bishop's fortitude and faith that he later converted to Christianity and was confirmed by Leonard Wilson.

The second moving moment, in the evening of the same day, was the first and final performance of *Crowning Glory*, written by Veronica Bennetts, the talented wife of the Bishop of Coventry, delightfully retelling the story of the Christian faith through words and music. In three short weeks Veronica, drawing on the skills and enthusiasm of the spouses, produced an impressive show which was one of the great successes of the Conference. It was fitting to be brought back on this day of Transfiguration to the roots of our faith and the way it transfigures all who walk the way of the cross.

*   *   *

How, ultimately, will Lambeth '98 be remembered? Those who attended will have their own personal memories and will have made their own judgements. The Bishops themselves rated it a great success. As President, and the one finally responsible for its success or failure, I considered it a great achievement for many reasons. It was the largest ever gathering of Anglican Bishops for mutual consultation and prayer, and that alone was significant. It was also a financial success, and will contribute a significant sum towards the next Lambeth Conference. The daily Bible studies, in which Bishops came together in small groups of about ten, led to deep friendships that will continue for years to come. But Lambeth '98 will also be remembered for finally demonstrating that power had swung decisively from the North to the South. The old adage that 'The Americans pay, the Africans pray and the British write the constitution' will never again ring true. The Bishops representing the southern hemisphere at Lambeth '98 were articulate, confident, and not in the slightest reticent about making their views known.

However, whilst for many Lambeth '98 will be remembered for Resolution 1.10 on homosexuality, the underlying issue that was exposed was an embarrassing ambiguity concerning the interpretation of scripture. The proud claim of Anglicans since the Reformation has been that truth emerges from a strenuous process of prayerful reflection on the threefold authority of scripture, tradition and reason, with primacy given to scripture. Those who claimed, as Martin Smith SSJE did following the Conference, that Bishops from the South had departed from this method of finding God's truth because they had 'no more theological education than a few months of Bible school, and the only form of discourse they know is a very simple form of biblical literalism' were very wrong. My many visits to Africa made me aware that theological training is taken seriously in all Provinces, although poverty and lack of resources affect its quality in some regions. There is certainly a need to strengthen theological education in Africa and elsewhere, but it is wrong to lay the blame at the feet of African Bishops. As I have already observed, the size of the vote on Resolution 1.10 revealed that the majority of Bishops, North and South, believe that practising homosexuality is in contravention of scripture.

The call that came from Lambeth for a deeper engagement with scripture in the light of human knowledge was well made, and is a challenge to all. To the conservative and traditional Christian the challenge must be to relate human experience and new knowledge to the teaching of the Bible. To the liberal Christian it will be a challenge not to empty the scriptures of all meaning when its testimony conflicts with cultural assumptions.

But Lambeth '98 left me with many questions concerning our unsatisfactory understanding of authority. The growth of the Anglican Communion had given rise to a conception of the Communion as a fellowship of independent or autonomous Churches. For many years I had challenged this notion on the grounds that if the Provinces are autonomous we cannot be, in any realistic or meaningful sense, a Communion. Indeed, in my Presidential Address I had remarked that 'We are not yet a Communion, we are becoming a Communion.' What makes us potentially a Communion is a common historical past, a common theological and liturgical framework, and a commitment to the See of Canterbury. In recent years this has been strengthened by annual Primates' Meetings, the creation of the Anglican Consultative Council and, of course, by the Lambeth Conference.

The desire for closer fellowship, for a clearer identity and theological coherence, led to the publication in 1997 of the Virginia Report, largely written by Bishop Mark Dyer. This important report, dealing with the issue of how the Communion arrives at theological truth, was unfortunately not debated by the whole Conference, but only by Section 1. Thus the underlying weakness of the Anglican Communion was not addressed adequately.

A failure to accept the primary authority of Communion, apart from that of scripture, was demonstrated by Bishops on both sides of the conflict. Some American Bishops made statements that disregarded the importance of Resolution 1.10. Bishop Fred Borsch of

Los Angeles, who remains a good friend, was not alone in telling homosexuals in his diocese that he had no intention of heeding a motion that was only 'advisory' in nature. Archbishop Michael Peers of Canada, in a more guarded letter to his Church, was critical of homophobic remarks made by some Bishops, and told homosexuals in Canada that 'we must not stop where this Conference left off. You, our brothers and sisters, deserve a more thorough hearing than you have received over these last three weeks.' It is difficult to avoid the conclusion that some supporters of more liberal policies towards practising homosexuals returned home more determined than ever to pursue the objective of their full inclusion in the life of the Church.

On the other hand, the blatant disregard of the Communion by Archbishop Moses Tay and Archbishop Emmanuel Kolini, in irregularly consecrating two missionary Bishops in Singapore in January 2000 and establishing Anglican Mission in America (AMiA) as a group of dissident parishes, was a regrettable example of the failure of Anglican ecclesiology to hold us together in unity. It has often struck me as profoundly ironic that Bishops who profess themselves anxious to maintain scriptural purity against the departure from scripture which they perceived to be the direction of the American Church, were quite prepared to ignore the same scripture's insistence on unity and walking together in love.

The overwhelming support given to Resolution 1.10 at Lambeth '98 is a test case for Anglican unity and identity. In 2002, despite many appeals to the contrary, Bishop Michael Ingham of the diocese of New Westminster in Canada gave the go-ahead for the blessing of same-sex relationships. Even more dramatically, on 5 August 2003, five years to the day after Resolution 1.10 was carried so decisively at Lambeth, Canon Gene Robinson, formerly a married man with two daughters, but now in a homosexual partnership, was nominated Bishop of New Hampshire, with backing from General Convention. Time will tell if the Anglican Communion will survive an action that so clearly goes against the wishes of the majority of the Communion and the grain of orthodox faith shared with other mainstream Churches.

18

Opening the Door

'Life may change, but it may fly not;
Hope may vanish, but it can die not;
Truth be veiled, but still it burneth;
Love repulsed – but it returneth!'

Percy Bysshe Shelley, 'Hellas' 1

ON BECOMING ARCHBISHOP OF CANTERBURY I automatically assumed a pivotal role in representing the Church of England and the Anglican Communion in their relations with other Churches. This was something that gave me the utmost pleasure, because of the importance of unity for the mission of the Church. The sad divisions of Christianity hinder effective mission and service by all Christians.

By virtue of my office I became one of the four Presidents of Churches Together in England (CTE). The others were Cardinal Basil Hume, representing the Roman Catholic Church of England and Wales, Dr Kathleen Richardson on behalf of the Free Church Federal Council, and Bishop Desmond Pemberton, representing the black-led Churches, the Lutheran Church and the Orthodox Churches. The Presidents met four times a year to assess the progress of our common journey together. These ecumenical colleagues were stimulating company and encouraging partners to work with. However, it often seemed that as far as the media, including even the religious press, were concerned, only Cardinal Hume and I mattered. Although all four Presidents spoke out with one voice on many different social matters, it was only the two of us the media wished to hear or photograph. This was understandable at one level, because the rotating leadership of the Free Churches inevitably meant that the public had little time to get to know their leaders. Sadly, this hid the real strength of nonconformism in England, which is numerically on a par with worshipping Anglicans and Roman Catholics. Over the years I endeavoured to challenge the Free Churches on this issue, but without success. One Church of Scotland President who agreed wholeheartedly with my argument stated frankly that the so-called democratic principle of the 'priesthood of all believers' at the level of synodical representation was 'inbuilt structural suspicion'.

I got to know Cardinal Basil Hume very well. He was one of the first people I met on becoming Archbishop, when I invited him to Lambeth Palace for tea. He observed that he too was a 'George' – George Basil Hume – and hoped that the press would not get us confused. I responded that although I trusted we would speak as one on many issues, there was hardly any chance of confusion, as he had been in office for fifteen years longer than I. That meeting was typical of the many times we had together. Basil was always courteous, kind and affable. Although I cannot claim to have got very close to him – there was a reserved side to his character that I never did penetrate – we worked well together, and shared quite deeply on many things, in spite of some difficulties.

Chief among these, as I have mentioned, was the ordination of women, which concerned Basil greatly because of its severe consequences for the move towards the visible unity of the Church, to which he was so committed. He confronted me frankly on the issue, and accepted my equally direct riposte that the lukewarm response of the Sacred Congregation for the Defence of the Faith to proposed closer Anglo–Catholic links was not encouraging enough for the Church of England to delay any longer. The matter, however, did nothing to harm our cordial and increasingly warm relationship. Indeed, the pastoral arrangements we set up to care jointly for Church of England clergy who sought to become Roman Catholics following the decision to allow the ordination of women led to stronger relationships between the Bishops of our Churches and the two of us.

What kind of man was Basil Hume? He was, as so many remember him, a delightful human being who could converse easily and naturally with anybody. He told me once that the only 'calling' that really mattered to him was to be a monk, and from that flowed everything else. He never professed to be a theologian, although his deep love of God and those he sought to serve made him an able and dedicated teacher of the faith. I often tried to draw him out theologically. My greatest frustration with the meetings of the Presidents of CTE was that we never grappled with the important issues that separated us. The structure of our meetings led us to focus on practical matters associated with our role in the bureaucracy of the unity movement. As a result of much complaining, largely on my part, we began to discuss the things that actually separated us. We started to meet in the evenings, and after a pleasant supper together, would discuss a subject relevant to us all. With his guard down, Basil revealed himself as a somewhat conservative pre-Vatican II Roman Catholic. Out would come expressions of pain about the rhetoric of the sixteenth-century Thirty-Nine Articles of Religion concerning the Roman Catholic Church, and the way his Church had been treated in England since the Reformation.

I had no difficulty in agreeing with him about the plight of Roman Catholics in England before freedom and equality were granted them in the early nineteenth century. While accepting his point about the polemic of the Articles (which at the time were certainly not restricted to the Anglican side), I would remind him that the starting point for closer co-operation and understanding between our two Churches today should be recent theological dialogues, which have achieved remarkable agreements between us, and which enable us to understand the Articles in a new light. He would agree, but would often return to the Articles as if they were at the heart of contemporary

Anglicanism. This led me to wonder sometimes if, in his heart, Basil viewed ecumenism in England as the return of the Church of England to the fold of Rome – as she now is – and not, as I saw it, as two Churches leaving behind what they are now and converging towards a wholly new reality.

But in many areas there was strong agreement that the Christian faith impacted on social life so profoundly that Church leaders could not remain silent when the very vulnerable were affected. An example was our common concern about the implications of the Asylum Bill going through Parliament in 1996. We decided to go together to see Peter Lilley, the then Minister for Social Security, about this Bill, which we considered too restrictive and lacking in the flexibility necessary to deal with the – not infrequent – sensitive exceptions to the proposed law. Peter Lilley saw our point of view, but did not seem to perceive the dangers that worried us. We shared the government's desire to address the failures of the present system, but felt that the Bill did not focus on the central issue – namely, the huge backlog of appeals which led to thousands of asylum seekers being kept waiting years for the resolution of their case. It remains an open question whether we had an effect on government policy, but Peter Lilley, as a practising Anglican, knew first-hand that the Churches had their fingers on the pulse of the issue, as we were often the first port of call for desperate people. Basil Hume was a very good person to have alongside one on such occasions. Behind his self-effacing and gentle nature was a clear mind and a willingness to speak up for the marginalised and oppressed.

In 1997 we were involved in overlapping plans for celebrating the 1400th anniversary of Augustine's arrival at Canterbury to re-establish the Church, following the successive invasions from the Continent that had driven the original inhabitants west, taking the Church with them. There was some sensitivity in commemorating these events. Which of us was the true successor to Augustine, sent by Pope Gregory I? The Anglican claim has consistently been that at the Reformation, Matthew Parker was legitimately consecrated

Archbishop of Canterbury by Elizabeth I, following the break with Rome. The national Church thus separated itself from Rome and the authority of the Pope, and has since regarded itself as the continuing Catholic Church in this country. Understandably, from the Roman Catholic perspective, the true continuing Church is the Catholic Church in union with Rome. Neither Basil Hume nor I wanted the issue to cause disunity, and our staffs were instructed to bear this in mind in the planning of the celebrations. They went very well indeed, with a great deal of co-operation.

Cardinal Hume was invited to the Anglican celebration on 26 May 1997, in Canterbury Cathedral with Prince Charles as the principal guest, at which I preached. It was a joyful occasion, with a real sense of celebration. The following day a Roman Catholic celebration took place, also in Canterbury Cathedral, and the Cardinal invited me to process with him for a Monastic Solemn Vespers service at which he preached. My impression, seeing the huge number of black-vested monks and nuns, was that every Benedictine in the country was there, including Anglican Benedictines. There were a great number of ordinary Catholics present, squeezed into every part of the nave, and they welcomed us enthusiastically as Cardinal Hume and I processed in side by side. Unlike the rather staid and over-organised celebration the day before, there was a sense of informality and homeliness that was very appealing.

An experience a few weeks later, when I was presiding over an ordination service at Canterbury Cathedral, indicated that Anglican–Roman Catholic relations are not always as friendly. The cathedral was packed with families and parishioners of an excellent body of ordinands, that included women. I had just begun the opening prayer when I saw from the corner of my eye an elderly woman moving in my direction. I waited for somebody to intercept her, but realised with increasing alarm that no one was going to do so. I paused. She looked extremely angry. Standing two feet away from me, she said in a thick French accent, 'You charlatan!' She spat, and walked down the aisle, glaring at each unfortunate woman ordinand in turn, then disappeared from view. I was mystified by the event, and could only guess that the recent celebrations had aroused her anger at the ordination of women. What a pity, I felt, that she could not appreciate that each ordinand, male or female, was seeking to fulfil Augustine's mission to bring Christ to our land.

It became clear that Basil Hume was suffering physically. I noticed that his hips appeared to be hurting him greatly, and that he was moving with less ease. On one occasion when we were together in my study, as he stood to leave he wobbled slightly. Recovering, he said, 'You know, I envy your Church's decision that all clergy should retire from active ministry at the age of seventy.' I made a gentle rejoinder, urging him to retire at the earliest moment and return to his beloved Ampleforth. He replied that he was under orders, and would have to stay on if that were Pope John Paul's wish. As we walked together down the steps of Lambeth Palace, Basil showed the weariness of advancing years.

In the light of the close links we shared as Presidents of CTE and in many other ways, I was quite astonished to be told by one of my staff at the beginning of 1999 that, in a tribute to Cardinal Hume on his seventy-fifth birthday, Ann Widdecombe had stated that 'Those who know him say that his [Basil Hume's] attitude to George Carey verges on contempt in private, but no trace of this has ever been publicly discernible.' Typically, on hearing of this, Basil immediately issued a statement denying it, and sent me a letter which also firmly contradicted it, adding, 'I have always valued your friendship and kindness towards me.' I replied at once to state that the assertion bore no relation to the reality of our friendship and contacts over the years, and that I would lose no sleep over it.

Unknown to most people, Basil Hume was dying of cancer. As soon as I received the news I phoned him to assure him that he was in my private prayers, and that I thanked God for his great witness over the years. Basil expressed gratitude, and said that although he was subject to anxiety and worry, he had found God's grace 'almost tangible'. He told me that the cancer had passed from gut to liver, and he had been told his life expectancy was three to six months. Shortly afterwards Sir Robin Janvrin, Private Secretary to the Queen, phoned me to ask on behalf of Her Majesty what my reaction would be if Cardinal Hume were given the Order of Merit. My unhesitating reply was that I would gladly support the honour. Basil Hume had been a notable Christian leader for over twenty-five years, and the influence of his witness and faith extended far beyond the Roman Catholic fold. Indeed, the honest truth was that his popularity took attention away from real problems facing Roman Catholics in England and Wales. The Church had a major crisis of vocations to the priesthood, and diminishing numbers of faithful Catholics. I was also told by several informants that the Archdiocese of Westminster faced a grave financial crisis.

Following Basil's death in June 1999, lamented by many from all Churches, Cormac Murphy-O'Connor was appointed Archbishop of Westminster. The good relations between our two Churches continued, and indeed developed. Whereas, as I have observed, there was a shyness and reticence in Basil's character, Cormac's was open, friendly and direct. Our friendship had begun some twenty years earlier in Rome, when he was Rector of the Venerable English College, and I had been impressed by his obvious commitment to ecumenism. As an Irishman he had none of the suspicion, and sometimes deep dislike, of Anglicanism that is often the result of experiences burned into the memory of English Catholics. I was delighted when Pope John Paul II made him a Cardinal at the beginning of January 2001. When I congratulated him on getting the 'red hat', Cormac modestly said, 'Oh, it comes with the job. It would have been surprising if I hadn't been offered it.'

Alongside the affirming and strengthening of the national relationships so important to unity between the Roman Catholic and the Anglican Churches in England, a great deal was also going on at the international level. My first visit to meet Pope John Paul II, in May 1992, got off to a shaky start, when two weeks or so before the visit I gave an interview for the *Daily Telegraph* on the environment, in which I expressed my views on the unchecked growth of world population and its impact on sustainable development. This led to the issue of contraception. I was fully aware that my opinions clashed with the position of the Roman Catholic Church set out in *Humanae Vitae*, issued by Pope Paul VI in 1968. I stated that our overcrowded planet demanded a responsible attitude to family planning, and that contraception was an entirely 'moral' decision. That was not a popular view in Rome, and drew disapproving comments from senior spokesmen in the Vatican. This spat, together with the possibility that the General Synod of the Church of England would authorise the ordination of women to the priesthood later that year, suggested that I was in for a torrid time.

In the event the visit went extraordinarily well. Rome knows how to charm its visitors, and I and my staff received nothing but kindness from the Vatican. Pope John Paul, although seventy-two, was still very able and alert, and my private conversation with him was friendly, frank and interesting. In attendance was Cardinal Edward Cassidy, President of the Pontifical Council for Christian Unity, and my Officer for Ecumenism, Canon Stephen Platten.

It was not long before we got round to the subject of the ordination of women. The Pope firmly stated his view that women had an honourable place in the Church, and that it was regrettable that the desire for equality with men had led some women to seek ordination. This, he argued, would set back unity considerably. I explained the process the Church of England had developed in considering the matter over nearly twenty years, and the way we had tackled the theological arguments for and against. I asked the Pope to state his objection to the ordination of women, and he gave a simple and direct reply: 'Anthropology.' That is to say, women *qua* women cannot be ordained. This was the very argument I had rebuffed before my installation as Archbishop, when I had stated that the idea that women cannot represent Christ at the altar was a great heresy.

We were clearly on opposing sides as far as this matter was concerned, but that did not detract from my enormous regard for Pope John Paul as a great Christian leader and inspiring personality. I could not fail to notice on this and other visits to the Holy Father how warmly he greeted Eileen. It spoke of his great regard for women and their enormous contribution to the human family, let alone the Christian family. On every occasion that we had the joy of meeting him he showed particular interest in her and in our children.

It was on that first official visit to Italy that I travelled north to meet Cardinal Carlo Maria Martini, Cardinal Archbishop of Milan, not principally because he was hotly tipped to be the next Pope, but because he was a well-known Biblical scholar and ecumenist. A tall, slim, distinguished man in a red cassock and bright red Cardinal's biretta, he welcomed me warmly. I felt immediately at home with him. We shared a love of the scriptures and had the same attitude to mission – that the Church was living in critical times and must urgently go to the young and seek to lead them to our Lord.

Cardinal Martini's own example was impressive. He explained his process to me. Several times a year he would invite young people to St Ambrose's Cathedral in Milan for a biblical meditation. Parish priests from designated areas would be invited to come with their young people to the cathedral to meet the Cardinal. Then there would be a ninety-minute service, separated into three parts. In the first, the Cardinal would introduce a passage from the Bible and expound its meaning and relevance. The second period was devoted to the young people themselves sharing together in reflection. In the final section the Cardinal would answer comments and questions, and conclude with encouragement. Over the years these meetings with their Cardinal had become the backbone of ministry to young people in his archdiocese, and had led many to seek ordination or other forms of Christian service. Cardinal Martini was a splendid illustration of the classical Christian and Catholic theologian – one for whom scholarship existed as a handmaid of the Church, not a discipline in its own right.

The following day we met again at St Ambrose's Cathedral, where we knelt together at the prayer desk in front of the skeletal remains of St Ambrose, who died in 397 AD. Still dressed in the now-faded remnants of his episcopal vestments, Ambrose was a visible sign to us both of the one faith that bound us together in spite of present divisions. We then visited the baptistery, where St Augustine had been baptised in 387 AD. As a student of the early Church I found this visit to the shrine of St Ambrose profoundly moving. Finally we visited the shrine of St Charles Borromeo, one of the giants of the Counter-Reformation movement, whose greatest contribution, in the opinion of Cardinal Martini, was the reform of the Church of Milan.

This successful trip to Italy, which took in Palermo and Venice as well as Rome and Milan, broadened my understanding of the Church in that land and its considerable hold on so many Italians, in spite of the inroads of secularism.

In May 1995 Pope John Paul II issued perhaps his most surprising encyclical, *Ut Unum Sint*. Although the Pope said he was addressing the Catholic Church and in particular his 'brothers in the Episcopate', he also directed his attention to other Churches and unity in the service of mission. In *Ut Unum Sint*, the Pope simply, movingly and gracefully offered his office as a service to unity. The long, reflective statement was generous in its estimate of other Churches, acknowledging the grace of God in all separated Churches. Whilst the Church of Jesus Christ 'subsists' in the Roman Catholic Church, the encyclical declared, the signs of Catholicity are not absent from other Churches. That is to say, God is at work in other Christian Churches, and they are not devoid of His grace.

Although the encyclical offered much, I could not greet the language of 'subsisting' – drawn from Vatican II's theology of '*subsistere in*' – with any great enthusiasm. It can be read to imply that one Church, namely the Roman Catholic Church, is more Christian, and closer to truth, than others. As I saw it, if this is taken as a '*fundamentum*' in ecumenical engagement, it automatically shifts ecumenism to a kind of Roman Catholic takeover.

On the whole, though, *Ut Unum Sint* represented a breakthrough. The Pope concluded by inviting other Churches to comment on his encyclical. It was greeted with enthusiasm by many, and no doubt much will flow from it in decades to come. It places a great responsibility on the Roman Catholic Church to follow up the responses, which the Pontifical Council has started to do. The most important challenge is to enable the Papal office truly to be an agent of unity. Having offered it as a 'gift', Pope John Paul II must make its exercise attractive and effective. That will most certainly be a major challenge for his successor.

The deteriorating physical condition of the Pope, who was eventually revealed to be suffering from Parkinson's disease, did little to halt his commitment to meeting the demands of his great office. His visits to other countries did not cease even when his powers of speech and movement became severely affected. The effects of his decline, however, inevitably meant that others in the Curia, notably Cardinal Ratzinger, President of the Sacred Congregation for the Defence of the Faith, and Cardinal Angelo Sodano, the Secretary of State, took on more responsibilities.

I became aware of the alarm this was causing many Roman Catholic scholars and Bishops around the world, who felt that it represented a hardening at the centre which worked against the personal mission of Pope John Paul. I recall meeting Cardinal Joseph Bernardin of Chicago, surely one of the great American Catholics of the twentieth century, in May 1996. He voiced his concern to me about the encroaching power of the Curia, which went directly against the policy of Vatican II to strengthen the authority and power of national Churches and the local Bishop 'in communion with the Holy See'.

However, on the occasions I met Cardinal Sodano and Cardinal Ratzinger I found them both charming and open to discussion. Cardinal Sodano's focus was clearly on structures and managing the huge and pluriform portfolio of Vatican ministries. I could see from his direct and blunt manner why he might seem a threat to some, but from his concerns I had no reason to doubt he was a man of prayer. I reached a similar conclusion on Cardinal Ratzinger. Our first meeting was in December 1996, when I was in Rome for the reopening of the Anglican Centre, a marvellous reordering through the leadership of its Director, Canon Bruce Ruddock. With me at the meeting was Bishop Mark Santer, then Co-Chairman of the Anglican–Roman Catholic International Commission (ARCIC).

I immediately noticed Cardinal Ratzinger's piercing eyes. A small, compact man with a thick mop of hair, his stillness and alertness impressed me. Mark and I had agreed that we wanted to understand what method the Cardinal's Congregation used in assessing ecumenical statements. In 1991 the convergence and consensus of the final report of ARCIC, affirmed so emphatically by Bishops at the 1988 Lambeth Conference, received only a half-hearted response from the Congregation, which called for further clarification. It seemed at the time that the Congregation had not fully understood the intention of ARCIC, which was not simply to repeat the language of past controversy, but to express the faith afresh together for today. Cardinal Ratzinger listened intently to our comments and questions. In what I can only describe as a thorough, Germanic approach he sifted each argument with care, and entered with energy into the debate. It was an enjoyable meeting, but the rigour with which he covered every point was exceedingly conservative, and showed little of the flexibility that characterised the approach of the second Vatican Council.

If Cardinal Ratzinger tended towards rigidity and conservatism, a different approach was manifest in the work of the Pontifical Council for Christian Unity under its President, Cardinal Edward Cassidy. Edward, a cheerful Australian with a gritty approach to life, was keen to use the constructive goodwill existing between the Churches to deepen dialogue. Though he is a competent theologian, his policy was more practical than theoretical. He thought, quite rightly, that if ecumenical discussion commenced with what we share in common and worked from agreement, we would be better able to handle the more difficult issues.

It was at Malines in Belgium in 1996 that Cardinal Cassidy and I agreed a plan to supplement the theological work of ARCIC. For some time I, and a number of others, had been increasingly concerned that the distance between the theologians of ARCIC and the Bishops, clergy and people of our two Churches was growing too great. There was a danger of ARCIC's valuable work being forgotten, ignored and considered irrelevant if something was not done. We concluded that we had to find a way of reconnecting ARCIC with the work of our Churches, and particularly with the ministry of our Bishops. If they did not own the theological agreements, the cause of unity would be damaged. We felt it was incumbent on the Bishops to focus and lead the vision of unity, and agreed to launch a supplementary initiative by bringing a representative group of Bishops from each Church to consider the implications of the theological agreements, to state together a common understanding of the goal of visible unity, and to consider what practical steps might be taken. For Cardinal Cassidy it was necessary to obtain the full agreement of the Pope; in my case I needed the support of the English House of Bishops and the Primates of the Anglican Communion. The exact date for this exciting development was left open-ended, and it eventually took place in the year 2000.

Another development from the celebrations in 1997 to mark the re-establishment of the Church in England by St Augustine was an invitation from the Pope to join him in an act of worship at St Gregory's church on the Caelian Hills in Rome, from where Augustine came. In my party were Njongonkulu Ndungane, Archbishop of Cape Town, and Canon John Peterson, Secretary General of the Anglican Communion. Their presence was a clear statement of the involvement of the wider Anglican Communion.

I was quite taken aback to get a message a few weeks prior to this visit that Pope John Paul hoped I might join him in wearing cope and mitre. This was an unprecedented request, and signified the importance he and the Vatican attached to the anniversary. Indeed, as symbols are often an important language in ecumenical circles, this remarkable suggestion was an encouraging statement of the way Rome saw its relationship with the Anglican Communion. It turned out to be a memorable visit, which commenced with a formal meeting with Pope John Paul II on 3 December at which speeches were read by both of us, welcoming the anniversary and expressing our indebtedness to the legacy of St Gregory in dispatching Augustine to England in 597 AD.

Two days later we were together again, this time for a private meeting. I was dismayed by how tired the Holy Father looked. He spoke in a low, expressionless voice, and seemed almost uncomprehending at times. Cardinal Cassidy had to prompt him occasionally, and he looked like a man at the end of his ministry. When I mentioned Ut Unum Sint, Edward Cassidy had to remind him that it was the encyclical he had written on unity. Later it became clear that the Pope's alertness and ability to function in public were significantly affected by the quality of the drugs he was being prescribed to combat his Parkinson's, and the time at which they were taken. An hour after our private meeting Eileen and I, together with Archbishop Njongonkulu and Canon Richard Marsh, were with him for midday prayers and lunch. The prayers were in silence in his private chapel, and it was impossible not to be impressed by his stillness and devotion at prayer. This was a man whose whole life was lived in contemplation and love of God.

Lunch followed, and a transformed Pope was our host. Sitting opposite me, he was alert, focused and engaged. There was none of the 'absence' I had felt earlier. We had a wide-ranging discussion about the mission of the Church and relations with Islam. He was particularly interested to hear the account of Archbishop Njongonkulu on how African leaders were confronting the crisis of HIV/ AIDS. On every topic his view was informed and intelligent. The contrast with his earlier exhaustion was staggering.

The main event, evensong, took place at the Basilica of San Gregorio in the Caelian Hills, the site of the monastery from which Augustine was sent to England. It was a simple yet beautiful act of thanksgiving for the lives of those early missionary monks whose legacy is the Church in Britain today. I noticed that Eileen was seated in the second row behind a whole line of Cardinals, including Cardinal Ratzinger. Shortly after I was robed in cope and mitre, I saw that she was now in the front row, on the other side of the aisle. When the Pope and I processed in side by side, she had been moved yet again, and was now sitting just inside the sanctuary. Neither she nor I was able to detect the liturgical significance of this three-fold move, other than perhaps signifying the care that the Pontifical Council takes with regard to protocol.

The Pope gave an encouraging homily in which he spoke warmly of the 'real yet imperfect' communion we already shared, and encouraged both Churches to walk together. In my address I spoke of my sadness that our Churches were victims of sixteenth-century bitterness. I said: 'It is tempting, especially in Rome, to feel particularly burdened by this historical rift in the body of Christ. Those of us who are heirs of division indeed regret deeply that the Western Church was split so widely. And yet for Anglicans and for other traditions such as the Lutheran Churches the Reformation was not a tragedy so much as a rediscovery of the Bible and its authority, of the importance of justification by faith, a rediscovery of the local Church and of the servanthood of ministry and priesthood.' But, I went on to say, both Anglican and Catholic Churches have much to share from each other's riches, and much to repent of. I concluded with an appeal for our Churches to 'walk together into a deeper unity which both of us know to be the will of our Lord'. As part of the service a Common Declaration was signed in which we committed ourselves and our Churches to share together in mission and service, and not to flag in the goal of seeking visible unity.

The extraordinary character of the Pope's determination to transcend, if not overcome, his illness showed itself in his refusal to give in and resign his office. For four years running I had been asked to do 'canned' TV interviews on the Pope and the Queen Mother in preparation for their deaths. In 1999 I ceased doing so for the Pope, as it was quite clear that he would outlast me in active ministry. He was determined to stay on for the millennium year, and lead the ecumenical celebrations at St Paul's Outside the Walls in Rome at which he, assisted by others, would push open the Holy Door, representing our commitment to seek full, visible unity. This was an event I looked forward to with enormous anticipation, yearning that it might move beyond symbolism to substance.

It turned out to be a wonderful occasion. There was a huge turnout, and as we gathered at Domus Santa Martha, the new residential conference centre in the Vatican, to be ferried in coaches to St Paul's Outside the Walls, I could see how very many denominations were represented. On arrival at the huge and ancient church it was with great difficulty that our buses managed to navigate their way through the crowds. We were told later that fifteen thousand people had applied for five thousand seats. It seemed that ten thousand at least were outside to greet 'il Papa' and his guests.

Leaning on his pastoral staff, the Pope slowly approached and greeted those of us who had been asked to be in his procession. His speech was now slurred, and he walked haltingly. Although his face was fixed in the mask-like rigidity characteristic of Parkinson's disease, his eyes sparkled his welcome. I was asked to be on his right and Metropolitan Athanasios, representing the Ecumenical Patriarch, on his left at the opening of the door. I was astonished that at such an important ecumenical moment the Ecumenical Patriarch, the head of the Orthodox Churches of the East, was not there, and feared it could be a sign of the strained relations between the Orthodox Churches and the Roman Catholic Church because of events in Eastern Europe.

We processed towards the great doors, and there was mounting excitement from the crowd as the Holy Father came into view. The deep reverence and affection in which he was held was clear. At the

Holy Door the three of us knelt for a few moments in silence, then at a given signal it was the Pope's role to push open the door. This was plainly an impossible task for this frail old man. I glanced across at Metropolitan Athanasios, our eyes met in agreement, and we pushed with him. This unscripted act was for me a real symbol of ecumenism and an unspoken expression of the truth that no Church can act alone in matters to do with unity – we have to push together.

Rising to our feet we processed through the crowded cathedral, with the Pope now bringing up the rear, to take our places in a semi-circle facing the huge congregation. This time I was on the Pope's left and Metropolitan Athanasios on his right. The service was crowned by a brief but masterly homily from the Pope who, although his delivery was heavy, managed to raise laughter by several asides. Lunch followed in the monastery refectory for the 120 or so ecumenical guests, to which Eileen and our eldest daughter Rachel had been invited. I was on the left of the Pope and, again, Metropolitan Athanasios on his right. On my left was Cardinal Ratzinger, with Cardinal Sodano immediately opposite. It was an extremely informal meal, with conversation ranging from Italian football to international politics. I raised with the Pope my concerns about the Middle East, and mentioned a suggestion that had been put to me by Professor Andrea Riccardi, leader of the well-known Sant'Egidio Community (see pages 435–6), that the Pope might consider calling all Christian leaders to join him that year in Bethlehem between 25 December and the Epiphany. Although I had my doubts whether political realities would allow such a gathering, I thought the idea had sufficient merit to pursue it. The Pope however seized on it, and said, 'I see, just like Assisi.'

'Yes,' I said, 'just like the meetings you have gathered at Assisi.'

He said he would talk it through with Cardinal Etcherray, whose department in the Vatican was concerned with issues of this kind.

In May 2000 Cardinal Cassidy and I convened the long-awaited Conference of Anglican and Roman Catholic Bishops at Mississauga, outside Toronto. There were fourteen Bishops from each Church, drawn from fourteen countries in which Roman Catholics and Anglicans already shared some degree of co-operation. We were supported by a few experts, including Dr Mary Tanner, my Officer for Ecumenism, Dr Richard Marsh and Dr David Hamid, Ecumenical Officer for the Anglican Communion. Supporting Roman Catholic Bishops were the Reverend Sister Dr Donna Geernaert, Monsignor Timothy Galligan from the Pontifical Council, the Reverend Peter Cross, and Father Jean-Marie Tillard.

The week-long meeting proved to be of great significance although it was not without its moments of tension, surprises, direct talking and drama. In the planning, Cardinal Cassidy and I had agreed that the Conference should take place in a context of a semi-retreat, so that the spiritual side might be uppermost. Each day would begin with a Eucharist or Mass. It was not surprising that the experience of being exposed to different forms of service was an ecumenical step forward for some. One Roman Catholic Bishop, amazed at the contiguity of the Anglican and Catholic liturgies, laughed and said, 'I can't see any reason why we should not unite immediately!'

Superficially, of course, that was and remains the case, but as our meeting progressed, helped by a number of strong friendships, the discussions revealed some differences in understanding and doctrine. Bishops from around the world described the relations between the two Communions in their region. Bishop Cormac Murphy-O'Connor introduced the theological agreements of ARCIC, and Bishop John Hind reminded the meeting of the official responses of each Communion to its final report. From this proceeded a thorough analysis of relations between the two Churches in different regions of the world, and the strengths and weaknesses of the dialogue. This led the Bishops in the following days to an appreciation of the strengths and weaknesses of both Churches. Under scrutiny came the hierarchical nature of the Roman Catholic Church and the dominance of the Curia. In one rather comical moment Alex Brunett, Roman Catholic

Archbishop of Seattle, said in an exasperated way to Cardinal Cassidy, 'Your Eminence, what are you asking us to do?' This received a laugh, but I could not but reflect that no Bishop in the Anglican Communion would ever put it quite like that to his Archbishop or to the Archbishop of Canterbury. Joke or not, it echoed the feelings of some Catholic Bishops present, who were worried about the power of the Congregation for the Defence of the Faith and its significance for unity with other Christians.

The honest criticism wasn't all directed one way. Father Jean-Marie Tillard, a graceful and distinguished ecumenist, pulled no punches when he observed that unity was hindered by internal Anglican incoherencies and the danger that moral inconsistencies were appearing. The issue of homosexuality was cited as an example of Anglican ambiguity, and in particular the way the Episcopal Church in the United States was drifting away from orthodox faith in moral matters. I was not the only Anglican to be made uncomfortably aware that the questions coming from our Roman Catholic brothers were exactly those raised in our own reports and at the 1988 Lambeth Conference. They could be summarised in one direct question that I had often asked myself: Can we Anglicans address our internal discords and moral inconsistencies so that we are worthy partners in dialogue with others? The evidence is not compelling that we can, nor that we intend to. This remains the Communion's greatest single theological challenge.

The Conference attracted much media attention, and not a little protest from extreme Protestant groups, although the threatened coachloads of Ian Paisley supporters did not appear, much to the disappointment of some of the Bishops, who I think fancied some spirited opposition. One group did turn up at the conference centre to deliver a petition accusing me of betraying Reformation principles and assigning us all a place in hell. Perhaps even that is better than apathy. Media attention focused on the one public event at St Michael's Roman Catholic Cathedral Church in Toronto, over which Cardinal Cassidy presided and I preached. It was a marvellous, heartwarming occasion, which made us all aware of how vital we were to one another if we were to bring the Christian faith to a needy world. Our Conference concluded by setting in place a structure to take the work forward and to deepen unity between our Churches throughout the world.

It had been a worthwhile and hopeful Conference, but within months many of us were angrily questioning the point of ecumenical dialogue, when on 5 September 2000 the Congregation for the Defence of the Faith issued *Dominus Jesus*. This new doctrinal statement of a mere thirty-six pages, authorised by the Pope, affirmed the Catholic Church's teaching that it was the 'one true Church of Jesus Christ'. I was astonished to read an advance copy and to note the different tone from the Pope's encyclical of 1995, *Ut Unum Sint*, which was so inclusive of other Churches. In its view that some Orthodox Churches had maintained the apostolic succession, but that all other ecclesial communities were not Churches 'in the proper sense', *Dominus Jesus* appeared to me to deny much of what had previously been affirmed about the ecclesial reality of other Churches.

I issued a press statement immediately, stating that the Anglican Communion 'believes itself to be part of the One, Holy, Catholic and Apostolic Church of Jesus Christ', and regretting the negative tones of *Dominus Jesus*. A phone call to Cardinal Cassidy elicited the admission that the Congregation had not discussed the contents of the doctrinal statement with his department. We agreed that the statement had many good things in it about the centrality of Jesus Christ, which Anglicans could also affirm, but I felt that it was crass in the extreme for the Congregation not to clear the ecumenical sections with its colleagues.

That same evening the Presidents of CTE assembled for one of our regular meetings, and Cormac Murphy-O'Connor, now Cardinal Archbishop, was clearly embarrassed. Although he could not be expected to criticise the Sacred Congregation or Cardinal Ratzinger publicly and outright, his evasive comments seemed to indicate that he was less than happy. The publication of *Dominus Jesus* suggested to me that the Anglican Communion does not have a monopoly on incoherence.

19

Rubbing Our Eyes

'In our ecumenical endeavours we should keep in mind that one day we will rub our eyes and be surprised by the new things God has achieved in His Church.'

Cardinal Walter Kasper, Mississauga, 2000

RELATIONS WITH ROME are not the only ecumenical occupation of an Archbishop of Canterbury. For many years the Church of England had had close relationships with the many Orthodox Churches throughout the world, including their tiny representative Churches in London. Although prior to my ministry as Archbishop I had had close contact with Roman Catholics, my contact with Orthodoxy amounted to nil. The importance of this tradition meant that I had much to learn. I knew at least that Orthodoxy fell into two clear branches. The senior See of Orthodoxy is the ancient See of Constantinople (now resident in Istanbul), and the holder of this office is known as His All-Holiness the Ecumenical Patriarch. Those in communion with the Ecumenical Patriarch of Constantinople include the Churches of Russia, Georgia, Greece, Romania and Hungary. The other Orthodox Churches are known as the Oriental Orthodox Churches, and include the Coptic, Syrian, Armenian and Ethiopian Orthodox Churches, and the Indian Malakara Church. These Churches are not in communion with the See of Constantinople.

My introduction to Orthodoxy was accelerated when the ailing

Ecumenical Patriarch, His All-Holiness Demetrios, died, and senior religious figures from all denominations were invited to his funeral in Istanbul on 8 October 1991. I stayed with the British Ambassador, Sir Timothy Daunt, who told me the news that a Turkish diplomat had just been murdered in Athens, and that the incident was thought to be linked with the funeral of the Ecumenical Patriarch the following day. There was deep distrust between the Greek and Turkish governments, not only because of Turkey's occupation of much of Cyprus but, just as importantly, because of the stranglehold the Turkish government had over the tiny Greek population in Istanbul and the ministry of the Ecumenical Patriarch. The situation was, and remains, scandalous, as the election of a new Patriarch is limited to clergy of the Phanar (the Church and headquarters of the Ecumenical Patriarch in Istanbul), who are compelled to be Turkish citizens. As a result the Greek population is steadily dwindling, and the future of that ancient centre of Christianity is increasingly at risk.

The following day the long and reverent Liturgy for the Departed started at noon and lasted most of the afternoon. As the Greek Prime Minister entered with his bodyguards, Archdeacon Geoffrey Evans whispered to me: 'If there's any trouble, dive to the ground!' This was the strangest liturgical command I had ever received, and I replied with a rather startled, 'What did you say?' Geoffrey murmured, 'If bullets start to fly, hit the ground.' In the event no dramatic incident occurred to spoil the service, and Patriarch Demetrios was duly laid to rest.

Almost exactly a year later I was back in Istanbul to meet the new Ecumenical Patriarch, Bartholomew, a jolly, stocky man with steady, twinkling eyes. The meeting was intended not only for us to get to know one another, but to consider the theological progress being made between the Anglican Communion and the Orthodox Churches. With me was Bishop Mark Dyer from the United States, the Co-Chairman of the Doctrinal Commission. We were made to understand that the approaching General Synod debate on the ordination of women would jeopardise the future of dialogue between the two Churches. I replied that we understood that perfectly, but believed there were strong theological grounds for the ordination of women. It was a spirited exchange, without rancour or bitterness, and led me to appreciate the Ecumenical Patriarch's theological rigour and warm personality. I was confident that we could establish a frank and positive relationship with him.

At a personal level, however, I was concerned about his delicate position in Istanbul. There was constant harassment from some rigid Islamic groups, and the Ecumenical Patriarch expressed his anxiety that the stream of very good priests and monks would dry up unless the Turks relaxed their rigid residential requirements. We were to see some of his problems first hand when, the following day, we visited Halki Island to view the monastery and the seminary there. In spite of its excellent facilities the monastery, which had once prepared generations of monks for service, now stood empty, with just three remaining monks. I could not help but muse that if the tables were turned, and Muslims in Britain or the United States were as badly treated as Christians in Turkey, there would be a huge outcry. On this and other occasions I wondered why we Christians are so silent when there are such clear infringements of human rights as this, and when other Christian denominations are treated so shabbily.

The most formidable and powerful Orthodox Church is without doubt the Russian Orthodox Church. Under its Patriarch, Alexis II, the Church had emerged from its Communist imprisonment and was one of the few institutions in the country left with some credibility. Patriarch Alexis II was the very first senior Orthodox leader to visit England as my guest, in October 1991. A burly, powerfully built man with a long beard, he was concerned to share the problems of the Orthodox Church after Communism. He spoke of the spiritual hunger of the people, and the way they had returned in their millions to the Church, but added, 'Whole generations are now unchurched and influenced by atheism.' In particular he expressed his anger at the 'invasion' of Mother Russia by American evangelicals, whose missionary methods appealed to the young, and he stated quite clearly that no other faith than the Orthodox Church had the right to evangelise in his country. From this extreme position emanated his hostility to the Roman Catholic Church establishing churches in Russia. He appealed to the Anglican Communion to help to set up theological training for his ordinands, and particularly to assist those capable of studying for advanced degrees. I was very sympathetic to this goal, and as a result of this visit the St Andrew's Trust was created, with its main office at Lambeth Palace. To this day it continues to give scholarships to Orthodox students.

The following day I took the Patriarch to visit the Queen, who was happy to give him a personal audience. She was not the slightest bit taken aback by this large Russian with his white Patriarchal hat, flowing robes and menacing beard. She had done her homework thoroughly, and was very much in command of the situation. She asked pertinent questions, and patiently endured the Patriarch's rather lengthy answers. As we drove back to Lambeth I could tell that he was delighted with the conversation, and impressed by the Queen's skill in conducting the audience. I believe he returned home very content with the visit, which had given him an opportunity to share his concerns and to develop new friendships.

Unfortunately, the return visit which I paid in April 1993 was not as happy, as the General Synod's decision in favour of the ordination of women was greeted with great dismay by the Orthodox Church. At the airport I was met by Sir Brian Fall, the British Ambassador to Russia, and taken to his famous residence overlooking the Kremlin. The forty-minute journey revealed the shocking legacy of Communism in the badly built blocks of flats, broken pavements, empty shops and clear evidence of neglect. That, together with the sight of a huge queue outside a bakery waiting for bread made from Australian wheat, suggested that we were in a Third World country with a Third World economy. On arriving at the Residence Eileen and I were greeted warmly by Delmar, Sir Brian's wife, and shown to the principal guest room to settle in.

Events over the following two days definitely signalled that my official visit had been downgraded because of the ordination of women. The first sign was that at the official dinner held by Sir Brian and Lady Fall the Patriarch was represented by Metropolitan Juvenale, a friendly man who seemed nervous and on edge. He wasted no time in telling me that the Russian Orthodox Church would tolerate no interference in its mission in its own land by either the Roman Catholic Church or 'American evangelical missionaries'. He was equally dogmatic about the ordination of women, which he declared had no basis 'in tradition'. I felt the hard tone had much to do with his unease at being required to act in opposition to his character, which seemed open and warm.

The following day the Patriarch met us at Danilovsky monastery. He welcomed us formally at the entrance, fully robed with mitre and pastoral staff. We greeted one another and went upstairs for lunch, consisting of six main courses with vodka, wine and fruit juice – I did not see much fruit juice consumed. Periodically there would be a toast, and generous amounts of vodka were drunk. Alexis II then stood and warmly welcomed Eileen and me, together with my staff and the British Ambassador. Then his tone changed, and a tough speech followed in which the ordination of women was forthrightly condemned. It was difficult to know how to follow that without giving offence, so I gave an off-the-cuff response thanking him for his hospitality – and indirectly reminding him of mine in 1991. Then, addressing his complaint, I made it clear that the Church of England had acted with theological integrity, believing that the time had come to ordain women to the priesthood. For myself, I was confident that time would show that the ordination of women would make a remarkable contribution to the ministry and mission of the Church.

We were all rather glad to leave Moscow for an official visit to the Orthodox Church of Armenia. A ramshackle Russian plane had been hired for the next two legs of our trip, and as we boarded it Francis Richards, number two at the Embassy, whispered to me, 'As you land at Yeravan, look for the trees.' None of us knew what to make of this comment. We were aware of course that Armenia was a very poor country, ruined by Communism and weary from its ongoing war with Azerbaijan. Just two years earlier an earthquake had devastated much of the country. The flight from Moscow took us over some spectacular countryside, but as we landed at Yeravan we understood what Francis meant – there were no trees. So destitute were the people that the trees had all been burned to keep them warm through the harsh winters.

This time the welcome was warm and heartfelt. We straggled from the plane to a wet and windswept tarmac, to be greeted by a long line of black-garbed clergy in their distinctive 'coalman' cowls. We were struck by how cold it was, even though it was May. Archbishop Nerses Bozabalian, formerly of Mirfield, greeted us and we were taken by car to Holy Etchmiadzim, the heart of the Armenian Church, fifteen miles away. The poverty of the people was evident from the small villages that we sped through. Buildings seemed in need of serious repair. Archbishop Nerses informed me that food was in short supply and essential goods were hard to obtain. Yet in spite of that the people seemed cheerful, and the children waved as the procession of cars sped through their villages.

Holy Etchmiadzim is a large monastery with a small cathedral founded in the fourth century, set in the middle of a huge compound. We were greeted warmly by the Catholicos Vazgen I, who in spite of his eighty-five years was alert and energetic. When we were shown to our room we discovered that we had no hot water and only one thin blanket on our beds. To our relief Diana and George Kurkjian, two London-based Armenians, came to our rescue with extra blankets. Following a good night's rest we were able to face the demands of a new day which included a formal welcome in the cathedral, and over the following days we saw something of the work of the Church in a very poor country. The Church of Armenia made a deep impression on us. Its brave Christian witness during hostile Communist rule, the distinctiveness of its traditions and faithful clergy, its courage during and after the massacre of its people by the

Turks at the beginning of the century, attracted us greatly. Over the years following this first visit we got to know Vazgen I's successors, Karekin I and Karekin II. Indeed, of all the Orthodox Churches we visited, we felt most at home in the Armenian Church.

Three days later we were back in the same plane, this time on our way to Georgia. This trip had not been without incident, because when we got to Yeravan airport there was no sign of our plane. Two hours later it arrived, and the pilot told us lamely that he had had to go to Tbilisi to pick up fuel. The view of the airport staff was that the aircrew had actually been gunrunning, and had used our fuel for their devious ends.

Whatever the reason, we were two hours late arriving at Tbilisi, where we were met by Patriarch Illya II and a huge entourage. Patriarch Illya, a tall, burly man with the obligatory white beard making him look ten years older than his age of sixty, greeted us with great warmth. We were bundled into cars in accordance with our ecclesial rank, which meant that Eileen was ushered into the seventh car, which had a broken suspension. The drive from the airport gave us the opportunity to note that Georgia was more prosperous than Armenia, but still very run-down and in urgent need of major improvements to its infrastructure. We were taken immediately to a government residence in a lovely area, and were shown to a large, comfortable room which even had hot water.

Talks with the Patriarch over the next few days made me aware not only of the problems of the country, but of the huge contribution the Church was making to its nation and people. Illya II struck me as a wise leader of a Church that is rich in spirituality but poor in material goods. Following the barren period of Communism, he said, the Church needed help in the training of clergy and teachers, in managing farms newly returned to Church ownership, and in repairing damaged Church buildings. I would become used to appeals of this kind, and all I could do on this occasion was to say that I would reflect on the challenges when I got home and see what I could do.

A private meeting the following day with President Eduard Shevardnadze confirmed the Patriarch's concerns. The President, who made no secret of being a practising Christian, launched into a description of the country's problems. Before any reconstruction of the economy, he said, must come resolution of the conflict between Georgia and the neighbouring Russian states. Following the collapse of Greater Russia those states were challenging Georgia's borders, encouraging armed gangs to menace outlying villages, leading to many thousands fleeing their homes to seek refuge in Tbilisi. I asked the obvious question: Who was responsible for this state of affairs? He replied that his comments were not a criticism of Russia's President Yeltsin, but rather of his subordinates in the regions who were disobeying his orders. It seemed a lame explanation, but with the media present Mr Shevardnadze was not prepared to go further. He did however offer a tribute to the Orthodox Church for its ministry to refugees and what it was doing generally to give hope to people.

The visit to the Church of Georgia made me more keenly aware of the nature of Orthodox spirituality, and particularly the way it handles the tension between mystery and intellectual questions. I remember especially the main service we attended in St George's Cathedral in the heart of Tbilisi. Although it was a weekday, and in spite of heavy rain, a large crowd had gathered. A great congregation filled the cathedral, and many more were outside enduring the downpour. The devotion of the faithful was palpable. The language barrier made it impossible for me to understand the liturgy, yet the shape of it was comprehensible and the singing was quite lovely. But it was only when I looked around at the standing congregation – no chairs in Orthodox churches – that I began to comprehend Orthodoxy. Young and old alike were absorbed in the divine liturgy. As I looked at them I began to realise that to ask 'How much do they understand?' is very much a Western preoccupation. While no doubt issues of meaning and truth are important questions for Orthodox worshippers, as they are for the British, they are not central. For most of the Orthodox there is a powerful sense of the mystery of God, in which they participate when they worship.

Further exposure to Orthodoxy over the coming years – in Romania, Syria, Lebanon and Greece, to say nothing of frequent contact with Archbishop Gregorius and Metropolitan Anthony Bloom, respectively heads of the Greek and Russian Orthodox Churches in the United Kingdom – led me to understand the strength of Orthodoxy, even though I found its liturgy overlong and remote. Although theological dialogue between Anglicans and the Orthodox has shown how much we share in a common understanding of the nature of the Church, there are so many issues to resolve that it is unlikely to lead to visible unity in the foreseeable future.

There was an amusing postscript to my experience of Orthodoxy during the return visit of Illya II to England. An enjoyable cruise down the Thames to Hampton Court had been provided by the river police. It was a fine summer's day, and as Illya and I were chatting I asked if there was anything I might be able to help him with. To my surprise he said that as security was one of the most urgent matters in Tbilisi, did I think I could obtain a Rottweiler bitch for him? He explained he had a male Rottweiler that needed a mate. I turned to the Police Superintendent on board and asked, 'Could you get us a Rottweiler bitch?' Taken aback, he replied, 'I will see what I can do, sir.' At once he was on the phone, and after speaking to someone in authority he told us that the police had a good line in German shepherds, but that they were out of Rottweilers. I cheerfully assured Illya that I would get my staff onto it. As I said this, I noticed Canon Richard Marsh, my Ecumenical Officer, blanching.

Over the next week Richard and Canon David Naumann at Canterbury contacted many dog handlers specialising in Rottweilers, and eventually found a delightful female puppy in East Anglia. At considerable expense and after much labour the puppy was duly delivered to the Patriarch's home in Tbilisi. I was greatly amused to learn later that Illya II christened her 'Meeess Carey'. In due time she produced a healthy litter to enable the Patriarch to sleep soundly at night. I am of course pleased that there are now many doggy 'Careys' on guard at the Residence in Georgia's capital.

If progress towards visible unity with the Roman Catholic Church and the Orthodox Churches has been slow, this has not been so with regard to the Protestant Churches. Anglicans and Moravians in England and Ireland have entered into a new relationship of closer fellowship on the way to full visible unity. I am also glad that the nineties saw the restart of the Anglican–Methodist conversations, resulting in the signing of a Covenant between the two Churches that is bound to lead to a much deeper relationship and perhaps, one day, full visible unity. Methodism, of course, sprang from the Church of England, and has now become a world Communion in its own right. It was my privilege to know many Methodist leaders, among them Donald English, and I am unable to regard Methodists as lacking in grace simply because they are Methodists, nor can I regard Methodism as being in any respect inferior to Anglicanism. These relations of closer fellowship in Britain and Ireland are paralleled in other parts of the Anglican Communion, for example in the United States and southern Africa.

Perhaps even more rewarding has been the progress made with the Lutheran Churches in Europe, North America and now in Australia. I was delighted in 1987 to be asked to be an Anglican delegate at the first official talks between the Anglican Churches of Britain and Ireland and the Nordic and Baltic Lutheran Churches, who met at Sigtuna, Sweden, under the Co-Chairmanship of Bishop David Tustin (Anglican) and Bishop Tore Furberg (from Sweden). Sadly, I had to surrender this role on my appointment as Archbishop of Canterbury, but I continued to follow the progress of the conversations with great interest. Building on the earlier theological work done in the Meissen Common Statement of 1988 (the result of conversations between the Church of England and the German Evangelical Church) and the 1988 Niagara Report on Episcope, from the Anglican–Lutheran International Continuation Committee, the conversations with the Nordic and Baltic Lutheran Churches achieved a remarkable breakthrough in understanding, particularly in the crucial areas of episcopacy, apostolicity and succession.

The key to this was a deeper understanding of the apostolicity of the whole Church, of the episcopal office within that, and of historic succession as sign, not guarantee, of apostolicity. The talks asked: Is there evidence to say that this or that Church is apostolic? Has it maintained an orderly succession of episcopal ministry within the continuity of its life? Has it kept the faith of the apostles? Are there signs of grace in the Church to convince that this body is truly Christian in spirit, in faith and in love? The talks broke new ground, and in October 1992 the final text was agreed at Porvoo in Finland. It is consequently known as the Porvoo Common Statement. The significance of this remarkable Agreement is the effective goal of visible unity between the four Anglican Churches of Britain and Ireland and the Lutheran Churches of Iceland, Finland, Norway, Sweden, Estonia and Lithuania. Latvia has not yet taken a decision, and unfortunately the Church of Denmark did not feel the time was right to sign. It continues to be hoped that both Churches will become part of this historic Agreement in the future. One significant feature of the accord is that it makes the Porvoo Churches the largest united body in northern Europe, and a sign of hope for the rest of the Christian world.

In April 1994 Eileen and I made an official visit to all eight Nordic/Baltic countries in a breathless fourteen days. With us came John Hind, the Anglican Bishop in mainland Europe; David Tustin, Bishop of Grimsby and Co-Chairman of the Porvoo conversations; and Canon Stephen Platten, my Ecumenical Officer. The purpose of the tour was to consolidate the work of Porvoo and to meet the leaders of all the Churches involved in the discussions.

All three Baltic nations – Lithuania, Latvia and Estonia – showed deep signs of the bitter yoke of Communism, and I did not meet a political leader in these countries who had a good word to say of their occupation by Russia. In Latvia I was particularly moved when I was taken to the Hill of Crosses at Sianliai, a short journey from Riga. In 1863 some Christians, in protest against restrictions on worship, started to plant large crosses on the hill. During the Second World War the Hill of Crosses became a sign of defiance of Nazi occupation, and after the war it continued as a silent protest against Russian oppression. Time after time German and Russian invaders bulldozed the crosses, but overnight they would spring up again. It was an amazing sight: thousands and thousands of crosses, large and small, plain and ornate, all shades of colour, crowded the small hill. I was invited to plant a cross alongside one planted by Pope John Paul II when he visited Latvia a few years earlier. It was moving to be reminded of the power of the cross as a symbol of the fight for freedom and also as a sign of hope. I saw one cross bearing the words 'We will overcome'. This, I thought, is truly the authentic language of Christianity. Then it was on to the Nordic countries, Finland, Sweden, Norway, Denmark and Iceland, where we were also given warm and generous welcomes.

If the Hill of Crosses moved me deeply on the Baltic leg, there was one unforgettable moment on the second leg when we visited a folk museum in Norway, where we saw three ancient Viking boats. The oldest was an ocean-going vessel dating from the mid-ninth century; one Runic line carved into the prow said it all: 'Man knows little'. Although separated by some 1200 years, I felt instantly one with that unknown traveller about to embark on a voyage into the unknown. Knowing so little, the human race is still compelled to reach out in faith and hope.

The visit brought home to me the fact that the Anglican Churches of the British Isles have much in common with the Lutheran Churches, and that the future journey of ecumenism must be to grow together in the faith we share as Churches profoundly influenced by the Reformation. Yet differences remain. I confess to finding Lutheran worship on the Continent rather severe, plain and uninteresting. Indeed, it makes God rather boring and dull. Perhaps the

Church of England, by and large, has escaped that by its greater closeness to Catholicism than most of northern Europe, and possibly also by the liturgical genius of Cranmer. We too, however, must find ways of making our worship far more interesting and relevant to a modern, seeking generation.

So it was that during the 1990s some encouraging advances were made with respect to Protestant Churches. These new relations of closer fellowship between Anglicans and Lutherans, Reformed and United Churches in Germany in the Meissen Agreement, between Anglicans and Lutherans and Reformed in France in the Reuilly Agreement, and between Anglicans and Lutherans in the Nordic and Baltic countries, have their counterparts in Canada in the Waterloo Agreement, and in the USA based on 'Called to Common Mission' and in other Provinces of the Anglican Communion.

What, though, are the prospects for ecumenism with Rome and the Orthodox Churches? At first sight the prospects do not seem encouraging. Hundreds of earnest and clever documents, representing millions of words and man hours, have appeared during the last forty years, and have hardly made a difference to the gulf separating us from these world Communions, let alone to their distance from each other. Yes, there are grounds for pessimism. There have been times when the cost-ineffectiveness of ecumenism has tempted me to call for a moratorium on ecumenical meetings for ten years, in order to focus the Church's limited resources on its mission. On the other hand, unity is inseparable from mission, and must remain at the heart of all that the Church does and is.

I cannot see conversations with the Orthodox Church yielding anything more than extremely modest results for some time, and in my view priority should be given to relationships with the Roman Catholic Church, focusing perhaps on the Mississauga initiative launched by Cardinal Edward Cassidy and myself. It remains to be seen how a new Pope will take forward his predecessor's great encyclical *Ut Unum Sint*. Indeed, the future of ecumenism lies to a considerable degree with the Holy Father and the Catholic Church. As the greater Church, it can either show generosity of spirit in recognising the fruits of grace in other Churches, or conclude in the spirit of *Dominus Jesus* that it has a monopoly of God's grace. The challenge for us all is to keep convergence in the faith together with convergence of life, and to take steps together on the basis of the theological agreements to reach new depths of shared life and mission.

In spite then of many dashed hopes regarding the journey towards affective and effective unity, the words at Mississauga 2000 AD of Bishop Walter Kasper, later to succeed Cardinal Cassidy, echo in my mind and encourage me to keep on hoping and praying: 'One day we will rub our eyes and be surprised by the new things God has achieved in His Church.'

20

From Crusades to Co-Operation

> 'We hear the bawling and din, we are reach'd at by divisions,
>   jealousies, recriminations on every side,
> They close peremptorily upon us to surround us, my comrade,
> Yet we walk unheld, free, the whole earth over, journeying up
>   and down
> Till we make our ineffaceable mark upon time and the diverse
>   eras . . .
> That the men and women of races, ages to come,
> May prove brethren and lovers as we are.'
>
>   Walt Whitman, 'To Him that was Crucified'

BEFORE I TOOK UP THE OFFICE of Archbishop, I had no inkling that inter-faith dialogue and co-operation with leaders of other faith communities worldwide would occupy so much of my time and energy. The way that this area has grown signifies the most important difference between my archiepiscopate and that of my predecessors. Rather than occupying a sliver of time that a busy Archbishop could simply slip into an already impossible diary, inter-faith activities would become one of my top priorities, and I expect them also to dominate the lives of my successors.

The first group to welcome me was, typically, the Jewish community. Long before I took up office, Eileen and I were invited to the Chief Rabbi's home in St John's Wood to meet some senior Jewish leaders. After we had been eyed suspiciously by the armed guard at the security gates, Dr Immanuel Jacobowitz greeted us warmly and ushered us in to meet his wife Amelia. I remember distinctly that his main concern that evening were the darkening clouds of anti-Semitism overshadowing Europe. He brought home to me the importance of the Council for Christians and Jews, and urged my full support. I had no difficulty in assuring him that I would follow Robert Runcie's practice of hosting the regular meetings of CCJ at Lambeth Palace.

Within a few months Dr Jacobowitz, feeling the demands of age, handed over the reins of his distinguished office to the young and dynamic Rabbi Jonathan Sacks. Jonathan and his wife Elaine quickly became good friends – a friendship which was established at a remarkable football match in November 1990. A Jewish businessman, Michael Moss, invited us to join him in his box to watch Arsenal play Manchester United in the League Cup before either of us had taken up office. Before the game we were taken out onto the pitch to be introduced to the crowd, then returned to the box. Sadly, Arsenal were trounced 6–2. When somebody suggested that if a losing team were supported by both the Archbishop of Canterbury and the Chief Rabbi it must mean there is no God, quick as a flash Jonathan responded, 'No, all it proves is that God is a Man U supporter!'

Peter Hill-Wood, Chairman of Arsenal, took a different tack with me. 'Archbishop,' he said, 'it's always nice to welcome you to Highbury, but if we're going to play like that when you come, please don't come too often!'

As Chief Rabbi, Jonathan has since become a significant influence in the life of the nation through his books, articles and television and radio broadcasts. Although his constituency in orthodox Judaism is small, he has proved an able spokesperson for all faiths.

Another key Jewish leader I met before becoming Archbishop was Sir Sigmund Sternberg. Sir Sigmund, known universally as 'Siggy', is an astute businessman whose contribution to inter-faith activity is as significant as it is legendary. A small, slight figure, he is one of the most tenacious and focused of religious leaders, and when he is possessed by a good idea he pursues it with energy. As a Vice-President of the International Council of Christians and Jews, he was keen to press upon me the urgency of inter-faith co-operation and dialogue. A few years later Siggy, Sheikh Zaki Badawi and a mutual friend, Marcus Braybrooke, would start an initiative called 'The Three Faiths Forum' bringing Jews, Muslims and Christians together.

As soon as I took up office I knew that I had a problem. Besides automatically being one of the Presidents of CCJ, I was also expected to be Patron of the Church's Ministry Among Jewish People (CMJ), as every Archbishop of Canterbury had been since William Howley in 1849. In many respects I was very sympathetic to the aims of CMJ. Christ's message began with Jews, and should never fail to include them. However, the impression of CMJ among some Jews was that it was a proselytising body which directly targeted Jews. This made me hesitate to take on the patronage of the society.

Over the years CMJ has had four changes of name – from 'Church Missions to Jews', to 'The Church's Mission to Jews', then 'The Church's Ministry Among the Jews', and in 1995 to 'The Church's Ministry Among Jewish People'. However, it is the earliest name that has stuck in the minds of British Jewry, and CMJ's close links with the 'Jews for Jesus' movement has helped to harden a view that CMJ's deepest instinct is for explicit evangelism.

A tactical reason also made me uncertain about whether or not I should take on this position. I had already decided to give priority to my role as President of CCJ alongside Cardinal Hume and other leaders, and separation from CMJ would send out a clear signal to the Jewish community that I had no hidden agenda. I shared my dilemma with Archbishop John Habgood, whose advice was unhesitating: an evangelical Archbishop could better sever the links than someone from a different tradition. I wasn't so sure about this; it seemed to me that it could create a far greater fuss than if the same decision were made by a non-evangelical, because it would seem an act of betrayal. Nevertheless, I made up my mind, and told CMJ that I declined to accept its offer of patronage.

Josh Drummond, the General Secretary, came to see me, and expressed his shock and distress. Was I aware that my decision would terminate a tradition going back 150 years? He felt it would marginalise CMJ from the rest of the Church of England. I replied that my priority must be how best to use my office as Archbishop for the good of the Church, and that I was convinced patronage of CMJ did not serve my strategy. The response was furious and bitter. Tony Higton, who later became General Secretary of CMJ, called it a 'shameful betrayal' and a 'grave undermining of the cause of the gospel'. The rumpus continued for years. The response from Jews, however, was of gratitude and respect. They knew that my decision did not represent any shrinking from offering the Christian faith to all; rather it meant clarity of purpose and an openness towards their place in the purposes of God.

This did not mean that my attitude to Jews was uncritical. On the one hand, I remain an admirer of all that the Jewish people have achieved through the ages. Christianity's debt to Israel is incalculable, although still not properly appreciated by the average Christian. The sufferings of Jews down the centuries in Christian Europe and particularly through the evil of the Holocaust is a story of shocking injustice and bigotry. The story of the renewal of the People and their 'return' to the Promised Land, in which Britain played a somewhat ambiguous part, is a remarkable tribute to a gifted people who had to overcome terrible odds to become a nation once more in 1948. What that land means to Jews was expressed very strongly by Prime Minister Ariel Sharon in 2001 when I told him I was going to lead a pilgrimage to the Holy Land in a few months. Although a secular Jew, his reply was as messianic as the most devout Jewish believer: 'Ah, yes, to you Christians it is the "Holy" Land – but to we Jews it is the "Promised" Land.'

It is in the tangle of the two words 'holy' and 'promised' that the tragedy of Israel and Palestine continues to be worked out. In my frequent visits to Israel I had no difficulty in agreeing with Jews that they had every right to return to that land, and every right to live in peace. I contended, however, that the Palestinians whose home it was too had the same claims for justice and security in their homeland, and that the violence would continue if Israel claimed entitlement to the entire land, as if it were promised to them alone. The continued building of settlements on occupied territory, and the blatant disregard of UN Resolutions urging Israel to comply with the request to withdraw to its pre-1967 border, has fanned the flames of deep hatred of Israel and its people.

I rather annoyed Prime Minister Benjamin Netanyahu when, at a private meeting in 1994, I drew a parallel between the Jewish Stern Gang, which had fought British occupation after the Second World War, and the terrorist tactics used by Palestinians. I drew his attention to the quiet British military cemetery hidden alongside the ancient wall of Jerusalem, south of King David's tower, where scores of young British soldiers of nineteen and twenty murdered by Jewish freedom fighters are buried. 'Are there not parallels today in the struggles of the Palestinian people?' I asked. He refused to see any equivalent, because the land, he claimed, did not belong to the Palestinian people. This obdurate attitude continues to poison the relationship between Israel and Palestine.

British Jewry, on the whole, seems more sensitive to the plight of Palestine than are most Israeli politicians. The late Hugo Gryn, one of the most able leaders of the Reformed Jewish Synagogue, often shared with me his concerns about the intransigence of successive Israeli governments in failing to heed the moral case for conceding land to allow Palestine to create a viable state. He and others, such as Rabbi Tony Bayfield and Greville Janner MP, later Lord Janner of Braunestone, were articulate advocates of a political settlement based on firm democratic values for both nations.

The Jewish faith has of course been a familiar part of British life for centuries, but Islam is a comparative newcomer, at least as far as the presence of a significant population goes. In 1951 there were a mere twenty-three thousand Muslims in Britain. By 1970 the numbers had risen to 370,000, and the figure given in the 2000 census was

1.6 million. In terms of the total population of the country, that is not a huge percentage. In fact the total of all members of non-Christian communities comes to only around 7 per cent of the population – the same as the percentage of Christians and non-Muslims in Pakistan. Despite these quite small numbers, other cultures and faith communities have brought a rich diversity to the cultural, culinary and faith map of Great Britain, and are greatly appreciated by the majority.

It was in connection with these relatively small percentages of the population that I caused a minor upset in the mid-nineties when I challenged the use of the term 'multi-faith society' to describe Britain. In an interview I said that Britain was certainly a multi-racial nation, but was no more a multi-faith nation than Pakistan. This was interpreted by some Muslims as suggesting opposition to other faiths. It was of course totally untrue, but it was largely as a result of this that I got to know Sheikh Dr Zaki Badawi, one of the most significant Muslim leaders in Britain and certainly one of the most open to dialogue. Zaki, an articulate and informed man, was born in Egypt but has lived in England for many years. As leader of the Regent's Park Mosque in London he was a moderate and respected voice of Islam.

Zaki initially misunderstood the point I had made in the interview, but very quickly cottoned on when I explained that I was anxious to protect the Christian identity of our nation. The constant repetition of the claim that 'Britain is a multi-faith society' was being used by many secularists to suggest that no one faith is special – that Britain is somehow neutral, and that Christianity is not entitled to a special place in the nation. I told him firmly that I was passionately committed to mutual respect and dialogue. The many different faith communities are welcomed and valued, and should have the same rights to religious freedom as the Christian Churches. Nevertheless, Britain is still a predominantly Christian country, and I was anxious that we should not downplay the huge impact that Christianity has had in shaping the nation, its laws, the monarchy, its education and its moral values. Zaki unhesitatingly accepted this, and out of the misunderstanding came a very strong relationship of trust.

Archbishops of Canterbury are ideally positioned to play the role of host to the varied faiths of the land, and that was a privilege I enjoyed as Patron of the Inter-Faith Network, which was founded in 1987. Led so well by its Director, Brian Pearce, the Network exists to give faiths a public face and voice. In addition to regular meetings of representatives of all faiths in England, it also meets annually at Lambeth Palace with the Archbishop for mutual consultation and the sharing of concerns. Within this context I got to know the leaders of faiths other than Islam and Judaism, and began to appreciate the values of Hinduism, Buddhism, Sikhism, the Bahai faith and others. Such meetings produced their share of drama and confrontation. I recall one afternoon when the Network had brought together representative young people from different faith communities. A lively discussion ensued as this group of teenagers and university students grappled with the necessity of dialogue. There was a flurry of discord when the topic turned to how much their faith meant to each person. One Muslim boy said fiercely, 'I would kill for my faith!'

There was a shocked and stunned silence, then an Irish girl who had earlier told her own story of conflict in Northern Ireland replied quietly, 'I hope you will never do that. My faith is important to me too – and I would be willing to die for my faith. But I would never kill for it.' It was a splendid riposte, and the sentiment was echoed around the room. I never found out if the Muslim boy agreed with that honest and searching reply.

It is in the widely held view that Islam is essentially a warlike desert religion that a great deal of suspicion arises, and that the roots of Islamophobia are to be found. It is often claimed in the West that Islam, more than any other religion, is capable of being misused by evil men for their own ends. In fact history shows Islam to be no worse than Christianity in its propensity to be used by the unscrupulous. A more mundane reason for Islamophobia, in my opinion, lies in a psychology of alienation or 'strangeness'. We recoil from the stranger because of his difference from us in dress, worship, cuisine, behaviour and habits. I saw this at work in three very different international contexts.

In the week before Christmas 1995, together with Eileen and two staff members, Dr Andrew Purkis and Canon Richard Marsh, I became one of the first Western Church leaders to pay an official visit to Bosnia-Herzegovina. Earlier attempts had been ruled out as unsafe and the very weekend I was there UN troops were being replaced by NATO forces. We travelled first to the Croatian capital Zagreb, and while staying with the British Ambassador, Gavin Hewitt, had dinner with Croatian leaders, several prominent businessmen, the local Roman Catholic Bishop and the Papal Nuncio.

I was astonished by the inability of the Croatians to accept any responsibility for the appalling human rights abuses and ethnic cleansing that had marked the Balkan war, and was told firmly that blame for the atrocities should be laid at the door of the Serbians, and particularly the Muslims of Bosnia-Herzegovina. The reasons given were that the Serbians have always been a warlike people, while the Muslims were driven by their faith to fight Christians and to take over the land. This highly educated group of people did not seem to be aware that such deeply-held prejudices were at the roots of the conflict, and that if they were left unresolved, even the advent of peace would amount to no more than papering over the cracks in racial understanding.

At 6.15 the following morning, suitably dressed in thermal under-wear, we boarded a UN flight for Split and then Sarajevo. We had never been on such a cold, uncomfortable and crowded plane. No concessions were made for Archbishops and their wives, nor did we expect any. It was a cargo plane, with huge containers in the middle, and the passengers, mainly troops, strapped to the sides. We sat in darkness for the duration of the flight to Split. After a brief stop we continued in the noisy, dark and uncomfortable craft until a gap in the clouds allowed us to land at Sarajevo airport.

We were met by Brian Hopkinson, the British Ambassador, a cheerful man who said abruptly, 'Let's go to the British Embassy for the Poetry Circle in honour of Seamus Heaney.' As we sped through the wartorn and shell-shocked city, I thought that surely only the British would be mad enough to refuse to allow hostilities to interrupt their poetry group. At the Embassy we met a dozen or so Bosnian nationals who were enthusiasts for Heaney's poetry, and grateful to the Ambassador for continuing to host the poetry circle in spite of everything. At times of stress and conflict, keeping the habits of normality enables people to endure and hope.

In the afternoon, a call on President Alija Izetbegovic of Bosnia-Herzegovina gave us a further insight into the bitterness behind the ethnic conflict. The President, a dignified moderate Muslim, spoke of the yearning of most Muslims for peace and the chance to live alongside their Serbian Christian neighbours. There was no alternative, he said, to building a pluralistic society in which all could live freely and worship as they wished. It was a vision I was able to applaud. When I asked his opinion of Slobodan Milosevic, the President of Serbia, he replied, 'He is a bad man, but behind him are even worse men.'

I then visited the leading Muslim in the country, the Reiss al-Ulema Dr Mustapha Ceric, who made a deep impression on me. Also a moderate, Dr Ceric was an energetic, highly intelligent man, acutely aware of his responsibility to lead his large Muslim community away from recrimination and retaliation to peace. He acknowledged that the behaviour of Muslims during the conflict had not always been exemplary, but said it was in defence of their families and homes that they had been led to commit atrocities against their neighbours. He told me harrowing stories of Muslim women whose husbands and sons had been taken away never to be seen again.

That evening the Ambassador held a dinner for about twenty guests at the Writers' Club. With signs of bomb damage all around and in flickering candlelight we ate mutton and potatoes, which was the best the restaurant could muster. Kate Adie, the BBC correspondent covering the conflict, was expected, but never appeared. We discovered later that on her way she had broken her leg in a fall. I spoke to a Muslim woman whose husband had been killed by a tank shell which blew him apart while he was feeding their baby in their flat. Miraculously, the baby was unharmed.

Dinner over, we left for the Ambassador's home, a simple flat in a building bearing the scars of the war – bulletholes, broken windows, wrecked cars outside. Mrs Hopkinson apologised for the conditions we would have to endure for the next two nights – no lighting, no heating, and no hot water. The temperature inside the flat was minus 14 degrees. Wrapped in layers of clothing, Eileen and I huddled close together and actually enjoyed a good night's rest.

The following morning we visited the headquarters of the United Nations Protection Force (UNPROFOR) to see General Sir Rupert Smith, who was in charge of the British forces, and then to a Roman Catholic Mass in the cathedral, where I met Cardinal Pulic, a forthright leader who publicly criticised me, as a token Westerner, for having let down the Christians in Bosnia-Herzegovina. He made it clear in his diatribe that this was not a personal attack – indeed, he was delighted and grateful that 'at long last' someone from Western Europe had shown up in Sarajevo and 'at last' identified with fellow Christians. The sarcasm was enjoyed by the large congregation.

In my address I chose not to respond, knowing that expressing anger is part of healing. Indeed, I acknowledged that Western indifference towards and ignorance of Christians in the Balkans may have contributed to the isolation the Cardinal felt so keenly. However, I reminded them that they had not been entirely overlooked, and that aid from the West had continued to flow into their communities from the beginning of the conflict. What now, I continued, should be the Christian response to the wounds of the past? Continuing bitterness and anger between the divided communities of Bosnia would never yield peace; peace comes not from the barrels of guns, but from women and men who are peacemakers. I urged them to remember that Christ tells us in the Sermon on the Mount that peacemakers share the nature of God Himself, and quoted the fine words of the priest and poet R.S. Thomas: 'They listened to me preaching the unique gospel of love, but our eyes never met.' What sort of gospel is it, what sort of Christians are we, if our message and our eyes do not match up?

A delightful though basic meal was shared afterwards with Cardinal Pulic, who like his Muslim counterpart Dr Ceric had served his community well. Sadly, for unknown reasons the Serbian religious leader never managed to meet me, in spite of several attempts on my part to make contact.

If the visit to Bosnia-Herzegovina showed the difficulty of bringing divided communities together, I was to see this even more vividly two years later in Pakistan.

The Church of Pakistan was formed in 1970, and comprises Anglican, Methodist, Presbyterian and other Churches. In a vast sea of Islam it is a tiny Christian body that seeks to live at peace with its neighbours. For many years concerns had been expressed about the indirect persecution of Christians in Pakistan, who tended to be among the lowest-paid workers in the land. The former Moderator, Bishop Alexander Malik, Bishop of Lahore, has been a powerful advocate for the Church, but it was my desire to see the situation for myself, and to seek to promote the Church's mission in such a hostile context.

In December 1997, with the Bishop of Rochester, Dr Michael Nazir-Ali, who many years earlier had been Bishop of Raiwind in Pakistan, I flew to Lahore. The first day was spent with the Christian community, and we were welcomed warmly by the Governor, Shahid Hamid. I particularly wanted to question him about the infamous Blasphemy Laws, which were a source of great offence to non-Muslims.

In my preparation for the visit I had discovered that in 1860 the British government had indirectly played a role in the formulation of the Blasphemy Laws when it introduced amendments to the Indian

Penal Code making it an offence to defile or damage a place of worship, or to utter words that might offend the religious feelings of others. However, the offences were clearly regarded as relatively minor, the maximum punishment being two years in prison or a fine. When Pakistan became a republic in 1947 its first leader, Muhammad Ali Jinnah, allowed the laws to be enforced in the new country although only a handful of cases were pursued. But in the 1970s President Zulfikar Ali Bhutto and his successor General Zia-ul-Haq saw the opportunity to use the Blasphemy Laws for their own ends, and they had them strengthened. In order to placate the religious authorities the death penalty was made mandatory if the name of the Holy Prophet Mohammed was defiled by word or deed, either directly or indirectly.

The Governor told me that the primary target of the Blasphemy Laws were not Christians but a Muslim sect known as the Ahmadis, 'who blasphemed the Prophet'. In any case, he said, the laws were seldom invoked, and Christians were not as a rule involved when they were. This was manifestly untrue, and I reminded him that at the very moment we were speaking, a young Christian man was under sentence of death on a specious charge of insulting the name of the Prophet. Later that evening Bishop Malik gave a courageous address on the subject of the iniquitous laws, which he said shamed Islam and mocked Pakistan's claim to be an enlightened democracy.

Yet, in spite of such barriers, Pakistani people do become Christian, and are quietly assimilated into the life of the Church. I met a young family who had been baptised recently but were terrified of being identified publicly because of the likelihood of persecution. Shamim, the wife of Bishop Malik, told me that her father had, improbably, become a Christian through reading the Koran. Such was the burden of law imposed by the Muslim holy book, she said, that when he heard of the deliverance Christ offers those who turn to Him, he 'found' Christ. Forever afterwards he felt immense gratitude to the Koran for leading him in the direction of the Christian faith.

The following day we were in Islamabad and met the acting President, Wasim Sajjid, who expressed his gratitude for the way the Churches provided education throughout the country. Indeed, that was a refrain sung by a succession of Muslim leaders on this visit, that the contribution of the Churches to education, health and social provision was outstanding. I tackled him on the excessive marginalisation of the Church that goes on in the name of Islam, and asked why, if Christianity was so good for his nation, the laws of the country made it so difficult for people to take advantage of its benefits?

The major event of my visit to Islamabad was a lecture at the International Islamic University. I intended to pull no punches in an address I entitled 'The Human Family and the Duty of Religion'. The large hall was absolutely packed, with many intense young male students and a scattering of females. I was given a warm welcome and polite attention as I developed an argument on the duty of religion to be a cement in society, not a cancer that destroyed the body. As I have done in so many speeches, I emphasised the importance of 'reciprocity', pointing out that although the percentage of Christians in the population of Pakistan is the same as that of Muslims in Britain, there is an insufficient balance between the rights of Christians in the Muslim world and that of Muslims in the West. Surely justice and human rights demand that minority groups should be honoured, respected and fully integrated? I touched on the theme of evangelism, and said it was important to honour faith commitment: 'One can, I believe, be a Christian as I am, wholly convinced of the uniqueness of Christ and his abiding relevance to humankind, and still affirm that other faiths possess value, significance and integrity.'

Afterwards I was tackled by an aggressive-looking student who said, 'How can there be peace between us? The Prophet said that Islam is the only true religion.'

I replied, 'But surely the Koran says that there should be no compulsion in religion. Even though there are great differences between Islam and Christianity, can't we live together? Surely we can find ways of living together.' I rather hope I managed to convince him.

Sadly, my address was not interpreted positively by the central religious authorities. I learned later that the following day a message was broadcast in every mosque in the land condemning my views on the Blasphemy Laws and the place of Christianity in Pakistan.

The following day we were in Peshawar, where we saw more of the outstanding work of the Church in serving the people. Peshawar is a frontier city, on the north-west border with Afghanistan, bustling, noisy, dirty, populous and exciting. There was traffic everywhere, with carts pulled by oxen jostling with Land Rovers, Jeeps and Mercedes Benzes. Old and modern were mixed in a splendour of colour and confusion. After lunch with the clergy we went to a Church mission hospital which was doing extraordinary work among the blind, those suffering from leprosy and the mentally ill.

We went next to All Saints' Church, right in the heart of the bazaars. Built a hundred years ago to look like a mosque, it was only when the cross was positioned on top that the local people realised it was a church. In a fit of pique, a marksman fired at the cross and put a bullet right through the middle, the mark of which is still visible. The local Christians claim that this shows that the cross at its heart can bear all things and heal all things. In a moving service in the searing heat led by Bishop Mano Rumalshah I gave my final address to the faithful clergy and people, encouraging them not to lose heart, but with faith, hope and love to follow our Lord to the end. Pakistan is a hard country for a native Christian.

The visit to Pakistan underscored for me the necessity for deepening the dialogue with Islam, and in frank but warm ways to plead the case for reciprocity in all things. In many respects Pakistan is not a good advertisement for Islam; it is undoubtedly an underdeveloped country where ignorance is rife, where poverty blights the lives of millions and where inequality robs many of their natural inheritance as human beings. So much more could be done if the Churches were truly free to play their full part.

I was worried too about the Anglican Church of Pakistan. Perhaps largely as a result of its social situation, I found its Bishops too concerned with status and power. Much of their energy and money was spent in pursuing legal claims against one another. Within a few years of my visit I was asked by the Muslim High Court to try to resolve a legal wrangle concerning the Bishopric of Karachi, with two claimants in an unholy deadlock. It is difficult for us all to follow the one who said, 'Who is greater, the one who sits at table or the one who serves? But I am among you as one who serves.' Only when we learn that lesson can ministry and mission flourish.

Back home, inter-faith matters started to move up my table of priorities. It is not only Archbishops and Bishops who have a stake in this important field. The Duke of Edinburgh has long been convinced of the importance of harnessing faiths with respect to nature and wildlife, and he was able to use his unique office and engaging personality to serve the wider community. He gained much respect as a result. The Prince of Wales has also become a powerful advocate for deeper understanding among the faiths, especially Islam, and has given some serious and thoughtful lectures on the values of Islam and the contribution this great faith can make to the West.

Prince Charles's most controversial contribution to this debate was in his television interview with Jonathan Dimbleby, when he spoke of his desire to be seen as 'defender of faith' rather than 'defender of *the* faith' (which ironically was the title given to Henry VIII by the Papacy before he rejected Papal authority). He later explained that this did not represent a rejection of the Sovereign's traditional role as head of the Church of England, but was rather to develop a quite different idea. He wished to be associated with the spiritual in all people and of encounter with a Divine reality, expressible in many different forms and ways.

Personally I did not share the view that this was somehow a defining statement by the Prince. I saw it more as an off-the-cuff remark about his desire to foster spirituality. In many different areas of thought Prince Charles has shown himself to be an independent thinker. I too have always been uncomfortable with the phrase 'defender of the faith', if it means no more than the role of the monarchy in protecting the vested interests of the Church of England. The most I would say in criticism of Prince Charles's statement is that it could have been expressed better. But that is forgivable in the light of his great concern for spirituality as opposed to the coldness of materialism and secularism.

As time went on, I became convinced that Britain needed a Christian–Muslim Council or Forum similar to CCJ. On 1 May 1996 therefore I convened a meeting of religious leaders to glean their views. My arguments for the establishment of such a body came from a number of related convictions. Britain's Muslim community had grown to the extent that it was now the most significant non-Christian faith group. Many Muslims however, especially the young, felt estranged from British society. I was concerned that this mood of alienation, feeding on social ills such as unemployment, was leading to the radicalisation of Islam. A great deal of dialogue was taking place in the country, notably in cities like Bradford, where Islam was strong and where Christian leaders such as Bishop David Smith and his predecessor, Roy Williamson, had been alert to the need to foster good relationships. But much of the effort was unfocused.

The problems facing the creation of such a Council or Forum were offputting. Not the least of them was the fact that Islam is not organised hierarchically as Judaism and Christianity are. Some Muslim leaders responded to my suggestion with the objection that the wide cultural and ethnic differences between Muslims from the Indian subcontinent and those from the Middle East made it impossible for them to speak with one voice. Furthermore, I was told that many religious leaders do not speak English. The most prominent spokespeople for Muslim communities were often community leaders rather than Imams.

In the face of these and other difficulties the idea of a Forum was delayed until resources could be found to research it. In 1999 the idea came to the surface once more, and the Bishop of Aston, John Austin, is currently chairing an initiative to look at it again.

I was to experience the tensions between Islam and Christianity yet again in January 1999, when I paid a visit to Syria as the guest of the Syrian Orthodox Church and the Cilician Armenian Church. I was immediately struck by how hospitable and picturesque Syria was. From the condition of its infrastructure – roads and buildings – it appeared to be one of the most economically advanced Arab nations in the Middle East. Relations between the faiths also appeared warm and friendly. The leader of the Syrian Orthodox Church, Mar Ignatius Zakka I, an old and genial man, told me that nothing hindered his Church's ministry under President Hafez al Assad. This was echoed by Aram I, the forceful Catholicos of the Cilician Armenian Church.

'Can we do direct evangelism?' he asked, anticipating one of my questions. 'No, we can't and shouldn't. Does evangelism go on? Yes, of course it does, but in modest and discreet ways.' While that sounded satisfactory, of course it wasn't. A faith that cannot be presented freely is a tolerated but an imprisoned faith.

I developed this point later that evening when I gave a lecture on relations between Islam and Christianity, and addressed once more the urgent need for reciprocity. Again, the questioning was lively and sympathetic. There was, it seemed to me, a clear difference between the acceptance of freedom of religion by Muslim intellectuals and the less enlightened views of grassroots Islam.

The following day began with a visit to the Ommayed Mosque, which as a building was onto its third faith. It started life as a Greek temple, then became a Christian cathedral, and finally, when Islam swept through the Near East, passed into the hands of Muslims. I was struck by the beauty of the building, and particularly by the words in Greek above its entrance: 'The Kingdom of Christ is the Kingdom of eternal life'.

That, I thought, was a fortifying message as we left to join the many thousands at Friday prayers in the great Abu Nour Mosque, in which the Pope would speak a few years later. The mosque, which I was told accommodates more than sixteen thousand people, was packed, and once again I was impressed by the devotion of the men and boys who were assembled in serried rows before the Grand Mufti, Sheikh Ahmed Keftaro. I was welcomed by the Grand Mufti, and then invited to address the Muslim faithful. In my ten-minute address I spoke of the urgent need for our two great 'missionary' faiths to respect each other and work together for the common good. The substantial common ground we shared, I said, should encourage us to face the challenges together.

As I was speaking I became a little uneasy when, one by one, twenty or so men sitting directly in front of me stood up and left. Since I had just spoken of my commitment to Jesus Christ as saviour of the world which called me to share him with everyone, I wondered if it was that which had caused offence. I had, however, followed it immediately by saying that 'It requires me to listen to others and respect the faith journey of another person and be challenged by it,' so only the ultra-sensitive could possibly have been offended.

When I had concluded, the Sheikh thanked me profusely, and we left. On my return to Ambassador Basil Eastwood's residence I was informed that the Grand Mufti had rung to apologise for the interruption caused by the men who had left. They were, he said, Imams whose job it was to take his message to other mosques in the city. I was comforted to know that.

The next day I was scheduled to meet President Assad, but as no precise time had been set, I fulfilled several Church engagements in the vicinity of the presidential palace. As the day dragged by I began to feel I was wasting my time, but Basil Eastwood assured me, 'Don't worry. The call will come.' The call in fact came at about 2.30 p.m., and I was invited to meet the President in the grand palace overlooking Damascus.

The ascent to it was obviously intended to make a statement about the importance of the President. After a long walk through a series of large rooms we entered a waiting room, where we were eventually joined by the President, who looked much older than he appeared in the posters that dotted the city. The customary photos were taken, and then we began what turned out to be a long and unsatisfactory discussion. President Assad looked back in a self-congratulatory way on his successes. His answers to questions took the form of long and involved speeches delivered in a tired and feeble voice. A question about Israel provoked a long historical survey of Israel's position in the Middle East since 1948, and how untrustworthy the Jews were in negotiations. It was interesting that President Assad started his peroration in 1948, as if there were no Jews in the Middle East before then. To a further question about whether he was optimistic about the prospects of a peace settlement between Israel and other Arab nations, the long answer conveyed a short, emphatic 'no'.

As we drove away from the splendour of the palace through the streets of Damascus, with the President's face on practically every corner and with his words ringing in our ears, the inherent flaws of a dictatorship were all too evident. Even among Christian circles in Syria I heard too often the President's name mentioned with respect verging on awe. The previous evening a young man at a lively Christian youth event had spoken with enthusiasm of 'our leader President Assad who has given us such peace and security'.

But Syria did not leave us without hope for Christian–Muslim dialogue. It was clear that the Grand Mufti was well disposed towards having closer relationships with Christians. It would be possible to build on that. However, I was left with a deeper and more troubling set of questions. I began to wonder if we Christians should learn from the experience of Muslims in the West, who are not reticent in calling for greater rights and privileges in the countries where they live. Could it be that there is a quietist strain in Christianity which makes us unwilling to mount protests, demonstrate or make a noise? Perhaps it is time for Christians to take to the streets peacefully in protest when circumstances demand it.

*   *   *

Back home, the dying years of the old millennium saw a mounting interest in the new one. The determination of both Conservative and Labour governments to spend millions of pounds of public and lottery money on a Dome in Greenwich was met by widespread scepticism and indifference among the general public. But as it became known that exhibitions were going to be mounted within the Dome, faith communities agreed that it was important to be involved. This, I recall, was met with some amazement by one government Minister, who was heard to remark, 'What has faith to do with the Millennium?' When it was pointed out to her that BC and AD had something to do with Christianity, she was suitably embarrassed.

It was not easy to get a foot in the door given these attitudes in government and in Whitehall, and as a result my Chaplain at the time, Colin Fletcher, was deputed to bring together an inter-faith group, known as the Lambeth Group. This body, representing the main faiths, did a splendid job in determining the shape of what eventually became the 'Faith Zone' – one of thirteen zones in the Dome. In the opinion of many it was one of the more imaginative and thoughtful of the zones, partly because of the way it found a sensible balance between celebrating the Christian inheritance of Britain and the impact of the Church on the landscape, while at the same time honouring the presence of other faith communities.

The Reverend Stephen Lynas, a former BBC journalist, accepted an invitation to be the Millennium Officer for the Churches – a post that included raising interest among the Churches as well as representing them in all matters to do with the millennium celebrations. My task was to launch the British millennium celebrations with prayers in the Dome at the stroke of midnight. In some ways it was not an enviable assignment: the association of prayer with New Year revelry is not an obvious one. To soften the impact, we agreed with the BBC and Dome staff that involving a few children with the prayers would help to create the right kind of spirit.

As I stood backstage on New Year's Eve waiting for my cue I could hear the boisterous and cheerful noise of the crowd – many of whom had been imbibing a different kind of spirit. When the Queen and Prince Philip entered there was a great welcoming cry which seemed to go on and on. The producer frantically waved at me to get going, but the noise was deafening, and I knew the children were extremely nervous. I waited a little while longer, although I could see the producer imploring the heavens. Finally the noise subsided, and then a brief moment was spent in turning to God to welcome the new era. The Queen said to me when I next met her: 'I felt so sorry for you when I saw you on the platform with the children. The noise around us was ear-shattering! We are glad you waited to get attention. Thank you.'

A much more thrilling millennium moment for me was the distribution of a copy of my booklet *Jesus 2000* with every copy of the *News of the World*. Over four million booklets were given away, courtesy of the paper's owner Rupert Murdoch. The idea was born the preceding September, when I decided to write to Rupert Murdoch to ask him if he would give away a copy of my booklet with every newspaper. I was aware that it was a cheeky initiative, not least because it would cost in the region of £400,000. To my surprise and joy he welcomed the idea. Many appreciative letters followed from readers, some of whom started on a journey into the Christian faith as a result of reading the booklet.

The tragedy of 11 September 2001 made no significant difference to my already burning commitment to inter-faith dialogue, but it brought home its importance with renewed urgency. The atrocity seemed to confirm to many Westerners that Islam had a darker side which fostered terrorism. Moderate Muslims were becoming increasingly troubled by alienated young men susceptible to the blandishments of radical clerics, who preached a barely veiled message of terror. Yet it was a revelation to many Westerners to learn that terrorists were prepared to take their own lives in order to kill as many innocents as possible, while reciting the Koran in the mistaken belief that they would have instant access to Paradise.

In the address I gave in St Paul's Cathedral following the attacks on the Twin Towers and the Pentagon, I appealed to the United States and the West in general not to respond with retaliation: 'For the flower of democracy to flourish it must grow in the soil of justice. Yes, those responsible for such barbaric acts must be held to account. But we must be guided by higher goals than mere revenge. As we battle with evil, our goal must be a world where such violence is a thing of the past.' The unspoken question, of course, was how do we touch the deep roots of hatred that some Muslims feel for the West, and for America in particular? As John Esposito points out in his book, *Unholy War*: 'How we understand Islam and the Muslim world will affect how we address the causes of terrorism and of anti-Americanism and whether we preserve our American values at home and abroad. We must be able to move beyond political rhetoric, beyond the world of black and white, of unadulterated good versus evil invoked not only by bin Laden and those like him but by his opponents as well.'

The Sunday after 11 September the Prime Minister phoned me, and asked if I felt the time had come to deepen the dialogue with Islam. I was cautious to begin with, knowing the weakness of politicians for being seen to be doing something. I asked him if he was aware of the range of inter-faith dialogue that was going on, not only in Britain but internationally. I rattled off several bodies with which I had direct links, including the Parliament of World Religions and the World Conference on Religion and Peace. No, the Prime Minister was not aware of such bodies, but he asked if I thought the present moment offered an opportunity to develop these contacts. If so, what form might an initiative take?

I asked him for time to reflect on the issue, assuring him that I shared his sense of urgency, but was wary of knee-jerk reactions. I immediately telephoned Bishop Michael Nazir-Ali, who is well versed in Muslim–Christian dialogue. His view was positive, and we agreed that a top-level international meeting of scholars from both sides could yield fruitful results. I contacted the Prime Minister and outlined the idea. He had already a similar scheme in mind, and a common approach was quickly agreed. I was asked to take the lead in organising the event, and he promised that I would receive every assistance from himself and his senior staff. I felt grateful that we had a Prime Minister with the breadth of vision to view faith as an element of statecraft.

The first meeting of the scholarly seminar took place at Lambeth Palace in January 2002, and attracted a great deal of attention. In a joint article in *The Times*, Sheikh Zaki Badawi and I stated that one of the key challenges was how to handle differences. Our goal was not only understanding, we wrote, but the building of new bridges of friendship and respect that would isolate the terrorists by bringing two great faiths closer together.

It was indeed the theme of 'Building Bridges' that focused the attention of the forty participants over the two-day conference introduced by the Prime Minister, His Royal Highness Prince El Hassan bin Talal of Jordan and myself. Drawn from every part of the world, the participants engaged in a high level of scholarship. We heard moving and telling stories. Dr Mustapha Ceric of Bosnia described the terrifying ordeal of living through a conflict in which he thought all Muslims, including himself, would be killed. Archbishop Henri Teissier of Algiers spoke softly of the terror of being hunted by Muslim fundamentalists a few years ago, and being rescued by a Muslim family.

It was a rich and fruitful conference, but no one was under any illusion that our job was done; it was in fact only a beginning, and would have to continue for years to come if it was to achieve its aims. The participants met again in Qatar in 2003, and will meet in Washington in 2004. It may be a top-down approach intellectually, but it could have an important role in changing the mind-set of fundamentalists.

Overlapping with the Muslim–Christian 'Building Bridges' initiative was a Middle East project which developed from modest beginnings. In July 2000 I heard that a long-promised United States

Episcopal Church visit to the Anglican Church in the Holy Land had been cancelled because of safety worries. Bishop Riah, the diocesan Bishop, was hurt and distressed; he had declared that his own brothers and sisters in the West were now deserting him. Partly to reassure him that this was not true, Eileen and I decided to pay a pastoral visit to the Holy Land, accompanied by Archbishop Robin Eames, Primate of Ireland, whose stature as a Church leader and respected role in the peace process in Northern Ireland made him an ideal companion.

This was to be the most revealing of all the visits I paid to that sad and damaged land. We went first of all to Beit Jalah, on the outskirts of Bethlehem, to see the damage to this once prosperous middle-class district where for many years Christians and Muslims had lived side by side. It was impossible for us to imagine the fear that must have been felt by the many families who huddled for safety in these formerly beautiful houses as Israeli tanks tore them apart. We went to the Bethlehem Arab Rehabilitation Centre, a modern hospital with ninety beds, to speak to some of those who had been caught up in the hostilities. We saw teenagers with the most horrific injuries – one young man had had part of his skull sliced off by a shell. This was the result, we were told, of random shooting by the Israel Defence Force. We had, of course, no way of assessing the truth or falsehood of the claim, but there was no doubt that the large number of young people in the hospital were evidence of shooting on a significant scale, largely unreported by the world's press.

Yet even in such calamitous situations, human fortitude and good humour shone through. I met Mr Shahadeh, an old, blind lawyer who told me of an amusing conversation with his four-year-old grandson, who said to him, 'Why do you have your eyes closed?' Mr Shahadeh replied, 'Because I'm blind. I cannot see.' The little boy then asked, 'How do you see then?' Mr Shahadeh replied patiently, 'I see with the eyes of my heart.' The boy replied, 'In that case, Granddad, you can see my new blue trousers!' Mr Shahadeh then observed to me, 'There are different ways of seeing, and perhaps

Jews and Arabs are blind to a new reality God is trying to show us.'

The following two days saw us, accompanied by Geoffrey Adams, the British Consul General to Palestine, in Gaza visiting Chairman Yasser Arafat. We were shown into his inner sanctum, where we had been several times before. Arafat was in very good form. There were signs of Parkinson's disease, but he was confident and bullish about his situation and 'his people'. He thought that the Israeli policy was to exterminate all Palestinians, but said they 'would never be defeated by this enemy'. By 'enemy' he did not mean the Jewish people but Prime Minister Ariel Sharon, whom he compared unfavourably with 'my friend Rabin'.

I asked him if he wanted peace. His answer was a clear 'yes', but in response to my probing about Palestinian atrocities he blamed them on Hamas and Jihad factions. He said he had no jurisdiction over extreme groups – a claim that sounded very unconvincing to me. If he indeed had no control over extremist groups, it was an admission of weakness and failure at the heart of his government.

Within a few hours we were to see fighting between factions at first hand. It was our desire to visit the Anglican hospital that for more than a century had given faithful care and attention to generations of Palestinians. As we approached the district we were turned away by police because, we were told, two feuding families were engaged in a fight to the death; already six people had been killed. Sadly it seemed that such internecine disputes were part of the Palestinian temperament, now deeply traumatised by Israeli occupation of their land.

Two days later, Robin Eames and I had a close discussion with Prime Minister Sharon. I was struck by his apparent jovialness. He said that he esteemed very highly the contribution that religious leaders made to peace, and was grateful for the work the Anglican Church was doing. But soon his tone hardened, and I could easily see his steel and determination. In his view the blame for the Palestinians' present terrorist tactics could be laid squarely at the door of Arafat. I repeated Arafat's words to me that he had no control over the wild men, at which the Prime Minister snorted in derision. Of course Arafat could call off Hamas, Sharon said. After all, he was paying each one of them!

I returned home from this visit more despondent than I had ever been about the difficulties facing peace talks. To some degree I saw Arafat and Sharon as mirror images of one another; two old men, living in the past, fighting for absolute positions for their own people and failing to realise that statecraft has to include compromise and negotiation.

I did not think of any follow-up until the autumn, when Canon Andrew White, Director of Coventry Cathedral's International Centre for Reconciliation, brought me a message from the Israeli Foreign Minister, Shimon Peres, who was keen to have my help in bringing all the religious leaders in the Holy Land together to make a statement calling for peace. I told Andrew that in principle I would be happy to assist, but that the Israeli authorities would have to contact me personally.

On Boxing Day, Rabbi Michael Melchior, number two in the Israeli Foreign Office, a distinguished and likeable Rabbi and politician, rang to plead for my help. Apparently all religious leaders in the Holy Land were very keen to be involved, but a senior outsider was required to chair a conference that was likely to be very demanding. The date suggested was only three weeks away, and he required an answer at once.

The short notice meant that my already overcrowded diary had to be rearranged, but the conference was an irresistible challenge. There would be the problem of overcoming deep distrust – many of the participants had never met. A further quandary was that a location outside Israel had to be found, because there was no neutral venue within it; eventually Alexandria would be settled upon. Then I discovered that the Co-Chair would be my old and good friend Dr Mohammed Sayed Tantawi, Grand Imam of Al-Azhar, who couldn't speak English, so the burden of chairing would inevitably fall on me. Whether the assembled Middle Eastern religious leaders would accept the authority of a complete outsider was another question. But these challenges made the request compelling to me.

On 19 January 2001 my party and I flew to Ben Gurion airport, where we were met by Sherrard Cowper-Coles, British Ambassador to Israel, and Rabbi Michael Melchior, who would lead the Jewish delegation to the summit. I went by car to see Yasser Arafat and get his view on the proposed summit. As we drove from Jerusalem in the early evening we could see the desperate conditions in which many Palestinians lived, and the deteriorating infrastructure. Arafat's HQ was no better – simply a squalid collection of buildings in a large compound. Arafat put on a brave and cheerful exterior, but his situation was clearly very worrying. He declared his support for the meeting of faith leaders and sent us off with a cheery wave.

The following morning I spent time with Israeli Foreign Minister Shimon Peres, who had given his backing to the conference. There was one interesting moment when, having welcomed the initiative, he remarked thoughtfully, 'Politicians have to compromise; religious leaders deal in absolutes.'

I challenged this immediately, on both political and religious grounds. 'Is not Israel in danger of dealing in absolutes?' I asked. Unless Israel backed away from building on the occupied territories, and negotiated according to UN Resolutions, the conflict would continue. Did he not realise that Israel had lost the moral high ground, as far as world opinion was concerned? Then, turning to religious leaders, I partly agreed with his viewpoint, but said that unless faith leaders accepted that their absolutes could be held with dignity and honour alongside other absolutes, violence would continue. The challenge facing us in Alexandria was that of humility. Could we make room for others?

Shortly afterwards we met Prime Minister Ariel Sharon once again. He was in cheerful mood, and welcomed 'all the help we can get'. But he added that while Israel was prepared to make painful concessions, he would not compromise on security.

We flew to Alexandria courtesy of the Norwegian government,

who had paid for the plane, and for three days sought to hammer out a document which allowed all three sides – Muslim, Jew and Christian – to share their anger, grief and disappointment. All three delegations comprised distinguished leaders with proven records in negotiation. Of Rabbi Michael Melchior's ability and integrity there was not a shadow of doubt. The Muslim delegation was led by Sheikh Talal Sidr, a quietly spoken man with a rugged face who I came to esteem very highly for his wisdom and faith. A former Hamas commander, he had become convinced that the way of violence represents a failure in statecraft. The leader of the Christians was the Latin Patriarch, Michel Sabah, whose fierce and outspoken support of the Palestinian people had made him a thorn in the flesh of successive Israeli governments.

Even though the most able and conscientious leaders were taking part, that did not guarantee a successful outcome. There were moments when it seemed that the conference was about to break up in disorder; then sanity would return, tempers would be calmed and the language of reason would replace that of bitter recrimination. It was, without exaggeration, the toughest meeting I have ever chaired. A significant turning point came at the end of one long day when the Sephardi Chief Rabbi Bakshi-Doron, a very eminent figure in Judaism, suddenly asked all the Muslims present to join him for an informal meeting in his hotel room. I was told the following day that the meeting went on for several hours, and the Chief Rabbi was deeply touched by what he heard about the suffering of the Palestine people. Just as significantly, the Muslims were impressed by the Chief Rabbi's humanity and concern. A few days later when we were sitting in the Presidential Palace waiting to meet President Hosni Mubarak, I idly asked him whether he had ever visited Egypt before. His reply was memorable: 'Not personally,' he said, 'but we came here three and a half thousand years ago, and have no desire to return!' It was the most perfect example of racial memory.

At the end of three days we had agreed a statement that was signed by all with great relief and euphoria. We were helped in achieving this not only by Canon Andrew White and his colleagues from Coventry Cathedral, but also by the drafting skills of John Sawyer, British Ambassador to Egypt, and Jeremy Harris, my staff colleague. The declaration unambiguously called on all people of faith to work for peace: 'We declare our commitment to ending the violence and bloodshed that denies the right to life and dignity ... killing innocents in the name of God is a desecration of His Holy name and defames religion in the world. The violence in the Holy Land is an evil which must be opposed by all people of good faith.' The declaration gave its support to political initiatives such as the Mitchell proposals, and gave an undertaking that it was not an end but a beginning.

The response was mixed. The Arab and Jewish press attended the press conference at the Sheraton Hotel afterwards, and news of the declaration hit the front pages in the Middle East. Disappointingly, though, there was hardly any sign of Western journalists, and even the BBC did not bother to send a team out to cover it. Once again, I thought this an example of dangerously narrow editorial policies, divorced from the realities of life in a region such as this. One can no more ignore religion in the Middle East than one can ignore people in politics – they belong together. It was appropriate that the last significant event for me as Archbishop, a week before I left office, was to be involved in the second summit of the religious leaders at Lambeth Palace. Under the faithful guidance of Andrew White and the leading participants the task of changing attitudes in Islam, Judaism and Christianity continues. There are no quick fixes; it is a patient, slow work of drawing out the best in each religion to confront and overcome the prejudice, bitterness and ignorance in all of us.

What is the future of inter-faith co-operation? I am glad that diplomats and politicians are beginning to place an emphasis on understanding religion. But more can and should be done. One cannot understand culture if one does not understand the abiding values that undergird societies and communities, especially in the developing world. I would like to see Christian politicians less apolo-getic or 'neutral' in stating what they personally believe. Such an approach would help to build trust rather than create suspicion from other faith communities. In the fine words of the leading Anglican writer on Islam, Kenneth Cragg: 'In order to be hospitable, one has to have a home.'

During my time as Archbishop I was profoundly impressed by the willingness of our Royal Family and the two governments I have been privileged to work with to include faith leaders in significant national moments. Those of other faiths have told me many times how much they appreciate this. Yet if politicians are to be challenged to take faith more seriously, religious adherents must realise that they are under judgement too. However exclusive the claims for our faith or sect, we have to live in pluralistic societies where no one group can impose its way of life upon another. Freedom, equality and fraternity are the key values that define good civil society. In our day it is Islam that faces the greatest challenge. In those communities where Islam dominates, the Muslim majority must be possessed of the grace to allow other faith communities to blossom and flourish. Equally importantly, in the light of the terrorism associated with Al-Qaeda, Islam must discipline, shame and marginalise those who disgrace its name.

Walt Whitman accurately foretold our time when he said: 'We hear the bawling and din, we are reach'd at by divisions, jealousies, recriminations on every side.' I would like to believe, with him, that one day 'the men and women of races, ages to come, may prove brethren and lovers'.

21

The Glory of the Crown

'To be a King and wear a crown is a thing more glorious to them that see it than it is pleasant to them that bear it. For myself, I was never so much enticed with the glorious name of a King or royal authority of a Queen as delighted that God hath made me His instrument to maintain His truth and glory, and to defend this kingdom from peril, dishonour, tyranny and oppression.'

Queen Elizabeth I

THE MONARCHY AND THE ROYAL FAMILY come under constant criticism in the British press. The institution is often accused of being a drain on public finances, and it is sometimes claimed that it is incompatible with the democratic principle. From time to time individual members of the Royal Family are slated for their lifestyle, and prurient eyes are continually on the lookout for any sign of misconduct. In spite of such disparagement and censure, the stock of the Royal Family remains high among the general public, and surveys indicate widespread support for it.

Before becoming a Bishop I had had very little contact with the Royal Family. If asked my opinion of the institution of the monarchy, I would have responded that on balance it should be preserved, because it was preferable to any of the alternatives. This assessment was to change radically from the moment I became Archbishop of Canterbury, and was thrust into close contact with the monarchy, its duties and responsibilities, its demands and its concerns.

On 16 April 1991 Eileen and I were driven to Windsor Castle, where I was due to pay Homage to Her Majesty. We were shown to a highly impressive suite of rooms overlooking the long drive leading through the park, and two valets immediately busied themselves unpacking our cases. Later we were amused to find that we had been given separate bedrooms, our underclothes had been packed neatly in gauze, and my white ecclesiastical 'rochet', needed for the Homage, which I hunted for frantically, had been put on a hanger alongside Eileen's nightclothes – my valet obviously thought I wore it to bed.

Homage is a form of commitment made by Bishops and Cabinet Ministers on taking up office. One is required to kneel before the sovereign, who places her hands outside the new Archbishop or Bishop's hands, and one remains in that position until the oath is administered by the Home Secretary and repeated by the Bishop. It was a moving and special moment, and is a ceremony that the Queen takes very seriously. Dinner followed with Prince Philip and Princess Margaret and a few guests, including Neil and Glenys Kinnock. At one point, when Eileen was serving herself from the meat dish being offered to her, the waiter quietly murmured in her ear, 'Please don't take three pieces, Mrs Carey. Mr Kinnock has taken three, and there won't be enough to go round.' It was reassuring to be reminded that economy reigns at Windsor as well as elsewhere.

Following dinner all the guests were taken on a personal tour of the Royal art collection and library by the Queen and Princess Margaret. Among the exhibits was a collection of Her Majesty's childhood drawings and diaries. She told us with great amusement of one Bishop who was so astonished at the extraordinary feat of a Princess doing something ordinary that he exclaimed on seeing her childish script, 'Did you write it in your own hand?' To which the Queen said, 'In what other hand could I have possibly done it?' More moving to me was to see for the first time the original treatise of Henry VIII's Defence of the Faith against Martin Luther, and the reformer's defiant response. There was a special poignancy in seeing documents that led to such momentous changes in the

Church and the nation long ago – including my own new office.

My meetings with the Queen from that moment on brought home to me the sacramental manner in which she views her own office. That God had called her from birth to fulfil her responsibilities as sovereign was very evidently her conviction, and it was founded on a firm Christian faith which also took the form of duty – not in the sense of a burden, but of glad service. She, like her great namesake Elizabeth I, viewed her role as being an 'instrument', in maintaining a noble service to all her subjects.

I grew to know other members of the Royal Family as time went by. I became a devoted fan of Queen Elizabeth, the Queen Mother, whose naturalness and deep interest in people were as attractive and endearing as her famous 'wave'. At state banquets it was often my privilege to escort the Queen Mother – indeed, it became such a habit that on one occasion, as the royal line was forming, Prince Philip hurried up his mother-in-law with the words, 'Come on, Mother – your taxi is waiting!' She would beam with delight, and holding firmly on to my arm we would enter behind the Queen to the strains of the National Anthem.

My first state banquet was memorable, not least for the reason that as we advanced past the standing guests to the top table, I realised with some dismay that I did not have the foggiest idea which was the Queen Mother's chair. Almost as if she had read my thoughts she said quietly, 'As a concession to my old age, my chair is the one with arms.' 'Ah, bless you, Ma'am!' I said under my breath. She was a wonderful conversationalist. I was astounded when on one occasion, after I had mentioned Cardinal Newman, whose preaching in Oxford around 1840 changed the lives of many young undergraduates, she commented thoughtfully, 'My grandfather was also deeply influenced by John Henry Newman.' In that one sentence she had travelled back nearly 160 years in a mere two generations. I was her eighth Archbishop of Canterbury, and she had some delightful anecdotes of my predecessors – some of a decidedly uncomplimentary nature, but never malicious.

There was a particular bond between the Queen Mother and Prince Charles, and she would speak devotedly of him and his great commitment to many causes. However, soon after my appointment I began to sense that the Royal Family were worried about his marriage. The press were beginning to scent a huge story, and by 1992 it was clear that the marriage was unravelling fast. The papers were speculating about the effects of Diana's rumoured bulimia on her physical and mental health. To make matters worse, before long claims were being made that Mrs Camilla Parker Bowles was very closely involved with Prince Charles, and that this relationship was putting great strain on an already fragile marriage. The questions I could not duck were: 'What can I do, and what ought I to do?' To do nothing would have been an evasion of responsibility. As the Royal Family's 'parish priest', I could not walk away from them when they were in trouble, and Charles and Diana were no ordinary couple. They were central to the Royal Family, and to the very future of the monarchy. It would have been irresponsible of me not to get involved, and to offer what guidance I could.

At a private meeting with the Prime Minister in July I was told that the couple were intending to separate in the autumn, and were likely to divorce the following year. John Major felt that this could precipitate a constitutional crisis, and that some preparatory work on constitutional matters should be undertaken by our staffs. We agreed that we should meet as soon as diaries allowed with the Lord Chancellor Lord Mackay, Cabinet Secretary Robin Butler and Foreign Secretary Douglas Hurd. In December the nation was rocked by the shockingly unscrupulous release of a recording of a private telephone conversation between Prince Charles and Mrs Parker Bowles, an affair popularly known as 'Camillagate'. From that moment any hopes for a dignified ending to the marriage were destroyed. It was hardly surprising that Her Majesty, following the dreadful fire which swept through St George's Hall at Windsor Castle that year, spoke so movingly of 1992 as an 'annus horribilis'. Indeed it had been, and her words touched many.

Conversations with both wounded people revealed the depths of pain and undisguised loathing, mingled with nostalgia and love, that are often present in dying relationships. Neither Charles nor Diana made any secret of the sadness they felt, and the deep emotional estrangement that went with it. In my opinion the relationship was doomed, and it was my pastoral duty to assist them to conclude their marriage with grace and understanding, and to bring a Christian perspective to bear on their situation and relationship. This was, frankly, very difficult, and I often found myself trapped between the moral guidelines of the Church and the situation of the couple whose marital troubles were the talking point of the entire world. Sadly, I never saw them together, because by the time I became Archbishop the marriage was all but over.

The pastoral situation was made more difficult by the admission of both that they had committed adultery. It may be that their advisers had encouraged them to be open, but in my opinion it was a mistaken policy. Although modern British society is very tolerant in its attitude to the sins and weaknesses of its members, it remains prurient about the behaviour of those in authority. The Royal Family in particular is expected to embody values that society does not necessarily expect others to uphold. My task was made more difficult by those who wanted me to raise my voice in condemnation of both parties for having committed adultery. To have done so would have been a betrayal of my duty of pastoral concern.

The deteriorating relationship between the Prince and Princess of Wales did not diminish my admiration for them both. Prince Charles was and is a man of great stature and vision. His commitment to young people through the Prince's Trust, his passion for excellence in architecture, care for the environment and concern for positive inter-faith relationships are all aspects of his ideological interests. He is deeply committed to the welfare of all, and a more caring and compassionate man would be hard to find.

I had first met Diana in 1989, when I conducted a wedding in Bath Abbey. She came with her two young sons, who greeted me politely, and I watched with admiration as she ushered them into the great congregation, encouraging them to smile and wave at people. It was clear that she was a devoted and caring mother. My first meeting with her in my new role as Archbishop came at the first state banquet I attended at Buckingham Palace, when I had the Queen Mother on my left and Diana on my right. She too was a good conversationalist, and she impressed me with her concern for the poor and the marginalised. I have never shared the view of some critics that her care for others was a sham, merely a way to get attention and a reflection of her craving to be loved. It was obvious that she had a caring heart and was a woman of great compassion, driven by clear ideals. She was also strikingly beautiful, and the eyes of all were drawn towards her. I had to admit to myself that at her wedding I had not perceived her as particularly beautiful – good-looking, yes, but not remarkably so. Now, however, she had matured and had been groomed to become one of the most beautiful women in the world. She knew it, of course, and consequently took great care of herself, exercising daily and worrying over her health.

Diana was always a pleasure to talk with. She had the common touch in abundance, and rather like the Queen Mother was able to reach out to people in an extraordinary way. There was clearly an actress in her – she could work a crowd in a style that would have done justice to any Hollywood star, yet she was also gifted at engaging with individuals and making them feel very special too. Her compassion for those suffering from HIV/AIDS is of course well known – less well known were the hours she spent with individuals suffering from that dreadful illness. Sometimes she would leave her home late at night to sit at the bedside of a sick person.

One of her role models was Mother Teresa, and there was speculation that Diana would one day become a Roman Catholic. I knew differently: if it ever crossed her mind, it was only a passing thought. Indeed, I don't think institutional religion had great importance to her. She had a faith, a real faith in God, but it had not yet blossomed into a full, explicit Christian commitment

Perhaps the uncertainty of her inner convictions related to the restlessness in her relationships. She often stated her desire to remain married to Prince Charles, but I had to conclude that there was little evidence that she was prepared to make the marriage work. Later, evidence was to emerge that the Princess herself was in contact with several journalists, and had given them her side of the story, thus further fuelling the intrigue and deepening the distress.

As the marriage moved towards total estrangement I considered it my pastoral duty to maintain strong independent links with both of them, and to steer a neutral course that would not suck me into taking sides. This was far from easy, as Diana was keen to secure the sympathy of the public. She managed that very successfully at a national level, but I was led to conclude with some sorrow that Charles was more sinned against than sinning. There was a streak in Diana's psychological make-up that would not allow her to give in – even though she claimed to the last that she never wanted a divorce.

In the press, the story was fast becoming a turf war between two tabloids in particular, the *Sun* and the *Mirror*. On 7 December 1993 the *Sun* had a front-page story that 'the Archbishop of Canterbury does not believe Charles should be King'. I issued an immediate denial as soon as my Press Officer told me about it, and phoned Sir Robert Fellowes, the Queen's Private Secretary, to assure Her Majesty that the story had no basis. The *Mirror* attacked the *Sun*, stating that I had declared its claims 'a pack of lies'. In the meantime discussions were proceeding between the Prime Minister, the Lord Chancellor, the Home Secretary and myself regarding the constitutional issues involved, particularly as it seemed that the relationship between Prince Charles and Camilla Parker Bowles would inevitably affect the delicate balance of monarchy, Church and state.

I was amazed by the ability of both Charles and Diana to keep going despite the personal trauma and the enormous public interest and intense media scrutiny. Diana would greet me in the same enthusiastic and charming way as ever, and would tell me about her visits to those suffering from AIDS/HIV and her deepening interest in other causes. Her commitment to these issues was deeply sincere, even if it was more rooted in emotion than in ideology. But from time to time her distress at the inevitability of divorce led her to express anger against Charles and his staff, who she felt wanted to remove her from the royal circle. Charles too kept going, with the media following every move he made. His dedication to his role followed the same pattern as his mother's – unswerving loyalty to the nation and to its betterment.

On 28 August 1996 Charles and Diana were divorced – the inevitable yet extremely sad ending of a relationship which had begun so promisingly fifteen years before. It meant that Diana was no longer, strictly speaking, a member of the Royal Family, although the Queen was determined to continue to treat her as such. Prince Charles, well aware of the anxieties aroused by his divorce and his continuing friendship with Mrs Parker Bowles, let it be known that he had no intention of marriage. This, I knew, would not be sufficient to satisfy the prurient intrusiveness of the international press, but I did not realise that I would soon be dragged into the controversy.

In August 1997 I visited the Church in Australia, and at a press conference in Sydney a question about Prince Charles was put. I replied that the Prince of Wales had stated he had no intention of remarrying. Back came the less than innocent question, 'But what if he did?' I responded, 'Well, that would constitute a crisis.' That gave the journalists the angle they were looking for. What I had said a moment before was entirely ignored. It did not matter a fig that the Prince had given an undertaking that he would not remarry – I had said that his remarriage would be a constitutional crisis, and that was the news that sped around the world.

My last meetings with Diana following her divorce revealed a Princess who was determined to go her own way and show the world what she was made of. The 'Jekyll and Hyde' sides to her character came out strongly in her deep upset and bitterness about Charles and the divorce, which she claimed she never desired yet to which, sadly, she had contributed greatly. The other side was her essential

compassion and desire to make a difference, and to use her prominence to help good causes. One that she took a great interest in was
the issue of landmines, in Angola and elsewhere. I sent her a letter
written to me by a Ugandan Bishop, MacCleod Baker, who had lost
his wife because of a landmine. Diana wrote a deeply sensitive reply
to me that she asked me to pass on to Bishop MacCleod.

The week that began with the news of Diana's death in Paris in
the early hours of Sunday, 31 August 1997 will always stay with me
as one of the most eventful and extraordinary of my ministry. We
were on holiday at the time. We had accepted an invitation to attend
a friend's seventieth birthday party in Altrincham, and had left Lambeth Palace the previous afternoon. We stayed overnight in a small
hotel, and I was in the shower at 7.55 a.m. when the strains of the
National Anthem came from the radio in the bedroom. Eileen called
out, 'I think there has been a Royal death during the night.' I grabbed
a towel and dashed into the bedroom, and we listened in silence to the
terrible news that Diana and her companion Dodi Fayed had been
killed in a car crash in the early hours of the morning. I telephoned
Lambeth Palace at once and spoke to Bishop Frank Sargeant, my
Chief of Staff. He had been trying to contact me since 5 a.m. For
the first and last time ever I had not given him an address at which
I could be contacted, and nor was my mobile phone turned on.

I was at once thrust into radio and television interviews for
most of the morning. Prime Minister Tony Blair made an impressive
off-the-cuff statement on his way to church and I felt he caught the
mood of the nation extremely well. I was less comfortable with the
description of Diana as 'the people's Princess', which I sensed might
encourage the temptation of some to make her an icon to set against
the Royal Family. These fears were to be realised that week. There
seemed to be a mounting hysteria, fuelled by the media's focus on
this very beautiful but in other ways unremarkable person. Now it
seemed she would have her posthumous revenge, by shaking the
Royal Family to its foundations.

On Monday morning I was in touch with the Dean of Westminster, Wesley Carr, concerning the funeral service which would be held that Saturday. I had every confidence that the Abbey would conduct the service brilliantly despite the short notice, but I was very concerned that Diana's brother Charles Spencer had been invited to give the address. I felt this was a great mistake. It is my conviction, backed by the Prayer Book, that only clergy and those authorised, such as Readers, should preach at funeral services, as opposed to memorial services. But there was little I could do other than advise, since the Abbey, as a 'Royal Peculiar', came directly under the authority of Her Majesty. I phoned Charles Spencer and offered my help, urging him to bring out the Christian message of hope and life evermore in God. He listened politely, but I had the impression that he already had clear ideas about what he wanted to say.

The death of the Princess of Wales struck a deep chord in the emotions and imaginations of people not only in Britain but around the world. So many tributes were left outside the gates of Buckingham Palace and Kensington Palace that within a few days the banks of flowers stretched almost as far as the eye could see. The Church responded magnificently. Many hundreds of churches laid on special services which were packed to the doors, and it was clear that people were grieving as if a dearly loved member of their own family had died. John Humphrys, in an interview for Radio 4's *Today* programme, suggested to me that it appeared a national spiritual revival was in progress. I replied that I wished that were the case, even though one could not discount the possibility that entangled in the sincere grief of so many, some groping after God and meaning was going on. I thought it more likely that it was simply an emotional reaction to the death of a popular Princess who through the virtual reality of television had become not only an icon of beauty and youth, but a presence in the lives of many people.

Nonetheless, the extraordinary display of public grief also suggested to me the basic 'niceness' of ordinary people, which I believe to be part and parcel of our spiritual nature and therefore not to be dismissed as 'unspiritual'. But I was uneasy at the hysteria being whipped up by some sections of the press. I gave the 'Thought for the Day' on the *Today* programme on the day of the funeral, and attempted to address the sense of loss that so many were feeling.

The prayers that I was preparing that week would be a crucial element of the funeral service, and I duly sent a draft to the Dean of Westminster to get comments from those directly involved. I was taken aback when the reaction revealed intense bitterness. It was reported to me that the Spencer family did not want any mention of the Royal Family in the prayers, and that in retaliation Buckingham Palace had insisted that there must be a separate prayer for the Royal Family, and that the words 'people's Princess' be removed. This was not an occasion to stand on one's dignity. It was a time of exceptional bewilderment, and the strain was affecting everybody. The final draft of the prayers satisfied all concerned.

The pressure on the Royal Family mounted during the week. Bitter, and in my view unjustified, criticism was directed at the Queen for remaining in Scotland instead of being with her people 'in their hour of need'. There seemed to be little comprehension that the Queen might have felt it better to stay out of the public eye for the sake of two young Princes who had just lost their mother. There were also complaints that the Royal Flag over Buckingham Palace was not at half-mast. A few days before the funeral a Lady-in-Waiting from the palace phoned me to say that, although she was only speaking for herself, she and many others were dismayed by the barrage of attacks directed at the Queen. 'Could you do something?' I shared her dismay, but felt that a public statement from the Archbishops defending the Queen could add fuel to the fire. Instead, the Archbishop of York and I issued an encouragement to the churches to lay on special services at the weekend, and to pray particularly for the Royal Family.

The Queen herself was more than capable of rising to the challenge. The day before the funeral, she addressed the nation. There had been such criticism of her that this was not without its risks. But her simple and moving address from the heart showed her compassion and understanding. It went a very long way towards silencing her critics and removing the misunderstanding that had developed.

On the evening before the funeral, Eileen and I together with my Chaplain, Colin Fletcher, and Bishop Frank Sargeant, walked among the crowds along Whitehall and outside the Abbey. Thousands were there, quite prepared to spend the night in order to get a good position for the pageantry of the day to come. One woman said she had come because this was a once-in-a-lifetime opportunity to share in a nation's grief, and so she would be able to say later, 'I was there.' A young man said that Diana's death had brought home to him the death of his mother, and given him 'permission' to grieve for her. But the majority were there because they had loved Diana, and wanted to be present as a tribute to her caring and compassion.

The actual day was bright and sunny, with large crowds around the Abbey and many, many thousands more watching the service on a giant screen in Hyde Park. Inside the Abbey the sense of loss of this beautiful young woman and mother was acutely felt. I intended also to mention Dodi Fayed in the prayers I was going to lead later. I felt very sorry for Mohammed Al Fayed and his family, whose grief was no less than that of the Royal Family, yet was ignored by the media. But I also felt very keenly for the Queen and the Royal Family, who at the same time as being in mourning were seen by some as being implicated in the tragedy. The two young Princes were magnificent, and bore the ordeal and the glare of world publicity with great dignity. They carried their grief silently and bravely.

The service itself was unashamedly populist and raw with emotion. We sang 'I Vow to Thee, My Country', Diana's two sisters read favourite poems, and the Prime Minister read St Paul's beautiful hymn to love from 1 Corinthians 13. John Tavener's choral anthem 'Alleluia: May Flights of Angels Sing Thee to Thy Rest' was deeply evocative, and Elton John's newly adapted version of 'Candle in the Wind' brought a contemporary element into the ancient Abbey Church. I led the prayers, and was told later that possibly the largest number of people in history had joined together in the Lord's Prayer.

Then Charles Spencer gave an eloquent and moving tribute to his sister, speaking of her rich qualities and her humanity. Addressing her almost as if she were listening to him, he said: 'There is a temptation to rush to canonise your memory, there is no need to do so. You stand tall enough as a human being of unique qualities not to need to be seen as a saint.' He spoke of her commitment to easing the anguish of AIDS and HIV sufferers, the plight of the homeless and the isolation of lepers, and her campaign against the random destruction of landmines. He spoke of her treatment at the hands of the press, and said he could only understand it because 'genuine goodness is threatening to those at the opposite end of the moral spectrum'. There was, sadly and noticeably, a sidelining of the Royal Family at the end when he said that 'on behalf of your mother and your sisters I pledge that we, your blood family, will do all we can to continue the imaginative way in which you were steering these two exceptional young men'. I felt deeply sorry for the Royal Family at those unnecessary words.

After the service, Cardinal Hume and I agreed that it was an eloquent and deeply moving tribute to the Princess, but that the address was gravely deficient. Grand music and prayers can go a long way in comforting the bereaved, but cannot bear the full weight of conveying the Christian hope of eternal life. That requires a message from someone entrusted by the Church to give it. Diana had been a woman of faith, and it was sad that there was no recognition of this and affirmation of the spiritual roots of her being.

Following the death of Diana I began to worry about how Mrs Parker Bowles was perceived by the media and the general public. I was unable to believe that she was the ogress and temptress portrayed by so many tabloid articles. That Prince Charles was absolutely committed to her and probably had been since they first met, long before he married Diana, persuaded me that I should see her as soon as possible. I wrote to her and received a warm letter agreeing to a meeting, as long as it could be kept strictly private.

We met a few weeks later at our son's home in East Peckham.

Eileen came along to make the encounter less forbidding for Camilla, and we had a very reassuring time together. Camilla was a most attractive and charming person, warm-hearted and intelligent, with a down-to-earth attitude. There was no doubt that she loved Charles and wanted to be a support to him. We were to meet several times, and a friendship grew. We came to appreciate the deep and affectionate relationship that existed between Prince Charles and herself; she was a dependable person, and was probably more aware of the importance of Charles's role in the nation than Diana ever was. Subsequent meetings gave us no reason to change our opinion that her future was irrevocably bound up with his.

Within three months of Diana's death there was another royal event in Westminster Abbey, this time to mark the golden wedding anniversary of the Queen and Prince Philip. There was a large crowd outside the Abbey to greet the royal couple, and the huge roar that greeted their arrival revealed the affection in which they were held. Fifty other couples who were also married in 1947 were there as special guests, and were invited to come forward for a blessing. It was a throat-catching moment as the royal couple knelt in front of me to receive God's blessing on their common life, and I found myself wondering if our nation was actually worthy of their devotion and unflagging sense of duty. I blessed the fifty nervous couples who shuffled uncertainly to the front, then moved to the pulpit to preach. It was my intention to make the address personal to the Queen and Prince Philip, and I offered thanks on behalf of so many: 'Thank you for the way you have, together, served us in your marriage with such devotion and dedication. And thank you for the gift you have given us, through these times of change, of a marriage which has endured.' It was a heartwarming occasion, and represented, I thought, a significant moving on from the sad events of the death of Diana.

There were other members of the Royal Family that we got to know well. We grew very fond of the Duke and Duchess of York, and it was with real sadness we saw their marriage disintegrate. We found Sarah a refreshing young woman who could relate to anyone, and Prince Andrew an outgoing, direct and entertaining man. I once had the great pleasure to be flown by him in a Sea King from Northolt to HMS *Illustrious* in the Channel, and much admired his skill as he dropped the helicopter neatly onto the deck of the aircraft carrier in a choppy sea. Princess Anne takes after her father in her sharp intelligence. Her devotion to the Save the Children Fund and her awareness of what is happening politically and socially throughout the world make her a penetrating thinker and speaker. The Duke and Duchess of Gloucester's charitable work is often out of sight, but is deeply appreciated. It is likewise easy to admire Princess Alexandra and the Hon. Angus Ogilvy, popular members of the Royal Family whose public persona is upheld by a firm but unobtrusive Christian faith.

With Princess Margaret a special friendship developed. She sometimes came for Holy Communion at Lambeth Palace with a close friend, Marigold Bridgeman. She had very firm views about religious services, and would have no truck whatsoever with 'newfangled' services, so the Book of Common Prayer rite would always be used when she was present.

There was one memorable Ash Wednesday service, when our practice was to mark the communicants with ash, a symbol of mortality and penitence. Princess Margaret had never encountered this before, and was slightly nervous at having to go to the communion rail with other people to receive the imposition of ash. But she was happy to take part, and said later that it was meaningful and reassuring to be reminded of one's mortality and need for God's grace day by day. She was a deeply spiritual person, but claims following her death that she longed to be a Roman Catholic were quite untrue. She was a rooted and firm Church of England person, and never once in my conversations with her did she express any interest in finding another spiritual home. It was only after her death that I discovered from her family and close friends that she often expressed her thoughts in written prayers and in verse. A beautiful hymn to the Holy Spirit went:

We thank thee, Lord,
Who by thy Spirit
Doth our faith restore,
When we with worldly things commune
And prayerless close our door,
We lose our precious gift divine
To worship and adore.
Then thou, O Saviour, fire our hearts
To love thee evermore.

Sadly, a series of strokes would lead to a deterioration in Princess Margaret's health, but her interests never declined. She spoke with enthusiasm of her love of ballet and art. She took a personal interest in her patronage of over eighty organisations, and had a lifelong commitment to the Girl Guides. She was a direct person, who would go to the heart of an argument very quickly. Some found this disconcerting; I didn't, preferring to deal with a person with clear views than with someone whose blandness hid indifference.

I took one communion service when she was bedridden in Kensington Palace, and anointed her with oil given to me by friends at Tantur Ecumenical Institute near Bethlehem. Eileen put the oil in an attractive little flask, and Princess Margaret was thrilled with it. The effect of the steroids she had been prescribed showed in her swollen face and she was rather depressed that evening, but she noticeably brightened up during the simple and short service. To encourage her, I suggested that she might like to anoint herself with the oil nightly, using the sign of the cross. When we went to pay our respects after hearing of her death, between the two candles flickering in the semi-gloom over her coffin was the flask of olive oil from Bethlehem.

Princess Margaret died just a few days before Ash Wednesday 2002, when we would have welcomed her once more to Lambeth for the service. Her funeral service in St George's, Windsor, was beautiful and dignified, but sadly lacked the personal touch. I was dismayed that there was no homily to pay tribute to a woman who had put her loyalty to Crown and country before her personal happiness.

Such reticence was due, I believe, to her own wishes, and to her desire to depart without a fuss. Apart from my prayer at the end, when I mentioned the Princess by name, it could have been anybody's funeral service.

During Princess Margaret's declining years the Queen Mother's health worried the Queen greatly. However, the Queen Mum continued to surprise everybody by her energy and positive attitude to life. Our hopes that she would make her hundredth birthday celebrations were happily fulfilled. The City of London was particularly keen to honour her with a special lunch, and I was invited to sit on her left. She was in sparkling form, witty, charming and intelligent. I had been told by the Lord Mayor of London that he intended to give an address and make a presentation to her, and I thought she ought to be warned. 'Oh dear,' she exclaimed. 'Should I say something?' I suggested a few words of thanks. In a determined way she then proceeded to rearrange the table before her, to prepare for action. She pushed the cutlery to the left and right, and moved her wine glass from her right to her left side. After the presentation she gave a warm and eloquent impromptu speech, expressing what the City of London had meant to her and King George VI, especially during the war years. She asked everyone to join with her in a toast to the Lord Mayor and the Corporation of the City of London. We stood, and I reached for the glass on my right, only to hear, to my horror, the Queen Mother protest, 'You've taken my wine glass!' It was an amusing moment, which delighted both her and the national press. In my address at the service of celebration and thanksgiving in honour of her hundredth birthday a few weeks later I took the opportunity to thank her for 'the recent loan of her wine glass'.

At the heart of the Queen Mother's popularity was her deep interest in people and her love of life. She shared the Queen's interest in horses, and I well recall being taken by her to see her own. But people came first. She loved meeting them, and when she was present with other members of the Royal Family no one was in any doubt who was the centre of attention.

I was particularly touched by her response when I wrote to her following Princess Margaret's death. In that letter I expressed my concern for her, because all parents dread the thought of their children predeceasing them. The day before Margaret's funeral, the Queen Mother phoned me herself. She apologised for not replying to my letter, as her poor sight made it difficult to write, but wanted to thank me for it. Margaret, she said, could not have borne another stroke. She said she agreed with what I had written, that Margaret was now with her beloved father and all was well. It was a touching phone call, and a typical example of her thoughtfulness for others.

Of course we knew that we would not have the Queen Mum forever, but her death grieved millions throughout the world, for whom this old lady had become one of the most important symbols of the monarchy. When, a mere seven weeks after Princess Margaret's passing, her mother joined her in the eternal love of God, the public reaction was deep, affectionate and sincere.

It was my role to receive the body at the door of the Palace of Westminster together with the Speaker of the House of Commons and the Lord Chancellor, and to process to the catafalque in the middle of the ancient hall, where the coffin was then placed. The Royal Family gathered to one side as I said two simple prayers, then the clergy and ceremonial party left, so that the Queen and her family could spend a few moments alone with the remains of a woman so greatly loved. Over the following five days large crowds came to pay their own respects to the Queen Mum.

It fell to me to give the address at a National Service in the Abbey, where Diana's funeral had taken place. I was initially very concerned about how I could sum up, in a mere eight minutes, one hundred years of life in my sermon for the funeral service in Westminster Abbey. How could I capture such a vibrant and loved person? Preachers and speakers will know that from time to time there are moments of inspiration. Two days following her death, early in the morning before the regular Lambeth Palace chapel service, I decided to look at Proverbs 31, which is a great passage about the 'noble

woman'. One sentence leapt out: 'Strength and dignity are her clothing, and she laughs at the time to come.' I knew that I could find
no better description in the whole of scripture to sum up the Queen
Mother. Strength, dignity and laughter – yes, that was it. I was able
to draft the address almost at once, and then, with the assistance of
a few of my colleagues at Lambeth, I hammered it into a shape that
attempted to catch the mood of the nation.

I could only imagine the Queen's sadness at losing both her
mother and sister in such rapid succession. Once more, I was amazed
at her resilience. At her mother's funeral in Westminster Abbey she
seemed one of the most serene and composed of the Royal Family.
Charles looked the most upset, which considering the very special
bond between himself and his grandmother was hardly surprising.

The sadness of bereavement did not diminish the sense of national
celebration of the Queen's Golden Jubilee, marking fifty years of
faithful service. Her reign began with the call to service to a young
woman crowned by Archbishop Geoffrey Fisher. She was now a wise
sovereign in her seventies, still devoted to her nation and people,
and still doing what she had been called to do with love and devotion.
On 30 April 2002 in Westminster Palace Hall, where a mere twenty-
five days earlier her mother's coffin had lain on the catafalque, both
Houses of Parliament assembled to present a Loyal Address to Her
Majesty. The Speaker, Michael Martin, and the Lord Chancellor,
Derry Irvine, gave warm tributes, but it was the Queen's own speech
that stole the show. In it she spoke simply of the values that had
upheld her service to the nation. As she finished we all stood and
applauded. The Queen stood there, embarrassed as the clapping
thundered around her. I believe she was moved very deeply by this
spontaneous act of gratitude. And the nation celebrated accordingly.
Street parties and pageants were organised up and down the country.
In Buckingham Palace itself two very special and very different con-
certs took place, encompassing pop and classical music.

On the Sunday before the National Service on 4 June the Christian
leaders of the country signed a Covenant committing our Churches

to continue a conversation that might one day lead us to a deeper unity. It was appropriate that our Christian ruler, together with Prince Philip, was in attendance to witness this special agreement.

Without false modesty, I think the British can claim that when it comes to ceremonies, both sacred and secular, we do it extremely well – and the events of 4 June 2002 lived up to the exacting standards of the past. Many thousands of people gathered outside St Paul's and up and down Pall Mall, armed with Union Jacks and picnic lunches. The weather was excellent, and a real sense of celebration filled the air. The service in St Paul's echoed the spirit in the streets around, with music from the choirs of Westminster, Windsor and St Paul's. In my address I attempted to express the nation's gratitude, drawing on the stirring words of Queen Elizabeth I, who in an address to Parliament towards the end of her reign said: 'Though God hath raised me high I count the glory of my Crown that I have reigned with your loves.' The theme of glory through service was the note I struck to celebrate the Queen's remarkable devotion to duty through-out fifty years on the throne. I was also keen to honour Prince Philip, 'whose unswerving support and energy of vision have been so crucial in the evolution of the monarchy during this time'.

But what of the future? There can be no doubt that the monarchy will continue to evolve, like all traditions in society, whether state or Church. What should be preserved, what remains valid and enduring, and what deserves to be relegated to history or the museum are questions that all institutions have to face. During my tenure as Archbishop I witnessed a gradual progression in the opening-up of the monarchy to the public, and that process is bound to continue. I began my period as a rather half-hearted royalist; I ended it as a committed one. I believe the Royal Family is an essential element of our society, whose gift to us far outweighs its cost to the nation, and that we would be foolish to yield to the siren tones of republicanism. Look at any other country you choose, and the alternatives are not attractive. What the monarchy adds to parliamentary democracy is an abiding sign of continuity that is above price. While governments come and go, the sovereign remains and holds all in place, not by power – she has none – but as a symbol. She is placed there by Almighty God, and held there by the affection and loyalty of her people. The question of how a modern monarchy might be both the linchpin and servant of a twenty-first-century democracy will continue to be discussed. But the answer lies, I believe, in the path Her Majesty has chosen – unswerving devotion to the task of serving and representing her people.

In the light of the changing nature of British culture, the next Coronation Service will have to take account of the multi-ethnic communities that are now happily part of the nation. Likewise, the Coronation Oath will have to reflect the changes in society since 1953. Personally, I would like to see some of the trappings of ceremony disappear from state banquets and the State Opening of Parliament. I am delighted that the Queen has taken the initiative in stopping the faintly ridiculous practice of two senior officials walking backwards before her. As for the State Opening of Parliament, let us bequeath such titles such as 'Gold Stick in Waiting' to the panto where they belong, and allow the Queen and Consort and party to process unencumbered by unnecessary ceremonial. That the Queen should deliver the political and social aims of 'her government' is entirely proper, but I know I am not alone in wishing that she might also speak directly and personally to her people, in the attractive and positive way she has done on other occasions.

Inevitably and regretfully, we have to look beyond Her Majesty to the succession. Prince Charles has already made a huge contribution to our land and the world. When the time comes, the nation will be ready to welcome him as our sovereign. He will wear the crown with distinction, and will continue to give noble and valuable service. I would welcome too his marriage to Mrs Parker Bowles. Their love is deep and goes back many, many years. It is surely time to formalise a relationship that is in all but name a marriage.

22

A World in Crisis

'In our world of six billion people, one billion own 80 per cent of global GDP, while another one billion struggle to survive on less than $1 a day. This is a world out of balance. The fact is that aid today is at its lowest level ever. It has fallen from 0.5 per cent of GDP in the early 1960s to about 0.22 per cent today, and this at a time when incomes in developed countries have never been higher.'

Jim Wolfensohn, President of the World Bank, 2003

IT IS OFTEN FORGOTTEN, even by Christians, that Christianity is a philosophy of life before it is a religion. Or, to put it another way, it is a world view, a *Weltanschauung*, that sees through the lens of faith untold possibilities of transformational activity through God's presence in the world. My constant belief and understanding has been that faith is about the action of carrying forward the mission of Christ, a mission that is summed up by the message of the Kingdom of God as preached and lived by Jesus Christ.

As a Christian shaped by the evangelical tradition I have long been familiar with the contribution that evangelical leaders have made in fields such as poverty, slavery, unemployment and child labour in the past. William Wilberforce, the seventh Earl of Shaftesbury and Dr Barnardo are among the glorious names of nineteenth-century evangelicals whose considerable contributions are still remembered with deep thanksgiving, along with the remarkable work of the Church Missionary Society abroad. But twentieth-century evangelicalism was a different story, as it retreated into pietism, creating a chasm between the gospel and social witness. The balance was restored by the historic National Evangelical Anglican Congress at Keele in 1967, when younger evangelicals reclaimed issues of poverty, human rights and social conditions as central to the Christian faith, and part and parcel of calling people to baptism and membership of the Church.

I have always been convinced that God's mission, His '*missio Dei*', includes action on behalf of the poor as much as it includes evangelism. But it was only when I became Archbishop that my head and my heart fully engaged in this action and service. Before that my thinking was almost entirely theoretical, but after entering office it became a passion and a commitment.

As Archbishop I was aware that I had an opportunity to be an advocate for the very poor, because of my newfound prominence together with the active role already being played by the Anglican Communion. The Communion already had a considerable track record in issues to do with social justice. Baroness Lynda Chalker, Minister for International Development in John Major's government, understood this very well, and John himself was very keen to deepen Britain's contribution to the relief of poverty worldwide. Baroness Chalker spearheaded our country's contribution, and we met several times in my first year of office.

It was shortly after my visit to Papua New Guinea in 1991 that a conversation between Lynda and myself helped to focus my concerns about poverty as a clear moral priority. In that meeting I told her of the problems I had seen in PNG which, although on nothing like the scale of those in Africa, were still worrying. There was much malnutrition in remote villages, illiteracy was high, and the infrastructure of the nation needed urgent attention if the growing population was to get adequate nourishment. Lynda had brought with her a new report from the World Bank which showed that, in spite of great improvements in some countries, Africa in particular was rapidly falling behind other continents. The statistics painted such a shocking picture of human misery that it could only be described as a moral indictment of the rest of us if we did nothing. There were now 1.3 billion people living on less than $1 a day, with another two billion on less than $2 a day. Squeezed between two evil forces of unpayable debt and insufficient aid, millions of human beings – particularly women and children – would soon be silent victims of the twin scourges of starvation and disease.

At that point Lynda did not have a clear view about the possibility of Western governments and banks waiving debt, but she did share my opinion that there was a serious moral problem looming, as desperate countries were not only piling up millions of dollars in debt, but were using Western aid to pay back the galloping interest. It seemed to me to be a clear case of having our cake and eating it, as Western nations congratulated themselves on giving generously to the world's poor, then took it all back with interest, in repayments on the capital. I was appalled by the apparent hypocrisy.

Shortly following that conversation with Lynda Chalker, a meeting with the Secretary General of the United Nations, Boutros Boutros Gali, helped to focus my thinking still further. A Coptic Christian, Mr Boutros Gali was personally aware of the impressive contribution of the Churches, but he chided me for not pulling our weight more, and for allowing divisions in the Christian Churches to stop them from being even more powerful participants in delivering aid. That was the first time anyone outside the Churches had, in my hearing, commented on one of the most important consequences of our disunity. He handed me a document – the United Nations Development Programme's Human Development Report for 1992 – which showed that in the 1960s the richer countries were thirty times wealthier than the poorer ones, but by 1992 the figure had grown to 150 times wealthier. Poorer countries were actually receiving less than half of the aid promised by richer nations, in part because of the debt scandal. The ecological implications of industrialisation were also noted: the exploitation of natural resources by richer nations had a direct impact on the poorest people, whose livelihoods depended largely on their environment.

The conclusion was obvious: the part of the world to which I belonged – largely white, Christian and Western – bore a responsibility for the gravity of the poorer countries' problems, and an obligation to shoulder a greater share of the financial burden. In more dramatic terms it could be said that 180 years after William Wilberforce's moral triumph over slavery, a new form of slavery was appearing that challenged our lip-service to our much-vaunted values of freedom and human rights.

Although I was delighted when Kofi Annan became Secretary General of the United Nations in January 1997, because I had collaborated with him closely at several conferences, Boutros Boutros Gali's contribution to the UN has been widely underestimated. I felt that he had a clear grasp of the debt problem, combined with a determination to make a difference. He drew my attention to the fact that the total debt for sub-Saharan Africa was at that date $235 billion, and that $33 million a day was being drained away in servicing that debt. Indeed, I discovered that Africa as a whole spends four times as much on debt repayments as she spends on health and education.

In 1996 I began to hear about the Jubilee campaign. In the early 1990s the idea of linking debt relief to the concept of Jubilee began to emerge. Jubilee in the Old Testament entailed the idealistic notion that every fifty years the land was to lie fallow, mortgage debts be remitted and slaves released. It was a brilliant concept. Much later, Chancellor of the Exchequer Gordon Brown would tell me of the impact of Jubilee 2000 on the meeting of G-7 leaders in Birmingham on 16 May 1998. The participants had been informed that a demonstration was likely, but they were unprepared for its scale or its peaceful nature. Tens of thousands of people were there, mainly from the Churches, with banners appealing to the world to 'break the chains of debt', and a petition was handed in. Gordon believed that Jubilee 2000 led to a fundamental shift in the thinking of the G-7 leaders, who from that moment on began to take the issue of the remission of unpayable debt seriously.

I wondered when New Labour came to power whether Lynda Chalker's impressive commitment could be rivalled. I need not have worried. Not only was Clare Short a very worthy successor, but I was thrilled to find that Gordon Brown was also totally committed to making a real difference to the state of the world. This was a remarkable partnership, and one firmly based on Christian principles. Clare often claimed to be a lapsed and 'cultural' Catholic, but there was no doubt that the influence of her Church shaped her passion for development and her compassion for the very poor. Gordon Brown's faith, forged through the remarkable influence of his father and the Scottish Church, was equally present in his intellectual development and in his determination to find solutions for seemingly intractable problems.

Soon after Labour's 1997 election victory the Chancellor and the Secretary of State for International Development commenced a regular series of breakfast meetings with NGOs and faith leaders. This totally unexpected initiative was welcomed by all. Gordon had intimated earlier to me his desire to gather people together, but worried that it might seem paternalistic. I did not think anybody would react in such a way, and responded that, on the contrary, it would change the nature of the relationship from opposition and hostility to partnership and co-operation. And so it proved. The meetings came to be significant moments of sharing concerns and raising worries. On several occasions I pointed out at these breakfasts that in spite of the government's strong words about development, the country's direct giving was still only 0.29 per cent of GNP, far below its 0.70 per cent commitment. Through Gordon and Clare's efforts the figure rose to 0.31 per cent, but that was still far below the goal. It is my firm belief that a government that had the boldness to make that magic 0.70 per cent of GNP a part of its policy would really signal its attention to get serious about the plight of the absolutely poor.

Initially Clare was not particularly impressed by the rhetoric of the Jubilee 2000 campaign, which she felt was too simplistic. In a remarkable address to General Synod in November 1998 she observed that 'The Churches' campaign on debt relief has been admirable and powerful, but there is a real danger that good people will believe that the debt relief is the "magic bullet" to end all poverty, and that debt is the cause of poverty. That is not true.' She was right about that. Debt relief could not be unconditional. It had to be linked with leadership in the debtor nations which was accountable to the people; this presupposed some form of democratic rule. Money released from debt repayments should be used to make a real difference to the lives of very poor people by being allocated to essential services such as education, health and social welfare programmes. Sudan provides a sad illustration of the impact of debt. Although it is a heavily indebted nation, it spends fifty times more on arms than on health. Debt forgiveness in the case of Sudan must be conditional on the establishment of peace between north and south, and of a responsible and trustworthy government.

Clare reminded Synod that there was much success to report. More people had been brought out of extreme poverty in the last fifty years than in the previous five hundred. However, the acceleration in world population meant that the number of those living on the edge of starvation had grown. But the situation was far from hopeless. Much had been achieved by the work of NGOs and the international community. In Clare's view it was possible to halve absolute poverty by 2015 if everyone pulled together.

I wondered as I listened to Clare if she was not in danger of underestimating the huge role that unpayable debt played in slowing down economic development in Africa. In short, for every £1 given in aid, £3 comes back in repayment of debt. Despite many promises by advanced countries, the burden of debt remains a moral issue that demands a moral and caring response.

It was with this perspective that I visited many different parts of the Communion, seeking also to raise awareness in the West. My first visit to Sudan in 1993 showed how easy it is to be blind to the problem. At first the Sudanese people seemed well-nourished and happy. It was only when I visited Ashwa hospital that I realised that those worst affected by chronic malnutrition are literally out of sight. As I walked through the wards I saw another building about sixty yards away, and asked to see it. The doctor explained that it was reserved for the terminally ill, and that I might find it distressing, but I insisted. As I entered the building I saw sixty or so patients lying on beds with tatty blankets covering them. No staff were to be seen, and no sound came from the sick people. A little boy with a distended tummy was sitting upright in the middle of a bed, sucking a corner of his blanket and looking lost and very, very ill. He was too weak to cry, and too emaciated and ill to eat. The embarrassed doctor explained that the child had been brought to the hospital a day or so before, and his mother had died a few hours ago. They could do nothing for him. 'But,' said the doctor, waving his hands in the direction of the north, 'out there hundreds of people never make it. Either the war stops them getting aid, or they wander in circles looking for grass and water for their emaciated cattle, and perish on futile journeys.'

On my return from one visit abroad, the Conservative MP Andrew Rowe offered a valuable suggestion: that in future when I met foreign government representatives, NGOs and Church delegates, I should ask who was responsible for orphans and children. It was sobering that in the scores of visits I made thereafter I never found one person whose job it was to represent children.

Late in 1997 a World Bank official contacted my office to ask if I would be willing to meet Jim Wolfensohn, the new President of the Bank. Jim was already making waves in the Bank through his hands-on approach and his dynamism. His willingness to think outside the box was beginning to alarm his colleagues as he sought to establish new partnerships, especially with religious communities. What brought home to him the importance of faith communities to development issues had been a recent report on Tanzania which revealed that nearly half of all health, education and social care in the country was delivered through the Churches and other faith groups. Jim said he found himself asking, 'Why are we processing all World Bank grants through the government, and ignoring the extensive religious networks of the country?' We decided to invite leaders of nine world religions to Lambeth Palace in February 1998 to meet senior staff of the World Bank, and to see if a partnership could be forged between these unlikely bedfellows.

The following February Jim and his team swept into Lambeth Palace for this historic gathering. Jim was an alert, friendly man in his sixties, with a shock of white hair. The most notable thing about him, I later decided, was his direct way of engagement. A typical Australian, he was friendly but blunt and to the point. That suited me, and we connected at once. I was thrilled to meet a leader who really wanted to make a difference and was prepared to enter a lions' den of religious leaders, some of whom had no time whatsoever for the World Bank.

As I looked around the conference room on that first morning, I mused that a more exotic group of religious leaders would be difficult to imagine. There were Bahais, Buddhists, Christians, Hindus, Jains, Jews, Muslims, Sikhs and Taoists. The variety of dress expressed the richness of their diversity. The seniority of all the participants in their respective communities indicated the importance each had placed on the conference.

Jim and I had decided that we would chair the meeting jointly, and we encouraged the delegates to speak frankly. And they did. One Indian woman hammered the Bank with such accusations that I could see the three-day conference ending within two hours of commencing. She regarded the Bank as a great secular evil inflicted on the very poor which, with its programme of structural adjustment programmes (SAPs) and its rigid policies, did more harm than good. In as civil a voice as he could muster, Jim defended the Bank against these remarks, but I could tell that he was having to exercise a great deal of self-control to master his temper. The woman had just said that the World Bank was the 'mother and godmother of all banks' when Jim interrupted her tirade with an explosion of his own. 'But we are not a bank! We are the largest foreign-aid agency in the world, and owned by all the governments, including your own. The World Bank has no money of its own; what it has comes from your governments, and we are accountable to your governments. If you think that the Bank tries to feather its own nest by extracting money from the world's poor, you have completely the wrong idea. The Bank exists for one purpose only – it wants to bring people out of poverty. Of course we make mistakes, and part of the reason why we are having this conference is to find ways of learning from one another.'

That tough exchange did not signal the closure of the conference, but rather the beginning of frank appraisals of the strengths and weaknesses of both religious communities and of the Bank and the IMF. There was recognition that the Bank and other secular agencies had been guilty of neglecting the role of faith in conflict resolution, poverty reduction and advocacy. Jim and others were well aware that religious communities were contributing a great deal towards development, and were close to the very poor. They were active in the provision of health care and education, and they gave poor people dignity and hope – in short, the World Bank had woken up to the great potential in faith communities.

However, religious communities were not without their shortcomings. One of Jim's senior assistants pointed out a structural problem with faith communities: they may have been very close to the most vulnerable, especially women and children, but traditional attitudes to the role of women often prohibited the changes that were urgently required to empower women – in education, contraception and work. An equally serious criticism was that the Bank's experience of faith groups had shown that some were 'survival-oriented' rather than 'transformative' institutions, limiting their care to members of their own religion, which sometimes led to deep divisions in the local community.

The World Bank was criticised for adopting a 'top-down' approach to the poor, and for working too often through governments. One African Church leader from Côte d'Ivoire wittily compared the Bank to a pangolin (a cross between an anteater and an armadillo), a creature that lives deep in the forest and is rarely seen. He continued: 'The visit of a World Bank official to our country is rather like the appearance of the pangolin. When he appears everyone gathers around to admire the strange creature. Which is a polite way of saying, "Where have you been all this time?"' Another delegate observed that the Bank's non-confessional and secular agenda limited its concept of human needs to poverty. Instead of affirming the importance of community so essential to the African and Eastern understanding of life, it was in danger of undermining it through its focus on the individual. The Bank's understanding of prosperity, one religious leader argued, seemed solely money-oriented. Nonetheless, there was recognition of the vital role that the Bank played in the alleviation of poverty, and its undisputed achievements over the years. The faith leaders were also quick to express their appreciation of Jim's commitment to work with faith communities.

From that historic encounter the World Faiths Development Dialogue emerged, with Jim and myself as co-founders. Our communiqué stated: 'This has been a precious opportunity for frank and intensive dialogue between religious leaders and development experts, drawn from nine of the world's religious faiths and leading staff of the World Bank ... We are strengthened in our conviction that the definition and practice of desirable development must have regard to spiritual, ethical, environmental, cultural and social considerations, if it is to be sustainable and contribute to the wellbeing of all, especially the poorest and weakest members of society.' It was agreed that WFDD would not be an 'aid-granting' body, but one that sought to maximise the considerable but unrealised potential of faith communities around the world. Its task should be to bring faith groups together to do more in eradicating poverty, and through a practical and probing reflection on development to deepen existing dialogue and overcome conflict and misunderstanding. A very light and flexible steering group was formed, and it was charged to help poor communities work more closely with World Bank officials and NGOs.

Jim and I were delighted with the success of the meeting, and within a few months were able to see significant progress made. We received considerable financial support from the Aga Khan, and much encouragement from Prince Philip and Prince Hassan of Jordan. And then a bombshell came. The Board of Executive Directors of the World Bank refused to endorse this unique agreement between the Bank and religious communities. The French representative particularly objected to it, arguing that the principle of separation of Church and state forbade such collaboration. This short-sighted argument won the day, leading to Jim having to agree reluctantly to break off official links with WFDD, although an informal partnership continued. He was deeply upset and outraged by his Board's decision, but there was little he could do. He made it clear however that he would continue his role as Co-Chair as an individual, even though he was unable to do so in his official capacity as President of the World Bank. While I was delighted that Jim would continue, the ban imposed by the Board meant that we could not depend upon the resources of the World Bank in the continuation of the work. An irony was that on 12 September 2001, the day after the terrorist attacks on the Twin Towers and the Pentagon, several members of that same Board said to Jim that the previous day's events had shown the importance of the initiative, and that religious communities needed to be drawn into closer collaboration with the Bank. It is a task that remains to be completed, but one that could bear much fruit.

In October 2002, just two weeks before my retirement, another meeting of world faith leaders with the President of the World Bank, together with Clare Short and Bono, the lead singer of the rock group U2, was unanimous in its affirmation of WFDD, and united in its common determination to support the Millennium Development Goals. These goals – to halve world poverty by 2015, to achieve universal primary education, to halt and reverse the spread of HIV/ AIDS, and to eliminate gender inequality – were seen by us all as attainable if we all pulled together. Bono, speaking with the passion of an evangelist, said: 'The Bible contains 2103 verses pertaining to the poor. Outside of personal redemption, the call to address the needs of the poor is the most important aspect and the main thrust of the scriptures. To ignore this misses the basic tenets of Judaeo-Christian values, indeed the values of any of the world's great faiths concerning the dignity of human life.'

My visits abroad also showed me that the Churches were making great contributions to relieving distress. However, the deepening crisis of HIV/AIDS presented an additional challenge to local communities. As well as the problem of feeding hungry stomachs, families were now finding that this terrible virus was taking away key members of their communities at an ever-growing rate.

When I visited Uganda in May 1998 I was taken to see a new clinic for HIV/AIDS sufferers in Namirembe. I did not expect to find a huge banner identifying it as 'The Archbishop Carey Centre'. A young priest, the Reverend Gideon Byamugisha, welcomed me warmly, and disarmingly asked me to become the patron of the day centre. If I had had any reservations about being put on the spot in this way, they would have been removed by Gideon's approach and vision. He told me how his wife had died after a terrible but short illness caused by the virus. He was encouraged to have his blood tested, and the result was that he too was HIV-positive. He said that at first it had seemed a sentence of death. He then started to reflect on it from a Christian angle, and decided that it did not mean death, but life. Christians believe in the resurrection, and that means there is always hope. He stated simply and memorably: 'I am not dying of AIDS, but living through AIDS.' Despite the social stigma attached to the virus, he felt he had no choice but to declare that he too was a sufferer. He became one of the first, if not the very first, African clergymen to acknowledge he was sero-positive.

But Gideon did far more than that. He decided to fight back against the disease by educating and caring for others. He took me to see some of those in advanced stages of the virus, and we prayed with them. We visited a clinic where doctors and nurses were busy caring for infected babies; we sat in on a class where a Christian approach to sexual practice was being taught; we talked with clergy and social workers of the needs of Ugandan society and what was being done to care for the growing numbers of orphans. I felt humbled by such dedication. Gideon's work continues to grow. He is now married to a young widow who is also HIV-positive, and they have dedicated their lives to helping others. I feel privileged to support this vital work and to have my name associated with it. Gideon and his wife are among the few fortunate African sufferers of AIDS so far to have benefited from anti-retroviral therapy.

It is perhaps openness like Gideon's that has made Uganda one of the few African countries where there are signs of hope as far as the pandemic is concerned. How different the situation was in South Africa when I visited just over a year later. The people of the country simply did not seem aware of the urgency and scale of the crisis. I visited a small clinic in Durban with Bishop Rubin Philips that catered for babies and toddlers suffering from AIDS. We held these tiny children in our arms and played with them for a while. I was particularly struck by a beautiful little girl who had been found under the body of her young mother several weeks earlier. Her mother had been dead for five days, and her twin sister was also dead. The little girl's foot had been trapped under her mother's body, and required physiotherapy. A more delightful child would be hard to imagine – but she had the virus too, and her life would be all too short. The Matron explained that death in Africa is not always terrible because of the faith and hope of the people. 'But,' she said, with her voice breaking, 'what cuts us all up as a staff is that when these little people die we have no resources to bury them properly; we send for the police, who take the bodies away for incineration.' I was horrified to learn this, and turning to Rubin said, 'Surely our Church can do better than that! You must find ways of giving these babies a proper funeral.' Rubin, who had had no idea of this state of affairs, readily agreed, and a firm relationship began between the clinic and the diocese. As we drove away in silence I reflected that had that clinic been for white children, it would have had all the resources it needed.

South Africa troubled me for a different reason too. Wherever I looked I saw signs with messages such as 'Be wise. Condom-wise!' or 'Carry a condom with you, wherever you go'. This seemed a sad reflection of the fact that, important though proper safeguards are, the really important messages of faithfulness in marriage and chastity in other relationships were simply not being emphasised sufficiently.

The following day I travelled to Johannesburg and went to meet Adelaide Tambo, the widow of the great Oliver Tambo, whose contri-bution to the dismantling of apartheid is legendary. We walked together to Oliver's memorial at the Church of the Resurrection at Weltville. A large crowd was there, and Mrs Tambo gave an impassioned speech lamenting the wild behaviour and crime of so many in South Africa. Her words electrified me as she tore into the crowd: 'Oliver did not make freedom his life's work for his people to destroy society by drugs, sex and theft,' she cried. 'We are dying within.'

A few days later I had a meeting with President Thabo Mbeki. He expressed an extraordinary view on AIDS, declaring that there was no such virus, and that people were simply dying of other identifiable diseases. There was no pandemic, and no need to panic; the govern-ment was well on top of the problem. I could see from Archbishop Njongonkulu Ndungane's face that he was as appalled as I was. South Africa's slowness in responding to the crisis, in stark contrast to Uganda, must owe something to an unwillingness on the part of some leading politicians to acknowledge the true nature of the problem.

Gender is another factor that is central to poverty. This struck me with particular force when I paid an official visit to Tanzania and went with a Church Development Officer into the depths of the countryside, where a widow was about to acquire a cow under the auspices of 'Send a Cow', an initiative that had originated in my last diocese of Bath and Wells. I asked the official why a woman had been chosen. He pointed to two groups of people. A long line of women were trudging steadily along the road with containers full of water on their heads, while a group of men were sitting playing cards in the doorway of a house. He said that he felt ashamed to say it, but the women could be better trusted than the men to care for the animal. The woman in question was bright and eager to learn. She was aware that both her own children and others in the village would be reliant on the way she treated the cow.

Gender is one of the most important keys to improving the lot of the very poor. Better-educated girls marry later, bear fewer children and have greater success in the work market. A World Bank report sums up the problem – and the opportunity – succinctly: 'Women are one of Africa's hidden reserves, providing most of the region's labour, but their productivity is hampered by widespread inequality in education and access to resources. Thus greater gender equality can be a potent force for accelerated poverty reduction.' I was pleased to see that in many areas of the Church's work abroad women were taking leading roles.

The many visits I made to different parts of the world showed me that the Church was faithfully working out its mission with a clear eye on the Kingdom of God. In the Church of Brazil, although Anglicans are small in number, the work among Indian tribes, street children, drug addicts and slum-dwellers was truly impressive. I was especially taken by a young Brazilian woman priest, Simiah, who worked among 'rubbish people'. She heard one day of a desperately poor couple who lived off what they could salvage from a huge dump at Orlinda, outside Recife, and of their distress when they discovered that the meat they had cooked and eaten was in fact cancerous human tissue discarded by a nearby hospital. The story was reported in the press around the world.

Simiah decided to take action. She found that over two hundred people lived off the rubbish at the dump. It was a scene of indescribable horror, a veritable 'gehenna' of human desperation. She decided to open a small church, which she called 'the Church of living water'. She raised money to aid the very poor, and badgered the local council to find ways of giving dignity to the people. Through her constant pressure on the Mayors of Orlinda and Recife, public appeals on radio and in the newspapers she became the voice of the rubbish people. A school was started, a clinic was opened, people were beginning to be housed properly, and little by little the place was being transformed.

When I visited the site the local Mayor told me with great pride that the council was now trying to create a recycling and environment project from the refuse, which would give the rubbish people jobs and a sense of worth. It was still a grim place as I looked over the huge acreage of rubbish with dozens of small fires burning. Scores of people – men, women and children – could be seen gathering rubbish and making neat piles for recycling. Later at the church I met some of these people and heard their stories. Simiah described their despair, and the assumption of many that those who lived here were 'garbage' themselves. A boy spoke of now being able to read for himself. A young mother told of her addiction to drugs and how she and her children had reached rock bottom. An older woman spoke movingly of losing all five of her sons through drug dealing: 'I was once a follower of Satanism [voodooism]. I now have a house built with brick thanks to the church and I am now a follower of Jesus.' A young girl presented me with a cross made from materials gathered from the tip, as a reminder that through God everything may be 'recycled' – nothing is ever over and finished. I felt moved by such a vision. Before I left I was asked to bless and dedicate a dentist's chair. Although this was a most unusual thing to bless I did so with a glad heart, knowing what a boon it would be to the needy people of this rubbish tip.

Anglicans are far from being exceptional in doing splendid work on the edges of society. On a visit to Mozambique I came across the work of the Sant'Egidio community from Rome. Founded by a young academic, Andrea Riccardi, this lay community had the vision of putting into practice the gospel of Jesus Christ. Andrea was not yet twenty when, in 1968, he invited a group of high-school students to meet with the intention of discussing politics and the Church in the light of the gospel. The group grew, and became like a religious community, based on prayer and practically living the Christian faith. Its work moved into advocacy and then reconciliation, and came to worldwide attention in 1990 when, at the headquarters of Sant'Egidio in Rome, the government of Mozambique and the guerrilla army Renamo, signed a peace treaty that signalled the end of a twenty-year war which had taken the lives of countless people. Through the quiet and untiring diplomacy of Professor Riccardi and his colleagues the two sides were led step by step to work for a constructive search for a lasting peace for their poor land.

Another key person in that peace was the Anglican Bishop in Mozambique, Dinis Singulane, who was closely involved in negotiations between the two bodies. Dinis was unstinting in his admiration of Sant'Egidio's work. Andrea Riccardi became a good friend, and whenever Eileen and I were in Rome we would visit the community in Trastevere and join in their prayers. Andrea is rarely without a huge smile on his face and a welcome for everyone. He is entirely dedicated to this remarkable work, and is always on the lookout for ways to bring people closer together.

This, in fact, is the heart of the Christian faith, and when reconciliation and the transformation of life are ignored the Christian Church shrinks. The challenge facing the Anglican Communion, and indeed all Churches, is to be a powerful voice for the poor. We are ideally situated to do this, because most of Africa's Christian children are among the very poor. We must enable their voices to be heard. We must tell their story of suffering and be their voice calling for food, for shelter and for education. To do any less would be to fail to walk in the steps of our Lord. Indeed, it is my firm belief that the health of our Churches should be assessed according to the degree to which they look away from their own interests to those of the world around, and seek to build the Kingdom of God there.

Without such a faith and hope, it is hard to feel confident about the future of the human race. The world's population is spiralling out of control, and we seem incapable of ending the wars that do so much damage to the very poor. The nations have set splendid Millennium Development Goals, but the chances of meeting them by the target date of 2015 seem slim unless all governments cease their policies of protectionism and begin to think globally. It is in our true interests to do so. As William Temple, Archbishop of Canterbury in the 1940s, said so memorably: 'The art of government in fact is the art of so ordering life that self-interest prompts what justice demands.' Justice is found in demanding that we must find ways of sharing the resources of the world with those who have equal rights to a Creator's generosity. However, Temple reminds us that it is in our own self-interest to do so, because no one is ever truly rich while another human being lacks clothing, food and love.

This, I am convinced, is at the heart of the Christian gospel. The God of love and justice I believe in, whose nature is expressed in the life, death and resurrection of Jesus Christ, calls the Church to move beyond charity to seeking justice for the world's poor. Anything short of that is less than the gospel demands.

23

———◦———

Quo Vadis?

'People today do not greatly care about secondary questions of
Church order, or the debates of ecclesiastical politics. They
want to know what is right and what is wrong, who God is
and how we can believe in Him. I earnestly long to hear the
Church again proclaiming a confident and positive faith.'

F. R. Barry

AFTER THE FURNITURE VAN had taken our belongings away from
Lambeth Palace on 31 October 2002, Eileen and I were left alone in
the now empty flat where we had lived for the past eleven and a half
years. It was after 7 o'clock in the evening, and the staff had gone
home. The huge building was peaceful and quiet. The long row of
portraits of Archbishops, from Cranmer to Carey, lining the main
corridor were silent witnesses to the fact that Lambeth Palace was
quite accustomed to Archbishops and their families coming and
going. It was impossible for me not to reflect on my place among
them. I had given of my very best. Yes, there were things I could
have done better, and some matters I should have tackled differently.
There had been times when I had been stretched to the very limit.
But through the good and bad times the grace and love of God had
been an ever-present reality. And now it was all over.

Suddenly the phone rang. It was Cardinal Cormac Murphy-
O'Connor, who was calling 'simply to wish us well', and to thank us
for what we had contributed to the mission of the Church. It was

good of him to phone, and was a reminder of the rich friendships Eileen and I had made along the way, and of our fellowship in the gospel of Christ. We drove out of the darkened Palace into the brightly-lit and noisy Lambeth Palace Road, and across the bridge to the Embankment. We were on our way home, with no regrets and no looking back – simply profoundly thankful to God for His guidance over the years.

Much had been achieved, by so many people working together. There was a deeper unity in the House of Bishops, and, more importantly, no one could now point the finger at so-called 'unbelieving Bishops'. The ordination of women to the priesthood was now a fact, and women were visible at practically every level of Church life. Indeed, I was sure that the ordination of women to the episcopate, although a contentious issue, would happen one day. The financial crisis created by the Church Commissioners' problems in the early nineties had resulted in reformed and clearer structures. Mission and evangelism were priorities in Church life, and Springboard was truly a 'gift' to the wider Church. Ecumenical relations were firmly on track, and beginning to bear fruit. Inter-faith co-operation and dialogue were significant realities in the Church and the nation, with the Archbishop of Canterbury taking a leading role. Relations with the monarchy and the government were also very healthy. The Anglican Communion was in good heart, and the Lambeth Conference of 1998 had revealed the strength of the Church in the developing world. As we drove away we felt confident about handing on to my successor, Rowan Williams, a national Church that was in good heart, even if, like other great institutions, it faces many challenges in the years ahead. I had no doubts that Rowan's considerable gifts would be appreciated by many, and would be used significantly in the time to come.

And what of that future?

'*Quo vadis?*' (Where are you going?) is the question that an apocryphal gospel tells us the risen Christ asked Peter as he ran away from his own martyrdom. Faced with this terrifying question, Peter returned with renewed resolve and courage to face death. It is a pertinent question to ask of the future of the Christian faith. What are the possible trajectories of faith as we leave the first two millennia of Christianity behind? Where are the different Churches of the Anglican Communion going? It is necessary to put these questions in the plural, because the answers point in different directions. I am very hopeful and optimistic for worldwide Christianity, especially in Africa, South America and South-East Asia. I am less hopeful for Europe and North America, where I believe a crisis of faith places traditional Christianity at risk.

Let us first consider the wider picture. The Church in what Westerners describe as 'developing' countries is in very good heart with, in spite of so many problems – AIDS/HIV, fundamentalist Islam, dire poverty, conflict and war – an abounding sense of mission. Churches are growing rapidly, and there is confidence concerning the future. Overall the twentieth century witnessed an astonishing explosion of Christianity, as the number of Christians in the world tripled. It is estimated that there were just ten million African Christians in the year 1900, representing a mere 9 per cent of the total population; today there are 360 million African Christians, representing 46 per cent of the total, and growing all the time. Africa is not the only continent where Christianity has grown remarkably and is flourishing. In South America there are now more than 480 million Christian adherents. The twentieth century also saw an astonishing growth of the faith in Asia, where there are now 313 million Christians.

This picture of buoyant faith, bubbling up from often depressing circumstances, contrasts vividly with the decline in so-called First World nations. In my lifetime I have witnessed a shocking and distressing change in the fortunes of the Churches in England. Although born into a non-observant family and a working-class culture indifferent to institutional faith, I was typical of most people in post-war England in believing myself to be Christian and being respectful of the Church. My family, like so many, was a Church of England family. It was the Church of England that we did not attend – the others did not come into the equation at all. Although like many families we were not grafted into the institutional Church, we still felt deeply Christian. We knew the rudiments of the faith: we were taught it at school, and most children could recite the Lord's Prayer and were familiar with the Bible and the rich traditions of Christianity. What is more, there was no talk of crisis. The Churches were healthy and in good heart.

What has caused our current predicament, within such a short period of time? It is easy to conclude that the Church itself is responsible for the decline of faith. Perhaps we have not done enough to halt the drift away from the Church, or perhaps we have betrayed the gospel in some way. Certainly we all could have done more. However, we should take a small crumb of comfort from the fact that the momentous and profound social changes shaking post-war Europe were bound to affect the role and position of the Church – and there was very little that the Church could do about it. Some Church leaders were far-sighted enough to perceive that social mutations were sure to affect all Christian denominations. Indeed, immediately after the war the Church of England leadership was worried about the problem, issuing a report entitled *Towards the Re-Conversion of England*. Largely inspired by Archbishop William Temple, who had died a few years before, the report is brilliant in its analysis of the challenges the Church was facing; but, like so many Church of England documents then and now, it was never properly followed through and implemented.

Perhaps we are reaping the whirlwind of neglect, as anxious and searching studies such as *Towards the Re-Conversion of England* continue to expose the Church of England's tendency to take the easy way out. But we should not berate ourselves too much, because as with so many social trends the reasons for the decline in church-going are much more prosaic than are sometimes realised. Most people do not leave institutions because they no longer believe, but because they no longer belong. The contours of the world have changed. The transformation of small towns into industrial centres, fed by changes in transport – the train, car and plane – have had their impact on community life, and correspondingly on our sense of where 'home' is located.

Leisure too has compounded the problem for Churches and all voluntary groups. Within the lifetime of many people we have witnessed a shift from the Church being at the centre of leisure and community, to a place on the periphery. When I was vicar of St Nicholas's, Durham, I remember seeing parish magazines from the 1920s and thirties which revealed that the church at that period had hundreds of children in its Sunday schools and youth groups. Annually that one parish church took over a thousand children on outings to the seaside, and it was also host to a great number of clubs and activities. On becoming vicar in 1975 I had to restart the children's work, which by that time had virtually disappeared, such had been the speed of change and its dramatic impact on the role of the Church.

Some might dismiss these thoughts as unduly pessimistic. After all, the sociologist Grace Davie, in a recent book, *Europe: The Exceptional Case. Parameters of Faith in the Modern World*, has argued that Western Europe is untypical of the rest of the world, where religious communities are growing strongly. She also notes that the Churches have fared better than most voluntary groups – far better than trade unions, for example. Moreover, the Church is still rooted in society through its great commitment to education and its army of clergy and Readers. It has not disengaged from its sense of mission to the entire community.

I agree with that; but we must not avoid unpleasant truth. The majority of churches up and down this land have congregations of fewer than thirty. A Reader in the Church of Wales told me recently that she took a service in a rural church where there had been only one worshipper. When I expressed astonishment, she said that this was far from unusual: in living memory that church has never had a congregation in double figures. Resistance to closure in that Welsh parish has come not from the church, but from the local community, who didn't wish to lose their church building. Like so many whose church attendance is infrequent, they want their church to be available and open to all, but are unwilling to support it sufficiently to secure its future. Caught between local intransigence and an irresistible logic that suggests closure, the diocese continues to put off the evil day.

Wherever we look, the signs are dire; but are they hopeless? I think not. There are other data that point in a much more encouraging direction, and suggest that the word 'crisis' should be replaced by 'crossroads'. Any organisation facing decline has to assess its message and what it offers people. In the light of that, the Church of England can ask what it should hold on to, and what it might learn from the vibrant faith of Churches in developing countries.

First, there is the message to consider. At the end of my working ministry I am more than ever convinced of the reality of the Christian faith and its transformative potential. Again and again I have seen it change societies, Churches and individuals. If people outside the Church doubt this, it is because they have never known for themselves the power of the gospel and the liberation it brings. The claim of the Church down the centuries is that when people turn to Jesus Christ they start on a journey that will lead to them discovering for themselves that 'the truth shall set them free'. It is this experience of transformation, of conversion – whether a slow gestation over many years, or the heart-throbbing experience of a personal encounter with the living God – that should underpin all Christian action and ministry, from being a Sunday-school teacher to being a Bishop. This, of course, transcends mere differences of Churchmanship. I am talking about being 'in love' with Someone, who is beyond description and who speaks '*cor ad cor*' – heart to heart. I am talking about spirituality, about knowing oneself captivated by something greater and better than we can ever comprehend. I am describing something which is authentically Catholic as much as it is evangelical. It is the experience that unites the disciples of Jesus Christ, who include such diverse followers as St Paul, St Augustine, Martin Luther, John Wesley, Billy Graham, Michael Ramsey and Pope John Paul II.

This experience of meeting God through Jesus Christ is the motivating force for leadership and therefore growth of the Church. Wherever we look, and whatever organisation is considered, leadership is the factor that contributes most to growth. If leaders lose their convictions, organisations eventually go out of business. Faith works. This does not mean that intellectual ability is unnecessary, or that rigorous theological exploration is futile. Indeed not. What it does imply is that our intelligence and scholarship are tools of faith, and not masters of it.

Regrettably, this has sometimes resulted in tension between faith and the intellect. There is a great deal of 'half belief' in our Church: clergy whose commitment seems less than wholehearted, living perhaps in that grim borderland world of doubt and convinced faith, not yet 'surprised by joy', as was C.S. Lewis's great experience. That journey into a mature and convinced faith can only come from a steady knowledge of God through prayer, study of the scriptures and living with the saints who have gone before. Churches move into growth when their leadership is fired by passion and deep commitment to the faith. Anglican 'coolness' has to be replaced by something considerably hotter if it is to win the hearts of people.

This of course is one of the lessons we learn from Third World Churches. No visitor to Africa, the West Indies, South-East Asia or Korea can fail to be moved by the warmth of their worship and the firm tones of their preaching and praying. I have heard British visitors say time and again how humbled they feel when they are in the presence of faith honed in the fires of suffering and tribulation. John Sentamu, Bishop of Birmingham, said in the course of an address to General Synod in November 2002: 'Our brothers and sisters from Africa are calling this Church, which took the gospel to Africa, to reclaim its evangelistic zeal and scriptural holiness so that it may yet again have that irresistible transforming presence. They call us to become a Church that is once again vitally connected with each other in love; and connected with the world around us in wholesome service.'

Another factor has been noted frequently in this book: a commitment to the Church's faith rooted in scripture. The Anglican tradition prides itself on its way of conducting its theology by an engagement with scripture, tradition and reason. But the three are not equal: scripture is the yardstick of theological science, and if something does not have the support of scripture it does not, or should not, have the support of the Anglican Communion. Scripture measures both tradition and reason, and in the light of that judgement our theology is shaped and reassessed. Tradition and reason, nevertheless, have important roles in our understanding of scripture, by correcting errors in understanding our faith and mistakes in the interpretation of the Bible.

Inevitably there are potential weaknesses as well as strengths in this intellectual position. It may lead to woolliness of belief, as expressed by A.D. Gilbert's description of Anglicanism in England as 'A religion demanding minimum commitment, and requiring neither deviation from the generally accepted ethical and social standards of the wider society nor burdensome donation of time, money or energy.'

Dr Stephen Neil agrees with this in part: 'To be a bad Anglican is the easiest thing in the world; the amount of effort required in a minimum Anglican conformity is so infinitesimal that it is hardly to be measured.' He adds, however: 'To be a good Anglican is an exceedingly taxing business.' It is taxing because the call to be an open Church which allows others to grow, to think, to dispute and yet to stay passionately committed to a historic faith in a world of doubt is very daunting and demanding indeed.

To see scripture as authoritative and binding on the Church for all time means to submit to its authority in our lives even when – especially when – it collides with the prevailing mores of our world or the Church. Perhaps one of our greatest challenges is to overcome the severe biblical illiteracy there now is in our Church, and no doubt most Churches. I witnessed the drift towards this when I returned to theological education in 1982 after seven years away in parish ministry. Even in Trinity College, Bristol – a college that prides itself on teaching the Bible – the level of Bible knowledge had dropped considerably. The teaching staff could not automatically assume that ordinands would know their way around the Bible and be able to find texts with ease, or that there was familiarity with the Old Testament or even New Testament epistles. If familiarity with the Bible is crucial for the clergy, it can be said without qualification that congregational vitality is linked to biblical literacy. A congregation out of touch with the Bible will be out of touch with God's vision for change and renewal. It will be susceptible to cultural fads, and may measure success and failure according to standards of our own making.

It is my firm view that only Christians and Churches rooted in orthodox faith and nourished by its worship and life can resist the drag of cultural relativity. Today's culture stresses riches, happiness, money and reason as the routes to fulfilment. There is of course nothing wrong with each in its rightful and proper place, but the implicit assumption that material blessings matter pre-eminently has sidelined spirituality and faith in God, and has penetrated religion itself. Little wonder that Bishop Lesslie Newbigin warned in many of his books that the conversion of our culture is the most important role confronting the Church today. I agree with that, with the proviso that it will only be accomplished if the Church is willing to become at times 'counter-cultural' in pointing unapologetically to values that transcend materialism and encouraging its members to adopt life-styles that testify to a better way. Without any doubt, British Churches need the help, encouragement and example of newer Churches to recover our nerve and to inspire our work. From their uncompromis-ing commitment to the Bible springs an emphatic and transparent belief in a God who acts powerfully in the present. It is hardly surprising therefore that the form of Christianity growing most strongly in developing countries, even within mainstream denominations, is the Pentecostal and Charismatic form.

We don't need to go abroad to find examples of lively Churches reaching out into their communities. There are many in Britain too, and it is time we learned from their experience and emulated key principles that are central to their success. In the main, growing Churches in our country are evangelical in character. This may challenge the comment of John Habgood, the Archbishop of York, who wrote some years ago: 'The future is Catholic.' I have the greatest respect for the 'Catholic tradition', and appreciate it greatly. I have to say, though, that I find little evidence today to convince me that 'the future is Catholic'. The Roman Catholic Church has many strengths, but if one considers the Western Roman Catholic Church, the problem of paedophilia in the American Church and the alarming shortage of priests caused by the obligation of celibacy has reduced the priesthood to an alarming degree, and has created a profound crisis of confidence. If one turns to traditional Catholicism in the Church of England, one has to conclude sadly that little growth will be forthcoming until opposition to the ordination of women is no longer its defining symbol. I trust it will recover, because it is a tradition that still has much to offer, not least in the form of Catholic evangelism and mission that used to typify it.

Liberalism is a difficult tradition to summarise. Its most extreme forms, expressed by groups such as the 'Sea of Faith', are essentially parasitic in character, and depend on believers drifting from other traditions to maintain their life. Very few 'seekers' will see anything attractive in forms of radical liberalism that deny fundamental tenets of the faith. As they have no secure moorings they will always remain 'at sea'. On the other hand, the experience of the Church of England is that the broad Church tradition, with its commitment to learning and scholarship, has a continuing role to play, as long as it remains loyal to the 'fundamentals' of the faith. Nevertheless, I have to conclude that liberalism is not an attractive option for those searching for faith, unless of course the search for truth, so central to the broad

Church tradition, is harnessed to mission. Frankly, there are not many examples of that around.

If then the future is not Catholic or liberal, does that suggest it is evangelical? I am tempted to say so, but I find myself pulling back. The temptation comes from the undeniable fact that evangelicalism is ascendant, and is where the energy in the Church is found these days. In my forty-two years of ministry I have seen this tradition emerge from the backwaters of the Church of England to being at its heart. There are more evangelical Bishops now than formerly, and each exercises dedicated and important ministries alongside other Bishops. In my eleven years of chairing the House of Bishops I saw with great interest how evangelicals grew in confidence and leadership. I am convinced that this will continue and deepen.

Although I do see this tradition becoming more and more important in the days ahead, I find myself hesitating in expecting it to hold the key to the future of Christianity in our land. There are several reasons for this. The first has to do with the fissiparous character of evangelicalism. Perhaps the reason evangelicals connect so well with modern culture is that the tradition is the mirror image of modern society – it is basically entrepreneurial in character. As such it is able to adapt quickly, react spontaneously and adopt liturgies and musical forms that appeal to the emotional needs of young people. However, its excessively individualistic outlook and character robs evangelicalism of the opportunity to be a significant force in the Church. Leadership is so often equated with charisma; unity to what 'I believe to be true'; and the Church is identified with 'me and my party'. Evangelicals are tempted more than others to act cavalierly with respect to outer conformity in terms of liturgical services and the wearing of robes. They are quick to condemn the theological errors of others when they contradict the faith of the Church, but conveniently ignore liturgical and canonical misdemeanours which also weaken the ordering of the Church's life.

In short, evangelicalism is not a tight, well-ordered and coherent body of believers embraced by common faith and common practice, but rather a diverse cluster of people united around a core body of evangelical tenets. There can be little doubt of its real strengths, particularly its devotion to Jesus Christ. Nonetheless, in spite of what some of its leaders claim, it has an inadequate understanding of the Church. An evangelical is likely to say, 'I am an evangelical first and foremost, then I am a member of the Church of England/Methodist Church.' But I learned long ago to put the Church first, because it is prior to my believing. Christians who put their own beliefs and tribal loyalties before their Church are likely to drift away from it when things get tough.

Can the future belong to Anglican evangelicals when that tradition has this fundamental weakness? I am quite sure that evangelicals have a critical and leading role to play in the resurgence of Christian belief in our country and the revival of the Church of England; I am less certain that they can dominate the Church in leadership and in theological learning. Perhaps evangelicals will always be at their best as the shock troops or commandos of the Church in their ability to challenge the status quo, but possibly they are at their weakest in attempting to hold all together. However, my greatest longing is not that one of the historic traditions should dominate the others and shape the future of the Church, but for each of them to combine in a true comprehensiveness, united in a common loyalty to the Church.

There is of course a third element of significance as one looks ahead. A challenge flowing from the last Lambeth Conference, which subsequent events have shown to our cost that we have not met, is the importance of valuing and honouring our Anglican inheritance. None of us can escape the importance of history. We are what we are because others have instructed and led us. Most of us are Catholics, Anglicans, Methodists and other denominations because we have been nourished from birth in these fine mansions of faith, and we see no convincing reason to live elsewhere. But the past also handed to us their divisions, and we are still living with the bitter squabbles of the Reformation itself – never mind who was right and who was wrong.

Valuing our heritage also carries within it a warning that no denomination is perfect and free from error. Even so, treasuring the Anglican tradition is something that must be emphasised and taught. To honour our tradition means valuing what makes us distinctive as Christians, so that we may offer it to other Christians and be able to receive from them. We do indeed celebrate the advances that have been made in ecumenical endeavour, and yearn for further implementation of unity. But nothing worthwhile comes from dismissing the past, or developing an ecclesiastical amnesia that suggests that what we have gained from it is worthless. I have already said that every ecclesiastical journey has had its shortcomings and terrible moments. We have not acted Christianly to one another. At times in our different pasts we have claimed to possess the whole truth, and have denied it to others. Anglicans, in common with others, have failed grievously. But a convenient forgetfulness is not the answer. We have to remember in order to go on. Knowing and treasuring our heritage has a vital role in reviving congregations not only to understand the weaknesses of the past and our all-too-evident humanity, but to recognise those key moments when the Spirit spoke to our forebears and authenticated the journey.

That is why Anglicans never start describing their Church from the Reformation. We are not a Reformation Church in the strict meaning of that term. The Reformers did not believe they were creating a new Church, but rather that they were reforming an old and precious one. To the claim at the Reformation that the Church of England was a new Church, unlike the Roman Catholic Church which was the living, organic Church of Jesus Christ, the answer was firmly given: 'Not so. Think of the Church as a garden which was once full of weeds. Now it has been cleared and once more is a garden. Or think of it as a face which has just been washed. After all, where was your face before you washed it this morning?'

But enough of such old polemical points. My point is that we are uneasy about tracing our Church from the Reformation. We acknowledge the sad necessity for such a terrible rupture in the unity of the Western Church, and wish it had not occurred. Because we see ourselves as a continuing part of historic, orthodox, confessional Christianity, we did not strip our tradition of all traditions that came from the ancient and medieval Church. Indeed, we recognise fully the Church of Rome, and its priests who leave to become Anglican are never required to be re-ordained, nor are its sacraments regarded as invalid.

Honouring our tradition does not mean a blanket refusal to accept new developments, or that we automatically assume that change is a good thing. New possibilities have to be weighed carefully, balancing the heritage we have received with all the baggage that went with it against the opportunities of a new world. And it is continuity with scripture, tradition and reason that we have to bear in mind as the future opens us before us. We have already encountered T.S Eliot's famous phrase 'Home is where we start from'. Heritage is a crucial aspect of home, in that it creates a sense of family.

Anglicans, wherever they are and whatever nation they originate from, are a recognisable entity by reason of a common history, liturgy, faith and order. This is, however, under strain as never before, and new attitudes towards homosexuality are posing the severest challenge to our nature of being in communion with each other. Actions taken in the United States and Canada to admit practising homosexuals to the priesthood and episcopate, and to legislate for liturgical forms of blessing of same-sex relationships, constitute a major threat to the integrity of the Anglican Communion, and could lead to a realignment of the Churches within it. Whether the Anglican Communion has within it the capacity to overcome these important disagreements is the question that confronts us now.

What I remain quite certain of is that, with or without us, God is working His purposes out, and establishing His kingdom in the hearts and homes of women and men. 'You shall know the truth and the truth shall set you free,' said Jesus to His disciples. That claim is as valid now as it was when first spoken – at the very least, I have found it so. The future belongs to those who are prepared to bow the knee to the God who confronts us in Jesus Christ. To them the Lord of history declares: 'Do not be afraid, little flock, for your Father has been pleased to give you the kingdom.' That is the only future I am sure about.

INDEX